REGULATION AND MARKETS BEYOND 2000

REGULATION AND MARKETS BEYOND 2000

Edited by
LAURA MACGREGOR, TONY PROSSER AND
CHARLOTTE VILLIERS

Routledge
Taylor & Francis Group
LONDON AND NEW YORK

First published 2000 by Dartmouth Publishing Company and
Ashgate Publishing

Reissued 2018 by Routledge
2 Park Square, Milton Park, Abingdon, Oxon OX14 4RN
711 Third Avenue, New York, NY 10017, USA

Routledge is an imprint of the Taylor & Francis Group, an informa business

Typeset by Manton Typesetters, Louth, Lincolnshire, UK.

A Library of Congress record exists under LC control number: 00044145

ISBN 13: 978-1-138-74063-1 (hbk)
ISBN 13: 978-1-138-74061-7 (pbk)
ISBN 13: 978-1-315-18336-7 (ebk)

Contents

Contributors

George Boyle, partner, Shepherd & Wedderburn

Noreen Burrows, Jean Monnet Professor of European Law, University of Glasgow

John Caldwell, solicitor, Shepherd & Wedderburn

Paul Carlyle, solicitor, Shepherd & Wedderburn

Gordon Downie, partner, Shepherd & Wedderburn

Robert Dunbar, lecturer in law, University of Glasgow

Philippa Gannon, lecturer in law, University of Glasgow

Jenny Hamilton, lecturer in law, University of Strathclyde

Sam Hamilton, solicitor, Shepherd & Wedderburn

John Huntley, Professor of Law, Glasgow Caledonian University

Colin Innes, partner, Shepherd & Wedderburn

Claire Johnson, Senior Records Manager, Archives and Business Records Centre, University of Glasgow

Thomas J. Long, Senior Telecommunications Attorney, The Utility Reform Network, San Francisco, USA, formerley Atlantic Fellow, University of Glasgow

Laura Macgregor, Dundas and Wilson Lecturer in Commercial Law, School of Law, University of Glasgow

Nick McKerrell, lecturer in law, Glasgow Caledonian University

Francis McManus, senior lecturer, Edinburgh Napier University

Elizabeth McRobb, partner, Shepherd & Wedderburn

Robin G. Milne, senior lecturer, Department of Economics, University of Glasgow

Duncan Osler, solicitor, Shepherd & Wedderburn

Tony Prosser, John Millar Professor of Law, University of Glasgow and Convenor of the Centre for Regulatory Studies

Charlotte Villiers, senior lecturer in commercial law, University of Glasgow and Visiting Research Fellow, Institute of Advanced Legal Studies, London

Alison White, associate, Shepherd & Wedderburn

Charles Woolfson, senior lecturer, Faculty of Social Sciences, University of Glasgow and Deputy Convenor of the Centre for Regulatory Studies

Preface

The advent of a new century and millennium is a time for reflection on the past and for contemplation of the future. The 20th century has witnessed the development of sophisticated technologies that have revolutionised transport and communications, and in turn have presented opportunities for improved living standards and more profitable trading activities. Such developments have at the same time presented us with increasingly difficult and complex challenges. Industrial and technological advances have generated threats to the environment and have created greater demands for accountability.

These developments have presented opportunities and challenges to lawyers as well as to industrialists, scientists and economists. If we are to benefit from these developments they must be regulated, and the regulatory systems chosen need to have a rational structure in order to be effective. As science and trade have advanced, new regulatory techniques and institutions have had to be found to meet the challenges, as law in its traditional form appears unable to control adequately these activities. The result is that the vast range of technologies and commercial activities is accompanied by a broad range of regulatory devices, many designed especially for the new conditions. This book seeks to provide the reader with an overview of these regulatory mechanisms by presenting them in their contexts. By bringing them together we hope to identify links and to provide the reader with a notion of their main characteristics. We also hope to provide the reader with a sense of the regulatory environment of the future and to stress the importance and sheer breadth of the regulatory phenomenon.

The Centre for Regulatory Studies has been established at the University of Glasgow since 1995 and this book reflects the interests of the members of that research group. From within the Universities of Glasgow, Strathclyde and Glasgow Caledonian, the Centre's membership comprises academics from a broad range of disciplines, such as law, accountancy, economics, social studies, politics, history, housing and management. An important further component of the Centre's membership is one of Scotlands' leading commercial law firms, Shepherd

& Wedderburn, WS. Many solicitors from that firm are active members of the Centre and most of the chapters in this book are the result of collaboration between academic and practitioner members of the Centre, so that theoretical and practical issues inform the various analyses presented.

The views in this book are those of the authors and do not represent the views of Shepherd & Wedderburn, WS. The law is stated as at 1 October 1999.

We would like to thank the publishers, especially John Irwin and Valerie Saunders, who have been generous in their support of this project. We would also like to thank Susan Holmes at the University of Glasgow for her support and assistance.

L.M., T.P., C.V.

Table of Cases

Table of Statutes and Statutory Instruments

1 Introduction

LAURA MACGREGOR, TONY PROSSER AND CHARLOTTE VILLIERS, *University of Glasgow*

Concepts of Regulation

Even a cursory examination of the contents page of this book would suggest that it covers a bewildering range of activities, some of which are outside the scope of what is normally regarded as regulation. A central aim of this chapter will be to suggest that regulation is a much broader phenomenon than it is often conceived to be, and that recent developments in the political world are changing its nature further. In particular, the frequent opposition of regulation to markets, in which regulation is seen as an outside intervention limiting the free play of market forces, only encompasses part of the picture; a central role for regulation is that of creating, and maintaining, the conditions which make the operation of markets possible. In this chapter we shall thus discuss different types of regulation, and some recent developments in the regulatory environment, notably competition law and corporate governance. The first is important as background to the more specific examples of competition regulation discussed in later chapters. The second will provide an example of what has normally been seen as a classic area for self-regulation, and suggest that in fact private and public responsibilities are inextricably mixed. Both of these themes are the subject of important developments likely to affect future regulation, and our discussion will set the scene for the discussion of particular areas of regulatory activity in later chapters.

Concepts of regulation are of course already legion, and some of them very broad in scope. For example, Majone has suggested that 'When one speaks of regulation today, in America and increasingly in Europe, one usually refers to sustained and focused control exercised by a public agency, on the basis of a legislative mandate, over activities that are generally regarded as desirable to society'.[1] Even this may be too narrow, however; as we shall see, much regulation may not be carried out directly by public agencies, nor may it be based on a legislative mandate. This definition has also been criticised as being limited to socially desirable activities, and so confusing a particular legal usage of the term 'regulation' with the broader concept itself.[2]

There is however a much narrower view of regulation in which it is treated as representing an external political or social intervention in markets which are normally self-regulating. For example, this usage,

> chiefly associated with the discipline of economics, *opposes* regulation to markets, and employs the former term to describe all acts of the state that control or alter the activity of markets. ... use of the term regulation in this way is particularly associated with writers (many of them grouped in the so-called Chicago School) who are optimistic about the capacity of markets to produce economic welfare and correspondingly suspicious of any state interference in them, casting doubt both on its motives and its effectiveness.[3]

Such a conception is characteristic of much of the currently influential schools of capture and public choice theory in which the operation of political bargaining results in both the creation of regulatory regimes and their capture by regulated industries; again, the dark world of politics sullies the purity of markets.[4] Finally, this opposition of regulation to markets is probably the most characteristic popular usage of the term; to quote no less elevated a source than Rupert Murdoch, 'Socialism is alive and well and living in regulatory agencies ... The growth of regulation has given enormous control to government ... Socialism has effectively reinvented itself.'[5]

This book will express a view of regulation which is radically different from this latter usage. Some regulation, such as that relating to the environment and genetic testing, does limit the operation of markets and, by doing so, aims to implement public interest goals. In other cases, however, it is impossible to conceive of markets without their being constituted by regulatory action. This is of course reasonably well accepted in the case of the allocation of property rights, though it is often seen as a different exercise from regulation itself. To quote Daintith once more:

> a key role of law may be seen as the underpinning of economic relations by the recognition and enforcement of property rights. ... This provision is seen as something anterior to regulation; it is the underpinning of the market system, into which the state intervenes by way

> of regulation, in order to correct market failures, furnish public goods, and redistribute wealth.[6]

A theme in other work, however, is that it is impossible to separate the constitutive role from regulation; 'Scholars of a variety of persuasions have for a long time argued that the conditions required for social interaction are not given by interaction itself. Interaction, they have argued, is not self-constituting. Markets are not self-ordering. Markets are always and necessarily regulated through careful constitutive work'.[7] Not only does this imply that markets and regulation are complementary rather than opposed, it suggests that both are means of delivering public interests, rather than regulation being the only means of doing so. A central purpose of this book will be to examine the role of regulation in constituting and structuring markets, a process in which economics, politics and law are inextricably intertwined.

Constituting Markets

Some examples should make these points clearer. An area which has been examined in detail in other work is that of utility regulation.[8] Even when the utilities were nationalised, serious tensions were evident between different purposes of public ownership and public intervention. On the one hand, nationalisation was seen as a means of implementing the (undefined) public interest, characterised as opposed to the profit motive and in many cases to market allocations. On the other hand, a later view was that, given proper governmental guidance, public enterprises could mimic the operation of markets and so act in ways which were economically efficient despite the monopoly nature of much of their activity.[9] Thus, rather than public ownership and markets being incompatible, such ownership would permit public intervention to mimic markets where private ownership would be subject to market failures.

With privatisation, only limited debate occurred about the purposes of the regulatory institutions which were established. The most influential document was the first Littlechild Report setting out the design for the price control to be used for the monopoly areas of British Telecom's business, a model also adopted for the other utilities. The report starkly opposed competition and regulation; thus 'Competition is indisputably the most effective means – perhaps ultimately the *only* effective means – of protecting consumers against monopoly power. Regulation is essentially a means of preventing the worst excesses of monopoly; it is not a substitute for competition. It is a means of "holding the fort" until competition arrives.'[10]

The reality has turned out to be somewhat different. Although regulation of monopoly through, for example, price control, has been one central task of the regulators, other tasks have included the constitution and policing of competitive markets. One example to be discussed in detail later, in Chapter 4, is that of electricity, where the regulator has been at the forefront of efforts to create and police markets against strong opposition from regulated companies, although serious doubts remain as to the degree to which generation is properly competitive. A similar story can be told of gas, this time with greater success, and also of telecommunications; again, regulators have been the key actors in developing competitive markets. In all these sectors, but especially in telecommunications, action to create competitive markets against strong opposition from some national governments has also been taken by the institutions of the European Union; as we shall see, the European Commission has become a key regulatory actor in many of the sectors to be described in this book. Nor has action by the regulators and Commission in relation to the utilities been simply a matter of creating competitive markets and letting them operate, for continued policing of their operation has also been required. This has included, for example, action by the telecommunications regulator to incorporate general conditions requiring fair trading into the licences of telecoms operators, and by the Commission to require separation of regulation and operation.[11] In the UK this has now been supplemented by the 1998 Competition Act (to be discussed below), which, apart from creating general prohibitions on anti-competitive agreements and behaviour, enables their implementation to be carried out by the utility regulators themselves.

A further example of regulatory intervention to constitute markets is that of competitive tendering and in particular compulsory competitive tendering in local government. The traditional position in the UK was that local authorities provided a wide range of services through their own staff with no requirement to seek competitive tenders from the private sector or to separate the provision of services from specifying what was needed and purchasing it. This was changed by legislation during the 1980s and early 1990s which required in many areas that competitive tendering took place and also required the actual service provision to be in the hands of direct labour organisations or direct service organisations at arm's length from the authority itself and subject to detailed accounting provisions and rate of return requirements.[12] In many ways the interventions involved have been characteristic of the worst forms of bureaucratic regulation; the legislation has been badly drafted, over-complex and stipulatory, in places mutually contradictory and involving a massive use of informal rule making in the form of ministerial guidance. Indeed, the current government is in the process of replacing it with a more flexible system of 'best value' giving more discretion to local government itself to decide how best to improve the delivery of services.[13] Despite the bureaucratic and over-specific nature of the regulatory interventions, however, the goal was not to restrict the operation of pre-existing markets but to bring new markets into existence where previously services had been delivered administratively. Thus, apart from the tendering requirements, much of the corpus of rules involved was designed to ensure that competition existed, not to limit it. Once again, this is supplemented by a body of rules at a European level designed to open up markets in public procurement, as we shall see in Chaper 13, when an assessment of their effects will be made.[14]

This is not to say, of course, that other regulation does not have a social rationale; important areas of social regulation exist for the utilities, although the legitimacy of entrusting them to unelected regulators is much debated and a new set of arrangements is to be established sharing responsibilities between government and regulators in social and environmental matters.[15] In other areas, such as broadcasting, social rationales for regulation are much more fully established and, apart from the familiar restrictions on explicit portrayal of sex and violence, include the norms, formal and informal, which constitute public service broadcasting. Here the debate is not whether social regulation is illegitimate, but how it can work successfully in the new media world of channel profusion and consumer choice, thus raising a further important theme in this book: the ability of regulation to cope with a rapidly changing technological environment.[16] Rather than social and economic regulation occupying different territories they are becoming closely intertwined, for example in requiring open access to essential facilities such as conditional access technology for digital television both on pro-competitive grounds and avoiding too great a share of media influence falling into the same hands and so subverting access to information necessary for democratic choice.

Competition Law and Policing Markets

The developments in utility regulation towards a model based on the creation and policing of competitive markets show in microcosm the general developments in competition law. Here the position adopted in the past in the UK has been that of applying a general 'public interest' test to assess the acceptability of restrictive practices, monopolies and mergers, something which has enabled a number of different rationales to be employed by the authorities and which has permitted considerable political influence in the process. This is now in the process of being replaced for anti-competitive agreements and abuse of a dominant position by tests based on Community law as a result of the Competition Act 1998. Similarly, an increasing proportion of mergers are now dealt with at a Community level, and there may be reforms of domestic merger control in the near future which are likely to bring it closer to the Community model.[17] The effect of these changes is to replace the broad public interest test with much more specific tests based to a large degree on economic rationales. Thus once more we can see a shift from regulation as public interest intervention to limit markets to regulation constituting and policing competitive markets. Given the importance of competition law as a background to the areas discussed in this book, and its importance for future policing of markets, this is worth examining in greater detail.

The shift from the use of a public interest test involving political influence towards the use of tests based on economic rationales can be illustrated by comparing the UK competition regulation before and after the coming into force of the Competition Act 1998 (the provisions of the Act described below come into force on 1 March 2000). The movement towards the use of tests based on economic rationales can be illustrated firstly by the change in the nature of regulation of restrictive practices. Under the older legislation, the Restrictive Trade Practices Act 1976, the secretary of state was able to use discretion in deciding whether or not proceedings would be taken on a registered agreement.[18] If proceedings were taken, the relevant test, administered by the Restrictive Trade Practices Court, was whether the restrictions operated against the 'public interest'. The restrictions would be upheld only if they could satisfy the criteria specified within one of the 'gateways' contained within section 21. However, even if they passed through a gateway, the restrictions had to be weighed against the wider public interest in the 'tailpiece'.[19] Therefore, ultimately, the system involved political discretion in the referral of cases to the court and a public interest test in the final decision. It is also interesting to note that the concept of public interest used here was not the same as that used in the context of the monopoly provisions under the Fair Trading Act 1973, commented on below.

The changes effected to regulation of restrictive practices by the 1998 Act are major. The system described above is replaced by provisions which are almost a direct reflection of the terms of Article 81 of the EC Treaty.[20] The new provisions will bring within their ambit a wider class of types of abuse. Whereas the UK legislation under the Restrictive Trade Practices Act 1973 focused on agreements,[21] the new legislation is less motivated by form and concentrates on the effect upon competition: agreements will be prohibited if they have as their object or effect the prevention, restriction or distortion of competition.[22] The ultimate aim of this European type of approach is the creation of a state of affairs – that is, a market which is not distorted by restrictive practices. It will be constitutive in the sense that it will attempt to create an outcome or order, not simply prohibit types of conduct.

In the field of control of monopolies, an analysis of the legislation before the 1998 Act reveals a similar pattern. The approach which the Fair Trading Act 1973 adopted was the very antithesis of an economic one. As an example, the Act did not place a legal obligation on the director general of fair trading (DGFT) and the secretary of state to define the relevant product market in which dominance was thought to occur. The monopoly situation could be defined by reference to goods or services of any description.[23] Once the market had been identified, the issue of dominance was analysed in an equally arbitrary way. The Act adopted a strictly numerical test of 25 per cent dominance of whichever market has been identified. This is in stark contrast to the position under the new legislation described below. Additionally, when the Monopolies and Mergers Commissoin (MMC) carried out its investigation the focus of the enquiry was whether the public interest was being harmed. As noted above, the concept of public interest used here differed from that used under the Restrictive Trade Practices Act 1973. Section 84 of the Fair Trading Act 1973 directed the MMC to all matters which appear to it in the particular circumstances to be relevant, before listing certain types of policies which it may take into account. Although public interest was the relevant test to be used, it is interesting to note that the concept was not used consistently in the UK legislation.

Another related criticism of the older system was that it was essentially discretionary, ultimate power lying in the secretary of state. That this is the case is illustrated by the fact that, after the MMC had submitted its report to the secretary of state, he or she could decline to accept both its advice and the advice of the DGFT.

The 1998 Act adopts an approach which is almost identical to that taken by Article 82 of the EC treaty.[24] Article 82 could be described as the article amongst all the articles relating to competition within the EC Treaty which most obviously uses an economic analysis. The analysis of the relevant market is highly sophisticated, including a threefold analysis of the product, geographical and temporal market. It is also not simply a numerical analysis of market share, but a search for indicators of dominance. Thus a large market share does not necessarily denote dominance. The analysis of market share is a fluid concept which depends on the structure of the market, the number of actors within that market and their relative shares.

In the field of merger control, it is less easy to say that the shift referred to above from political control by way of public policy tests towards economic analysis has been made. The pre-1998 Act landscape is a curious mixture. On the one hand, it is essentially pro-merger and so one could say that the UK system is influenced by ideas which are similar to those of the Chicago school, assuming the rationality of private economic action. On the other hand, this can be disturbed on broad and undefined 'public interest' grounds. The secretary of state for trade and industry and the MMC (now the Competition Commission, or CC) both have an important role to play in merger control. Mergers are referred to the CC by the secretary of state.[25] The CC decides whether the merger operates against the public interest. Following its investigation and report, if the CC does not conclude that the merger would be against the public interest, the secretary of state cannot block the merger. However, if the CC concludes that the merger would be against the public interest, the secretary of state is not obliged to block the merger. Thus the system assumes that mergers are generally beneficial and the decision to refer and block the merger is essentially one of political discretion. Although the CC can refer to criteria within the Fair Trading Act in order to decide whether the merger operates against the public interest, these criteria are highly discretionary.[26] In practice the DGFT has an important practical role in deciding which mergers should be referred to the CC, advised and assisted by the mergers panel. This is a panel of civil servants whose deliberations are not published, but who nevertheless appear to have significant influence on merger control.

Merger control is left relatively unchanged by the 1998 Act, aside from the transfer of the powers to the new CC. However, recent proposals point towards the possibility of change in the UK in the near future.[27] They would considerably reduce the involvement of the secretary of state in the vast majority of merger cases, and would replace the public interest test with a new competition-based test, although the secretary of state would retain a role in cases involving exceptional public interest matters, the criteria for which would be set out in law. It must also be remembered that the financial thresholds which trigger Community competence over a merger have recently been lowered.[28] This should lead to a small increase in the proportion of mergers falling within Community competence and outside the UK system. Mergers with a Community dimension are, under Regulation 4064/89,[29] subjected to a type of regulation which is very different from the UK approach. Most importantly, a public interest test is not used. The main test is to ascertain whether the merger is compatible with the common market.[30] The Commission may take into account matters such as the structure of the markets concerned and the position of the undertakings concerned within those markets – matters which necessarily involve an economic analysis. In a similar manner to the operation of Article 82, the legislation directs the Commission to search for the creation or strengthening of a dominant position.[31] This task involves the Commission in an analysis of the relevant product and geographical markets, a task which involves a high degree of economic analysis.

It may seem surprising that we have included such a discussion of competition law reform in a book about regulation. It is, however, important for two reasons. Firstly, it is essential background to a number of the discussions of regulatory developments in individual sectors included below. Secondly, the reform of competition law is itself a regulatory development. It involves changes in the way in which public authorities act to mould conduct and to set limits on actions within the market; in this sense it provides a good example of the market-constituting regulation discussed above. It also involves making generally applicable a function which regulatory bodies, in particular the utility regulators, have already performed. What is particularly striking is a shift away from public interest-based interventions to market-based tests; we shall see later that this represents part of a more general shift away from 'command and control' regulation towards models which shape markets with the goal of increasing their efficient operation rather than replacing them. In other words, regulation has created a constitution within which markets are to operate.

A substantial area of recent regulation has thus constituted and policed markets, and this role has become central to public policy in recent years. Not only has it constituted markets in the sense of creating them but it has provided them with a constitution in the sense of laying down the basic rules and procedures which will determine their operation – for example, in prohibitions on anti-competitive practices and setting tendering and accounting requirements; more examples will become apparent from later chapters of this book. We are currently witnessing an important shift towards this model of regulation with the reform of UK competition law.

The Institutions of Regulation

If we adopt the broad concept of regulation proposed above, incorporating the constitution and policing of markets, we also widen considerably the range of institutions involved in regulation.[32] In most of the older economic writing and in popular usage, regulation is associated with the state, once more as an undifferentiated and external source of interference in the operation of markets. However, the complexity of the modern state makes its nature far from undifferentiated; public authorities operate at a range of different levels, often with different interests and cultures. Thus:

> public competence and power to take economic decisions may today be exercisable at levels above the state, in international organisations; it may also, within the state, be diffused among public authorities with specific territorial or functional competences. In addition, the boundaries between the action of the state, and private economic action, may often be blurred, either by reason of the purposes of the action or, more important for our discussion, of the nature of the institutions involved.[33]

A considerable amount of regulation already takes place at supranational level, most notably through the institutions of the European Union and European Community law.[34] Indeed, in many of the areas to be covered in this book there is already considerable tension between the European and the UK or other national levels of regulation, notably in competition law, telecommunications and energy. The choice of level often has important implications for regulatory style; thus European regulation gives a far greater role to the European Court of Justice than that given to the judiciary at a domestic level, and the conception of democracy involved in Union politics may be very different from that which has characterised UK politics, at least so far.[35]

A further important development has been the rapid change from direct regulation by government departments to regulation by independent or semi-independent agencies.[36] These have a long history in the USA with, for example, the Federal Trade Commission and the Federal Communications Commission as central regulatory actors. There have been isolated examples in Europe for many years, the most famous being the German Cartel Office created in 1957. However, the employment of this model really took off with the establishment of the UK offices to regulate privatised utilities from 1984, although technically these take the form of 'non-ministerial government departments' with legal powers vested not in the office but in an individual director-general. Since then, various forms of regulatory agency have spread throughout Europe, examples being the regulation of broadcasting, telecommunications and energy in Italy, of telecommunications in Germany and of telecommunications and competition in France. This of course partly reflects the process of liberalisation of public utilities in the European Union, although such liberalisation does not require any particular form of regulatory institution and the degree of real independence from government of the agencies varies widely. The model of agency rather than direct ministerial regulation has also been adopted in areas other than those of the utilities; a particularly controversial UK example is the proposed creation of a food standards agency. Further institutional developments include the increasing use of specialised agencies at the European Union level.[37]

Finally, it must not be forgotten that important regulatory powers may often be retained at a local level: in the UK important licensing functions and food and trading standards responsibilities, for example. Indeed, the development of tiers of government between local and national, such as the new Scottish Executive, will complicate the division of functions further. One example of the complexities which may result can be seen from Germany where telecommunications regulation is the responsibility of a federal agency whilst broadcasting regulation remains in the hands of the regions or Länder, a recipe for serious boundary disputes in an era of convergence between the two technologies.[38]

The result of all this institutional complexity is not simply to complicate the concept of regulation itself but to cast doubt on some of the more familiar views of the way regulation works. For example, an influential theme in both academic and popular analysis of regulation has been that of regulatory capture, according to which it is inevitable that regulatory bodies become dominated by producer interests which subvert public interest goals for their own private benefit.[39] However, if the regulatory map is as complex and multidimensional as we have suggested, it is no longer possible to assume that producer groups have the same power to dominate, or that regulatory bureaucrats have same interests, at each level. Rather than capture, a better metaphor becomes that of regulatory space. Thus 'different institutions have come to inhabit a common regulatory space. The critical question for the analyst of the European regulatory scene is not to assume "capture", but rather to understand the nature of this shared space: the rules of admission, the relations between occupants, and the variations introduced by differences in markets and issue arenas.'[40] This clearly provides important opportunities for sociological research, but it also has implications for lawyers, for it is law which will police boundary disputes between the different regulatory institutions (and indeed this is already occurring) and will determine common principles – for example, those relating to fair procedures applicable across all agencies.[41]

Private Regulation, Corporate Governance and Self-regulation

The analysis above has stressed the range of public institutions which may be involved in regulation. However, even this is not extensive enough for our purposes as the broad concept of regulation to be used in this book also includes private techniques for constituting and policing markets and reflecting elements of the public interest. Thus the 'regulatory space' analogy referred to above includes private actors as forms of 'governing institution'.[42] Indeed, calls for 'self-regulation' of one kind or another, often portrayed as an alternative to regulation by law, suggest that private governance is becoming seen as an increasingly attractive regulatory form. The classic examples of private regulation in this sense are of course the rules and principles of corporate governance, and these merit examination in greater detail here as background to more detailed analysis elsewhere in this book; corporate governance is prominent in current debates about corporate activities and the role of company law and it illustrates just how complex regulatory systems may be.[43]

Defined as 'the system by which companies are directed and controlled',[44] corporate governance concerns issues such as the composition and structure of boards of directors and the accountability of boards to shareholders.[45] A striking feature relevant to this book is its apparent reliance on best practice and internal company arrangements for accountability rather than on legal rules. The Hampel Committee Report on Corporate Governance states: 'Business prosperity cannot be commanded. People, teamwork, leadership, enterprise, experience and skills are what really produce prosperity. There is no single formula to weld these together, and it is dangerous to encourage the belief that rules and regulations about structure will deliver success.'[46] The perceived problem with 'hard and fast' legal rules is that they do not provide enough flexibility to accommodate the different types of companies and their individual circumstances.[47] Another problem is that legal regulations create burdens on companies such as time and monetary costs of compliance. In addition, the procedural barriers faced by shareholders who seek to challenge directors' actions in the courts[48] and the generally known reluctance of the judiciary to intervene in commercial decisions[49] act as a further discouragement of the use of public authorities or legal regulation. For these reasons the corporate governance debate has moved towards an internalisation of control of directors within the company rather than controlling their behaviour by use of legal measures and public institutions or agencies. This would appear a straightforward recipe for self-regulation.

The above approach places directors at the centre, linked to the role of the shareholders who appoint them. This requires the directors to develop effective control policies and for there to be monitoring and enforcement of those policies by directors and shareholders collectively. However, pure reliance on the internal relationships within the company does not guarantee an effective corporate governance system. One problem is that independence of those entrusted with control of management behaviour is an essential ingredient of corporate governance. Yet there is often a lack of independence of the non-executive directors and auditors.[50] Another, crucial, problem is information asymmetry; many of those who are required to make independent judgments about the performance of directors lack the information to make informed judgments. Often the executive directors themselves rely on company managers for their information. The procedures and structures of company general meetings also provide the directors with an information advantage over the shareholders.[51] A further difficulty lies in the apparent lack of willingness of shareholders to monitor the behaviour of their directors. In large companies especially, the shareholders are dispersed and have small proportional holdings in the enterprise. The practical effect of these shareholdings is that the costs of monitoring often outweigh the benefits of monitoring, thereby reducing the incentives for vigilance.[52] To some extent this problem has been alleviated by the growth of institutional investors who, by economies of scale, are better able to bear the monitoring costs. Overall, however, to rely on internal procedures and parties alone offers no guarantee of an effective corporate governance system.

It is therefore necessary to provide an external mechanism for directing and controlling corporate activities. The UK's reluctance to use legal rules and procedures for corporate governance has again led to a preference for non-binding codes designed to encourage best practice. According to the Department of Trade and Industry, 'Best practice is more flexible: individual companies can apply it in the way that best fits their own circumstances and it can be kept up-to-date more easily.'[53] These codes have been issued by all three of the committees that have reported on corporate governance during the 1990s, culminating in a *Combined Code of Best Practice* implemented by the London Stock Exchange in July 1998, comprising principles of corporate governance and a code of best practice. The aim of the Combined Code is to allow companies to create and establish their own governance policies in the light of the principles set out in the Code. Again, it is possible to deduce an emphasis on flexibility and internal governance controls, but within a framework of guiding principles.

This is not, however, a purely internal process and it is also important to note the involvement of the London Stock Exchange. The Stock Exchange, in addition to publishing the Combined Code, is to impose an obligation on listed companies to make a disclosure statement of compliance with the Code. It is not clear what sanctions the Stock Exchange will adopt for non-compliance with the Code, but in other situations it is clear that the Stock Exchange has stringent sanctions available to it, not least the denial of listing for breach of the Listing Rules. Internal regulation still requires external scrutiny.

External scrutiny can also be illustrated through the operation of the Takeover Code through the Takeover Panel and Executive. The Takeover Panel is a regulatory body concerned with takeovers of companies the shares of which are held by the public; it was set up in 1968 at the recommendation of the governor of the Bank of England, in response to mounting concern about unfair practices. The chairman, deputy chairmen and further non-representative members of the Panel are appointed by the governor of the Bank of England, and the rest of the Panel's membership comprises representatives of other private professional and regulatory bodies such as the Association of British Insurers, the Institutes of Chartered Accountants for England and Wales and for Scotland, and the Securities and Futures Authority. The objective of the Takeover Panel is, through its Code, to 'ensure good business standards and fairness to shareholders',[54] and the Panel states that maintaining fair and orderly markets is crucial to this objective.[55] The Panel also emphasises the need for its system to have characteristics such as flexibility, certainty and speed and that such characteristics should be retained in order to avoid over-rigid rules and the risk of takeovers becoming delayed by litigation of a tactical nature.[56]

Although the Takeover Panel is a private institution, it clearly performs public functions in its operation of the Code.[57] Indeed, its decisions affect citizens as well as shareholders. The Panel may also use a range of possible sanctions from private reprimand, to public censure, to reporting the offender's conduct to another regulatory authority and to requiring further action to be taken.[58] Cold-shouldering of a company could have severe effects on that company's business and profits.

It is now common to propose self-regulation as a more flexible alternative to regulation by public authorities; it has been employed in areas as diverse as financial services, health and safety and Internet pornography. However, as the discussion above makes clear, the relationship between self-regulation and other forms of regulation is highly complex.[59] In particular, self-regulation is not the antithesis of legal regulation. Thus it is not a useful way of characterising a whole legal regime as almost inevitably it is accompanied by more direct interventions on the part of public authorities, including use of criminal or civil sanctions; self-regulation is thus a technique of regulation rather than an alternative to it. Indeed, even in the classic 'private' area of corporate governance, company law, and even criminal law, play an essential background role. Recognising this, recent attention has shifted to 'co-regulation' or 'enforced self-regulation' in which regulation is undertaken by an industry association with some oversight and ratification by government, or through negotiation between the state and individual firms to establish appropriate standards and norms which can then be publicly enforced.[60] Later in this book we shall see just how complex the relationship between public regulation and attempts at self-regulation can be when we examine the area of financial services (Chapter 12). The key point to be made here, however, is that regulation in areas often seen as essentially private is a complex mix of different normative and institutional systems; neither those of public authorities nor those of private organisations have a monopoly on the exercise of regulatory functions. In addition, availability of information is crucial in the operation of self-regulation.

Conclusion

This book will thus employ a broad concept of regulation in determining both the activities and institutions which are covered; a particular interest will be the use of regulation to constitute and police markets.[61] This is a particularly interesting time to examine developments of this kind. Firstly, the UK has seen important changes since the 1997 election, reflecting both developments in economic policy and constitutional reform. Regulatory legitimacy has been rethought with a move from 'deregulation' to 'better regulation', as we shall see in our discussion of the role of the Better Regulation Task Force below. Simplistic notions of self-regulation have been discarded, especially in the area of financial services. Perhaps most importantly of all, European developments have had a greater impact within the UK. This is most notably the case with the move to European-based competition law, but can also be seen in the partial revival of a concept of public service, itself recently more closely associated with other European jurisdictions.[62] The range of material covered in this book will be wide, but only in this way will we be able to provide an adequate analysis of regulation in a state of major change and development.

Notes

1 Majone, G. (1996), *Regulating Europe*, London: Routledge, p.9. The definition is itself derived from P. Selznick (1985), 'Focussing Organizational Research on Regulation' in R.G. Noll (ed.), *Regulatory Policy and the Social Sciences*, Berkeley: University of California Press, pp.363–4.

2 Daintith, T. (1997), 'Regulation', in R. Buxbaum and F. Mádl (eds), *International Encyclopedia of Comparative Law*, Tübingen: Mohr Siebeck, vol. XVII, 10–5.

3 *Ibid.*, 10–3, emphasis retained, footnotes omitted. For good general accounts of concepts of regulation in economic thought, see A. Ogus (1994), *Regulation: Legal Form and Economic Theory*, Oxford: Clarendon, ch.2; Majone, *Regulating Europe* (n.1, above), ch.2.

4 Any such one-sentence summary can be no more than a caricature of a vast and diverse body of work; for more information, see T. Prosser (1999), 'Theorising Utility Regulation', *Modern Law Review*, 62, 203–6; P. Dunleavy (1991),

Democracy, Bureaucracy and Public Choice, Hemel Hempstead: Harvester Wheatsheaf.

5 Quoted in 'Murdoch Rails Against Regulators', *Financial Times*, 28–9 June 1997.

6 Daintith, 'Regulation' (n.2, above), 10–16, footnote omitted.

7 Shearing, C. (1993), 'A Constitutive Conception of Regulation', in P. Grabosky and J. Braithwaite (eds), *Business Regulation and Australia's Future*, Canberra: Australian Institute of Criminology, p.70.

8 See, for example, Prosser, T. (1997), *Law and the Regulators*, Oxford: Clarendon.

9 Prosser, T. (1986), *Nationalised Industries and Public Control*, Oxford: Blackwell, chs 2–3. A particularly clear expression of the latter view was the 1978 White Paper, *The Nationalised Industries*, Cm 7131.

10 Littlechild, S. (1983), *The Regulation of British Telecommunications' Profitability*, London: Department of Industry, para. 4.11 (emphasis retained).

11 For the former, see Prosser, *Law and the Regulators* (n.8, above), pp.76–8; for the latter, Hunt, A. (1997), 'Regulation of Telecommunications: The Developing EU Regulatory Framework and its Impact on the United Kingdom', *European Public Law*, 3, 93–115.

12 Local Government, Planning and Land Act 1980, Part III; Local Government Act 1988; Local Government Act 1992, Part I.

13 Department of the Environment, Transport and the Regions, *Modern Local Government: In Touch With the People*, Cm 4014 (1998), ch.7; Local Government Act 1999.

14 An overview is Arrowsmith, S. (1995), 'Public Procurement as an Instrument of Policy and the Impact of Market Liberalisation', *Law Quarterly Review*, 111, 235–84. For the general process of 'contractualisation' of government, see I. Harden (1992), *The Contracting State*, Milton Keynes: Open University Press.

15 Majone, *Regulating Europe* (n.1, above), ch.13; Foster, C.D. (1992), *Privatization, Public Ownership and the Regulation of Natural Monopoly*, Oxford: Blackwell, esp. ch. 9. For the reforms, see Department of Trade and Industry (1998), *A Fair Deal for Consumers: The Response to Consultation*, London: Department of Trade and Industry, paras 10–14, 57–62.

16 Goldberg, D., T. Prosser and S. Verhulst (eds) (1998), *Regulating the Changing Media: A Comparative Study*, Oxford: Clarendon, esp. ch.1. For an indication of the economic role of what has been conceived of as a social regulator see *R* v. *Independent Television Commission, ex parte Flextech plc*, *The Times*, 27 November 1998.

17 Department of Trade and Industry (1999), *Mergers: A Consultation Document on Proposals for Reform*, London: Department of Trade and Industry.

18 Section 21(2) Restrictive Trade Practices Act 1976.

19 Sections 21(10) and (19).

20 The change in numbering following the ratification of the Amsterdam Treaty is adopted here.

21 Section 43(1). The restrictive effect of this section is mitigated by ss.8 and 16 the provisions relating to information agreements as to goods and services in ss.6, 7, 11, 12 and 14.

22 Article 81 includes agreements, decisions by associations of undertakings and concerted practices.

23 See in particular s.10(7) of the Fair Trading Act 1973.

24 The monopoly provisions are contained in the Chapter II prohibition.

25 Sections 64–75 Fair Trading Act 1973.

26 Section 84 Fair Trading Act 1973, which allows the MMC to take into account 'all matters which appear to them in the particular circumstances to be relevant'.

27 *Mergers: A Consultation Document* (n.17, above).

28 Council Regulation 1310/97/EEC OJ L180/1, 1997.
29 OJ [1989] L 395/1, [1990] 4 CMLR 286.
30 Article 2(1).
31 Articles 2(2) and 2(3).
32 This is not the place to deal with the recent institutional theories of regulation, important as they may be. See, for example, Majone (n.1, above), pp.34–44, for an introduction.
33 Daintith, 'Regulation' (n.2, above), 10–47.
34 For general analysis, see Majone, *Regulating Europe* (n.1, above), esp. chs 4, 12.
35 *Ibid.*, p.285.
36 For an overview see ibid., ch.3.
37 *Ibid.*, pp.274–82.
38 Kleinwächter, W. (1998), 'Germany', in Goldberg *et al.* (eds), *Regulating the Changing Media* (n.16, above), pp.29–60.
39 For a brief summary and critique, see Prosser, 'Theorising Utility Regulation' (n.4, above).
40 Hancher, L. and M. Moran (1989), 'Organizing Regulatory Space', in L. Hancher and M. Moran (eds), *Capitalism, Culture and Economic Regulation*, Oxford: Clarendon, p.276.
41 For recent examples of such judicial decisions, see *R* v. *Independent Television Commission, ex parte Flextech, The Times*, 27 November 1998, and *R* v. *Monopolies and Mergers Commission, ex parte Stagecoach Holdings plc, The Times*, 23 July 1996.
42 Hancher and Moran, 'Organizing Regulatory Space' (n.40, above), p.275; Shearing, 'A Constitutional Conception' (n.7, above), p.73. For an outstanding statement of this view, see Stokes, M. (1986), 'Company Law and Legal Theory', in W. Twining (ed.), *Common Law and Legal Theory*, Oxford: Oxford University Press, p.155.
43 During the 1990s there have been at least three influential reports on corporate governance and a vast literature on the subject: Cadbury Committee (1992), *Report on The Financial Aspects of Corporate Governance*, London; Gee; Greenbury Committee (1995), *Report on Directors' Remuneration*, London: Gee; and the Hampel Committee on Corporate Governance (1998), *Final Report*, London: Gee. For a useful introduction and helpful bibliography on corporate governance, see Sheikh, S. and W. Rees (eds) (1995), *Corporate Governance and Corporate Control*, London: Cavendish.
44 Cadbury Report (n.43, above), para. 2.5.
45 Department of Trade and Industry (1998), *Modern Company Law for a Competitive Economy*, London: HMSO.
46 Hampel Report, (n.43, above), para. 1.1.
47 *Ibid.*, paras 1.10 and 1.11.
48 All UK company lawyers are familiar with the difficulties caused by the case of *Foss* v. *Harbottle* (1843) 2 Hare 461.
49 In the USA, this is known as the business judgment rule. The UK adopts a similar approach: see, for example, Lord Greene MR stating in the case of *Re Smith & Fawcett Ltd* [1942] Ch304 (CA) that directors are bound to exercise the powers conferred upon them 'bona fide in what they consider – not what a court may consider – is in the interests of the company' (p.306).
50 On the lack of independence of non-executive directors, see Cosh, A. and A. Hughes (1997),'The Changing Anatomy of Corporate Control and the Market for Executives in the United Kingdom', *Journal of Law and Society*, 104, 111 and 121. On the problem of lack of independence of auditors, see Macgregor, L. and C. Villiers (1998), 'Independence of Auditors', *European Business Law Review*, 318.
51 See Butcher, D. (1995), 'Reform of the General Meetings', in Sheikh and Rees (eds), *Corporate Governance* (n.43, above).

52 See Finch, V. (1992), 'Company Directors: Who Cares About Skill and Care?', *Modern Law Review*, 55, 179.
53 Department of Trade and Industry, *Modern Company Law for a Competitive Economy* (n.45, above), para. 3.7.
54 See The Takeover Panel, *1997–1998 Report*, p.6.
55 *Ibid.*
56 *Ibid.* For these reasons, the Panel is opposed to the adoption of the draft Thirteenth Company Law Directive (latest draft at COM(97) 565 final, 10.11.97) which would necessitate statutory implementation, thereby creating a legal regulatory framework. Despite the fact that the draft Directive is expressed in very flexible terms and bases itself on the UK's system, it is the creation of a legal framework which embodies those rules that is problematic for the Panel. See also the House of Lords Select Committee Report, July 1996, which expresses the same opinion (1995–6) HL 100.
57 Consequently, the Panel is subject to judicial review by the courts. See *R* v. *Panel on Takeovers and mergers, ex parte Datafin plc* [1987] QB 815.
58 *1997–1998 Report* (n.54, above), p.6.
59 For introductions, see Majone, *Regulating Europe* (n.1, above), pp.23–6; Daintith, 'Regulation' (n.2, above), 10–39–10–45.
60 An influential statement of the case for these types of regulation is Ayres, I. and J. Braithwaite (1992), *Responsive Regulation: Transcending the Deregulation Debate*, Oxford: Oxford University Press.
61 In this we share the approach of Daintith (n.2, above), 10–7.
62 See Prosser, T. (forthcoming), 'Public Service Law: Privatization's Unexpected Offspring' [2000] in D. Nelken (ed.), *Law and Contemporary Problems*. Cf. the rewriting of the Citizens' Charter Programme as 'Service First', available at <http://www.servicefirst.gov.uk/sfirst/>.

2 Essential Facilities and Utility Networks

GORDON DOWNIE, *Shepherd & Wedderburn*
AND LAURA MACGREGOR, *University of Glasgow*

Introduction

In competition law terms, the essential facilities doctrine has developed as a means by which a general prohibition of monopolistic conduct is applied in the context of the ownership and control of infrastructure bottlenecks. The doctrine originates from the USA, where it was first considered in the case of *United States* v. *Terminal Railroad Association of St Louis*.[1] In the USA it has benefited from much academic and judicial analysis.[2] In contrast, it remains relatively unexplored in European law.[3] It is even less well understood in the context of UK competition law, where no comparable prohibition has historically existed.

The recent case of *Oscar Bronner* v. *Mediaprint and Others*[4] provided the European Court with an opportunity to examine the proper role of the doctrine in Community law. In anticipation of this review, Advocate-General Jacobs in his opinion provided a strongly worded warning against the over-use of the doctrine. In his opinion, this could lead:

> Community and national authorities and courts into detailed regulation of the Community markets, entailing the fixing of prices and conditions for supply in large sectors of the economy. Intervention on that scale would not only be unworkable but would be anti-competitive in the longer term and would scarcely be compatible with a free market economy.[5]

This chapter explores a number of the ways in which the essential facilities doctrine, as it may be developed in the UK under the new Competition Act in the context of utility networks, could give rise to the sort of concern expressed by Advocate-General Jacobs. It also focuses on the fundamental institutional and procedural weaknesses which would be exposed by any widespread application of the doctrine. One of the questions which the writers seek to answer is whether alternative means of regulation provide a more legitimate and efficient method of control of the problems classically posed by essential facilities cases.

Background

In 1974, in the *Commercial Solvents* case,[6] the fundamentals of the doctrine were established in European law, although without reference to the term 'essential facilities'. The Court of Justice stated:

> An undertaking which has a dominant position in the market in raw materials and which, with the object of reserving such raw material for manufacturing its own derivatives, refuses to supply an existing customer which is itself a manufacturer of such derivatives, and thereby risks eliminating competition on the part of such customer, is abusing its dominant position within the meaning of Article 86 EEC, read together with Article 3(f).[7]

Certain of the facts of this case are characteristic of many subsequent essential facilities decisions. The undertakings in dispute usually operate on two different levels. In *Commercial Solvents*, the first level was production of raw materials and the second, manufacturing. In essential facility cases, the owner of the essential facility attempts to extend its monopoly power into the second level (the second level being referred to in this chapter as 'the downstream market'). The result of this is that competition on the downstream market is restricted or excluded altogether. In *Commercial Solvents*, the essential facilities were raw materials necessary for manufacture of a product on the downstream market. The applicant, active on the downstream/manufacturing level, objected to Commercial Solvents' refusal to supply raw materials for manufacturing. The applicant alleged that the reason for the refusal was that the owner of the essential facilities was attempting to reserve all of the raw materials for its own use or use by a related company. The potential effect of such a reservation could be to eliminate all competition at the manufacturing level, although this will depend upon the structure of the market, the number of undertakings operating at manufacturing level and the existence of alternative outlets for raw materials.

Many of the early essential facilities cases concern natural monopolies such as ports or harbours.[8] The facility is indispensable to, for example, a ferry operator, and duplication by the ferry operator of the facility is not reasonable either for economic or for environmental reasons. The Commission first used the term 'essential facilities' in two interim measures cases of this type: *B&I Line plc* v. *Sealink Harbours Ltd and Sealink Stena Ltd*[9] and *Sea Containers/Stena Sealink*,[10] in the latter of which it explained:

> A company in a dominant position may not discriminate in favour of its own activities in a related market. The owner of an essential facility which uses its power in one market in order to strengthen its position in another related market, in particular by granting its competitor access to that related market on less favourable terms than those of its own service, infringes Article 86 EEC where a competitive disadvantage is imposed upon its competitor without objective justification.[11]

Sea Containers/Stena Sealink[12] provided a definition of an essential facility as follows: 'a facility or infrastructure, without access to which competitors cannot provide services to their customers'.[13] Early case law confirmed that the facility could be raw materials[14] or a service.[15] It is clear from later cases, notably *Magill*,[16] that incorporeal property such as information is included within the term 'facility or infrastructure',[17] and that this term is not limited to corporeal structures such as ports and harbours.

It is not clear from the definition whether a right which is less than ownership is sufficient to impose duties on a potentially dominant undertaking. There seems no reason why actual ownership itself should be necessary. The focus of the enquiry is abuse by a dominant undertaking. It is possible that such abuse may take place where the undertaking has a contractual right less than ownership.

The analysis of whether the facility is 'essential' is perhaps one of the most difficult parts of the definition.[18] Obviously, there are many ways in which a facility could be essential. It may be financially too expensive for a third party to replicate, or replicating it may be physically impossible or unreasonable owing to planning or environmental concerns. The language used by the Commission in *Sealink/Stena* established a high test: that it is 'impossible' for the competitor to provide services without access to the facility. Later cases have focused on the practicality of duplication. For example, in *Tiercé Ladbroke* v. *EC Commission*,[19] the Court of First Instance referred to a facility being essential where there was 'no real or potential substitute'.[20] US antitrust law adopts a similar approach.[21]

In some cases assessing whether the facility is essential will be relatively simple. In *Magill*, there was only one actual physical outlet for the information/facilities, and duplication was factually impossible. Applying a standard of replication being impossible or practically unreasonable is not an easy task, particularly where replication is difficult for economic reasons. Whether an objective or subjective analysis is adopted makes a large difference to the outcome of the enquiry.

In *Oscar Bronner*, the definition was reduced to two components: (1) access to the facility is indispensable in order to compete on the market;[22] and (2) duplication is impossible or extremely difficult owing to physical, geographical or legal constraints (or is highly undesirable for reasons of public policy).[23]

The potential outcome of a successful essential facilities case is that the owner of the facility can be ordered to commence supply to the complainant, or to supply on non-discriminatory terms. However, it must be remembered that the general principle of law is that undertakings are able to choose with whom they wish to contract. The owner of an essential facility will only be under an obligation to contract in exceptional circumstances.[24]

Key Components of the Doctrine

Form of Abuse or New Rule?

One of the main difficulties in this area is that the Court of First Instance and Court of Justice have avoided the use of the term 'essential facilities'. Instead, cases have been classified as part of the jurisprudence concerning refusal to supply under Article 82. One might argue that this is perfectly understandable. It would be incorrect to classify the essential facilities doctrine as an independent, *sui generis* concept of European competition law. Essential facilities cases occur mainly in the context of Article 82[25] and, consequently, cases are decided by an application of Article 82 principles. The court must therefore establish the relevant product and geographical markets, an effect on trade between member states, the existence of dominance and the abuse of the same. Rather than a substantive principle of law, the doctrine is more in the nature of an 'abstraction designed to assist courts in determining whether the statute has been violated'.[26]

However, increasingly in EC case law, the doctrine has been applied more as a substantive principle of law rather than as a tool or aid in the application of Article 82. The development of the concept occurred implicitly at first, through the use of an analysis similar to the US essential facilities concept, but without use of the exact name. Thereafter the Commission has applied the concept overtly. Refined definitions of the concept appeared in cases such as *B&I Line plc* v. *Sealink Harbours Ltd and Sealink Stena Ltd*,[27] *Sea Containers/Stena*

Sealink,[28] *GB-INNO-BM*,[29] and more recently in *Oscar Bronner* v. *Mediaprint*.[30]

Requirement for Dominance

The essence of the essential facilities doctrine is that a dominant undertaking on one market is seeking to extend that dominance into another market.[31] One US commentator has suggested that it is a requirement in US antitrust law that dominance exist in both the upstream and downstream markets.[32] This requirement is not stressed in the European cases. If the undertaking is not already dominant on the downstream market the negative effect on competition will be less severe and therefore there will be less need to intervene. If the undertaking is dominant on the downstream market, the need to intervene will be heightened. To stipulate that dominance must always exist on both markets would, however, constrain the doctrine. The focus of the enquiry should be the discrimination/unfair treatment of competitors. This can occur regardless of dominance on the downstream market.

Although dominance in the downstream market is not a requirement, it is logical that the undertaking in control of the facility should at least be present on the downstream market. The nature of an essential facilities case is that the controller of the facility is seeking to use it to improve its position on the downstream market. There would seem to be no reason for the dominant undertaking to exclude access to the downstream market if it is not already active on the market or planning to be active.[33] However, this was, in fact, the case in *Tiercé Ladbroke* v. *Commission*,[34] where the owner of the facility had no position on the market to which the complainant was seeking access to. Given that the court considered that there was no abuse, it did not specifically consider the issue of dominance. However, at several points in the judgment the court stressed the fact that the owner of the facility was not present on the Belgian market.[35] In fact, the owners of the essential facility had granted no licences to any operators on the Belgian market, where the complainants were, in fact, already dominant.[36]

Abuse through Discrimination

Certain abuses will have a more pernicious effect on competition than others. Conduct may range from making access difficult for the competitor, offering access on unreasonable terms or terms less advantageous than those which the owner of the facility enjoys, to an absolute refusal to grant access. Where access is offered on less advantageous terms than those enjoyed by the dominant undertaking and its affiliates such as related companies, the essence of the abuse is discrimination. An abuse may occur unless it can be shown that new entrants are able to benefit from reasonable terms which equate with those enjoyed by the owner of the facility. An example of this is the *Telemarketing* case, where a television station had subjected the sale of broadcasting time for telemarketing to the use of a telephone number of an exclusive advertising agent which belonged to the same group. It was therefore seeking to reserve to itself an ancillary activity which could be carried out by another undertaking. What was involved was not an explicit refusal to supply but rather the imposition of tying conditions in the contract. This constituted discrimination given that the dominant undertaking was imposing conditions on competitors which it was not required to fulfil itself, and thereby obtaining an advantage, namely the ability to use its own telephone number.

Similarly, in the *Sealink/Stena* case, the owner of the facility had altered the schedule of ferry sailing times of its ferry division. This alteration was detrimental to the only other ferry company which operated out of the harbour, owing to the unique layout of the harbour. Thus the timetable alteration had the practical effect of favouring the owner of the essential facility and discriminating against the competitor.

Abuse through Refusal to give Access

The most severe abuse lies in seeking to close off the market entirely, reserving it to the dominant undertaking or one of its related companies. This could remove all competition from the downstream market. Early cases such as *Commercial Solvents*[37] and *United Brands*[38] were in effect cases of refusal to supply, given that they concerned cessation of supply to an existing customer rather than refusal to supply a new entrant to the market. Both cases confirmed that cessation in this manner could constitute an abuse. Denying access to a new entrant is arguably more severe, given that it acts, not only as a barrier to entry to that particular entrant, but also as a disincentive to potential entrants. In the Commission decision in the case of *Sea Containers* v. *Stena Sealink*,[39] the Commission confirmed that to exclude a new entrant to the market could amount to an abuse.[40]

Once the court moved into the realm of refusal to grant access to new entrants, it was inevitable that it would face a clash between principles of competition law and intellectual property rights. This is because the very essence of intellectual property rights is the protection of a specific part of the market for one particular undertaking. A full examination of the application of the clash between the essential facilities doctrine and intellectual property rights is outside the scope of this chapter. However, the case of *Magill*[41] is of importance to the development of the doctrine and therefore merits brief consideration.

In *Magill*, ITP, RTE and the BBC had provided information on their viewing schedules to daily newspapers under a system whereby a licence was granted free of charge. Magill, a small independent publisher, attempted to publish a comprehensive weekly television guide, but had been prevented from doing so by the appellants, who had obtained injunctions prohibiting publication. The appellants sought to use the previous case of *Volvo* v. *Veng*[42] as authority to the effect that the mere exercise by the owner of an intellectual property right could not in itself be considered an abuse of a dominant position. In delivering judgment in favour of *Magill*, the Court of Justice highlighted the importance of special circumstances which could turn a mere refusal to license/supply into an abuse. It listed the fact that the TV companies were the only source of the information and the fact that the refusal to supply had prevented the emergence of a new product which the TV companies could not provide, and for which there was consumer demand. The judgment suggests that the essence of the abuse lay in the effect of the refusal to grant access – that is, the reservation by the dominant undertaking of the secondary market and exclusion of all competition on that market.[43] Interestingly, that market was only a potential and not an actual one.

Damage to Competition, not Competitors

Under Article 82 the applicant must establish that the conduct involved has an actual or potential effect on competition. In this context it must be recalled that Article 82 is directed towards the protection of competition through prevention/punishment of abuses of a dominant position. The effect on competition is therefore more relevant to the court's enquiry than the arguments of the complainant concerning its own position.

The level of seriousness of the actual or potential effect must be established. The most serious effect would be actual elimination of all competition on the downstream market, but the effect may be short of this extreme. The judgment in *Commercial Solvents* refers to the 'risk'[44] and in *Telemarketing*[45] to the 'possibility'[46] of eliminating all competition. The *Commercial Solvents*[47] judgment also indicated that the focus of enquiry should be on the effect on the competitive structure[48] of the market, whether that be direct or indirect,[49] and expressly considered the effect on consumers.[50]

If the conduct of the dominant undertaking has eliminated all competition, then this will almost certainly be classed as an abuse. The conduct in *Magill* was a particularly extreme abuse: not only was the market reserved to the dominant undertaking but a new product which would have competed with the dominant undertaking's product was prevented from entering the market. The negative effect on competition was emphasised many times in the judgment. The judgment in *Oscar Bronner* emphasised that *Commercial Solvents* had rested on the basis that the conduct was likely to eliminate all competition.[51]

Objectively Justified Refusals?

It is clear that it is only if the conduct is not objectively justified that an actual abuse will take place.[52] This has been emphasised many times by the Court of Justice, at first in *Commercial Solvents* v. *Commission*[53] and *CBEM* v. *CLT and IPB (Telemarketing),*[54] and more recently in *Magill.*[55]

Obviously, there may be several reasons why conduct may be objectively justified. One potential reason might be the creditworthiness of the potential entrant. Generally, the dominant undertaking is seeking to prove that there are valid business reasons for the refusal and that it was not simply an arbitrary attempt to corner the market for themselves. Thus, in *Telemarketing,* the judgment refers to 'technical or commercial requirements relating to the nature of television'[56] as a potential objective justification. The Office of Fair Trading (OFT) has commented that cases where the conduct will be objectively justified are likely to be rare.[57]

Areeda has argued that there are two types of legitimate business purpose (as this defence is classed in US law). Justifications can occur at micro and macro level.[58] At micro level the justification focuses on the circumstances of the particular case, whereas at macro level the justification is a 'proposition of general policy'.[59] An example of the latter might be the general economic effect such as discouraging research and development, or the fact that the undertaking would not have acquired the facility in the first place had it known that access would have been enforced. This distinction is useful, in that it directs the court to the wider public policy issues, and not simply to issues concerning the parties.

Treatment of Capacity Constraints

The capacity of the facility is a practical consideration which is also a potential objective justification. The court must analyse whether the facility has sufficient capacity to cope adequately with the competitor's business in addition to the dominant undertaking's business. The US *Hecht* case confirms that undertakings should not be put under a duty to share if 'such sharing would be impractical or would inhibit the defendant's ability to serve its customers adequately'.[60] Thus, in *Oscar Bronner*, Mediaprint argued that the inclusion of Oscar Bronner's publications would be impossible owing to the limited capacity of the scheme.

The mere existence of extra capacity should not mean, however, that it must be made available for a competitor. The dominant undertaking may be able to point to plans to utilise the facility in the future which are central to its development and support the argument that access by a competitor is impossible. Such plans are more likely to be relevant where the dominant undertaking is new, and less likely to be relevant where the facility is well established.[61]

It seems logical that there should be no obligation to create extra capacity, and indeed US case law supports this view.[62] However, the OFT has indicated that, in its opinion, the owner of an essential facility may be obliged to create new capacity. As an example, it refers to obligations on utility network operators to connect new customers and provide access to competitors.[63] Given the fact that the essential facilities doctrine is the exception rather than the rule (of freedom of contract), it is suggested that the obligation to create new capacity should only be possible in exceptional cases. It may be that utility networks are one such special case.

Application to Network Industries

Oscar Bronner

As stated above, the particular focus of this chapter is the effect of essential facilities doctrine on networked industries. The case of *Oscar Bronner* v. *Mediaprint* provides an example of its application to an attempt to gain access to a network. Oscar Bronner was an editor and distributor of a daily newspaper in Austria. It brought a case before the Austrian competition court against Mediaprint, one of the largest suppliers of daily newspapers by way of home delivery. The national court brought an Article 177 reference to the Court of Justice.

Oscar Bronner maintained that it was unable either alone or in cooperation with other publishers to set up its own home-delivery scheme on economically reasonable conditions. It therefore sought access to Mediaprint's distribution network as it was the only economically viable home-delivery scheme in Austria. It argued that the service was an essential facility because it was indispensable to its business, there being no actual or potential substitute.[64]

The court found that no dominant position existed. Other methods of distributing daily newspapers existed and those methods were used by publishers of daily newspapers. The court stated that, in order to prove that access was 'indispensable', it would be necessary at the very least to establish that a second home-delivery network was not economically viable. The applicant's small circulation of newspapers was insufficient in itself to establish that setting up an alternative system was not economically viable. The court could see no technical, legal or economic obstacles to the setting-up of a further distribution system, either alone or in conjunction with other publishers.[65] This judgment confirms that an objective test is appropriate. Subjective factors such as the complainant's small circulation were not relevant.

The Advocate-General specifically addressed the issue of the standard of difficulty of duplication. He referred to a 'genuine stranglehold' on the related market, and stated that this would exist 'where duplication of the facility is impossible or extremely difficult owing to physical, geographical or legal constraints or is highly undesirable for reasons of public policy'.[66]

Issues Unanswered by Bronner

There are several questions left unanswered by *Bronner* which are of particular importance to utility networks. Problems of access are exacerbated where there are several complainants: must they all be treated alike and admitted on the same terms? What happens if only one undertaking has brought a complaint but other undertakings are present on the downstream market: must they also be taken into account?[67] If there is only capacity for one further undertaking in addition to the dominant undertaking, how does the court choose which undertaking should be admitted? These are all questions which would require to be answered were the essential facilities doctrine to be expanded and applied to utility networks.

Some of the potential problems can be briefly summarised. There is a perceived danger that to grant a decree requiring access penalises economically efficient undertakings and protects those which are economically inefficient. The true position may be that the dominant undertaking has reached the position of control of the facility through efficiency, or successful research and development. If this efficiency receives the 'reward' of compulsory access to competitors, this may act as a disincentive to undertakings to acquire useful assets and carry out research and development.[68] There is also a danger that the competitor requiring access is simply looking for a 'free ride'.[69] To grant access is to reward this type of behaviour.[70]

Other commentators have pointed out that vertical integration can involve economies of scale or savings in terms of cost and efficiency.[71] This could occur, for example, if one undertaking consolidated two different levels of the market, such as production of raw materials and manufacturing. The efficiency occurs because the firm itself is producing some or all of the raw materials which it requires in the manufacturing process.[72] Others again have argued that facilities should only be shared where such sharing is likely to have a positive effect on competition: it is possible that the new entrant may be less efficient or set prices similar to the incumbent's, in which case there is no competitive benefit.[73] Creation of access terms and conditions inevitably involves transaction costs. Such costs also increase with the number of undertakings seeking access to the facility.

One of the most forceful objections is that to impose a continuing relationship is an extreme remedy, and should only be used if the negative effect which would otherwise ensue is severe. It must be remembered that, as stated above, the general principle is and should remain freedom of contract.[74]

Interface with UK Utilities Regulation

If the essential facilities doctrine is to feature in any use of the Chapter II prohibition of the Competition Act 1998 in the context of vertically integrated network utilities, it may create unwelcome conflict with the existing licence regimes governing those utilities. This conflict may arise either because the doctrine duplicates the licence regime, or because it extends it. In either case, however, the problem is that use of the doctrine deprives the regulated entities of the legal certainty which they are entitled to expect.

In order to appreciate the nature of the conflict and the threats which it poses, we will examine two specific aspects of the current licensing regime. First, we will look at the licence arrangements governing the operation of the electricity interconnector between Scotland and England. Second, we will examine the arrangements for inset appointments in the water industry in England and Wales.

Electricity: The Scottish Interconnector

Scottish Power plc is the successor company formed to acquire the assets and undertaking of the former South of Scotland Electricity Board. It is vertically integrated – that is, it is engaged in the generation, transmission, distribution and supply of electricity. One of the assets of its transmission business is a set of electrical circuits, or 'interconnector', connecting the Scottish electricity 'grid' to that in England.

On the transfer of assets on privatisation, Scottish Power was granted a number of licences pursuant to the Electricity Act 1989 which regulate the operation of different parts of its electricity operations. These licences are granted by the Secretary of State and are administered by the Director-General of Electricity Supply. The licence granted to Scottish Power's transmission business contains detailed provisions regarding operation of the Scottish transmission system owned and operated by it and, in particular, the interconnector. Certain key elements of these provisions can be summarised as follows.

- *Price control*: charges for use of the interconnector (or of any upgrade – see below) are required to be set at a level which will enable Scottish Power to recover no more than a reasonable rate of return on the capital invested by it. Further, Scottish Power must not, in setting its charges for use of the interconnector restrict, distort or prevent competition in the transmission, supply, distribution or generation of electricity.[75]
- *Capacity statement*: Scottish Power is required to prepare and publish annual statements detailing amounts of interconnector capacity under use and available for use.[76]
- *Non discrimination*: in the provision of use of the interconnector, Scottish Power must not discriminate between any person or class or classes of persons, or between itself (in providing use of the interconnector to its own upstream or downstream activities) and any person or class or classes of persons.[77]
- *Offer of terms*: on application made by any person, Scottish Power must, generally speaking, offer to enter into an agreement for use of the interconnector to transport electricity in such quantities and for such periods as may be required by or on behalf of such person (and if the terms of the agreement cannot be settled between the parties, the Director has the power to settle the terms for them).[78]
- *Offer to upgrade*: in the event that there is insufficient available capacity on the interconnector to accommodate a third party request for use, Scottish Power is required to offer terms for increasing or 'upgrading' that capacity. In fixing its charges for use of that upgraded capacity, Scottish Power is obliged to have regard to the benefit (if any) to be obtained or likely to be obtained by it or any other person from the increase in capacity and to its ability or likely ability to recoup part of its costs from third parties.[79]

Water: Inset Appointments

The Water Act 1989 established a regime under which the ten water authorities in England and Wales were privatised and licences were granted to vertically integrated successors, known as water and sewerage undertakers, to operate geographical monopolies for all aspects of water and sewerage services. A Director-General of Water Services was appointed to administer the licence regime.

The statutory regime (as altered by the Water Industry Act 1991) provides for competitive entry into the water and sewerage industries in England and Wales. The Director may appoint new companies in either (or both) capacities with the agreement of the incumbent undertaker, or where the new appointment covers an undeveloped site, or the customer concerned uses or is expected to use above a threshold amount of water per year. In making such an appointment (known as an 'inset' appointment), the Director is empowered to require an incumbent undertaker to provide a bulk transfer of water to the new undertaker or to permit it to connect its sewerage system to the incumbent's system, including the use of its treatment works.

Under section 40 of the 1991 Act, where the Director is satisfied that an applicant and the undertaker from which it requires a bulk supply cannot agree on the terms for the supply, he may make a determination requiring the supplier to give and the applicant to take such a supply for such a period and on such terms and conditions as may be provided in the order. Any such determination must have regard to factors such as the need for the supplier to recover the expenses of complying with its obligations under the order and securing a reasonable return on its capital. Similar powers exist under section 110A of the Act with regard to the determination of terms of sewerage connection agreements.

Importantly, the limited competition in the downstream (retail) supply market introduced by the 1991 Act was not supplemented by any measures promoting competition in the upstream (wholesale) market. In other words, the inset appointee must still purchase a bulk supply from the incumbent rather than being able to obtain a bulk supply from a third party and require the incumbent simply to transport it.

Assessment

It can be seen that both of these licensing arrangements provide means for regulating the operation of facilities, an interconnector and a water transport grid, access to which is 'essential' if downstream competition is to develop and thrive. Clearly, they do so in quite different ways. In the interconnector context, third parties are given the right to obtain access to the infrastructure in question, whereas in the water context such access rights are more limited, but are supplemented by a right to obtain bulk supplies in the downstream market from the facility operator itself.

The next section of this chapter looks at the role which is already being mapped out for the essential facilities doctrine in these same areas, notwithstanding the existence of licensing solutions, and points to the threats to legal certainty which this may create.

Application of the Doctrine in the UK Utilities Sector

The threats posed by the development of the essential facilities doctrine in the context of the UK utilities sector can best be appreciated in the context of two major policy reforms, both running in parallel and due to crystallise at the turn of the century: first, the proposed reform of utilities regulation in the shape of the promised Utilities Reform Bill; and, second, the continuing reform of competition law via the Competition Act 1998.

Reform of Utilities Regulation

A number of factors, such as the increased competition in the period since privatisation and the emergence of multi-utility players, has led the government to propose modernising the framework for UK utility regulation. The proposals were set out in the Green Paper published in March 1998, entitled 'A Fair Deal For Consumers – Modernising the Framework for Utility Regulation'. The response to the consultation exercise was published in July 1998 and the government introduced a bill to amend telecommunications, gas, electricity and water regulation in January 2000.

One of the key themes of the Green Paper and the response document was that of 'better regulation'.[80] The government envisages that each sectoral regulator will be placed under a statutory duty to consult on, publish and follow a code of practice governing their consultation and decision-making processes. Crucially, the codes would include the procedures regulators intend to adopt in determining when a market has moved from a pre-competitive state to a state which is fully competitive.[81] This is a key point, according to the government, since 'it will determine when regulatory controls are lifted. It affects, for example, the stage at which price controls on a dominant supplier can be lifted, and the stage at which service standards set by the regulator may give way to an approach based on the publication of comparable information on performance.'[82]

Reform of UK Competition Law

The Competition Act 1998 introduces two new prohibitions, closely modelled on Articles 81 and 82 EC. Chapter 1 prohibits agreements which prevent, restrict or distort competition and may affect trade within the UK and Chapter II prohibits abuse of a dominant position in the UK or part of it, where this may affect trade within the UK. As with Article 82, there is an illustrative list of the kind of conduct which may constitute an abuse. Behaviour which infringes the prohibition will be unlawful and subject to penalties. Third parties affected by anti-competitive behaviour in breach of the prohibitions will be entitled to seek compensation.

The prohibitions will be enforced primarily by the Director-General of Fair Trading, although the utility regulators will have concurrent powers in their particular sectors. This means that, in any one context, they will have the ability to choose between these powers and their existing licensing powers for the purpose of imposing a solution. The Chapter II prohibition, which is planned to become the principal tool for dealing with anti-competitive conduct by monopolists, is of particular interest to utility regulators.

In one of its guidelines, the OFT talks specifically about the role of the essential facilities doctrine in the context of utility networks. It suggests, for instance, that utility distribution networks (electricity wires, water and gas pipelines) are all potential candidates to be treated as essential facilities for the purposes of the Chapter II prohibition.[83]

The Concerns Raised by Essential Facilities Doctrine

The development of an essential facilities doctrine in the context of regulation of utilities in the UK would appear potentially to undermine the government's three key stated means for improving industry confidence in the regulatory regime: transparency, consistency and accountability.

The transparency issue Despite its flaws and the acknowledged need for reform, the rules of the current UK regime for utilities regulation are at least clearly established in the various privatisation statutes and licensing regime. Where 'essential facilities' exist, in terms of vital and unique infrastructure assets, there are clear rules to determine both the means of gaining access to them and the terms upon which access rights are to be enjoyed. The interconnector example mentioned above is a case in point. To the extent that the relevant licence does not provide the answer itself, it empowers the relevant Director to impose a solution based on his expert determination.

It is difficult to express the same confidence as to precisely how any essential facilities doctrine developed under the Chapter II prohibition will operate in this context, which is worrying for regulated utilities who will be exposed to fines and legal actions for compensation if they are found to be in breach.

This transparent regime contrasts starkly with some regulators' perception of their new powers to apply the essential facilities doctrine. To return to the water example, the Director's draft guidelines on the essential facilities doctrine and common carriage state that, where

> a facility is *deemed by the Director* to be essential, the onus will be placed on the facility owner to prove that a refusal to share access has an objective justification. In addition, the *unreasonable* refusal by an undertaker to expand the capacity of an essential facility to meet the demands placed on facilities by an undertaking requesting common carriage, or to offer *reasonable* terms for network expansion, may also be regarded as an abuse. (Emphasis added)[84]

This statement could hardly be described as transparent or comprehensive. Indeed, the paper also suggests that, in a case where he has chosen to act, the 'Director *may* also publish his reasoning in deciding that an infringement had occurred, including relevant analysis of the costs involved' (emphasis added).[85] Contrast this statement with the government's commitment in its July 1998 Response Paper that it 'intends to introduce a duty on the regulators to publish reasons for key decisions'.[86]

It would seem that there is also a fundamental confusion on OFWAT's part as to the difference between the Director enforcing Chapter II, on the one hand, in the essential facilities context, and adjudicating on access disputes under his licence powers. The draft guidelines assert:

> Where the Director has reasonable grounds for suspecting that an infringement of the Chapter II prohibition has occurred, he will ask the owner of the facility to justify his offer of terms for network access or expansion. He may also require the owner of the facility and the person seeking access to provide an expert assessment of the case. The assessment should offer an opinion of what would be reasonable terms to achieve access. *If the parties involved cannot agree terms, the Director may find that there has been a breach of the prohibition, and use his powers under the Act to apply a remedy.* (Emphasis added)[87]

The consistency issue The boundaries of each of the current UK utility regulatory regimes are fairly well defined. We have also seen that the government has proposed that regulators provide clear indications of when and how those boundaries are to be rolled back in light of increased competition. It would appear that there is little or no acceptance on the part of the OFT or the regulators that they ought to respect those boundaries in applying the Chapter II prohibition in the utilities sectors. Rather, there is the suggestion that Chapter II –

and the essential facilities doctrine – will both supplement and potentially overlap the relevant regimes.

This is revealed in one of the OFT's own draft guidance papers, where it discusses the role of the essential facilities doctrine. It is stated that 'In the case of UK utility networks, there are licence or statutory obligations on network operators to connect new customers and to provide access to competitors (subject to conditions). Refusal by the owner to permit the creation of further capacity to accommodate additional users is likely to constitute an abuse.'[88] No attempt is made, it would seem, to identify the boundary between those licence or statutory obligations and the occurrence of abuse. Indeed, the impression given is of the new prohibition effectively 'filling a gap' in a somehow incomplete regime.

Confirmation of this approach can be seen in the current round of consultation on concurrent application of Chapter II in the water and sewerage sectors in England and Wales. There, OFWAT has seized the opportunity provided by the essential facilities doctrine to 'plug' a perceived regulatory 'gap' in relation to inset appointments. According to OFWAT's consultation paper, it 'regards "common carriage" as the shared use of assets by undertakings. In many circumstances it would be uneconomic for a competitor to duplicate the provision of large assets, such as a pipe network or treatment facility. Common carriage, therefore, has the potential to increase customer choice by facilitating the entry of competitors (whether existing undertakers or new entrants) into a local market.'[89]

OFWAT acknowledges that there is no specific statutory framework under the Water Industry Act 1991 for common carriage. However, it believes that:

> the [Competition] Act provides an effective legal framework for the development of common carriage, where there are genuine opportunities for improved services to customers. Refusal by one undertaking to grant access to facilities that would allow another undertaking to compete in its market could be seen to be an attempt to restrict competition. Similarly, the imposition of unreasonable price or non-price terms could have the effect of restricting or preventing competition. Both could be considered infringements of the Chapter II prohibition.[90]

It must surely be a matter for some concern that regulators ostensibly charged with applying a statutory regime and exercising licensing powers in a particular sector consider themselves in a position to extend their jurisdiction over unregulated aspects of the sector under cover of identifying abuse. Is it permissible for regulators to take this course when there exist other means (licence modifications and primary legislation) for achieving the same ends? In fact, the government's Green Paper specifically concluded:

> The scale monopoly provisions of the Fair Trading Act should be retained for the regulated utility sectors. Because of the special circumstances of the utility sectors, and the difficulty of establishing competition, use of the scale monopoly provisions should be possible whether or not there has been a prior finding of abuse of a dominant position under the Competition Bill when this becomes law.[91]

Clearly, the 1973 Act's scale monopoly provisions (which are closely linked, in terms of process, to the licence modification provisions of the utility statutes) would provide a means of remedying regulatory deficiencies which was not dependent on any finding of abuse on the part of the regulated utility. But why should this matter? This question prompts an examination of the third area of concern, that of accountability.

The accountability issue It is the writers' view that the powers conferred on legal institutions ought to be consistent with the means by which they can be held to account. Bodies which are called upon to apply legal norms ought to be accountable in ways different from administrative agencies which apply policy. It would be inappropriate, for instance, for a court to give members of the public or users of a service the opportunity to influence its decision as to whether the relevant service provider had or had not breached its legal duties. On the other hand, a regulator looking to fix the price for that service would certainly need to involve them.

The corollary, in the writers' view, is also true: that is, the method of accountability prescribed for a legal institution ought to determine the powers legitimately exercisable by an institution. In other words, if a body is required to act judicially and is subject to control by the appellate courts on points of law, then it is not entitled to apply policy considerations in a way that ought to involve wider and different forms of participation.

It is this same institutional dilemma that so concerned Advocate-General Jacobs in the *Oscar Bronner* case. It is therefore worth pausing to look at the some of those concerns in more detail, particularly in relation to the crafting of remedies by courts.

The issue of remedies in an essential facilities case is a particularly difficult one. In general, under an Article 82 case, the judgment can decree that the abuse should terminate, or that a fine be payable. However, in cases of refusal to grant access, what the complainant is seeking is the reinstatement of supply, or, if the applicant is a new entrant, the commencement of supply. In essential facilities cases, therefore, the court may instruct the dominant undertaking to carry out positive action, much as a decree of specific implement or performance would require.

Some might argue that the difference between a positive and a negative decree is semantic rather than substantive. However, generally, decrees requiring positive action are more problematic.[92] This is because, in order to ensure that a decree is effective, the court must effectively 'police' the decree, ensuring compliance by the undertaking. The decree must also be sufficiently certain, so that the undertaking is in no doubt as to what is required of it. Continuing supervision is particularly difficult for a court to carry out, and is more characteristic of the functions of a regulator. These difficulties have meant that in English law the primary remedy for breach of contract is damages, specific performance providing a secondary remedy should, for some reason, an award of damages be unsuitable because it does not provide adequate compensation.[93]

However, essential facilities cases involve even greater difficulties than other cases of decrees requiring positive action. The terms of access require to be set out in the decree. Setting such terms will be an extremely difficult exercise for a court, having no investigatory powers, and one which, one might argue, courts are unqualified to carry out. The task involves knowledge of the industry which the court, comprising lawyers and not businesspersons, simply does not have. Courts are able only to rely on expert evidence which may not give a clear picture of the overall structure and content of the market. The complexity of the task may vary depending upon the nature of the facility. Creation of terms of access to, for example, a bridge is probably simpler than creation of terms relating to intellectual property rights. However, the task clearly seems better suited to sector-specific regulation. If a pre-existing regulatory structure is in place, it seems advisable to leave it to that structure to find a solution. However, if the industry is not regulated, this option is not available. Should this be the case, setting prices and conditions is an even more difficult task for a court.[94] As was explored in the introductory chapter of this book, what is required here is regulation of the rules of admission and relations between occupants in the shared regulatory space.

Where the problem is not refusal to grant access, but the fairness of access terms already granted, the courts may be required to determine the fairness of the fee charged. Again, this involves knowledge of the industry, and so the objections stated above are equally applicable here. Clearly, the analysis will be an economic one requiring careful consideration of the structure of the market and previous behaviour of undertakings on that market.

It seems to the writers that OFWAT and others, in their enthusiasm to embrace their concurrent Chapter II powers, risk ignoring the warning of Advocate-General Jacobs in *Bronner*. It is not good enough to dismiss this simply as concern about the structural failings of courts in this context. The warning applies equally to any agency (whether a court or the sectoral regulator) which applies Chapter II. In other words, if a regulator is called upon to penalise an abuse of a dominant position, it risks subverting that duty by crafting forward-looking remedies designed to pursue market opening or any other policy agenda.

The authors suspect that sectoral regulators, in their attempts to craft detailed remedies aimed at correcting anticipated or threatened 'abuse' by utility network operators in terms of the Chapter II prohibition, will end up recreating something not unlike a licence regime under which the same entities have operated since privatisation. The key difference, of course, will be that such a 'meta' regulatory scheme (which will evolve on a case-by-case basis rather than by licence modification) will not be capable of amendment or review by political means in the same way as the conditions in traditional regulatory licences.

In light of the government's stated desire to see a clear divide between the regulated and unregulated sectors of the utilities sector, this 'creeping regulation' and lack of accountability will, it is submitted, seriously undermine efforts to inspire confidence among the regulated in those wielding regulatory authority (however described) over them.

Conclusions

The essential facilities doctrine takes competition law to the very limit of its legitimate scope, and possibly across the border into regulation. Whether this strays across the line can best be ascertained by looking at the strain which it is likely to place on the legitimacy of those legal institutions called upon to apply it in practice.

There is little doubt that vital infrastructure assets, bottlenecks or other essential facilities do need to be regulated. Control of essential facilities thus aptly illustrates the ideas explored in Chapter 1 of this book, given that the area illustrates the requirement for regulation to create the conditions necessary for the market to operate. However, it is properly for elected politicians to establish comprehensive, transparent and forward-looking regulatory regimes for such assets at the outset. It is not for the courts or competition authorities to develop parallel or overlapping regimes which have none of these characteristics, in the name of preventing or remedying past abuse. Unless that is accepted, the losers will be not only those operating essential facilities but also the consumers and shareholders they serve.

Notes

1 224 US 383 (1912), although the actual term 'essential facilities' was not used until *Hecht* v. *Pro-Football Inc* 570 F.2d 982, 992–3 (D.C. 1977). One of the most significant cases for the development of the doctrine was *MCI Communications* v. *AT & T* 708 F.2d 1081 (7th Cir.).
2 See the influential article by Areeda, P. (1990) 'Essential Facilities: An Epithet in Need of Limiting Principles', *Antitrust Law Journal*, 58, 841.
3 For analysis see Furse, M. (1995) 'The 'Essential Facilities' Doctrine in Community Law', *European Competition Law Review*, 8, 469; D. Ridyard (1996) 'Essential Facilities and the Obligations to Supply Competitors Under EC and UK Competition Law', *European Competition Law Review*, 8, 438; S. White (1995) 'Is There a Role for an "Essential Facilities" Doctrine in Europe', *Communications and Technology Law Review*, 4, 110.
4 Case C-7/97 [1999] 4 CMLR 112.
5 *Ibid.*, para. 69 of his opinion.
6 Cases 6 and 7/73, *Commercial Solvents* v. *Commission* [1974] ECR 223, [1974] 1 CMLR 309.
7 *Ibid.*, para [25] of the judgment.
8 *B & I Line plc* v. *Sealink Harbours Limited and Sealink Stena Ltd* Commission Decision IV/34.174 [1992] 5 CMLR 255; *Sea Containers/Stena Sealink* Commission Decision EC/94/119, OJ 1994 L15/8; *Port of Rodby* Commission Decision EC 94/119, OJ 1994 L55/52; *Port of Roscoff* [1995] CMLR 677.
9 Commission Decision IV/34.174 [1992] 5 CMLR 255.
10 Commission Decision EC/94/119, OJ 1994 L15/8.
11 *Ibid.*, at para. [41] of the decision.
12 [1994] OJ L15/8.
13 *Ibid.*, at para. [66] of the judgment.
14 Cases 6 and 7/73, *Commercial Solvents* v. *Commission* [1974] ECR 223, [1994] 1 CMLR 309.
15 Case 311/84, *CBEM* v. *CLT and IPB (Telemarketing)* [1985] ECR 3261, [1986] 2 CMLR 558.
16 Cases C-241 & 242/91, *RTE and ITP* v. *Commission* ('Magill') [1995] 1 ECR 743, [1995] 4 CMLR 718.
17 This is also the position in US antitrust law; see, for example, *Aspen Highlands Skiing Corp* v. *Aspen Skiing Co* 738 F.2d 1509 (10th Cir.1984).
18 Seelen, C. (1997) 'The Essential Facilities Doctrine: What Does it Mean to be Essential?', *Marquette Law Review*, 80, 1117–8 states that there is no precise definition of 'essential' in US antitrust law.
19 Case T-504/93 [1997] ECR II – 923 [1998] appeal pending C-300/97 P.
20 *Ibid.*, para. 131 of the judgment.
21 The 'competitor's inability practically or reasonably to duplicate the essential facility'. This is part of the four element test established in *MCI Communications* v. *American Telephone and Telegraph Co* 708 F.2d 1081 (7th Cir).
22 Above, n.4. Advocate-General Jacobs' opinion at para. 65 refers to a 'genuine stranglehold on the related market'.
23 *Ibid.*
24 This point was emphasised in both *Magill* and *Oscar Bronner*.
25 However, if an agreement between rival undertakings exists, an Article 81 analysis is relevant.
26 Kezbom, A. and Goldman, A.V. (1996), 'No Shortcut to Antitrust Analysis: The Twisted Journey of the "Essential Facilities" Doctrine', <http://www.ffhsj.com

/firmpage/cmemos/011204.htm> reprinted from *Columbia Business Law Review*, 1(1), 15.
27 Note 8, above.
28 Note 8, above.
29 Case C-18/88: [1991] ECR I-5941, para. [18] of the judgment.
30 See, in particular, the Advocate-General's (Jacobs) opinion at para. 34, and paras [37] to [46] of the judgment.
31 Seelen (n.18, above), 1122.
32 Harz, M.H. (1994), 'Dominance and Duty in the European Union: A Look Through Microsoft Windows at the Essential Facilities Doctrine', http://www.law.emory.edu/EILR/volumes/ spg97/HARZ.html at 14 and at 12, where he refers to Venit, J.S. and J.J. Kallaugher (1994), 'Essential Facilities: A Comparative Approach', *Fordham Corporate Law Institute (Proceedings of)* 317.
33 Tye, W. (1987) 'Competitive Access: A Comparative Industry Approach to the Essential Facility Doctrine', *Energy Law Journal*, 8, 338.
34 Note 19, above.
35 *Ibid.*, paras 130 and 133 of the judgment.
36 *Ibid.*, para. 124 of the judgment.
37 Note 6, above.
38 Case 27/76, *United Brands* v. *E C Commission* [1978] ECR 207; [1978] 1 CMLR 429.
39 Note 10, above.
40 *Ibid.* para. 67.
41 Note 16, above.
42 Case 238/87: [1988] ECR 6211; [1989] 4 CMLR 122.
43 Note 16, above, paras [30] and [56] of the judgment.
44 *Ibid.*, Para.[25] of the judgment.
45 Note 15, above.
46 *Ibid.*, para. [27] of the judgment.
47 Note 14, above.
48 *Ibid.*, paras [32] and [33] of the judgment.
49 *Ibid.*
50 *Ibid.*
51 *Ibid.*, Para. [38] of the judgment.
52 See OFT draft Guidelines on the application of the Competition Act 1998: Assessment of individual agreements and conduct, 7.17. US antitrust law recognises a similar defence of 'legitimate business purpose': see Areeda, 'Essential Facilities' (n.2, above), 852, although it is not explicitly included in the four element test in *MCI*.
53 Note 14, above.
54 Case 311/84 [1985] ECR 3261 at paras [23] and [27] of the judgment; [1986] 2 CMLR 558.
55 Note 16, above, para. [55] of the judgment.
56 Note 15, above, para. [26] of the judgment.
57 OFT Draft Guidelines on application of the Competition Act 1998: Assessment of individual agreements and conduct, 7.17.
58 Areeda, 'Essential Facilities' (n.2, above), 850–51.
59 *Ibid.*
60 *Hecht* v. *Pro-Football Inc* 570 F.2d 982 at 992–3 (DC Cir. 1977).
61 This is pointed out by the OFT Draft Guidelines on application of the Competition Act 1998: Assessment of individual agreements and conduct, 7.12.
62 See cases cited by Pengilley, W. (1994), 'Hilmer and "Essential Facilities"', *University of New South Wales Law Journal*, 17(1) at fn. 27.

63 OFT Draft Guidelines on application of the Competition Act 1998: Assessment of individual agreements and conduct, 7.13.
64 See *Magill* (n.16, above).
65 *Ibid.*, paras [42] to [47] of the judgment.
66 Note 4, above, para. 65 of the Advocate-General's opinion
67 Werden, G.J. (1987), 'The Law and Economics of the Essential Facilities Doctrine', *St Louis University Law Journal*, 32, 477.
68 *Ibid.*, 473.
69 Tye, 'Competitive Access' (n.33, above), 347.
70 See discussion of policy factors in Advocate-General Jacobs' opinion in *Oscar Bronner*, para. 57.
71 Tye, 'Competitive Access' (n.33, above,), 338; Hay, G.A. and K. McMahon (1994), 'The "Duty to Deal" Under s.46: Panacea or Pandora's Box?', *University of New South Wales Law Journal*, 17(1), 61.
72 Werden, G.J. (1987), 'The Law and Economics of the Essential Facility Doctrine', *St Louis University Law Journal*, 32, 474 describes downstream integration into distribution of one's own goods as 'competitively benign and efficient'.
73 These concerns are recognised in the Draft Guidelines on the application of the Competition Act 1998: Assessment of individual agreements and conduct, 7.14; Areeda, 'Essential Facilities' (n.2, above), 852.
74 See Advocate-General Jacobs' opinion in *Oscar Bronner*, 56.
75 SP Licence, Part VI, Conditions 3(1) and 3A(4).
76 *Ibid.*, Condition 3(7).
77 *Ibid.*, Condition 3A(1).
78 *Ibid.*, Conditions 3B(1) and 3C(1).
79 *Ibid.*, Condition 3B(3).
80 'Fair Deal for Consumers: Modernising the Framework for Utility Regulation – The Response to Consultation' (July 1998), para. 68.
81 'A Fair Deal for Consumers: Modernising the Framework for Utility Regulation – Consultation Paper' (July 1998), conclusion, 7.3 ('Fair Deal For Consumers').
82 'Fair Deal for Consumers', para. 7.
83 'Assessment of Individual Agreements and Conduct' OFT 414 (September 1999), para. 7.3.
84 'Competition Act 1998: Application in the Water and Sewerage Sectors', OFT 422 (July 1999), para. 3.35.
85 *Ibid.*, para. 3.36.
86 'Fair Deal for Consumers', conclusion 7.5.
87 'Competition Act 1998: Application in the Water and Sewerage Sectors', OFT 422 (July 1999), para. 3.36.
88 'Assessment of Individual Agreements and Conduct', OFT 414 (Formal Consultation Draft), para. 7.13. Interestingly, this paragraph has been removed in the final version of the guideline.
89 'Competition Act 1998: Application in the Water and Sewerage Sectors', OFT 422 (July 1999), para. 3.28.
90 *Ibid.*, para. 3.30.
91 'Fair Deal for Consumers', proposal 4.5.
92 See MacQueen, H.L. and L.J. Macgregor (1999) 'Specific Implement, Interdict and Contractual Performance', *Edinburgh Law Review*, 3, 39, for an analysis of the position in Scots law.
93 See *Co-operative Insurance Society Ltd* v. *Argyll Stores (Holdings) Ltd*, 1998 AC 1 at 11, per Lord Hoffman.
94 Pengilley, W. 'Hilmer and "Essential Facilities"' (n.62, above), 3.

3 The Regulation of Trans-European Networks

SAM HAMILTON,* ***Shepherd & Wedderburn***

Introduction

Within defined geographical boundaries there are a number of factors that distinguish a single economic area from a collection of individual economic areas. A recurring theme in a single economic area is a commonality of laws, systems and structures, the existence of which is both a prerequisite for the creation of such an area and an indication that such an area exists. The European Union (EU) is in the process of transforming the area within its geographical competence into a single economic area, or single market, from the collection of individual economic areas that exist at present. As part of this process the laws, systems and structures of the Member States within the EU are moving toward parity with one another.

The EU considers that an important element in the realisation of the single market is the creation of infrastructure networks that span the EU. It is envisaged that the development of these networks, known as trans-European networks (TENs), in areas such as energy, transport and telecommunication will help bring about the single market by aiding political and social cohesion and facilitating competition in network products. Although mature networks exist in the areas of energy, transport and telecommunications in most Member States, the historical lack of European political integration has resulted in diverse national infrastructure networks that are not, with limited exceptions, interoperable or interconnected.[1]

* This chapter is in part based on research carried out by the author at the Australian National University in 1997 for the course in Law and Economics as part of the degree of Master of Laws. The author would like to thank John Grady for his extensive and insightful comments on earlier drafts of this chapter.

At present TENs exist only as a concept. Their development involves both the creation of physical infrastructure and the development of a regulatory framework that will allow an equivalence of competitive conditions throughout the single market. The inherent administrative, physical and financial difficulty of linking disparate networks[2] has resulted in a disproportionate emphasis being given to the physical creation of TENs and consequently insufficient consideration being given to the development of a dedicated regulatory structure that will govern TENs in both their development and operational stages. Although in the short term the physical existence of TENs may fulfil certain EU social and political objectives, in the long term the lack of a coherent regulatory structure will lead to the inefficient provision of network services across the EU and so inhibit the development of the single market.

Trans-European Networks

The term 'trans-European network' could be applied to any number of networks that are European in their scale, and indeed the EU's programmes for the development of TENs in energy, transport and telecommunications cover a wide range of networks in addition to those normally associated with such activities.[3] For the purposes of this chapter, however, attention will focus on the main networks associated with energy, transport and telecommunications, such as electricity grids and gas pipelines, roads and railways and fixed line and mobile communications networks.

History

The imperative for creating TENs is twofold. In social and political terms, TENs can be seen as a catalyst in cementing a new unified European political structure: as a report into the creation of TENs in energy and transport noted, 'The emergence of new political entities has led historically to corresponding adaptations of the infrastructures of trade and communication, which in turn help consolidate the new entities.'[14] On an economic level, however, TENs can be seen as a benefit of a unified political structure creating economic conditions that allow competition between or along networks where previously this was not possible.

The Maastricht Treaty was the first EU treaty to give a mandate for the development of TENs, inserting Article 154 into the Treaty Establishing the European Community, which reads:

1. To help achieve the objectives referred to in Articles 14[5] and 158[6] and to enable citizens of the Union, economic operators and regional and local communities to derive full benefit from the setting up of an area without internal frontiers, the Community shall contribute to the establishment and development of trans-European networks in the areas of transport, telecommunications and energy infrastructures.
2. Within the framework of a system of open and competitive markets, action by the Community shall aim at promoting the interconnection and interoperability of national networks as well as access to such networks. It shall take account in particular of the need to link island, landlocked and peripheral regions with the central regions of the Community.

Article 155 of the Treaty further states:

1. In order to achieve the objective referred to in Article 154, the Community:

   – shall establish a series of guidelines covering the objectives, priorities and broad lines of measures envisaged in the sphere of trans-European networks; these guidelines shall identify projects of common interest;
   – shall implement any measures that may prove necessary to ensure the interoperability of the networks, in particular in the field of technical standardisation;
   – may support projects of common interest which are identified in the framework of the guidelines referred to in the first indent, particularly through feasibility studies, loan guarantees or interest rate subsidies.

The guidelines envisaged in terms of the first indent of Article 155 created three TEN programmes:[7] TEN-Energy,[8] TEN-Transport[9] and TEN-Telecom.[10] As detailed in Articles 154 and 155, the EU's role in the physical creation of TENs through the TEN programmes is that of a facilitator, coordinating the creation of interconnecting infrastructure and ensuring that such infrastructure is interoperable by standardising network operating systems. The physical infrastructure will be largely developed by the private sector.

Regulation

At EU level the regulation of network industries is a relatively new phenomenon and has initially been developed through a series of internal market Directives. Following the principle of subsidiarity, these detail general principles of regulation that require to be incorporated within the regulatory structures of the Member States.[11] In terms of regulatory principles the internal market Directives have two central themes: structural separation and open access.

Structural separation involves separating the provision of network infrastructure from competition in network services in order to remove the incentive for market participants engaged in both activities to act anti-competitively.[12] The principle of open access requires network operators to offer access to third parties on non-discriminatory terms and conditions. These principles are easily discernible in the internal market Directives that relate to electricity,[13] transport[14] and telecommunications.[15]

A third principle that will be applicable to TENs, and which is not detailed at length in the internal market Directives, is that of the application of general competition law. The Competition Directorates-General department of the European Commission has produced a number of notices on the application of competition laws to the various network industries.[16] In the context of TENs, and specifically in relation to the interconnectors that will complete the TENs, the Commission has acknowledged that the application of competition rules to all interconnectors *per se* may be unfeasible and has indicated that it will be prepared to consider such interconnectors on a case-by-case basis.[17]

Before considering the adequacy of the proposed regulatory structure that will govern TENs, consideration will turn to the principles that underlie the regulation of networks in general and the application of such principles in comparable jurisdictions.

The Regulation of Networks

The principles governing the regulation of networks are most readily understood when considered in the context of the historical development of networks. In most industrialised nations the provision of networks has historically been entrusted to a monopoly. It is often assumed that this was because the provision of network services was a natural monopoly and, although networks display a number of characteristics of natural monopoly,[18] a more significant reason for the historical monopoly status of network industries was the requirement for universal network coverage[19] in a standardised way,[20] objectives that at the time were best served by a single entity. These objectives were further advanced by insulating such entities from competition as, at the time, competition in a developing market was seen as destructive, leading to the duplication of networks, a lack of standardisation and coverage only in profitable areas.[21] It has been said of the American telecommunications industry, for example, that 'The early days of multiple telephone companies were referred to as the era of "destructive competition". A public consensus emerged favouring only one telephone company.'[22]

While the monopolistic provision of networks can been seen to have advantages in an era when networks are developing, once networks have become established, the advantages of monopoly provision are usually outweighed by the inefficiencies traditionally associated with monopolies.[23] When this stage is reached many countries have attempted to expose networks industries to market forces promoting a structural transformation from state monopoly to competitive environment.

Once the decision has been taken to subject network industries to competitive forces, there are generally three options available: network competition, service competition or a combination of both. Network competition encourages the development of alternative networks, whereas service competition involves facilitating competition over the same network by rivals differentiated only by price and service. In most cases, however, whichever competitive environment is chosen, a combination of network and service competition is likely to result, as there is usually a part of the network that cannot be replicated, whether through financial or physical impossibility,[24] resulting in certain parts of existing infrastructure being the only medium along which market participants can compete. For this reason the issue of access to essential network infrastructure is perhaps the most important issue in the field of network regulation.

Network Access

The issue of access to infrastructure facilities that cannot be replicated has received little consideration in the EU in comparison to in the USA, where the issue has been extensively considered and has resulted in the development of a doctrine known as the 'essential facilities' doctrine.

The essential facilities doctrine relates to the ownership of, and access to, infrastructure facilities that cannot practicably be replicated.[25] The purpose of the doctrine is to assist in the consideration of questions of access by providing a test that can be applied to any given piece of infrastructure in order to determine whether access should be granted. In short, the doctrine states that the owner of a piece of infrastructure that cannot be replicated should be required to give access to that infrastructure on equitable terms if doing so would promote competition. The doctrine overwrites conventional rules of property ownership on the basis of public policy: that in certain circumstances the benefit to society of granting access to such a facility is greater than the benefits of exclusive property ownership. The test used to establish whether a particular infrastructure facility can be considered an essential facility is not universally accepted,[26] although the two central issues will usually be concerned with whether the facility can be replicated and, secondly, even where a facility cannot be replicated, no alternative facility or means of facilitating competition in the market to which the facility relates exists.[27]

It is necessary in considering whether a particular facility is an essential facility, having determined that the facility cannot be replicated, to define the particular market in question in order to assess whether there are alternative means that could provide competition rather than through access to the facility in question. A good example of this was the European Court of First Instance decision in the *European Night Services* case,[28] which concerned an agreement to reserve capacity through the Channel Tunnel. It was argued that the Channel Tunnel was an essential facility as the cost and difficulty of construction make it impossible to replicate. The court held, however, that the Channel Tunnel could not be considered an essential facility as, although it could not be replicated, access to the Tunnel was not necessary to facilitate competition in the market for business and leisure travellers between certain European cities. This was because passage by train was not the only means of passage between cities, as transport by air and road were substitutable.

The scope of this chapter does not provide the opportunity to consider the essential facilities doctrine in detail, although even a basic understanding of the doctrine provides a useful background to any consideration of the regulation of networks as it is used as the basis of utility regulation in a number of jurisdictions.

Access Pricing

Even if the issue of access to network infrastructure is resolved, it should not be assumed that a competitive outcome will result. A third party gaining access to a network will have to pay for access and the price paid will be significant in determining the level of competition that results. Indeed, it would be fair to say that access pricing can have such a significant effect on competitive outcomes that, if an inadequate access pricing arrangement is in place, the effect of any infrastructure access regime could be made redundant. Access pricing is a notoriously difficult enterprise engendering vigorous debate as to the most appropriate pricing structure for a particular industry.

Access pricing is contentious because it is primarily an instrument of policy. An access price has two components: fixed charges, those that contribute towards the capital cost of the infrastructure, and variable charges, which encompass both the cost of capacity and the cost of transit. In terms of the fixed charge element, the level of costs that can be recovered will be a matter for policy makers to decide. Implicit in such a decision will be the economic signals that the policy maker will wish to send to both network operators and other market participants. For example, in an industry phase where policy makers wish to increase the augmentation of a single network, the access pricing formula chosen will allow those who augment the network to recover the costs of doing so at a level that will provide an incentive for further development of the network.[29] Conversely, in an industry phase where policy makers wish to encourage the development of an alternative network, the price of access to the old and new networks can be set at levels that discourage the use of the old network and encourage the construction of a new network.[30]

The variable charge element of an access price is an attempt to recompense the facility operator for the use of the network. However, in many network industries it is notoriously difficult to determine exactly how much consumption of network capacity has cost for any given network transaction.[31] This often results in 'postage stamp' pricing or averaging of prices which does not reward the efficiency of particular network users.

A detailed consideration of access pricing is beyond the scope of this chapter,[32] although it is sufficient to understand that no matter how non-discriminatory and fair an access regime may purport to be, price discrimination can render any access regime ineffective.[33]

Comparative Regulation

In considering the experience of other jurisdictions it becomes quickly apparent that relatively few are directly comparable to the EU in terms of political, social and economic development, particularly in the context of network industries. Two jurisdictions that are suitable for comparative purposes are Australia and the USA, both of which have broadly similar economies to the EU and need to regulate network industries on a trans-continental basis.

In both the USA and Australia, certain trans-continental networks have existed, at least in a physical sense,[34] for a long time although, for the most part, fully functional trans-continental networks have yet to become a reality.[35] This is despite the historical advantage the USA and Australia have enjoyed in terms of network standardisation, where a single network standard was developed at a time when the networks themselves were much simpler and the markets for their services immature.

Australia

Since Australia became a federal state in 1901, the Australian States and Territories have retained a significant influence, both in the development and in the regulation of network industries. As a result, inter-state trade in network products has not developed as quickly as may have been anticipated. However, Australia is, like many other nations, attempting to introduce competition into its network industries and this has necessitated the fostering of competition, and indeed regulation, on a federal basis. In terms of the electricity industry, for example, the parallels with the development of TENs are obvious, as Professor Allan Fels, the chairman of the Australian Competition and Consumer Commission (ACCC)[36] commented: 'The Australian electricity supply industry traditionally consisted of state based vertically integrated public utilities. As such, at present there is little interconnection between the jurisdictions of the National Electricity Market.'[37]

The Australian government has taken a proactive approach to the regulation of network industries, as part of its general approach to competition policy. In 1995, it adopted a Comprehensive Competition Policy (CCP) which applied competition principles to all aspects of the Australian economy, including network industries. The Australian government believed that such a systematic and wholesale reform of Australian competition policy would have significant benefits for the Australian economy.[38] A substantial part of the competition reforms was the concept of equitable access to essential infrastructure facilities, as was stated at the time:

> The operation of effective regimes of access to pipelines, transmission wires, telecommunications exchanges, and other assets of national significance ... has the potential to achieve considerable national savings in infrastructure investment while bringing about upstream and downstream competition – the best of two worlds, recognising a wider obligation of owners of essential facilities to maximise community welfare.[39]

As part of the CCP, the ACCC was given the responsibility, in addition to that of applying general competition law, for administering the national access regime.[40] The basis of the Australian access regime is the essential facilities doctrine, which has been adapted from the US doctrine and is governed by the Australian Trade Practices Act 1974 (TPA) Part IIIA.[41] Under the TPA a third party may obtain access to an essential facility in three ways: (1) by seeking to have a facility declared an essential facility, (2) by negotiating with an essential facility operator who has already made an access undertaking, and (3) by negotiating with an essential facility operator who is subject to an industry-wide access code.

In terms of the first option, a third party may request that the National Competition Council (NCC) recommend to the designated government minister that a particular service be declared an essential facility.[42] In order to make such a recommendation the NCC must first be satisfied of the following:

> (a) that access (or increased access) to the service would promote competition in at least one market (whether or not in Australia), other than the market for the service;
> (b) that it would be uneconomical for anyone to develop another facility to provide the service;
> (c) that the facility is of national significance, having regard to:-
> (i) the size of the facility; or
> (ii) the importance of the facility to constitutional trade or commerce; or
> (iii) the importance of the facility to the national economy;
> (d) that access to the service can be provided without undue risk to human health or safety;
> (e) that access to the service is not already the subject of an effective access regime; and
> (f) that access (or increased access) to the service would not be contrary to the public interest.[43]

In the context of the network industries, it is much more likely that a third party seeking access to a particular network would face an existing access regime. In terms of the TPA, a facility owner may enter into an access undertaking with the ACCC, which the ACCC must approve, detailing the terms and conditions of access to their particular facility.[44] The TPA also permits an industry body to propose an access code to govern rights of access to infrastructure within a particular industry. In considering whether an access code proposed by an industry body is acceptable the ACCC must have regard to:

> (a) the legitimate business interests of providers who might give undertakings in accordance with the code;
> (b) the public interest, including the public interest in having competition in markets (whether or not in Australia);
> (c) the interests of persons who might want access to the service covered by the code;
> (d) whether access to the service is already the subject of an access regime;
> (e) any other matters that the ACCC thinks are relevant.[45]

The preparation of a specific industry code by an industry body has been utilised in both the gas[46] and electricity industries. Once an industry-specific access code has been approved by the ACCC, access to infrastructure is negotiated between the third party and the facility owner. The ACCC retains a role as an arbiter of access disputes.

Like the EU, many Australian infrastructure networks are not yet complete and will be completed by the construction of interconnectors. In the case of electricity, the access code makes specific provision for network expansion and interconnection. Interconnectors that existed at the time of the acceptance of the access code are considered an integral part of the network. When it comes to the construction of new interconnectors, to use the electricity industry as an example, the Network Access Code allows network service providers to apply for interconnectors to become part of the regulated network and be subject to a regulated rate of return if the network service providers can pass a market/customer benefit test in relation to the construction of the interconnector.[47] In short, this means that, if the interconnector brings a market/customer benefit, it will be subsumed within the existing network. If a new interconnector becomes a regulated interconnector, the investment in the interconnector is effectively underwritten and the cost is borne by system users.[48]

Alternatively, if a new interconnector does not meet the market/customer benefit test, or no application is made for the interconnector to be regulated, the interconnector will be unregulated and commonly known as an entrepreneurial interconnector. Although then not subject to the industry access code, the interconnector will be subject to the general access regime. In terms of access pricing, a pricing mechanism is developed as part of the code and is applicable to the entire network.

USA

Under a simplistic analysis, the USA would seem to have achieved, in political terms, what the EU is trying to achieve, only centuries earlier: a federation of states. In these circumstances it would be easy to assume that network industries within the USA would operate on a trans-national level and be subject to federal regulation. However, this is not the case. Despite the USA's level of political maturity as a federation, as far as network industries are concerned, regulation and indeed infrastructure development has, like the EU, historically been developed on a state-by-state basis. For this reason, the USA remains in a transition period in the introduction of competition on a trans-continental level, although in the cases of certain networks federal regulation has been implemented and regional if not trans-national networks have been developed.[49]

The regulation of networks, on both a state and national level, differs markedly according to the industry involved. A common thread of regulation between the various industries is the essential facilities doctrine, which has historically underpinned any rights of access. In addition to the application of the essential facilities doctrine through the courts, most network industries have industry-specific access policies allowing third party access.[50]

As a result of the essential facilities doctrine, the central tenet of US network regulatory policy is the principle of structural separation,[51] the most obvious example of which was the divestiture of AT&T in 1984 to form AT&T as a long-distance carrier and the Bell Operating Companies as regional telephone companies, responsible for local calls and prohibited from entering the long-distance market. Another example is the electricity industry, where the Federal Energy Regulation Commission (FERC),[52] in proposing the creation of regional transmission organisations, stated: 'The objective of FERC's policy promoting regional transmission organizations (RTOs), is that the electricity transmission grid be operated by a corporate entity not controlled by any seller of generation or other market participant. ... We want market participants to be able to trust that the grid is being operated without discrimination or preference.'[53]

In structural terms, the USA is fairly well advanced in achieving trans-continental or, in some cases, trans-regional networks in most network industries. The most significant problem faced by the USA, in terms of creating markets for network industry products that are truly competitive, is the problem of regulation and this is a problem that is predominantly political. Commenting in the context of energy markets, a commissioner of the FERC recently stated, in response to his own question:

> Can national pro-competition goals be achieved in a reasonable time frame when authority is split between federal and state policy makers? This is perhaps the most critical question in the US. Roughly 80% of electricity revenues are regulated by 50 state regulatory bodies. The FERC has jurisdiction over wholesale power sales and unbundled electricity transmission. States have authority over retail sales, bundled retail transmission, local distribution and the siting of all electric transmission facilities. Obviously, no single regulatory body is in charge of the electric restructuring debate, and there is a patchwork of policies among the states.[54]

Network infrastructure is therefore subject to regulation from both a state and federal level and additionally may be subject to the jurisdiction of the Federal Trade Commission or the Justice Department in terms of general competition laws.

The Regulatory Framework for Trans-European Networks

In considering the EU's proposals for the regulation of TENs, there are a number of issues that deserve further consideration. In terms of regulatory principles, the first area of concern is the application of competition law to TENs and in particular to the interconnectors that will facilitate the creation of TENs. *Prima facie* there would seem to be an inherent conflict between encouraging interconnector development, on the one hand, and subjecting such interconnectors to general competition rules, on the other. This conflict was recognised by the Christophersen Report in the context of interconnectors between transport networks, which stated:

> transport undertakings can only make a financial commitment if they receive guaranteed access to the infrastructure to provide their own services. It is therefore conceivable that the infrastructure operator may give a contractual undertaking to reserve part of the available capacity for these undertakings. The lawfulness of such agreements must be assessed in the light of the competition rules on a case-by-case basis. However, two general principles can be identified:-
>
> (ii) the restriction on competition, i.e. the reservation of capacity, cannot go beyond what is strictly essential for the success of the project;
>
> (iii) the agreement in question must not eliminate competition on a substantial part of the market, which in principle precludes the reservation of all available capacity for one undertaking or group of undertakings.
>
> In any case, competition imperatives must be reconciled with the specifics of major infrastructure works: very long timescales and construction risks, difficulties of forecasting traffic, insufficient financial profitability, operating risks etc.
>
> When examining such agreements, the Commission will take account of the fact that the Trans-European Networks have been designed from the outset from a European perspective and that commercial use thereof must be considered from the same perspective.[55]

The Christophersen Report's recognition of the problem will be of little comfort to network developers as the internal market Directives do not distinguish between existing and new parts of TENs. As the Second Electricity Harmonisation Report noted, in the context of electricity interconnectors, 'As the Directive does not provide for any exception from the obligation to grant access to the interconnector network, non-discriminatory access to third parties has to be given'.[56]

While the Commission has acknowledged that interconnectors require specific regulation, there is no specific legislatory exception for interconnectors, and the uncertainty this creates will have several consequences. The first and most significant is that the development of TENs will be inhibited. As the Christophersen Report noted, 'the conditions for access to the infrastructure, once it has been completed, can have a decisive impact on the search for private funding at the design construction stages'.[57] Secondly, where development does proceed it will do so in the most profitable areas first. This concern was noted by the Economic and Social Committee of the Commission when considering the then proposed guidelines that subsequently established TEN Telecom:

> In the Committee's view the Commission's competition-based regulatory approach and its concentration on the private sector is bound to lead to the emphasis being placed on services and projects which are marketable and yield a profit in the market place. The Committee thinks that the Commission's duty is to make sure that the information society serves the whole society. The prerequisite for this must be that the widest possible range of universally accessible networks and services is available and that cost efficient use can be made of them.[58]

A second area of concern relates to the structure of the proposed regulation of TENs and in particular the principle of subsidiarity. While the motivation for this is understandable from a social and political perspective, from a regulatory standpoint it is not clear that this will be sufficient to create regulatory parity throughout the single market. Although there is parity in terms of regulatory principles, the discretion of Member States in implementing those principles is wide. Nowhere is this more evident than in the area of access pricing, which has been left to Member State regulators. If Member States are only required to set prices and terms at levels that are non-discriminatory, their discretion is so wide that it is difficult to see how any level of equivalence can be established throughout the single market.[59] Furthermore, because of the different political structures of the member states of the EU and the different attitudes to risk and reward, substantial variations in pricing will exist. Although the EU has mechanisms for correcting imbalances between member states, the process for doing so is cumbersome and, in a fast-moving area such as telecommunication, largely redundant.[60] The experience of the USA shows that the failure to regulate effectively on a trans-national basis fundamentally undermines trans-national regulatory policy.

A third issue of concern is the principle of open access to network infrastructure. It is not clear why such service-based competition has been preferred to network competition, that the principle of open access is applicable to all TENs, or how the principle of open access will be administered in practice. Although both Australia and the USA have ostensibly opted for open access regimes, these are firmly based on the essential facilities doctrine and so an essential facilities test which is not, as is the EU system, a system that allows blanket open access.[61]

The open access principle means that as soon as an interconnector is built it is subject to open access in terms of the internal market Directives, effectively constituting all new interconnectors as essential facilities, which is clearly not the case.[62] This issue was noted in the Second Electricity Harmonisation Report which stated, in the context of electricity interconnectors and the internal market in electricity Directive:

> In order to encourage the construction of new interconnector lines, or the reinforcement of transit lines, it could be necessary to provide for timely limited exceptions from the general [competition] rules under case by case regulatory control. This being said, it must be maintained that any new line, irrespective of whether constructed as part of the Transmission System Operators system or as direct line according to Article 21 of the Directive, is fully subject to the principle of third party access, as soon as it is connected to the interconnected system.[63]

The EU regulatory system, by allowing third party access without guaranteeing an investment return, is a disincentive to investment in network infrastructure. By comparison, the Australian system provides investment certainty and strongly encourages efficient network interconnection and expansion, neutralising the bitter pill of access to new infrastructure facilities with the reward and comfort of a guaranteed pricing mechanism that will repay the investment in the new facility.

Conclusion

The purpose of establishing TENs is to help create and thereafter sustain the single market, and accordingly significant efforts have been channelled towards the physical construction of infrastructure that will connect the currently disparate national networks of the EU Member States. In terms of regulation, however, it is clear that the currently envisaged regulatory structure that will govern TENs has not been devised with the development of TENs in mind. In order to redress the balance it will be necessary to develop a regulatory regime that will be effective in regulating TENs in both their development and operational phases.

Such a regime should encourage efficient interconnection and network augmentation by providing investment certainty and specifically allowing the development of entrepreneurial interconnectors. Historically, network development in a competitive environment has not been achievable and, although advances in regulatory theory have now made this possible, it is only possible within a system that is designed to cater for both objectives. At the moment the EU regulatory regime does not make adequate provision for either.

Notes

1 For example, as highlighted by the report by the Christophersen Group in the areas of energy and transport (*Report of the Group of Personal Representatives of the Heads of State or Government: Trans-European Networks*, Luxembourg, 1995) ('Christopherson Report'), p.89, a Eurostar train operating through the Channel Tunnel from the UK to the centre of Europe must be able to use three types of power supply and four types of signalling. A train running on one of the current priority projects under the TEN Transport Programme, the Paris–Brussels-Köln/Frankfurt–Amsterdam–London line (PBKAL line), will not be able to run on the Eurostar network.

2 A very clear example of these difficulties was the construction of the Channel Tunnel, which is an interconnector between the road/rail systems of the UK and the rest of Europe. For an overview of the colossal difficulty involved, see (1996), 'The Channel Tunnel Experience and Other Mega Projects' *International Business Lawyer*, 24, 1–48. The Channel Tunnel forms part of the PBKAL line, see the Christophersen Report (n.1, above), p.115 for details of the project.

3 For example, the TEN Telecom Programme: see TEN Telecom web site (http://www.echo.lu/tentelecom/home.html) which covers up to ten different areas of application, only one of which relates to the physical creation of TEN infrastructure.

4 The Christophersen Report (n.1, above), p.10.

5 Article 14 gives the imperative for the creation of the single market.

6 Article 158 is concerned with removing the disparity between the stages of economic and social development of the various regions of the EU.

7 The guidelines were developed following the recommendations of the Christophersen Group, (n.1, above) in the areas of energy and transport and the Bangermann Group in the area of telecommunications, (*Report of the Members of the High-Level Group on the Information Society: Europe and the Global Information Society*, Luxembourg, 1994). Both reports provide a useful introduction to the development of TENs in their respective areas.

8 Decision No. 1254/96/EC. TEN-Energy's main focus is the interconnection of electricity and gas networks throughout the EU with a view to facilitating the completion of the internal market in energy. Further details regarding the TEN Energy programme can be found at the Energy DG web site (http://europa.eu.int/comm/dgs/energy/index_en.htm).

9 Decision No. 1692/96/ EC. The TEN-Transport programme envisages an intermodel transport network throughout Europe which will be based on the concept of transport users linking a variety of methods of transport to complete a single journey. Further details regarding the TEN Transport programme can be found at the Transport DG web site (http://europa.eu.int/comm/dgs/transport/index_en.htm).

10 Decision No. 1336/97/EC. TEN-Telecom aims to develop interconnecting and interoperable telecommunications infrastructure throughout the EU, and like TEN-Transport this will be an intermodal network as it is acknowledged that, owing to the number of fixed, satellite and mobile networking technologies

available, it is unlikely that one single network will emerge. The programme does, however, concentrate initially on the creation of two TEN-Telecoms: TEN-Euro-ISDN (Integrated Service Digital Network) and TEN-IBC (Integrated Broadband Communications). Further details regarding the TEN Telecoms programme can be found at the TEN Telecom web site (http://www.echo.lu/tentelecom/home.html).

11 For example, see recital (11) in the preface to the internal market in electricity Directive 96/92/EC.

12 The structural separation envisaged in terms of the internal market Directives can be best described as 'soft' structural separation as only the separation of accounting/management functions is required, see Article 8(2) of Directive 97/33/EC or Article 15 of Directive 96/92/EC.

13 In the case of electricity, Directive 96/92/EC specifically requires the electricity transmission system to be operated independently and access to be given on non-discriminatory terms.

14 In terms of rail infrastructure, Directive 91/440/EEC requires that railway businesses operate separate accounts for their network facilities and gives them the option of operating a separate management system for such network facilities. Railway undertakings must also offer access to their network to associations of railway undertakings from Member States in order to enable those associations to run passenger rail services between their domiciles.

15 In telecommunications, Directives 97/33/EC and 98/10/EC, respectively, require operators with significant market power to meet all reasonable requests for access to their network and for guaranteed open and efficient access to the voice telephony service network.

16 For example, in the field of telecommunications, see 'Notice on the Applications of the Competition Rules to Access Agreements in the Telecommunications Sector; Framework, Relevant Markets and Principles' (OJ C265) 1998.

17 See the 'Second Report to the Council and the European Parliament on Harmonisation Requirements', pp.6–14, SEC 1999/470; speech by Michael Albers, 'Views and Expectations on the Competition Developments in the EU Electricity Market', Brussels, 1999, available on the Competition DG web site (http://europa.eu.int/comm/dgs/competition/ index_en.htm).

18 A natural monopoly can be said to exist where it is more efficient for one economic entity to supply the market than for several entities to do so. In the case of most networks significant economies of scale and scope will result in natural monopoly elements. See Carlton, D.W. and J.M. Perloff (1994), *Modern Industrial Organisations*, 2nd edn, New York: Harper Collins, pp.151 and 850.

19 This has traditionally involved cross-subsidisation, where revenues earned from a profitable area of the market are used to subsidise the cost of service provision to an unprofitable area and which, if left to the markets, would not justify service provision by itself or service provision at a much greater cost. The universal service obligation placed on a network operator has the aim of ensuring countrywide coverage of infrastructure at a similar price.

20 For example, in both Australia and the USA the development of trans-continental networks was only achieved after the responsibility for the development of such networks was given to a single monopoly entity.

21 Conversely, a monopoly can achieve the objective of universal coverage more readily and overall costs can be reduced as a result of standardisation, less duplication and forward planning.

22 Wiley, R.E. (1988), 'The End of Monopoly: Regulatory Change and the Promotion of Competition', in W. Sapronov (ed.), *Telecommunications and the Law*, Computer Science Press, Rockville, p.48. The use of a monopoly to develop a network with standardised universal service has also been seen in modern

times, the most notable example being the development of the telecommunications network in Germany; see Stehman, O. (1995), *Network Competition for European Telecommunications*, Oxford University Press, Oxford, at 187.

23 See Carlton and Perloff (n.18, above), p.143.

24 Obvious examples of such pieces of infrastructure include the 'Local Loop' in telecommunications, inter-state interconnectors in the case of electricity, and major bridges and tunnels in transport.

25 The case of *United States* v. *Terminal Railroad Association* 224 US 383 (1912) originally developed the essential facilities doctrine. In this case the defendants formed a company that, by purchasing bridge access land and terminal facilities, controlled the rail traffic over the Mississippi river at St Louis, and consequently rail access between the eastern and western United States. At that time there were two bridges crossing the Mississippi river and one ferry. The bridges were toll bridges able to be used by all upon equal terms. However, access to the bridges was only possible through the terminal facilities owned by the Terminal Railroad Association (TRA). The TRA charged for use of their facilities, which their competitors believed to be discriminatory. The company was formed by a number of rail operators who claimed that the common ownership of such facilities was in the public interest as it was more efficient. While the court accepted that common ownership could benefit society, it was held that exclusive common ownership did not. The court ruled against the TRA and held that the access land was an 'essential facility' to which all competitors should have access.

26 The standard test used in the USA is derived from the case of *MCI Communications* v. *AT&T*, 708 F.2d 1081, (7th Cir. 1983) where the court described four elements necessary to establish an essential facility: (1) control of the essential facility by a monopolist; (2) a competitor's inability practically or reasonably to duplicate the essential facility; (3) the denial of the use of the facility to a competitor; and (4) the feasibility of providing the facility (1132–3). The Australian essential facilities test is discussed below. For a discussion of the essential facilities test in the EU, see the consideration given in Chapter 2.

27 The standard essential facility tests that have arisen have the common theme of access being given if competition will be promoted. The *Terminal Railroad Case*, on the other hand, essentially espouses allocative economic efficiency as the determinant for access, giving access in order to prevent uneconomic replication of essential facilities, although in the *Terminal Railroad Case* replication was physically, but not economically, impossible.

28 Judgment of the Court of First Instance: *European Night Services*, 1998, T-374/94, T-375/94, T-384/94 and T-388/94. In this case the court held that the plaintiffs should succeed because the Commission did not give adequate reasons for their decision, which limited the court's analysis of the issues.

29 As is the case with the Australian National Electricity Market, discussed below.

30 An access pricing mechanism model that was adopted in New Zealand is worthy of note. In 1990, the government of New Zealand privatised the state telecommunications company to create New Zealand Telecom. Rather than appoint an industry-specific regulator, the government decided that the telecommunications industry would simply be subject to the country's general competition laws. As a result of the inevitable access dispute, Clear Telecommunications brought an action against NZ Telecom centring on access pricing. The court decided on pricing according to the Efficient Component Pricing Rule (ECPR), or the Baumol–Willig Rule, as it is also known. The rule makes entry into the market efficient if the new entrant is more efficient than the incumbent. The rule is controversial and is discussed more fully in Valletti, T.M. and A. Estache (1998), *The Theory of Access Pricing: An Overview for Infra-*

structure Regulators, The World Bank, Policy Research Working Paper No.2097, available on the World Bank web site (http://www.worldbank.org/).

31 This is particularly true in the electricity industry. If electricity is being supplied by generator A to customer B, the laws of physics dictate that electricity will flow down the path of least resistance. This will invariably not be the path from A to B, and it will be difficult to ascertain the precise route taken, the percentage of the network used and how much of the electricity has been used up in transmission. For an overview of access pricing in relation to electricity networks, see 'Review of Australian Transmission Pricing – A Report for the Australian Competition and Consumer Commission', *London Economics*, April 1999, available on the ACCC web site (http://www.accc.gov.au).

32 An excellent summary of access pricing theory is given by Valletti and Estache, *The Theory of Access Pricing* (n.30, above).

33 Non-price discrimination, where access is given but with inadequate levels of service and quality, can have a similar effect.

34 For example, in Australia by 1901 the Commonwealth postmaster-general was the sole provider of telecommunication services across Australia.

35 In jurisdictions like the USA and Australia, vast areas of sparsely populated land may prevent the creation of truly trans-continental networks and in these circumstances trans-regional networks may exist. A good example is Australia where the vast distances and sparse population between Western Australia and the more heavily populated eastern side of Australia preclude the creation of many networks between the two. However, the size of trans-regional networks that exist in the USA and Australia are comparable with TENs.

36 The ACCC is the body responsible for the implementation of Australia's competition policy.

37 'The Regulatory Framework', speech given by Professor Allan Fels, chairman of the Australian Competition and Consumer Commission, to the National Power Conference, Melbourne, 9 August 1999, p.1, available on the ACCC web site (http://www.accc.gov.au).

38 The Australian Productivity Commission went as far as to estimate that the competition reforms would generate annual growth of 5.5 per cent of Gross Domestic Product.

39 'Network Industry Regulation and Convergence in Service Delivery: Challenges for Suppliers, Users and Regulators', ACCC, 1999, p.3, available on the ACCC web site (n.37, above).

40 The ACCC is not responsible, however, for the regulation of networks *per se*. In the electricity and gas industries, for example, the ACCC is responsible for the regulation of the transmission system, while the states retain responsibility for the distribution system, although in the long term it is anticipated that regulation will gravitate towards the ACCC.

41 The Competition Policy Reform Act 1995 inserted a new Part IIIA into the Trade Practices Act 1974.

42 TPA, s.44F(1).

43 TPA, s.44G(2). In terms of s.44H, the designated government minister must take the same considerations into account in deciding whether or not a service should be declared an essential facility.

44 *Ibid.*, s.44ZZA.

45 *Ibid.*, s.44ZZAA.

46 The *National Third Party Access Code for Natural Gas Pipeline Systems* ('the Code') specifies that the service provider of a gas pipeline covered by the Code is required to establish an access arrangement and submit it to the regulator for approval.

47 The test was originally a 'customer benefits test' which was reviewed when the South Australia–New South Wales interconnector failed the test and the application for the interconnector to be a regulated interconnector was rejected. Following its review, the ACCC recommended a 'market benefit test'. See the ACCC 'Preliminary View on the Assessment Criterion for New Interconnectors and Network Augmentation', April 1999, available on the ACCC web site (n.37, above).

48 See the ACCC 'Decision Relating to the Application for Acceptance – National Electricity Market Access Code 16', September 1998, 142.

49 This is the case in the electricity industry. See Energy Information Administration, 'The Changing Structure of the Electric Power Industry: Selected Issues, 1998', available on the EIA web site (http// www.eig.doe.gov/).

50 In the case of the electricity industry, access to the transmission system is governed by FERC Order No. 888, and in telecommunications access questions are governed by the Telecommunications Act 1996. It is interesting to note that US access codes such as FERC CO 888 follow more closely the *Terminal Railroad Case* in promoting common ownership of essential facilities that are open to all: see 'The Changing Structure of the Electric Power Industry: Selected Issues' (n.49, above).

51 In contrast to the EU concept of structural separation, in the USA this has historically meant 'hard' structural separation in the form of divestiture.

52 The body responsible for the regulation of the inter-state transmission of, among other things, gas and electricity.

53 Massey, W.L., Commissioner of the FERC, 'Regulatory Principles and Trends in U.S. Energy Markets', speech to 1999 CGA/CEA Senior Executives Conference–Energy Restructuring:Blueprint for the Future', 24 June 1999. Available on the FERC web site (http://www.ferc.fed.us/default3.htm).

54 *Ibid.*

55 The Christophersen Report (n.1, above), p.88.

56 The Second Harmonisation Report, (n. 17, above), p.14.

57 The Christophersen Report, (n.1, above), p.88.

58 Opinion on 'Towards the Information Society – Communication from the Commission to the Council from the European Parliament, the Economic and Social Committee and the Committee for the Regions on a Methodology for the Implementation of Information Society Applications – Proposal for a European Parliament and Council Decision on a Series of Guidelines for the Trans European Telecommunication Networks' (96/C 39/02).

59 For example, in the case of Telecommunications, Articles 7(1) and 7(2) of the Interconnection Directive (97/33/EC) only require charges for interconnection to follow the principle of transparency and cost orientation.

60 This point is also made by Ungerer, Dr. H. (1998), 'Ensuring Efficient Access to Bottleneck Facilities. The Case of Telecommunications in the European Union', p.20, available on the Competition DG web site (http://europa.eu. int/comm/dgs/competition/index_en.htm).

61 In both the USA and Australia, industry-specific regimes that effectively allow blanket open access do exist in order to avoid the uncertainty and inconvenience of continual access attempts by third parties. However, such access regimes are specific to the existing network and new pieces of infrastructure are not automatically subject to them.

62 By comparison, in Australia, a new interconnector, although subject to the statutory access regime, is not subject to open access in terms of the specific industry access code. The facility owner can choose whether or not such a facility should seek to become part of the network and, where a decision is

made not to join the network, third party access will only be mandated if the third party can satisfy the statutory essential facilities test.

63 The Second Harmonisation Report (n.17, above), p.14.

4 Regulating Electricity

ELIZABETH McROBB, ***Shepherd & Wedderburn*** **AND TONY PROSSER,**
University of Glasgow

Introduction

It might appear that in the case of electricity there were particularly good reasons why a regime of light regulation, gradually reducing in scope, would have been possible after privatisation. Whereas gas regulation was plagued by the fact that the industry had been privatised as a single vertically integrated unit, in electricity the industry was split not just vertically but so as to create what were intended to be competitive markets in generation and, eventually, in supply. Thus the dominant task for the gas regulator, that of ensuring that transport and supply separated (as eventually occurred) and that access to the monopoly elements of the industry were offered to competitors on fair terms, should have proved much easier in the case of electricity as the separation was already in place. Moreover, the first Director-General of Electricity Supply was Stephen Littlechild who, as author of the influential price control arrangements for British Telecom at the time of its privatisation, was more responsible than anyone else for the British model of ostensibly light regulation which would wither away as soon as it could be replaced by a competitive market.[1]

However, light regulation which reduces in scope and complexity is far from an accurate description of the arrangements for electricity. It has proved remarkably durable and, in important ways, regulation has grown in scope and in complexity in the years since privatisation. A major aim of this chapter will be to suggest some of the reasons for this. It would be easy to suggest that it has occurred because of a liking for regulation for its own sake, or because of a desire to extend regulatory empires on the part of regulatory staff.[2]

Rather, we shall suggest that the continuing regulation is due to the nature of the markets involved; their own very complexity and their interrelated character actually requires continuing regulation to make them work, and indeed what is happening at the moment is a correction of underregulation in the years immediately following privatisation. This does not mean, however, that regulation must be carried out directly by the regulatory office itself and we are seeing the development of new forms of delegated regulation emerging. A second characteristic is that the role of government is now becoming more clearly defined and a legitimate role for social regulation has also emerged more strongly, although there is still some doubt as to the best allocation for this between government and regulator.

We shall begin with a brief description of the electricity industry after privatisation and of the regulatory arrangements adopted.[3] One point should be noted at the outset: different industry structures were adopted in England and Wales on the one hand, and in Scotland, on the other, and these have affected regulation in each regime. We shall cover both in this chapter, and indeed the differences may be instructive for comparative purposes.

Industry Structure and Regulatory Institutions

The structure adopted for the electricity industry after privatisation was highly complex, but some brief description is necessary to understand the regulatory issues. In brief, in England and Wales, two generating companies were established, National Power and PowerGen. The split was made more complex by the withdrawal of the nuclear facilities at the last moment, although the more modern stations have since been privatised as British Energy. This resulted in the two companies being of different sizes, though together they were able effectively to dominate the generation market. As a natural monopoly, the high-voltage transmission system was vested in a company originally owned by the regional supply companies, but since floated as the National Grid Company. Twelve regional supply and distribution companies were established (now universally known as regional electricity companies or recs) which have also been able themselves to generate electricity. In Scotland, a different structure was adopted through the creation of two vertically integrated companies combining generation, transmission and supply functions.[4] There are thus two key markets in the system: that for generation and that for supply, with a natural monopoly in transmission and in distribution. Perhaps unexpectedly, the director-general has also had a role in relation to the market in corporate control through advising government on the consumer and regulatory implications of the takeovers and mergers which have become a dominant characteristic of the industry.

The regulatory system adopted was similar to that in the other utility privatisations.[5] Legal powers were vested in an individual, the Director-General of Electricity Supply, assisted by the Office of Electricity Regulation (OFFER), now combined with the Office of Gas Supply as the Office of Gas and Electricity Markets (OFGEM). A deputy director-general for Scotland was also created, given the different regime. Consumer protection was through regional Consumers' Committees established and appointed by the director-general and through a National Consumers' Consultative Committee, composed of the chairs of the Consumers' Committees and chaired by the director-general.

These regulatory arrangements are now in the course of substantial change.[6] This has been a result of the new approach to utility regulation adopted by the Labour government elected in 1997 and the fast-converging markets for gas and electricity after liberalisation of the supply markets. The objective is to establish by new legislation (to be introduced in the 1999–2000 session of Parliament) a combined energy regulator in the form of an executive board in place of the directors-general of electricity supply and of gas supply. In the meantime, the two positions have been combined through the appointment of a single person, Callum McCarthy, to both through administrative integration of the two offices as OFGEM. The government has also announced its intention of legislating for new arrangements to protect consumers which will involve the appointment by government of independent national councils with powers to establish regional committees and offices.[7]

Companies operate under licences granted by the secretary of state but enforced by the director-general. There are also provisions for licence modification, either by agreement with the licensed company or, if that cannot be obtained, through reference to the Competition Commission for a report on the issues involved in the modification. This process has been of considerable importance, especially in setting price controls. It should finally be mentioned that the opening up of electricity markets is now happening on a European scale with the agreement of a directive on common rules for the internal market for electricity.[8] Although this will require some minor changes in the licensing regime, the progress in electricity liberalisation in the UK is already far more advanced than the directive requires, so the substantive effects will be very limited.

The Generation Market: England and Wales

The generation market is in many ways the most important of all the markets in the electricity industry; in 1996, generation costs represented 52 per cent of the final price paid by consumers. As one commentator has noted, privatisation 'was accompanied by complete liberalisation of the generation sector, with minimal regulatory oversight compared with the rest of the industry'.[9] To over-simplify dramatically, coordination of the purchase of electricity from the generators was to take place through the pool, a form of spot market, though in practice most electricity is purchased under contract at a fixed price from a generating company by the recs through contracts for differences which provide a degree of hedging against fluctuations in pool prices. However, the pool is not a licensed activity and so the director-general has had no role in monitoring, enforcing or modifying any licence obligations relating to the pool itself. Nor has he been able to make licence modification references of the pool to the Competition Commission to permit a thorough-going review of its operation, which could result in power to enforce its conclusions through new licence conditions. Crucially, at the time of privatisation, no price controls were set on generation prices, the intention being that pricing should be a matter for the competitive market. Supply companies were permitted to pass through the costs of purchase of electricity from generators, though their licences require them to purchase electricity economically.

Two problems in particular have characterised the operation of the pool. The first is that of market distortion. Although there has been considerable new entry into generation, for technical reasons National Power and PowerGen were able to dominate the forms of supply which effectively fix the pool price.[10] There have also been strong allegations, especially from large industrial consumers, of anti-competitive practices in relation to the pool. As a result, the director-general was not able to distance himself effectively from the operation of the pool and from February 1994 a two-year generation price cap was imposed in all but name after he had concluded that the extent of competition in generation was not sufficient to restrain the two large generators from increasing prices; it took the form of an agreement that they would bid into the pool in such a way as to ensure that the average pool purchase price would not exceed specified sums per kilowatt hour.[11] Action was also taken to limit the market power of the dominant companies by requiring the disposal of 6000MW of generating plant by the end of 1995, amounting to just under 10 per cent of capacity in England and Wales. After some delays, the capacity was sold to a rec by the end of 1996. Further undertakings to divest were later sought from PowerGen as a condition for approval of its acquisition of a rec, and similar undertakings have also been required from National Power.

The second problem of the operation of the pool related to that of market distortion but also involved other public interest arguments. This was the 'dash for gas'. After privatisation there was a major shift from coal generation to the use of new, small gas generators. This has had potential environmental advantages and in the short term increased fuel diversity; however, in the long term it seemed likely to lead to over-dependence on gas as a fuel; according to a study commissioned by the government, the UK would become a net importer of gas early in the new millennium and by 2020 might need to import between 55 per cent and 90 per cent of its gas. The major sources for imports would be Norway, Russia and Algeria, the latter two not being known for their political stability.[12] The effects on the already severely contracted domestic coal industry would be devastating. It was alleged that, apart from the arguments for security of supply, the pool system involved market distortions which favour gas stations at the expense of coal plants. As a result, the government imposed a partial moratorium on the construction of new gas generation stations from June 1998 and organised a major review of the electricity generation market. The results appeared in the form of a set of proposals for the review of electricity trading arrangements issued by the director-general in July 1998 and a White Paper from government itself in October of that year.[13]

The proposals are highly complex.[14] In brief, they involve major reform of the trading arrangements and a clarification of the role of government. The trading arrangements will involve forwards and futures markets organised by the market participants, with, in addition, a voluntary short-term bilateral market and a voluntary balancing market, imbalances being settled through a further process. Further measures will also be taken to limit market distortion through divestment and through new legislation to separate the licensing of distribution and supply businesses.

At first sight this appears to be a straightforward retreat of regulation in favour of the market. However, it is more complex than this, as the proposed arrangements for governance and regulation of the trading system make clear.[15] The director-general's review noted the criticism of the limited provision for the role of regulation in the pool, and that many respondents to consultation had suggested that there should be a continuing and more explicit role for regulation. The new markets will be to some extent regulated through the Financial Services Act 1986 (itself soon to be replaced by new legislation). However, in addition a Balancing and Settlement Code will be established containing the basic rules to cover the new balancing markets and other pricing mechanisms, and setting out the relations of the participants and their responsibilities and duties. This will be required by licence obligations, and administered by a Balancing and Settlement Code Panel whose responsibilities will include modification of the Code and settling disputes. Its membership will include representatives of the National Grid Company and of other interested groups including customers, OFGEM itself and perhaps independent members; the director-general will appoint the chairman. The Panel will be required to consult widely before making its decisions. All modifications to the Code, as well as its initial provisions, will need approval by the director-general, who may also have the power to propose rule changes.

Apart from the reform of the trading arrangements, the White Paper also attempted to clarify the role of government in relation to the electricity industry.[16] This was characterised as setting the legal framework for competitive energy markets and the economic development of Britain's energy resources, providing for regulation in the consumer interest, and monitoring the wider public interest. Within this, energy security would play a particularly important role. As a result, the government confirmed its policy of adopting a stricter consents policy for gas generation, using powers under the Electricity Act 1989 and the Energy Act 1976.[17] It also supplemented the director-general's proposals for reform of the trading arrangements with a need to explore further how to protect long-term security of supply.

The reforms thus involve two important regulatory themes. The first is to take a new approach to the regulation of trading arrangements. In the past this has been characterised by the unstable combination of, on the one hand, a pretence that regulation is unnecessary and that no special powers are needed by the regulator, with a reality of ad hoc interventions such as the unofficial price cap and the pressure for divestment. Under the new system, clearly trading will be market-based but with a recognition that the operation of the markets will need administrative underpinning. The day-to-day administration of this underpinning will be undertaken not by the director-general himself but by the new Code Panel representing a number of interests, although the director-general will have important powers of veto. This illustrates very clearly two themes in the introductory chapter to this volume: that of the necessity of some form of regulation to make it possible for markets to operate at all, and the growing role of the delegation of regulatory powers to private actors but with considerable oversight and ratification by public bodies.

The clarification of government's role is also welcome, though it has proved far from uncontroversial, with accusations that the restriction on new gas generation consents will restrict competition and result in higher prices.[18] However, whatever one's views on the merits of the policy, it is surely right to make it clear that some public concerns do go beyond the immediate objectives of a particular regulator and that there is a broader context within which markets operate. This was implicitly accepted in the legislation privatising the industry, which included extensive powers of governmental intervention.[19] Previously, there had been a marked reluctance to set any sort of framework to establish when governmental powers would be used, but the White Paper does go some way towards doing this. We shall return to this point about the potential role of government in discussing supply competition below.

The Generation Market and the Scottish Trading Arrangements

In Scotland at the time of privatisation there were various views as to the appropriate structure for the market, but a pooled generation market was rejected. There appeared to be less scope for establishing viable competition in generation in Scotland for reasons which included the relative size of the Scottish market (approximately one-tenth of the size of the market in England and Wales) and the substantial existing generation capacity as compared with expected customer demand. In 1988, the government's White Paper, *Privatisation of the Scottish Electricity Industry*,[20] acknowledged that 'the present level of excess capacity on the Scottish system makes it unlikely that major new entrants into the generation market will be forthcoming in the short to medium term'. By adopting a structure which created two vertically integrated Scottish companies rather than one, however, the potential for competition in certain areas was created.[21]

Ownership of generation plant in Scotland at privatisation was split three ways between Scottish Hydro-Electric, ScottishPower and Scottish Nuclear (now part of British Energy). In order to provide each of the Scottish companies with a balanced portfolio of plant and fuel diversity, a number of restructuring contracts were entered into which effectively gave ScottishPower around 70 per cent of the generation market and Scottish Hydro-Electric the remaining 30 per cent. This was achieved partly via the Nuclear Energy Agreement which provides for ScottishPower and Scottish Hydro-Electric to purchase all of Scottish Nuclear's output until 2005. This and the other restructuring contracts largely remain in force today and, while renewable power has developed in Scotland and a number of independent generators including PowerGen and National Power have sought to establish plant in Scotland, the level of plant in independent ownership remains relatively low.

In the absence of a pool from which second tier suppliers can draw their energy requirements, the two Scottish companies are obliged by their respective public electricity supply licences to establish and comply with 'relevant second tier supply arrangements'.[22] The arrangements established in 1991 to enable second tier supplies[23] to large industrial customers were approved by the director,[24] and created a basic framework within which generators and suppliers could contract. The Scottish companies also agreed to supply energy at a pool-related price to any second tier supplier requesting it. A bilateral contract market therefore emerged with most second tier suppliers purchasing their energy requirements from the relevant Scottish company at the administered Scottish wholesale price. To cater for those second tier suppliers who purchased their energy requirements from an independent generator, the arrangements approved by the director in 1991 included a basis for balancing mismatches of generation and supply. Briefly, if a supplier contracts for less generation than is required to meet its customer demand, the shortfall is deemed to have been supplied by the host Scottish company. Equally, if the independent generator supplies more than is required to meet the customer demand, the excess is deemed to have been purchased by the host Scottish company. The price of these sales of 'top up' and purchases of 'spill' energy (known as residual requirements) were again agreed between the Scottish companies and the regulator. A basic framework (the Trading Code) was also established by the Scottish companies under their licences[25] to permit generator-to-generator trades. The Trading Code applies only to generators with over 50MW of plant in Scotland and until 1998 the only signatories were the two Scottish companies.

The trading regime in Scotland, by contrast with England and Wales, was, therefore, very basic. The regulator's role in establishing the Scottish wholesale price, approving the relevant second tier supply arrangements including the prices for residual requirements and in overseeing the Trading Code reflected the limited stage of development of competition in generation and contrasted with the director's retreat from active regulation in the early days of the England and Wales pool. The bilateral contracts between the Scottish companies and suppliers did not, however, involve any input by the regulator other than with respect to the price cap and the trading arrangements operated on a very informal footing.

Early in 1996, a consultation exercise was carried out by OFFER which concluded that trading in Scotland would continue on a bilateral basis but with a structure which catered for more flexibility and therefore sophistication in the underlying contract market. The two Scottish companies then carried out a review of the second tier supply arrangements in terms of their licences which led to detailed consultation on the principles behind the new market rules and the drafting, negotiation and signing of a settlement agreement, the Settlement Agreement for the electricity industry in Scotland (SAS) in August 1998. The SAS provides the market rules for the calculation of the volumes of electricity traded between generators and suppliers and for the volumes of top-up and spill energy traded by market participants with the Scottish companies. Scottish Electricity Settlements Limited was established as a 50/50 joint venture by the Scottish companies to oversee the design, implementation and operation of the settlement systems required and the Scottish companies accepted a new licence obligation underpinning the creation of the SAS.[26] The governance of this multilateral agreement provides for the creation of industry panels split 50/50 between Scottish company representatives and non-Scottish company representatives. Ultimately, however, the director has powers to veto the decisions of these panels and to approve or reject all changes to the SAS.

It is interesting to note that the governance structure adopted in Scotland in 1998 owed more to the structure of the gas industry and its Network Code than to the more cumbersome structure of the England and Wales pool. It also avoided the problems of lack of regulatory oversight in the pool by giving the director a key role in decision making. The new trading arrangements for England and Wales appear to be going down a similar route.

Whilst the SAS represented a major development in the Scottish market by formalising the basis for settlement and creating a greater flexibility for wholesale trading, the lack of significant incoming generation in Scotland has continued to inhibit the development of the bilateral trading market. OFGEM has now embarked on a review of the Scottish trading arrangements in which it argues that the lower level of market entry in generation in Scotland has arisen as a result of a number of significant barriers to entry.[27] Independent generators argue that the absence of a scheduling and despatch code, the lack of clarity on treatment of ancillary services and their inability to gain access to the Scotland/England interconnector all create a high degree of uncertainty for any generator seeking to build plant in Scotland. Equally, the government's partial moratorium on gas-fired power stations has had an impact in Scotland. The Scottish companies have indicated their willingness to move towards a market structure which creates a single system operator for Scotland, but there are material issues to be addressed, including the continuing impact of the restructuring contracts.

A key issue for the Scottish review will be the interaction with the introduction of new trading arrangements in England and Wales. OFGEM has now published a further consultation document on the Scottish market which proposes major structural change in a number of areas.[28] Briefly, the changes suggested seek to introduce new trading arrangements to Scotland which reflect more closely both the structures and trading mechanisms which are currently being implemented in England and Wales. The key components in Scotland will, therefore, be the introduction of Scotland-wide trading arrangements via a Scottish system operator which is separated from the Scottish companies. This system operator would operate under a balancing and settlement code for Scotland and would contract for imbalances in a manner similar to that proposed for the new England and Wales market. The paper also discusses possible changes to the current interconnector framework to allow non-discriminatory access on the basis of capacity auction. It appears, therefore, that the regulator is seeking to establish a Scotland-wide market which mirrors that in England and Wales. Whether or not the long-term aim is to combine the two markets is not clear at this stage.

The generation market in Scotland has, therefore, been characterised by the existence of two incumbent market players and the commitment of most Scottish generation under long-term restructuring contracts entered into at the time of privatisation. It was recognised at the time of privatisation that the vertical integration of the Scottish companies of itself would necessitate strong regulatory intervention and, in contrast to the experience of England and Wales, there has never been a retreat from regulation as was evidenced by the limited role taken by the director in the pool. The different market structure has meant that continuing price regulation in generation was inevitable. The regulator is now considering substantial structural change which may mean that the Scottish market develops towards the model currently being implemented in England and Wales. Given the proposed active involvement of the director in the new English arrangements, and the fact that a similar role has already been taken by the director in the Scottish market, it is clear that there will be continuing regulation in Scotland even following any significant structural change.

This does not mean, however, that the regulator necessarily wishes to direct the market and, indeed, to do so would go well beyond his statutory powers. A constant theme of the 1998 arrangements in Scotland was the need for the director to approve all changes to the SAS; however, the structure of panels established to oversee the market aims to devolve decision making to market participants. In addition, the director envisaged that Scottish market governance may develop in such a manner as to remove the need for this degree of regulatory oversight, and the licence condition underpinning the SAS[29] specifically allows for at least the partial withdrawal of the director from that role at a future date following consultation on an alternative governance mechanism. Experience in England and Wales has suggested that complex markets do require continuing regulation, but the degree of involvement taken by the regulator can be limited to what is necessary to fulfil his statutory functions with appropriate delegation of decision making.

Another issue of relevance only to the Scottish market will be the interaction between the Scottish Parliament and Westminster in areas of energy policy. Whilst energy policy is a reserved matter, there are a number of ways in which the Scottish Parliament may still develop a role. It will be interesting, for example, to monitor how future applications for generation consents will be dealt with in Scotland. The government's partial moratorium on gas-fired power stations will be implemented, at least in part, via the giving or withholding of consents in terms of the Electricity Act.[30]

Following devolution, the powers to grant such consents are delegated in Scotland to Scottish ministers who are legally obliged to act consistently with the terms of the Act.[31] The government's *Conclusions of the Review of Energy Sources for Power Generation*,[32] however, makes the implicit assumption that Scottish ministers will exercise their powers under the Electricity Act in accordance with energy policy as determined at UK level and therefore in a manner which recognises that new gas-fired generation would normally be inconsistent with the government's energy policy. This type of policy issue will be governed by non-legally binding 'concordats' currently being finalised between Whitehall departments and their counterparts in Edinburgh. Tensions are likely to arise, particularly in this area, given that policy on planning, environment, social inclusion and sustainability are otherwise devolved matters but, in the context of energy policy, are established in London. While the political party in power in both jurisdictions is common this may be less of an issue, but there is certainly the potential for conflict where this is not the case in future.

Transmission: England and Wales

High-voltage transmission requires quite different regulatory techniques. This is a classic area of natural monopoly, and so is subject to indefinite price control. The system adopted is that of the RPI-X formula familiar from the regulation of other utilities and derived from Professor Littlechild's recommendations for British Telecom referred to above. Under this system price increases are limited to a figure below the rate of inflation as determined in the Retail Price Index (RPI). The difference between the Index and the permitted increase, the X-factor, represents the expected efficiency gains from the enterprise over the period of the price control.

The formula for the National Grid was originally set at RPI, then tightened by the director-general to RPI-3 from April 1993 to 1997. In

1995–6, he issued consultation papers for a new formula from 1997 and engaged consultants to examine the company's business plan and proposed capital expenditure. The outcome was proposals for a new control involving a 20 per cent cut in prices followed by RPI-4 for three years, which the company accepted.[33] This will expire in 2001 and a further control will be set. Distribution by the recs has also been subject to price control of a similar pattern, in this case very controversially, as the controls for England and Wales covering 1995–2000 had to be withdrawn and amended at a late stage after it had become clear that information supplied to the director-general had seriously understated the finance available to the companies.[34] Once more, further distribution controls will be set from the year 2000.[35]

This is not the place to undertake a general critique of the RPI-X system of price control, especially as the government remains committed to it.[36] It may be mentioned, however, that one of the issues which has become very clear is that setting the formula requires considerable discretionary assessment on the part of the director-general. This then puts the emphasis on to the need for open procedures to permit views to be gathered fairly and exposed to criticism before the formulae are set. There was considerable early criticism of the director-general as having adopted procedures which were not sufficiently transparent.[37] A more open approach was adopted in the transmission review of 1995–6 with the issue of four consultation papers; consultants' reports on operating costs and on capital expenditure were discussed with the company and published in summary form, although the full reports were not made available to the trade unions involved, despite a request for them. For the new distribution formulae the first consultation paper was issued in February 1998 and they were made part of a wider programme of reviews of the recs; other detailed papers have followed. Legal requirements to consult and to give reasons will be imposed as part of the government's general review of utility regulation.[38] Given that regulation of transmission prices will be necessary indefinitely, this concern with improving the legitimacy of regulation is the most important practical route for reform.

Transmission: Scotland

In Scotland the vertical integration of the Scottish companies and the contractual and regulatory regime surrounding the Scotland/England interconnector give rise to their own specific regulatory issues. On privatisation, the transmission business in Scotland was left within the two Scottish companies. In their capacity as transmission licensees they have obligations to establish transmission as a separate business and to keep separate accounts. The transmission charges and terms upon which the business offers to enter into connection and use of system agreements with competitors are all regulated.

One impact of the different structure in Scotland can be seen in the qualification to the statutory duty imposed on the Scottish companies as transmission licensees to facilitate competition in the supply and generation of electricity.[39] This is qualified in that it is to be interpreted as a duty only to make the transmission system available to competitors on terms which neither prevent nor restrict competition. In the context of its consultations on business separation generally, OFFER has indicated that the removal of this qualification would be desirable. The Scottish companies have questioned whether or not this is appropriate in the absence of full separation of ownership of the transmission businesses.

In the area of price controls the Scottish transmission price control is also based on an RPI-X formula and was first set in 1990 for four years and was revised in 1994 for the period to 1999. It has been agreed that the review will be deferred until April 2000 to bring this into line with the Public Electricity Suppliers' reviews of distribution and supply pricing. Historically, the price controls in Scotland for both transmission and distribution have been more demanding than their counterparts in England and Wales, again demonstrating that regulation in Scotland has tended to be stronger than that south of the border.[40]

A number of factors have combined to give rise to OFFER's current proposal to separate the transmission businesses. Experience from England and Wales, where ownership of the grid is independent and competition in generation and supply is more developed, is often cited.[41] Whilst that difference in structure may or may not have contributed to the development in competition, it is interesting that, in its May 1998 consultation paper on separation of businesses, OFFER states that in 'England and Wales the independence of the transmission company and the unqualified duty to facilitate competition have worked with the grain of regulation and competition. In Scotland, the absence of these factors has tended to work against it.'[42]

Equally, the restructuring of the gas market following the MMC report on British Gas in 1993 was driven by the view that the dual role of supply and transport gave rise to an inherent conflict of interest which did not create conditions within which competition could develop. Other influences include convergence with the gas market heralded in the government's Green Paper as requiring an integrated approach to promoting competition between the two markets. The directive on common rules for the internal market for electricity[43] is also relevant, in that OFFER has commented that the lack of independent operational and managerial control of the transmission system in Scotland may not meet the requirements of the directive.[44] It is worth noting, however, that this view has not been endorsed by the UK government.

It is clear from the current consultation on separation that the director has viewed vertical integration of the transmission businesses as inhibiting the development of competition in the generation and supply markets notwithstanding the harsher price control regime adopted for Scotland. This suggests again that the complexity of the market and particularly the need for the transmission licensees in Scotland to interact with competitors to the two Scottish companies give rise to concerns which have not been capable of being addressed via the existing licensing framework. Strong regulation on price will clearly have had an impact, but the regulator has not been able to establish the degree of transparency in the operation of the transmission businesses which market entrants require. Further regulatory change is now proposed in this area, given the current review of Scottish Trading Arrangements.[45] The proposals to establish Scotland-wide trading via a Scottish system operator will mean that certain important functions of the current transmission licensees will be carved out and taken over by the system operator.

The Scotland/England interconnector which links the two systems and provides an opportunity for generators in Scotland to trade with the market in England and Wales operates within a contractual and regulatory framework which was put in place at the time of privatisation.[46] Whilst the White Paper on the structure of the industry refers to the Scottish industry having the benefit of excess capacity and being able to export to England and Wales,[47] in fact the framework adopted reserved all of the existing capacity to the two Scottish companies and to British Nuclear Fuels (which had always exported its entire output to the English market) and has not shown itself to be conducive to providing access for independent generators. One of the key economic factors for any incoming generator in a market which already has substantial excess capacity will inevitably be an assessment of the costs and availability of interconnector access.

In the course of 1998, the director issued his determination on certain applications for access to the interconnector and reservation of capacity by National Power, British Nuclear Fuels and ScottishPower and in 1999 OFFER is again consulting on interconnector issues as a result of a revised application for reservation of capacity by ScottishPower.[48] It would also appear that a major overhaul of the interconnector contractual and regulatory framework is now likely via the current consultation on new trading arrangements for Scotland, which suggests changes to create greater transparency in interconnector pricing and the introduction of an auction process on which available interconnector capacity can be allocated on non-discriminatory terms.[49] There is a good example here, then, of another recurring theme in regulation which has been particularly true of the Scottish market. Decisions which were taken at the time of privatisation on market structure, contracts which were entered into and licence conditions which were drafted in the light of that structure are all currently being questioned. The degree of change now being suggested for the Scottish market will require change to that licence framework and may require the alteration or replacement of some of the major industry agreements. If the director is to be capable of the continuing role which will be required after market reform, the contractual and regulatory framework put in place to achieve this will be crucial.

Supply Competition and Social Regulation: England and Wales

In our discussion of the reform of the trading arrangements above we suggested that an important role of the regulator had been to create the systems making a working market possible. This is also a theme in the liberalisation of supply to consumers, where an important regulatory role has been to oversee market creation and to set the boundary conditions within which such markets will operate.

The opening of the supply markets has occurred in three stages. The first was that for the largest users, those with a maximum consumption of over one megawatt, and was achieved relatively easily; by 1997 in England and Wales, nearly 64 per cent of such sites were supplied by a second tier supplier – that is, a supplier other than their local rec. From April 1994 (1995 in Scotland) markets were opened for medium-size customers with a consumption of over 100KW and, by 1997, 42 per cent were supplied by a second tier. In Scotland, the respective second tier shares were smaller, at 27 per cent and 16 per cent. The second opening of the market, however, illustrated the likelihood of serious administrative difficulties in extending competition further. It was planned that all consumers would be given the opportunity to choose a competing supplier by 1998, but the process of implementation was initially slow. The Trade and Industry Committee was highly critical of preparations in a 1995 report, claiming that there had been little analysis of the costs and benefits and no clear allocation of responsibility for seeing the changes through.[50] In response, the director-general agreed to take a more proactive stance and took a number of measures to prepare for implementation. However, he was concerned about foot-dragging by the recs themselves. They were after all in an enviable position as the gas market had already been successfully liberalised and they were in a position to compete in it while not themselves facing competition in their core markets. The implementation of full competition was delayed, beginning in September 1998 and completed in June 1999.

In a further report the Trade and Industry Committee was critical once more, stating that '*neither the* [director-general] *nor the* [recs] *can be proud of their collective inability to open up the domestic electricity market to competition within the eight years since Vesting, particularly given the speed with which competition was introduced in the domestic gas market*'.[51] It blamed the delay once more on inadequate leadership by the regulator and lack of commitment by some recs. Moreover, the Committee also stressed that '*firm regulatory oversight and action will be required even after competition commences to ensure that liberalisation of the electricity market is a success and not an expensive failure*'.[52]

What is evident from these events is that regulation does not simply disappear with the creation of liberalised markets. Firstly, strong regulation is necessary to bring the markets into existence. This is best carried out by a specialist regulator; only the director-general of electricity supply was in a position to provide leadership in the complex and arcane matter of ensuring that electricity consumer markets could be opened without disruption of supply. Secondly, even after the markets have been opened, regulation remains necessary to supervise their operation. This is true in the sense of avoiding anti-competitive conduct; once more a specialist regulator will be much better placed to detect this than a general competition authority would be. A further purpose of regulation has also become apparent, however: that of social regulation. This is partly due to the change of government in 1997; the incoming Labour government stressed that 'we are concerned that the current framework does not fully reflect the importance of the utility industries to the achievement of wider social and environmental objectives. We are determined that the benefits of better services and lower prices are shared fairly by all sectors of society.'[53]

The reform plans include arrangements for guidance to regulators on social matters from government as a way of reflecting these concerns. Moreover, the opening up of the household market to competition created strong concerns that new entrants would 'cream skim' – in other words, offer services only to the most profitable consumers, leaving the poor with a deteriorating service at higher prices from the former monopoly supplier. A number of regulatory steps were taken by the regulator to avoid this. The new suppliers were made subject to broadly similar obligations to those of the recs; these include obligations to supply on request on published terms and to offer a range of payment options, including pre-payment meters. They are also subject to special duties relating to elderly, disabled and chronically sick customers. Moreover, supply price controls for the dominant public electricity suppliers are likely to be retained until at least the year 2002 and these controls set maximum price limits for domestic customers.[54]

The energy regulators were also required by the incoming government to produce a social action plan relating to the supply of energy to disadvantaged customers. First drafts of the plans were published in 1998; however, these suffered from a limited time for preparation and did little more than restate a number of existing policies while expressing serious concerns about some mechanisms proposed by the government for further help.[55] The Trade and Industry Committee expressed its disappointment that the preparation of the plans had only been undertaken after a direct instruction from government and that the proposals were highly qualified.[56] The director-general has since prepared a much more detailed draft of the action plan for consultation, listing nine priority measures to assist the disadvantaged; the National Electricity Consumers Council has also published its own proposals.[57]

Social regulation is thus in a state of transition with the development of the liberalised household market. However, it seems clear that it will not go away with liberalisation; indeed, the opening of markets has raised social concerns with new force. Although, when legislation has been passed to implement the government's reform proposals, regulatory guidance will be issued by the government, implementation will still be for the regulator; it also remains to be seen to what extent the power to issue such guidance will actually be used. Nevertheless, social regulation is another area of regulation which is unlikely to wither away.

Supply: Scotland

The supply market in Scotland is subject to a regulatory regime similar to that in England and Wales, and full supply competition started its phased roll-out in ScottishPower's area in September and in Scottish Hydro-Electric's area in November 1998. Market penetration figures are not yet available for the domestic market but, to date, second tier supply has not established itself in Scotland at the same levels as in England and Wales.[58] The lower levels of second tier supply are attributed by second tier suppliers to the limitations on the bilateral contract market in the absence of significant independent generation and the continuing vertical integration of the transmission businesses. An important aspect of the trading arrangements put in place in Scotland in 1998 was the decision that the settlement arrangements, and therefore the systems required by suppliers to compete in Scotland, should be as similar as possible to those being introduced in England and Wales. Thus the industry avoided creating a barrier to entry in Scotland due to a requirement to fund the development of different systems.

The structural and regulatory change now envisaged for Scotland to bring trading arrangements more in line with those in England and Wales will involve a major programme of work which is potentially more wide-ranging than the already complex implementation of new trading arrangements south of the border. To be in a position to introduce the regime now proposed there will need to be alterations in Scotland which have no parallel in England and the exercise of delivering that change will require strong central leadership.

Conclusions

The immediate future of electricity regulation will see important developments which could shape its operation for many years. Reform of the pool and other trading arrangements will be controversial and complex, but will utilise a new form of regulation through the administration by a representative Code Panel within the context of powers of veto on the part of the director-general. In supply we shall see the implications of the liberalisation of the household market, raising both competition and social concerns for the regulator. Moreover, the Competition Act 1998 grants to the director-general concurrent powers of enforcement of the new, European-based prohibitions on anti-competitive agreements and conduct. Thus in all these areas regulation has moved on from the regulation of natural monopoly which was the model which was most influential after privatisation; important areas of natural monopoly will remain in transmission and in distribution, but these will not be the most characteristic types of regulatory activity.

What we have seen in recent years is a growing realisation that regulation and market operation are complex and interdependent phenomena. Thus pool trading arrangements were unsatisfactory largely because they were expected to operate without any serious regulatory supervision; supply competition for small consumers was difficult to produce precisely because there was insufficient regulatory action to overcome the initial resistance of the companies involved, and the social implications were at first underestimated. Moreover, the legitimate role of government in relation to such matters as fuel diversity and security of supply has only recently been properly recognised. As a result, in electricity there will clearly be a permanent role for regulation and one which will not necessarily reduce. However, it is changing from control of monopoly to the creation of competitive markets, their coordination and setting the boundary conditions in which they will operate.

Notes

1 Littlechild, S. (1984), *Economic Regulation of British Telecommunications' Profitability*, London: Department of Trade and Industry.
2 For a general critique of such 'public choice' theories of regulation, see Prosser, T. (1999), 'Theorising Utility Regulation', *Modern Law Review*, 62, 203–6.
3 Fuller discussion is contained in Prosser, T. (1997), *Law and the Regulators*, Oxford: Clarendon, ch. 6.
4 Scottish Power plc and Scottish Hydro-Electric plc (now Scottish and Southern Energy plc) referred to in this chapter as the Scottish companies.
5 See the Electricity Act 1989, Part I, and Prosser, *Law and the Regulators* (n.3, above).
6 The key documents are Department of Trade and Industry (1998), *A Fair Deal for Consumers: Modernising the Framework for Utility Regulation*, Cm 3898, London: Department of Trade and Industry; Department of Trade and Industry (1998) *A Fair Deal for Consumers: The Response to Consultation*, London: Department of Trade and Industry; and Department of Trade and Industry (1998), *The Future of Gas and Electricity Regulation*, London: Department of Trade and Industry.
7 Department of Trade and Industry (1998), *A Fair Deal for Consumers: Public Consultation Paper on Consumer Councils*, London: Department of Trade and Industry; Department of Trade and Industry (1999), *A Fair Deal for Consumers: Modernising the Framework for Utility Regulation Consumer Councils: The Response to Consultation*, London: Department of Trade and Industry.
8 Directive 96/92/EC, OJ 1997 L27/20.
9 McHarg, A. (1999), 'Reshaping the Electricity Generation Market in England and Wales', *Utilities Law Review*, 10, 34. This article is highly recommended as a clear introduction to an extraordinarily arcane and complex subject.
10 For details, see the Trade and Industry Committee (1994–5), *Aspects of the Electricity Supply Industry*, HC481, paras 32–46.
11 OFFER (1994–5), *Annual Report 1994*, HC 432, 22–3.
12 *Conclusions of the Review of Energy Sources for Power Generation and the Government's Response to the Fourth and Fifth Reports of the Trade and Industry Committee*, Cm 4071 (1998), para. 2.9.
13 OFFER (1998), *Review of Electricity Trading Arrangements: Proposals*, Birmingham: OFFER; see also now OFGEM (1999), *The New Electricity Trading Arrangements*, London: OFGEM.
14 Once more the reader is referred to McHarg (n.9, above) for details.
15 See in particular OFFER (1998), (n.13, above), ch.7; OFGEM (1999) (n.13, above), ch.10.
16 *Review* (n.12, above), paras 2.2–4 and ch.3.
17 Sections 36 and 14 (1–2), respectively.
18 See, for example, Shuttleworth, G. (1998), 'The Electricity Industry 1997–8', in Centre for the Study of Regulated Industries (ed.), *Regulatory Review 1998/9*, London: CRI, 19–33.
19 See, for example, the Electricity Act 1989, s.34.
20 Industry Department for Scotland (1988), *Privatisation of the Scottish Electricity Industry*, Cm 327, para. 30.
21 *Ibid.*, para. 33.
22 See, for example, OFFER (1998), *Generation, Transmission and Public Electricity Supply Licence for Scottish Power plc*, Birmingham; OFFER, Part V, Condition 23, which defines these as 'arrangements which the Director shall agree to be the most appropriate for securing the objective of eliminating barriers to the eco-

nomic and efficient supply of electricity by relevant second tier suppliers to relevant premises caused by relevant constraints'.

23 Second tier supply is the supply of electricity to customers in an area by a supplier where the supplier is not the local franchise supplier for that area.
24 See OFFER (1998), *Scottish Trading Arrangements Consultation Paper,* Birmingham; OFFER, para. 3.2.
25 See, for example, OFFER, *Generation* (n.22, above), Part IV, Condition 5.
26 OFFER, *Generation* (n.22, above), Part V, Condition 24.
27 OFFER, *Scottish Trading* (n.24, above), paras 2.24–31.
28 OFGEM (1999), *Review of Scottish Trading Arrangements – A Consultation Document,* London; OFGEM.
29 OFFER, *Generation* (n.22, above), Part V, Condition 24, para. 3(c).
30 Section 36.
31 See *The Scotland Act 1998 (Transfer of Functions to the Scottish Ministers etc.) Order 1999* (S.I. 1999/1750), Schedule 1.
32 See *Conclusions of the Review of Energy Sources for Power Generation* (n.12, above), 11, para. 1.2.
33 OFFER (1996), *The Transmission Price Control Review of the National Grid Company: Proposals,* Birmingham: OFFER.
34 For details, see Prosser, *Law and the Regulators* (n.3, above), pp.162–6.
35 OFFER (1999), *Reviews of Public Electricity Suppliers 1998 to 2000: Distribution Price Control Review Update,* Birmingham: OFFER.
36 See Department of Trade and Industry, *A Fair Deal for Consumers* (1998) (n.6, above), para. 3.27; for critiques, see, for example, Helm, D. (1994), 'British Utility Regulation: Theory, Practice and Reform', *Oxford Review of Economic Policy,* 10, 17–39; Rees, R. and J. Vickers (1995), 'RPI-X Price Cap Regulation', in M. Bishop, J. Kay and C. Mayer (eds), *The Regulatory Challenge,* Oxford: Oxford University Press, pp.358–85.
37 For details, see Prosser, *Law and the Regulators* (n.3, above), pp.177–8.
38 See Department of Trade and Industry, *A Fair Deal for Consumers* (1998) paras 7.17–27.
39 See the Electricity Act 1989, s.9(3).
40 See, for example, Monopoly and Mergers Commission (1995), *Scottish Hydro-Electric Plc, A Report on a Reference under Section 12 of the Electricity Act 1989,* para. 3.33, London; HMSO.
41 See, for example, OFFER/OFGAS (1999), *Separation of Businesses: Proposals and Consultation,* para. 5.8, Birmingham; OFFER.
42 See OFFER (1998), *Reviews of Public Electricity Suppliers 1998 to 2000, Separation of Businesses Consultation Paper,* para 5.11.
43 Directive 96/92/EC (n.8, above).
44 See, for example, OFFER/OFGAS (1999), *Separation of Businesses* (n.41, above), para. 2.4.
45 See OFGEM, *Review of Scottish Trading Arrangements* (n.28, above), para. 10.4.
46 See Chapter 2, on essential facilities.
47 See Industry Department for Scotland, *Privatisation of the Scottish Electricity Industry* (n.20, above), para. 33.
48 See OFGEM (1999), *Access to the Scotland-England Interconnector: A Consultation Document,* London; OFGEM.
49 See OFGEM, *Review of Scottish Trading Arrangements* (n.28, above), para. 10.3.
50 Trade and Industry Committee, *Aspects of the Electricity Supply Industry* (n.10, above), paras 7–31.
51 Trade and Industry Committee (1997–8), *Developments in the Liberalisation of the Domestic Electricity Market,* HC 781, para. 8 (emphasis retained).
52 *Ibid.,* para. 47 (emphasis retained).

53 Department of Trade and Industry, *A Fair Deal for Consumers* (1998) (n.6, above), para 1.14.
54 See OFFER (1999), *Reviews of Public Electricity Suppliers 1998 to 2000: Supply Price Control Review Initial Proposals*, Birmingham: OFFER.
55 OFFER/OFGAS (1998), *The Social Dimension: Action Plan*, Birmingham: OFFER.
56 Trade and Industry Committee, *Developments in the Liberalisation of the Domestic Electricity Market* (n.51, above), para. 38.
57 OFFER/OFGAS (1999), *Social Action Plan: Discussion Paper*, Birmingham: OFFER; National Electricity Consumers Council (1999), *Assisting Disadvantaged Electricity Consumers – Practical Proposals*, London: NECC.
58 See, for example, OFFER, *Scottish Trading* (n.24, above), paras 2.18–21.

5 Telecommunications Regulation in the USA: Seeking the Right Balance between Regulation and Competition

THOMAS J. LONG,* *The Utility Reform Network*

Introduction

As the new millennium dawns, casual observers of the US telecoms market-place could easily conclude that the days of significant economic regulation are numbered. Each day brings reports of emerging technologies and services that have the potential to revolutionise our communications capabilities. A multitude of new telecoms operators and service providers spring on to the business pages, promising to inject competition into this or that market. Mobile operators tell us that our tiny portable phones will soon handle all of our information and communication needs far better than our current computers and fixed link phones. Satellites and electricity lines are touted as future telecoms pathways. The impression one gets is that we will soon be deluged with a choice of affordable and astounding communications

* Senior telecommunications attorney, The Utility Reform Network (TURN), a non-profit consumer advocacy organisation based in San Francisco, California. In the 1998–9 academic year, he was an Atlantic Fellow in Public Policy based at the University of Glasgow School of Law and researched telecoms regulation in the UK.

options. The best action for regulators, it would seem, is simply to get out of the way.

On closer inspection, however, the USA has a different, and far more complicated, story to tell. If you believed the prevailing wisdom that accompanied the passage of the Telecommunications Act of 1996 (TA 96),[1] you would have expected, at the end of 1999, that most US residents would have a choice of local telephone operators. And you would have expected competition to spur sharp decreases in prices for telephone services. Such expectations have been proved wrong. As the decade closes, almost no residential or small business customers (collectively the 'mass market') have any choice of local operator. Local line charges are increasing. And many customers with modest usage levels have found that their long-distance bills are increasing, not decreasing.

The reality in the USA is an extremely uneven pace of change and, where competition has taken hold, a skewed distribution of benefits. To be sure, new markets, most notably the market for fast Internet access, are emerging and growing rapidly. At the same time, the residential market for local telephone service remains monopolistic despite extensive regulatory intervention to attempt to inject competition. In the more competitive long-distance market, high-volume customers can obtain steadily decreasing rates that reflect lower input costs, while low-volume customers are saddled with rising bills.

Consequently, regulation is neither disappearing nor becoming simpler. This chapter will address four areas in which US telecoms regulators can be expected to be busy in the years ahead. First, regulators will continue to use regulatory tools, such as 'unbundling' and non-discrimination requirements, to break down monopolies in existing markets while attempting to prevent monopolisation of new markets. Second, regulators will need to use price and service quality regulation to protect consumers in markets where market power persists or develops. Third, even for relatively competitive markets, regulators will be busy attempting to make markets work better, such as by fashioning rules to permit effective comparison shopping and to ensure that all groups benefit from the lower prices resulting from competition. Fourth, regulators will continue to confront universal service issues both in the context of traditional voice service telephone service and in connection with emerging markets for fast Internet access service. In all of these endeavours, enlightened regulators will find that regulation and competition are not mutually exclusive, but must work together to serve the ultimate goal of satisfying the needs of the public.

Regulating to Promote Competition

Continued Construction of the Framework for Local Competition for Voice Service

In the second half of the 1990s, the primary focus of US policy makers and regulators has been to extend competition from long-distance markets into the local market. US long-distance markets have been open to mass-market competition since 1984. As of late 1999, the market share of the incumbent, AT&T, had fallen just below 50 per cent. While there is some controversy regarding whether the long-distance market can be deemed fully competitive for all market segments (a point that will be further addressed below), all US consumers have a variety of options for long-distance service.

In contrast, it did not become US policy to open local markets to competition until the enactment of TA 96.[2] In the US scheme, where the local and long-distance markets are separated, it made sense to save for last the chore of creating local competition. Local telephone networks, which include lines running into each home and business, are the most costly part of the telecommunications business. Because of the massive expense (and the disruption to streets and neighbourhoods) involved in replicating existing local networks, local competition is the hardest type of competition to bring about. Furthermore, the number and complexity of technical issues (such as telephone number portability,[3] access to rights of way, and distribution of telephone numbers) associated with allowing new companies to compete in a domain that was designed to be a monopoly dwarf those associated with long-distance competition.

While Congress described TA 96 as deregulatory,[4] the Act actually has required the construction of an elaborate framework of federal and state regulations to support the development of local competition.[5] In contrast to the case of the UK, where the initial focus was on infrastructure competition, TA 96 offers three potential paths for competitors to follow.[6]

First, through *resale*, competitors can use the incumbents' facilities entirely and simply rebrand the local service as their own.[7] In the UK, this would mean, for example, that a competitor pays British Telecom (BT) a wholesale charge for the customer's line rental and local calls and then bills the customer directly for those services. All of the customer's interactions would be with the competitor and the customer could therefore be oblivious to the fact that BT was actually providing the service.

Second, competitors can use their own infrastructure (usually called *facilities-based competition* in the USA).[8] The customer's calls travel initially over facilities owned by the competitor, but ultimately will pass over other networks to reach customers served by the incumbent or other competitors.

Third, competitors can use a hybrid of the previous two, called 'unbundled network element' or *UNE-based competition*,[9] which permits competitors to lease unbundled elements of the incumbent's exchange networks and use those elements in conjunction with facilities supplied by the competitor.[10] The unbundled network element (UNE) that Congress expected competitors to make use of the most was the incumbent's local loop.[11] A competitor who uses the incumbent's local loop would pay the incumbent a one-off and recurring wholesale charge for the rental and then connect its own facilities to the incumbent's network on the customer side of the incumbent's switch. Calls would then be diverted to the competitor's switch. As with resale, the customer could be oblivious to the fact that any facilities of the incumbent were being used. The competitor would be responsible for billing and all other interactions with the customer.

Each of these forms of competition requires its own set of rules and regulated prices. For example, resale requires regulators to establish the level of the discount off retail rates,[12] UNE-based competition requires regulated prices for the network components leased from the incumbent,[13] and facilities-based competition requires regulatory intervention to ensure fair rates when a competitor uses the incumbent's network to complete calls.[14]

Whether three forms of competition are permitted or just one, local competition is not possible without extensive regulatory intervention. Without regulation, incumbents could simply refuse to do business with potential competitors, or, more discreetly, go through the motions of cooperation while steadfastly denying competitors the terms and access to facilities that they need to mount a challenge. Almost four years after the enactment of TA 96 and after devoting hundreds of thousands of hours to local competition issues, regulators still have more work to do to construct the basic edifice to permit competition.

TA 96 was ushered in with a wave of bold predictions that most customers would have a choice of two or more local operators by the end of the century. However, the reality as of late 1999 is that only about 2 per cent of residential and small business customers have an alternative to the incumbent for local service. US policy makers and regulators were too optimistic about the technologies to be used by competitors, especially the still unproven capability of most US cable networks (which, unlike UK networks, do not incorporate copper wire) to carry voice conversations in a cost-effective manner. At the same time, they underestimated the ability of the incumbents to impede competition through overt tactics (such as litigation) and more passive tactics (such as failing to process competitors' orders for service in a timely and efficient manner). In addition, for a variety of reasons, UNE-based piggy-back competition, in which a competitor leases the incumbent's local loop, has not yet proved to be a viable vehicle of mass-market competition.[15]

As the 21st century begins, however, federal and state regulators will not give up the effort to promote local competition for voice service. They will continue to develop and refine the rules that are the necessary preconditions for such competition. These include reform of outdated and illogical telephone number allocation rules, continued scrutiny of systems used by incumbents to process competitors' service orders, and further refinement of regulated prices for competitors to lease components of incumbent networks.

However, at the same time that regulators are conducting this work, they will also need to decrease their expectations for local competition. The huge investments necessary to replicate even just portions of the incumbent's networks and the need to obtain a sizable critical mass of customers pose daunting barriers to entry, as the UK's experience shows. Despite highly favourable conditions for infrastructure competitors in the UK – including an incumbent with a history of deficient service quality and an absence of US-type requirements to provide access to other long-distance operators – the UK's decade-long efforts have resulted in only limited duopoly competition. Unless and until mobile networks become fully competitive with fixed link networks in terms of price, quality and data transmission capability, most mass-market customers in the USA will be lucky if they have even one alternative to the incumbent for local voice service.

Promoting Competition in the Emerging Fast Internet Access Market

Although competition for voice telephone service has been disappointing, the policy of opening local markets to competition has been successful in speeding the deployment of fast Internet access. Before local competition was permitted, incumbent local operators were painfully slow to deploy improved technologies such as ISDN,[16] out of concern for undermining the profitability of other more expensive services. Local competition, however, has spurred the incumbents to bring their next generation of fast Internet access to market much more quickly. Called DSL (Digital Subscriber Line), this technology uses existing copper wire phone lines to allow Internet access up to 50 times faster than analog (28.8 kbps) modems. Since 1998, incumbents have been rolling out DSL in major markets across the USA, and it has been popular with residential and small business customers.

The competitive threat that spurred the incumbents to act is coming from two fronts. First, in 1998, US cable operators began mass-market deployment of cable modems, which can allow Internet access at speeds even faster than DSL permits. Second, TA 96's requirement that incumbents unbundle their local loops (that is, lease the connections between customer premises and telephone switches) has permitted competitors to offer their own DSL services over the incumbent's lines into offices and homes. Incumbents have been forced to rush their own DSL services to market in order to fend off these competitive challenges.[17]

The quickly emerging market for fast Internet access poses new challenges for regulators. Such high-speed services are likely to become the dominant mode of gaining access to the Internet and thereby promise to become essential services for businesses and households. Regulators will need to act proactively to ensure that this market develops as competitively as possible. In this vein, US regulators are already facing a key issue, whether to require 'open access' to cable modems. Cable operators, led by AT&T (which in 1998 acquired the largest US cable operator, TCI), seek to restrict customers who buy their service to use of a single Internet Service Provider (ISP) – one that is affiliated with the cable operator. They claim that their network design only permits such restricted access and that a requirement of open access to other ISPs would require cost-prohibitive upgrades that would stifle their incentives to continue deployment of the service. Proponents of open access, which include ISPs and most consumer organisations, argue that customers should be able to gain access to the ISP of their choice, which would promote price competition and limit the ability of cable operators to act as 'gatekeepers' for the information that citizens seek to obtain from the Internet. Open access essentially is a non-discrimination requirement that requires cable operators to offer non-affiliated ISPs access to their cable modems on the same terms as are enjoyed by affiliated ISPs. Incumbent telecoms operators are required to make their DSL service available to any ISP and contend that cable operators should be subject to the same requirement.[18]

As of late 1999, the FCC had thus far deferred decision on this issue in favour of waiting to see how well competition would develop without regulatory intervention.[19] The FCC has coined the term 'unregulation' to describe its favoured approach to issues such as this.[20] In the vacuum left by the FCC's inaction, cities and counties, which have authority over the terms and conditions of cable franchises, have begun requiring open access.

This issue illustrates the ideological opposition to government regulation that holds sway with a large, though not necessarily dominant, segment of American policy makers. In the author's view, AT&T's

threats of curtailing cable modem deployment ring hollow in light of the huge revenues available in this rapidly expanding market. Open access can only promote lower prices and enhanced consumer choice, which are clear goals of US policy. Even though it was regulation that helped to speed DSL deployment by requiring incumbent telecoms operators to unbundle their local loops, there is still considerable resistance in the USA to the use of regulation to promote competition. However, the importance of maximising competition for access to the Internet will probably overcome such resistance with respect to this and other issues that are sure to arise in connection with the market for fast Internet access.

Continued Regulation of Voice Telecoms Markets to Constrain Market Power

By now, US regulators should be realising that local competition for voice service will progress extremely slowly and that the local market may never have enough competitors for incumbent prices to be disciplined by the market. If the snail-paced growth of competition in the USA is not sufficient to make this apparent, US regulators can learn from the experience in the UK, which fully opened its local market to competition five years before the USA. Buoyed by the ambitious business plans of fixed radio access operators, in 1997, OFTEL projected that most UK consumers would have a choice of three local operators by the end of the century and that all price controls on BT would end in 2001.[21] Instead, with the close of the century, the fixed radio access operators have all but disappeared and, for the 50 per cent of customers who have a choice, the market is a duopoly. Price controls are almost certain to be continued beyond 2001.

Just as OFTEL saw its optimistic predictions evaporate, many US regulators are now coming to realise that they have been unduly optimistic. For the foreseeable future, US incumbents will retain significant market power in the residential and small business markets and will need to be regulated. Regulating prices in markets that are opened to competition poses new challenges and presents some traps for the unwary regulator.

First, competitors are likely to join forces with incumbents in arguing for lenient regulation of incumbent retail rates. Competitors stand to gain from a high price umbrella set by the incumbent, especially in markets such as local voice service where duopoly operators can sustain supracompetitive prices with little fear of entry by other firms. Exactly such a coalition emerged in the UK with respect to its 1997 price cap consultation, in which the cable operators threatened to curtail investment if BT's rates were reduced too sharply.[22] When faced with such a seemingly unusual coalition of powerful interests, regulators must remember their priorities. The ultimate goal of regulation is not to promote competition, but, as OFTEL puts it, to secure the best possible deal for consumers in terms of quality, choice and value for money. Competitors who need a high price umbrella in order to survive may be inefficient. Consumers are best served by setting rates that are in reasonable relation to efficient costs, mimicking, to the extent discernible, prices in a robustly competitive market. If prescribing such rates for the incumbent drives a competitor out of the market, it means the competitor was inefficient and did not deserve to survive. Thus regulators should take their best shot at setting reasonable rates for incumbents, without regard to the impact of those rates on competitors.

Second, incumbents are likely to appeal to regulators' concerns about anti-competitive pricing as a pretext for gaining rate increases for services facing little competition. For such services, incumbents will have an incentive to exaggerate their costs to justify higher rates. For example, in California, the incumbent local operator is seeking large increases in the rate for directory enquiries (DQ) on the grounds that its current rates are below cost and therefore anti-competitive. However, no competitor has ever expressed concern about DQ rates, and TURN, the consumer organization for which the author works, presented evidence showing that current rates exceed the utility's cost. Regulators must be suspicious whenever incumbents take on the mantle of their competitors in their arguments. This is a tip-off to potential price-gouging for non-competitive services.

Third, incumbents can be expected to seek price and service quality deregulation before the interests of consumers would warrant, in an effort to collect monopoly profits. In aid of this objective, they will attempt to flatter the regulator by arguing that the regulator's efforts to promote competition are highly successful and will soon produce vigorous competition. They will cite projected business plans of competitors to support their predictions. Regulators should resist the invitation to reduce regulation based on anything other than a proven diminution in market power. As the UK's experience with fixed radio access shows, business plans can fail and should not be relied upon in assessments of the extent of competition.

Need for Regulation Even in Relatively Competitive Markets

As previously noted, the US long-distance market has been open to competition for 15 years and, compared to the local market, is relatively competitive. For high-volume customers, rate decreases have kept pace with industry cost savings. However, low-volume customers of the major carriers have not fully shared in those cost savings and, in the late 1990s, have seen their long-distance bills increase. The industry has achieved this result through complex rate structures that effectively discriminate between the two types of customer. In 1998 and 1999, the major operators began imposing a variety of fixed fees and minimum charges on customer bills, making the per-minute prices significantly higher for low-volume users.

For example, customers who subscribe to AT&T, the largest US long-distance operator, now must pay a minimum of $5.50 per month, even if they make no long-distance calls. Table 5.1 shows the disparity in per-minute rates for AT&T customers as of October 1999. A customer who makes 10 minutes of calls in a month will pay an effective per-minute rate over 400 per cent higher than the rate paid by a customer with four hours of usage.

Table 5.1 Rate disparities for AT&T low- and high-volume customers (best available per-minute inter-state rates)

Monthly minutes of use	Best available rate
1	$5.50
5	$1.10
10	$0.550
20	$0.275
40	$0.213
60	$0.192
120	$0.140
180	$0.117
240	$0.105
300	$0.098

The uneven distribution of benefits has sparked an outcry from consumers and consumer organisations, who allege that long-distance operators are taking advantage of the relative price-insensitivity of low-volume customers, many of whom are poor. As discussed below, it is extremely difficult and time-consuming to research and compare long-distance rates, and many low-usage customers lack the time and inclination to do so. In response to this problem, in 1999, the FCC took the controversial step of inviting comments regarding whether it should reregulate part of a market that it completely deregulated several years earlier.[23]

Regulators are likely to consider two approaches to addressing the problem of uneven price competition in relatively competitive markets. First, they will seek to improve the information that is available to consumers. In the USA, there is no readily available and trustworthy source of information about long-distance operators and their rates. Instead, consumers are bombarded with confusing advertisements and telemarketing calls, the latter featuring salespeople working on commission who often provide half-truths and misleading information. Moreover, long-distance operators are not obliged to put their rates in writing, other than in their tariffs, which are, for all practical purposes, unavailable and unintelligible to the general public. The result is that many consumers find the prospect of comparison shopping a daunting chore.

However, regulators who seek to assist consumers by preparing price comparisons will find this an extremely difficult task, largely because of the many operators (over one hundred serving residential customers, most with a minute fraction of the market) and the industry's practice of offering complex and non-comparable pricing structures. For example, some rate plans offer different rates for different time periods and different days of the week. As noted above, others use minimum charges and still others use fixed fees that are added to per-minute rates. It is challenging, and perhaps impossible, to reduce all rate offers to comparable per-minute rates without making the comparisons undesirably complex or inaccurate. The complexity of rate comparisons is compounded in the USA by the fact that each operator has separate rates, usually with considerable variation, for inter-state, intra-state and regional calls. Consequently, for a customer to decide which long-distance operator will produce the lowest bill is a major research exercise that, to do properly, requires creation of a matrix of mind-numbing complexity. While regulators certainly should take all possible steps to improve the availability of information to consumers, this is not likely to be a solution to the problem of uneven competition.

The second approach will be to use price regulation to limit the unreasonable disparities between high- and low-volume rates. The goal should be to ensure that all consumers benefit from competition by linking rates for the low-volume market segment, in which competition is not effectively restraining prices, to those available to high-volume users, a market segment in which competition is serving to discipline prices. For example, recognising that some level of volume-based price discounts can be cost-justified and is therefore consistent with a competitive market, regulators could establish a maximum permissible disparity between rates for the two segments of the market. To determine the appropriate maximum disparity, regulators could observe rates in effectively competitive markets. One candidate would be the wholesale market, where US long-distance operators typically offer discounts of about 50 per cent to resellers who buy large volumes of long-distance service. This 50 per cent discount would represent an upper range on an appropriate disparity since the wholesale discount reflects the avoidance of all retail costs (such as marketing and billing). Whatever specific benchmark were used, the idea would be to use the behaviour of rates in truly competitive markets as a guide to regulate effectively a less competitive sector.

Reintroducing even a limited measure of price regulation in the long-distance market will be highly controversial in the USA, as it clashes with the ideology of many policy makers that such regulation stifles, rather than promotes, competition. However, when markets are demonstrably not delivering benefits to all consumers, regulation is necessary in order to satisfy the ultimate goal of fair rates for all.

Regulation to Promote Universal Service

In the next century, regulators will face universal service issues with respect to both traditional voice telephone service and the emerging fast Internet access services. In the USA, there are two main types of universal service programme for voice services.[24] The first category includes 'Lifeline' programmes to support discounted voice service for low-income households,[25] and programmes to provide specialised equipment for disabled customers. These are paid for by surcharges that are ultimately borne by all consumers. These programmes are popular and successful and will certainly be maintained for the foreseeable future.

The second category consists of so-called 'High Cost Funds', which are being redesigned as required by TA 96. Section 254(*b*)(3) of TA 96 requires that rates in high-cost areas be 'reasonably comparable' to those in urban areas. Such funds support affordable service for customers living in areas where it is extremely costly to provide service. Local operators serving high-cost areas can claim the difference between a designated benchmark rate and the cost to serve such customers. For these new funds to work, regulators must determine the cost to serve customers. Incumbents (who will get most or all of the money) have an interest in maximising the costs, whereas consumers (who have to pay) and competitors (who are unlikely to be able to reach high-cost areas) have an interest in minimising them. Under TA 96, ensuring affordably priced service in high-cost areas is a joint responsibility of state and federal regulators.

The end of 1999 marked a full three years during which, at the federal level, the FCC and interested parties had been attempting to develop extremely complex models to estimate the cost of serving customers in high-cost areas. Some states, such as California, have developed their own cost models and implemented their own high-cost funds. Other states are awaiting final FCC action before implementing their own funds. In retrospect, it is not clear that any high cost fund is necessary, given the lack of local competition. Nevertheless, Congress and the FCC, backed by the incumbents, are not likely to renounce the need for high-cost funds. Federal/state coordination and controversies over the cost studies (which will need to be reviewed periodically) are likely to bedevil regulators for years.

With respect to fast Internet access, the key question in coming years will be whether to redefine the concept of universal service to embrace such services. If fast Internet access is considered essential and therefore an element of universal service, regulators and policy makers will be called upon to decide whether to extend the Lifeline and High Cost Fund programmes to include high bandwidth services. In light of the increasing concern already being expressed about a 'digital divide' in the USA, such an expansion of universal service programmes is likely. Controversy will surround the issues of, first, when the existing programmes should be expanded and, second, how deep a discount to support. Today, fast Internet access charges are at least double or triple voice service charges, though prices are likely to drop. Whether to expand the concept of universal service is likely to be a key issue in the early years of the 21st century.

Conclusion

As in the 20th century, regulators in the 21st century can be expected to grapple with the proper relationship between competition and regulation. At the end of the 20th century, many US policy makers and regulators appeared to be striking a schizophrenic stance towards this issue. On the one hand, the last five years of the century saw a frenzy of interventionist regulation designed to promote local competition. At the same time, many supporters of such activity nevertheless hold regulation in contempt and stand ready to jettison economic regulation at the first signs of emerging competition. In this idealist view, competition becomes a goal in itself and the main purpose of regulation is to promote competition.

Consumers are best served by a more practical and harmonious relationship between competition and regulation. Competition should be regarded as one of the regulator's tools for achieving the ultimate goals of fair rates, meaningful choice and high-quality service. Competition can be a potent tool for achieving these goals since, for example, it has already hastened the availability of attractively priced alternatives for fast Internet access in the USA. However, in telecoms, as in most markets, perfect or even near-perfect competition is not a realistic expectation. Regulation remains necessary to supplement competition when markets alone are not serving the needs of all groups of consumers. Such regulation should capitalise on the benefits of competition – for example, by pegging regulated rates in poorly competitive sectors to rates available in more competitive sectors. Moreover, as even idealists sometimes acknowledge, regulation can make markets work better – for example, through non-discrimination requirements such as open access for cable modems or rate disclosure and comparison programmes. As useful as competition can be, it should not take precedence over the fundamental goal of ensuring that essential services are provided in a way that serves the public interest.

Notes

1 The provisions of TA 96 have been incorporated into the Communications Act of 1934, 47 USC s.151 *et seq*.
2 TA 96 has been integrated into the Communications Act of 1934, 47 USC s.151 *et seq*. The provisions of TA 96 can be found in isolation at http://www.fcc.gov/telecom.html.
3 The ability to keep your telephone number if you switch local operators.
4 House of Representatives Report No. 104–58, 104th Congress, 2d Session, p.1
5 See, generally, Long, T. (1999), 'Will the US Telecoms Act Bring Real Local Competition? Three Years Gone and Still Too Soon to Tell', *Utilities Law Review*, July–August, 193–205, for a more detailed analysis of the provisions of TA 96 designed to create local competition.
6 Throughout this chapter, the term 'incumbent' will refer to the traditional monopoly local operator and the term 'competitor' will refer to any new local operator that attempts to challenge the incumbent.
7 47 USC ss.251(*c*)(4), 252(*d*)(3).
8 47 USC ss.251(*c*)(2), 252(*d*).
9 In US regulatory-speak, UNE is usually pronounced 'yunie'.
10 47 USC ss.251(*c*)(3), 252(*d*)(1).
11 The local loop refers to the wire connecting the customer's premises with the local operator's switching facility.
12 47 USC s.252(*d*)(3).
13 47 USC s.252(*d*)(1).
14 47 USC s.252(*d*)(2).
15 Such piggy-back competition still requires the competitor to make a considerable investment in switches. To finance this investment, the competitor needs to quickly switch over their customers from the incumbent's network to the competitor's network without significant interruption in the customer's telephone service. This requires a high level of cooperation and coordination between the incumbent and competitor. Thus far, competitors have found that they cannot switch sufficient numbers of customers to their networks quickly enough and reliably enough in order to obtain the revenues they need to stay in business. For a more complete discussion of the reasons for the absence of

local competition in the USA, see Long, 'Real Local Competition?' (n.5, above), pp.196–200.

16 ISDN permits Internet access at 128 kbps, which is three to five times faster than the speeds otherwise available over a conventional analog telephone line and modem.

17 At the time of preparing this chapter, the best available government statistics were already out-of-date. In a January 1999 report, the Federal Communications Commission (FCC) cited estimates that between 350 000 and 700 000 residential customers subscribed to cable modems and 25 000 customers subscribed to DSL service (*Inquiry Concerning the Deployment of Advanced Telecommunications Capability to All Americans,* FCC 99–5, CC Docket No. 98–146, paras 54, 58 ('*Advanced Services Report*'). These numbers are increasing rapidly.

18 In this brief review, it is not possible to do justice to the nuances of the arguments on both sides. To delve deeper into this important debate, readers could start at www.nogatekeepers.org (pro open access) and www.handsofftheinternet.org (anti open access).

19 *Advanced Services Report,* para. 101.

20 See Kennard, W. (1999), 'The Unregulation of the Internet: Laying a Competitive Course for the Future', prepared text for speech delivered 20 July, available at <http://www.fcc.gov/Speeches/Kennard/spwek924.html>; see also Oxman, J. (1999), 'The FCC and the Unregulation of the Internet', FCC Office of Plans and Policy, July, available at <http://www.fcc.gov/Bureaus/OPP/News_Releases/1999/nrop9004.html>, which attempts to explain how the FCC has consistently followed the policy of 'unregulation'. In my view, the paper actually shows the importance of affirmative regulation by the FCC over the years, particularly to force the firms in control of key transmission facilities to open their networks to permit innovative uses by competitors and customers.

21 Don Cruickshank, director-general of telecommunications, speech to FT World Telecommunications Conference: 1 December 1997, <http://www.oftel.gov.uk/speeches/dgft112.htm>.

22 See OFTEL's second consultation in connection with the Pricing of Telecommunications Services from 1997, June 1996, para. 2.10.

23 *Re Low-Volume Long-Distance Users,* Notice of Inquiry, FCC 99–168 (20 July 1999). An initial decision, which may lead to further consultations, in not expected until early to mid-2000.

24 For an explanation of universal service programmes in the wake of TA 96, see *Re Federal-State Joint Board on Universal Service,* FCC 97–157, CC Docket No. 96–45, 8 May 1997.

25 In California, low-income households can pay as little as $3.00 per month for basic telephone service.

6 Competition in the Telecommunications Sector

JOHN HUNTLEY, ***University of Middlesex,***
WITH PAUL CARLYLE, ***Shepherd & Wedderburn*** **AND JOHN CALDWELL,**
Shepherd & Wedderburn

Introduction

The regulation of the telecommunications industry has been the object of intensive study.[1] The industry has been in the vanguard of the turbulent regulatory shifts of the last two decades. Once universally recognised as a natural monopoly (whether as a state-run PTT like the Post Office or as a vertically integrated private monopoly like the Bell system of AT&T in the USA) the industry became the test-bed of often radical experimentation with competitive structures. There is little doubt that such experimentation was heavily influenced by radical new ideas of the advantages of, and potential for, such structures. A distinguishing feature of telecommunications regulation over the last 25 years has been the impact of technology which continues radically to transform telecommunications and challenges 'conventional wisdom' about the nature and scope of telecommunications markets.[2] Technological change has therefore been a key driver for regulatory change. The pace of that change and the regulatory change it generates make telecommunications particularly worthy of study as a regulatory paradigm. Britain, as the first to deregulate and introduce competition in Europe, is in a particularly special position as a guide to the effect of competition in these utilities. Indeed, regulatory developments in Britain are often a benchmark for other European telecommunications regulatory regimes.

Underlying assumptions about the scope of the 'natural' telecommunications monopoly were challenged in the immediate post-war period in the USA. The AT&T monopoly appeared to some to impede the introduction of new technology at reasonable costs.[3] The technology in question was the computer. By the late 1950s, the transfer of data in digitised form in certain key industries from one computer to another in a different location demanded the use of modems coupled to telephone lines. Apart from the obvious control which the monopoly telephone provider had over things attached to its network and equipment, such as the modem, there was no guarantee that the monopolist would not charge a monopolist's price for the provision of this service. Not surprisingly, business users began to look for alternatives. That came in the form of a very limited network provider, MCI, which used microwave technology to establish links between towns, primarily for the transfer of such data.

The MCI experience raised an issue which has plagued regulatory agencies ever since. In order for MCI to connect customers at two locations – say, for example, X Corporation's site in Los Angeles and Y Corporation's site in St Louis – a link would have to be made between MCI's network and the AT&T network, to which X's and Y's telephones would be connected. The alternative would be for MCI to lay a new local network connecting its trunk network to the premises of X and Y, which in most cases is prohibitively expensive. This bottleneck gives the monopoly telecommunications network provider the ability to regulate access to the local loop.[4] Access by other companies to the telecommunications monopolist's network would have to be sanctioned and regulated by the regulatory agency (in the case of long-distance providers in the USA, the Federal Communications Commission). Control of the network, or rather of access to it, was seen as control over an essential facility which was at the root of the network provider's 'natural' monopoly. What MCI and the new technologies demonstrated was that this monopoly was increasingly contestable.[5] Over the ensuing decades, the challenges to the stable regulatory structure of US telecommunications increased and notions of competition and antitrust challenged the very structure of the regulatory regime. The UK was not, of course, immune to such developments. The decision was taken not simply to privatise British Telecommunications, but also to introduce competition into network provision, initially in the form of a duopoly with Mercury plc, now owned by Cable & Wireless plc. The duopoly,[6] which was originally a feature of the UK network provision market, introduced competition into telecommunications and thereby questioned fundamental assumptions about the regulated telecommunications industry.

Although technological change is a feature of the recent regulatory history of telecommunications, the current pace of change is phenomenal. There is constant pressure to redefine the *scope* of what is regulated and what is capable of regulation, what is competitive or potentially competitive.[7] More significantly, technological change has led to convergence, sometimes of entire industries. In particular, the convergence between the telephone and the computer and the creation of the Internet creates a host of problems for regulation in a competitive environment. Data traffic is now more important, almost by any measure, than voice telephony.[8] Most significantly, consumer use of Internet technology and the emergence of e-commerce are opening up entirely new markets.[9] Should this potentially massive market be regulated? Who, and on what criteria, should regulate it?

Other technologies have had a similar impact. The development of fibre optic technology and the bandwidth that it makes available has led to the convergence of telecommunications and broadcasting. The development of wireless and satellite technology and the ability to exploit the radio spectrum much more efficiently has created a far greater variety of methods for delivering telephony services. Mobile, cellular telephony is now prevalent as an alternative or supplementary to provision of fixed telephony. The traditional and distinct regulatory paradigms for telecommunications and broadcasting are being re-examined.[10]

The Impact of Internet Technology

From the earliest days of telecommunications deregulation, much of the pressure for change has come from business users or those wishing to provide services to business customers. The race is now on to develop mass markets for Internet and e-commerce, on a scale similar to radio and television. The stimulus is the developing transformation of Internet technology into multi-media provision which could seriously challenge existing print or broadcast entertainment media and an interactive virtual shopping mall which could operate as a retail channel for domestic and business use.

Telecommunications, the platform for Internet technology, is now being subjected to massive technological shifts. It is an industry where technologies converge and markets converge. It is therefore *the* paradigm of a globalising market. The subject of this chapter is how the regulatory framework adapts to these trends.

A telephonic network is essentially a network of copper wires with relatively simple transmitting and receiving devices – telephones. When business users of telephones turned to computers for the transmission of data, the use of the modem proliferated, particularly in the financial services industries. A simple coupling device to begin with, it increased data usage of telephone lines to the extent that they were neither technically nor economically capable of meeting demand. Gradually, business users demanded and received dedicated (or leased) lines for data usage. The digitisation of data formerly transmitted as analog signals on a copper wire massively expanded the capacity and demand for data usage. Packet switching technology facilitates the transfer of such data from one machine to another in the blinking of an eye. These key developments more than any others led from such simple beginnings to the present.

The Internet is a development of the digitised transmission of data. From modest origins as a system for academics to communicate data via computer over the telephonic network, a series of technical developments transformed the utility and efficacy of the Internet. The first was the development of a 'user-friendly' interface for the personal computer (PC). Prior to Netscape, the use of the Internet demanded a fair understanding of programming; after Netscape, a Windows environment simplified the computer/user interface greatly. The second development was the standardisation of search engines. These are devices that permit the user to search interconnected sites for data within parameters that the user prescribes, thereby minimising the amount of searching. Most users of the Internet would now look for such data as files on the World Wide Web. Using HTML, a standardised document formatting language, documents of almost any description and content can be placed in files on different computers and linked through standard, digitised telecommunications connections. Such files can even be electronically transferred from one computer to another, using a standard File Transfer Protocol (FTP). Interactive communications can be established through electronic mail, relying on one of the many e-mail packages available.

The proliferation of Internet sites, users and material now supports a significant number of Internet Service Providers (ISPs), which provide individuals and organisations with access to the Internet and services like Web building and hosting. On-line service providers (OSPs), such as Freeserve and America Online (AOL) also provide access, but are generally more dependent on the telecommunications network than are ISPs. One estimate is that there are about three million Internet subscribers and that the figure is increasing by 100 per cent annually.[11] About 24 per cent of the adult population have used the Internet.[12] About 300 ISPs offer Internet access in the UK.[13]

Internet technologies raise several competition issues. Most notable, in the context of telecommunications, are pricing and the charging system for access to BT's PSTN (Public Switched Telephone Network) network by ISPs.[14] OFTEL has identified two specific issues: whether BT, through its position of dominance, can discriminate against other Internet providers or cross-subsidise its own Internet provision; and the effect of BT's pricing mechanism for Internet calls.[15] In both cases, BT's market power, derived from its ownership of the former nationalised network, creates a competitive advantage over other operators in almost all market sectors.[16] It is at this point that regulatory and competition issues converge. OFTEL is increasingly performing the dual role of economic regulator of markets in which competition is nascent, such as the Internet, and of competition regulator. It is increasingly applying *ex post* competition principles in *ex ante* regulation of telecommunications markets. Moreover, it is doing so at the frontiers of its jurisdiction, such as the Internet, where its brief merges not only with that of the competition regulator, the Office of Fair Trading (OFT), but with that of other industry regulators, notably broadcasting regulators. This interrelationship between competition and regulatory principles will, it is submitted, form OFTEL's regulatory policy towards the Internet.

Competition and Regulation in Telecommunications

OFTEL was set up in 1984, when its prime function, as an economic regulator, was to control the BT monopoly so that it would not disadvantage competitors or consumers. That function has changed over time. As competition becomes established in telecommunications, OFTEL's function is increasingly *ex post* regulation of competition: remedying the anti-competitive effects of the structural and behavioural terrain of the industry. The 1984 Telecommunications Act itself gave the director-general power to investigate anti-competitive conduct and to refer matters to the then Monopolies and Mergers Commission (MMC). As competition increasingly became a feature of the telecommunications landscape, the emphasis on competition controls became a central OFTEL preoccupation. The preoccupation was, to a great extent, the result of activity in Brussels. The major initiatives in telecommunications regulation came, at first, from the Competition Directorate General of the European Commission, DG IV, but increasingly from the Telecommunications Directorate General, DG XIII.[17] This inevitably gave the first European regulatory principles for telecommunications a competition law complexion. Even the emanations from the Telecommunications Directorate General itself, DG XIII, showed a similar tendency.[18]

The result has been convergence of regulatory and competition criteria and a convergence between EC and domestic provision. This convergence became even more marked when British competition laws were revised to bring them more into line with European practice. The Competition Act 1998 has given the utilities regulators extensive concurrent powers.[19] This raises the question: how should the director apply those competition powers in the regulated telecommunications industry? In a series of publications, the director has attempted to indicate this. In reality, the director must apply a variety of 'competition' criteria to different circumstances.[20]

Key Competition Features of Telecommunications Markets

Several features of the telecommunications industry are significant from the competition law perspective, features which 'necessitate a different emphasis or a slightly different approach in the application of competition rules'.[21] The primary distinguishing feature has been the bottleneck in access provision which results from the high levels of fixed costs associated with telecommunications networks. This is likely to be eroded over time. As far back as 1987, the Triennial Review carried out by the US Department of Justice under the AT&T consent decree[22] pointed out that new technologies were facilitating bypass of the fixed copper wire telecommunications network at relatively low cost. Similarly, telecommunications regulation has itself resulted in easier access to the BT network for other providers.

The conventional wisdom is that such a bottleneck gives the incumbent telecommunications operator a position of dominance. The incumbent's ability to 'leverage' anti-competitive advantage from such a position has been the focus of competition controls in telecommunications since deregulation began and is likely to remain a major focus for the foreseeable future.[23]

Even where competition is feasible and actively encouraged, significant barriers to entry exist. The high fixed and sunk costs are in themselves barriers which, in network provision at least, can be surmounted only by substantial capital resources. Even though telecommunications markets might no longer be natural monopolies, significant economies of scale and of scope dictate that the minimum economic size for competitors is relatively high. In some telecommunications markets, there are both regulatory and physical barriers to entry. For example, in mobile telephony and wireless local loops, the limits imposed by the availability of radio spectrum determine the number of players: currently four, in the case of mobile telephony in the UK. Such barriers have a tendency to reinforce the dominance of established operators and will differentiate the assessment of each telecommunications market.[24]

OFTEL points out that 'few sectors in competitive markets exhibit the range of externalities that exist in the telecommunications sector which arise because of its network nature and the fact that a call always involves two participants'.[25] In other words, the mere fact that telecommunications markets are invariably networked creates specific competition problems. OFTEL has identified three significant externalities. The 'network externality' 'is the simple welfare effect that the more people attached to the network the more value it has to those already on it'. Although OFTEL does not consider the network externality particularly significant in competition matters, it is more concerned about the competition implication of other externalities which relate to network access. The dominant operator has control over interconnection by competitors to its network: the so-called 'interoperability externality'. The terminating operator in a call which originates on a different network can, where the caller pays, raise the price of the call without directly affecting its own customers: the so-called 'call termination externality'.[26]

Perhaps because of these inherent features of the market, OFTEL sees as a major part of its role 'the management of change in the telecoms market from monopoly towards competition'.[27] It sees such competition gradually reducing the need for 'intrusive regulation' and confirms that

> there is already a presumption in the current framework against the need to impose the full force of regulatory rules ... on new telecoms services as they emerge. In the longer run, OFTEL expects that the telecoms industry in the United Kingdom will operate like many other private sector industries without the need for detailed regulation (except perhaps in the field of interconnection).

OFTEL sees its role as changing from that of a company or industry specific regulator to 'that of a specialist competition authority for the telecoms industry in the United Kingdom'.[28]

The Development of Common Competition Principles in Telecommunications Regulation

The extent to which OFTEL, as a competition law authority, has developed a common set of principles from these disparate sources – a converged set of principles – is a key issue. More particularly, the extent to which these principles have affected or will affect the regulation of the Internet is a central theme. The peculiarities of telecommunications competition are, at first glance, writ large in the markets for Internet provision. The next two sections will assess, first, the extent to which OFTEL has developed common principles for the regulation of competition in telecommunications; and secondly, the extent to which such principles have been applied – or are applicable – to the regulation of competition in Internet provision.

OFTEL has attempted, in its *Effective Competition Review*, a common methodology for market definition which 'would be the same whether the relevant market was being identified in the context of considering a complaint about anti-competitive behaviour or in considering whether regulatory controls should be relaxed'.[29] There are in fact four different sources of competition principles affecting the regulatory structure for telecommunications: the Competition Rules of the European Communities, the United Kingdom Competition Act, the regulatory principles of the Telecommunications Act, and the regulatory principles of the Open Network Provision framework. The principles which the European Commission relies upon to establish dominance under Article 82 are now generally well known and were reiterated by the Commission in its 1991 *Guidelines on Telecommunications*.[30]

Dominant Position under the Fair Trading Condition

These influences were such, and the investigative burden placed on OFTEL of such a nature, that the director introduced a Fair Trading Condition (FTC) in BT's licence and the licences of other providers. This condition, in general terms, imposes on the licensee, *inter alia*, an obligation not to abuse a position of dominance.[31] To a great extent, discussion of the condition, in terms of future policy, is now academic. OFTEL makes it clear that 'the FTC would automatically cease to apply to all types of agreements and conduct which would otherwise be caught by both the FTC and the Competition Act once the provisions of the Act come into force in March 2000'.[32] OFTEL will seek to remove it from all licences by that time. Nevertheless, the condition and the *Guidelines on the Operation of the Fair Trading Conditions*[33] have been relied on by OFTEL.[34] Furthermore, the FTC has played a key role in conferring on OFTEL the power to enforce Articles 81 and 82 of the EC Treaty. It can now act directly against operators, without having to go through the European Commission, or enforcing competition standards through the cumbersome procedures of the Telecommunications Act and the Monopolies and Mergers Commission (now the Competition Commission). Nevertheless, as has been pointed out,[35] there are clear differences between 'dominant position' as used in EC legislation and Commission Guidelines and in the FTC and its Guidelines, both in the definition of dominance and in the interpretation given to it by OFTEL.

In its *Draft Guidelines*,[36] OFTEL has attempted to indicate the factors special to telecommunications in defining the relevant market by reference to 'practical examples' from previous investigations. More significant is the discussion in the *Guidelines* of the relevance of market share in the assessment of market power.[37] OFTEL confirms that, in relation to the Chapter II prohibition of the 1998 Act (the UK equivalent of Article 82), a persistent market share above 50 per cent establishes a presumption of dominance. The implication is that a share below this might still be enough to establish market power. Thus, in its *Statement on Fair Trading in the Mobile Telephony Market*, OFTEL determined that Vodafone and Cellnet, with market shares well below 50 per cent, nevertheless had market power. Although OFTEL was here applying the FTC standard, which replicates the criteria in Article 82, OFTEL explicitly applied the 25 per cent threshold of the Fair Trading Act 1973 'as a rule of thumb below which firms are unlikely to possess market power'.[38] Although the FTC might be obsolescent, there is no indication that OFTEL will apply any stricter market share criterion in applying the Competition Act 1998 to telecommunications. The indication is, if anything, that it will apply the now repealed (for the purposes of establishing a dominant position) criterion of the Fair Trading Act.

Dominance and 'Significant Market Power'

In the *Interconnection Directive,*[39] Directorate General XIII introduced the concept of 'significant market power' (SMP). The significance attached by regulators (and DG XIII is no exception) to interconnection in telecommunications markets dominated by often nationalised incumbents has already been noted. In attempting to regulate the power of such operators to influence often nascent markets in telecommunications, the Commission introduced the lower threshold of 25 per cent market share for establishing SMP.[40] OFTEL is clearly of the view that SMP is not the same as dominance and that an investigation under the directive would not preclude the application of the competition rules.[41]

Dominance and 'Market Influence'

Market influence replaces the term 'well established operator' (WEO), used frequently in telecommunications regulation.[42] The definition is, in fact, identical to OFTEL's definition of 'market power', as opposed to '*significant* market power': 'the ability to raise prices above the competitive level for a non-transitory period'.[43] The intention is to establish a mechanism for regulating the behaviour of firms which could not be described as 'dominant', but which OFTEL wishes to regulate through specific licence provisions to forestall anti-competitive behaviour.

There is, therefore, a multiplicity of standards for determining the position of a firm in the relevant market, a variety of thresholds in the form of market share and a confusion of consequences, depending on which criterion is applied. Such diversity reflects the confusion of the regulatory and competition functions of OFTEL. It also reflects a preoccupation with bottlenecks and leverage. The extent to which either phenomenon predominates is diminishing.[44] The extent to which either is or could be a feature of Internet markets is even less certain. Ultimately, the issue is whether OFTEL will view development of the Internet as a market subject to 'light', *ex post* regulation of competition, or a market demanding heavier, *ex ante* regulation.

OFTEL's Approach: The Current Internet Debates

Reference has already been made to the OFTEL Statement, *Promoting Competition in Services over Telecommunications Networks*, which set out its views on the relationship between BT and competing independent service providers, or ISPs. Although the main focus of the Statement is the pricing of BT's network services to service providers generally, it is the first where OFTEL deals at length with the position of ISPs. Of particular interest are OFTEL's comments on the 'unbundling' of network services. Services or products are 'bundled' when the supply of one product or service is tied to the supply of another product or service. On the grounds that 'bundling of services can be an example of anti-competitive behaviour which could be prohibited under the Fair Trading Condition',[45] OFTEL concluded:

> where BT plans to develop a new enhanced service it should, from the outset, configure it in such a way that the underlying network service, or its functional equivalent, is capable of being provided to independent service providers and is charged on the same basis as to the SSB [Supplemental Services Business]. OFTEL's view is that the very fact that BT itself requires the network service as an input to its own enhanced service implies that demand exists, and suggests that there could be demand from independent service providers. In other words, for the purpose of establishing whether demand for a network service exists, BT should treat the SSB as though it were an independent service provider.[46]

OFTEL does concede, however, 'that there are limits to the degree of disaggregation that is economically or technically feasible'.[47] On this basis, OFTEL confirmed that it would consider on a case-by-case basis any complaints made to it about BT's refusal to provide unbundled services. The clear indication is that OFTEL intends to take a pragmatic approach to the issue of unbundling. This can be contrasted with the rather doctrinaire approach taken by the Telecommunications Act 1996 in the USA, which is already creating difficulties in enforcement of the legislation.[48]

Of perhaps greater significance is OFTEL's approach to the difficult issue of defining Internet services markets. Much regulatory impact hinges on whether such provision is network provision (in which OFTEL might have a *prima facie* dominance) or service provision. Since its June 1996 Statement, OFTEL had kept under review the treatment of Internet services. The major concern was ensuring that BT was supplying Internet services competitively. The 1996 Statement introduced the distinction between BT's Systems Business (SB) and its Supplemental Services Business (SSB). The objective was to ensure 'that BT does not leverage the dominance it has in many network services into the enhanced services market, in particular, by means of unfair cross subsidy between the SB and the SSB or by means of undue discrimination and undue preference'.[49]

The question whether to place Internet provision and services into the SB category thus assumes great significance in OFTEL's planning. This dichotomy determines the prices which BT charges itself for the provision of network services (SB) to its own enhanced service (SSB) provider subsidiaries. As the Statement continues: 'BT is a vertically integrated company providing both network services and enhanced services and it is dominant in the supply of many network services. BT is subject to a number of requirements which are placed upon it in order to ensure that it does not abuse its market power. These include a requirement to provide separate accounts for its SB services (i.e. network services) and SSB services (i.e. enhanced services).'[50]

Service providers need to be able to buy network service at the same price as BT's SSB. Furthermore, the distinction between SB and SSB, based originally on the distinction between voice and data (data services being placed in SSB), is becoming blurred. This is a result of digital technology applied throughout telecommunications and the technologically converged network technology of ATM (Asynchronous Transfer Mode), which makes packet switching generally available.

OFTEL's views on Internet services were fully articulated for the first time in the 1996 Statement.[51] OFTEL drew a distinction between IP[52] Access Service[53] and IP Routing Service.[54] OFTEL's view is that BT's IP Routing Service should be regarded as a basic SB service. At the time of the Statement, IP Routing Service was provided by BT Net and BT Internet, both SSB trading divisions of BT, which purchased transmission from the SB usually in the form of private circuits, added routers, servers and so on, and sold these as a package. Such packages included IP Routing Service or simple routing and conveyance of packets of data. These services should now be provided as SB services, whereas the more enhanced aspects of such services, 'e-mail, Usenet feeds and high level support services',[55] should continue to be provided by SSB.

The decision highlights the definitional problems which Internet provision raises. The logic is simple: IP Routing service is a basic conveyance service involving the provision of high-capacity connections that any Internet provider would need, so it is sensible to regard it as a part of basic network provision. Transparency of BT prices and costs would thus be enhanced. Nevertheless, as OFTEL acknowledges in the Statement: 'the precise elements of Internet services are difficult to enumerate and differentiate, given the various methods available of supplying these elements and the different services that service providers decide to offer to their customers'.[56]

Furthermore, it concedes, 'Internet services give rise to a number of apparent anomalies.'[57] The general view it seems to have come to is that, regardless of the complexity of the particular service, if it provides simple conveyance (whether access or routing), it should be regarded as network service. As a result of OFTEL's position, it is now possible for BT to provide its IP Routing Service as a stand-alone SB service both to its own enhanced services providers and to independent service providers. This could give BT flexibility to develop a special access service for linking to the Internet which did not rely on 0345/0845 or geographic number dial-up. It would also allow BT to price such SB IP Routing Service at a discount, so that Internet service providers who do not need the enhanced services provided in BT's SSB offerings need not purchase them. It is a form of unbundling of the IP service.

So conscious was OFTEL of the potential for BT to bundle basic IP Access Service with more enhanced IP Routing Service that it concluded:

> OFTEL expects BT, when pricing components of IP Access and IP Routing services, and when developing new offerings bundling such services which are or could be aimed at those in the Internet service provider business, or who compete directly with such businesses, to exercise extreme care in order to ensure that its prices, tariff structures or any other aspect of its offerings do not give rise to any possibility of a contravention of Conditions 17 and/or 18A of its licence. OFTEL expects BT to liaise very closely with it in developing products for this market and will take prompt action to secure compliance with those provisions if evidence of a breach is apparent.

In particular, OFTEL drew attention to the fact that, under Condition 16 of its licence, BT must notify OFTEL at least 28 days before the launch of any new product offering to sell IP Access or Routing Service from its SB.[58]

It is clear from this line of decisions by OFTEL that it regards the questions of unbundling and BT's market dominance in network provision as so closely interrelated, and the potential for market distortion so significant, that it is prepared to impose regulatory criteria on BT. Despite the logic behind such action – the need to protect newcomers in these quickly developing markets – their efficacy in such unchartable territory must be doubted. The most that can be said is that, at least, OFTEL's approach is one of constant review, rather than active intervention.

Internet pricing has become so prominent an issue that it has become a topic for wide discussion. In its March 1999 Memorandum to the Trade and Industry Select Committee's Inquiry into Electronic Commerce, OFTEL raised several issues concerning telecommunications infrastructure and the effect on Internet use.[59] The main issue of debate was whether the cost of using the Internet was relatively high in the UK and therefore acting as a disincentive for residential users in particular. The focus of OFTEL's concern therefore was dial-up access. This, it estimated, costs between £8 and £15 per month for unlimited access in subscription to the ISP. In addition, a UK subscriber normally pays a metered local charge when 'on-line'. The introduction of 'free' access by ISPs like Dixon's Freeserve means that a subscriber need pay only the local metered telephone charge, as there is no subscription charge. OFTEL is conscious of the pressure from some quarters to permit unmetered access on a local basis or, at least, to reduce the cost of local calls for Internet access, but was not convinced by arguments that Internet access in the UK is more expensive than elsewhere in Europe. Nor was it convinced by arguments that we should introduce 'free' local calls on the US model. OFTEL raised the usual argument that such calls are 'free' only because they are subsidised by other services, notably long-distance calls. Such 'free' access is also normally accompanied by a higher fixed 'rental' charge, which 'may cause problems for lower income families for whom the line rental charge is typically a significant element of the phone bill'.

Furthermore, such 'free' access could lead to congestion at peak times, unless additional capacity is installed, which would be an additional cost. Even if 'free' access were permitted only in off-peak periods, 'this would create a very strong incentive to increase usage, possibly to the extent that previously *off-peak* periods become peak periods – with a direct impact on network capacity required at that period, i.e. creating a cost'. OFTEL points to the fact that the average Internet call in the UK is 25 minutes, whereas in the USA it is about 2.5 hours. 'Such long connection times have created congestion and prevented other calls from being carried. Quality of service in some areas of the US has declined quite significantly and it has been known, in some instances, for calls to emergency services to not get through.'

OFTEL also suggests that investment in the local telephone network might be unattractive if it is not possible to recover the costs from local charges. It concludes, 'if they are unable to recover the costs of "free" calls from other services these operators are put at an overall commercial disadvantage'. The real question is, therefore, whether or not such costs are recoverable from usage of the Internet, either by way of advertising revenue or by way of a fixed access charge, as in the USA. The argument could thus be reversed and free calls could be seen as an incentive to investment in local networks. OFTEL is also concerned about the effects on competition were BT to offer free local calls and points out that there is little competition for the local network provider in the USA. OFTEL's position is that it would wish to avoid such problems associated with free calls and concludes that it would prefer to see 'innovative tariffs' which may involve an element of 'free' calls. It clearly does not want to regulate pricing in this area.

In a sense, events overtook OFTEL's initial position. In its *Additional Memorandum,* it referred to the 'explosion' in the number of subscription-free ISPs.[60] Similarly, it drew attention to new alternatives to metered calls, notably off-peak dial-up access through freephone 0800 numbers or at specific off-peak times. OFTEL views such developments as indicative of a competitive market and regards regulatory intervention as inappropriate. The main concern is that the market remain competitive – and this means ensuring that BT's tariff charges are not anti-competitive and do not discriminate unfairly between customers. OFTEL expressed particular concern to ensure that BT should not cross-subsidise, thereby restricting competition. In particular, it echoed its concerns that we should not emulate the position of US telecommunications, where business/long-distance users are often seen as subsidising a free local service. The signals are clearly that OFTEL will resist going down the 'toll-free', US route. Its purpose seems to be to permit competition to determine price structures wherever possible and to generate diversity in Internet service provision. Such a strategy would, undoubtedly, lead to asymmetric pricing structures, but 'free' service seems an unstoppable trend. Even AOL, with its US background and strong resistance to removal of its significant monthly rates, has now succumbed to market pressure. The scope for the development of OFTEL's 'variety pack' of prices seems limited. Yet the reality is that such 'free' service is highly dependent on the interconnection charges which BT (primarily) is allowed to charge such service providers.

Interconnection Charges

OFTEL drew attention to a particular issue that might act as a brake on the development of unmetered tariffs. Even where access from the customer to the ISP is unmetered, the ISP's interconnection payment to the network provider (normally BT) will be time-based. Unmetered access will not generate income that can be directly passed to the network provider. Again, OFTEL's view is equivocal:

> We acknowledges [*sic*] that providing unmetered calls for a fixed [*sic*] with metered interconnection presents significant risks for operators because the amount of revenue from fees from consumers might be insufficient to meet interconnection charges if usage is higher than expected. Operators are free to come to commercial agreements that

> mitigate this risk, provided that charges meet licence conditions. In BT's case, this would means [*sic*] that charges would need to conform to Network Charge Controls, that they were offered on a non-discriminatory basis and that they were not anti-competitive. The scope for facilitating different bases for interconnection payments is an issue that we intend to examine as part of the review of controls on BT's interconnection charges which is now getting underway.[61]

Again, OFTEL's preference is to leave it to competitive forces to establish interconnection charges which, it also points out, it does not require to be time-based.

The key factor in Internet tariff determination is the use of Number Translation Services (NTS). A standard, end-to-end telephone call is geographic. The price charged to the customer will depend on the number of switches through which the call is routed. A national call is switched more than a local call and therefore attracts a higher rate. If the originating operator and the terminating operator are different – say, for example, the call originates on a BT line, but terminates on a Telewest cable line – the originating operator pays a termination charge to the terminating operator and retains what remains of the charge to the customer. The amount of the termination charge will be based on cost, which in turn is based on the number of switching stages used by the call.

NTS calls are treated differently. All users of the telephone are now familiar with what is now a very wide range of special tariff services. They include freephone numbers (such as 0800, used primarily for telemarketing), local rate access numbers (0x45 numbers, such as 0845, used notably for Internet access), national rate access numbers (such as 0870) and premium rate services numbers (such as 08xx). Such services involve 'number translation', in the sense that calls to such numbers are not sent to a specific geographic location, but are routed intelligently through the PSTN to a prearranged destination. As with geographic numbers, the revenue from such calls is shared between the originating and terminating operator. The allocation is based on an interconnection charge. The charge is based on a formula, the 'NTS formula', devised by OFTEL but, essentially, the price paid is determined by the call, not the distance the call travels.

In March 1999, OFTEL issued a consultation paper that signals a fundamental review of the NTS formula.[62] Several issues prompted this review, but prominent amongst them was the rapid expansion of Internet provision. Most dial-up Internet access is through local rate NTS numbers, notably 0345/0845. Most such calls originate on the BT network, as BT controls over 85 per cent of the local loop to residential and small and medium size enterprise customers. They currently amount to around 15 per cent of all BT's calls and are estimated to grow at 200 per cent per annum.

This use of local rate NTS numbers has been particularly significant in the development of subscription-free provision like *Freeserve*. As OFTEL points out, 'the revenue passed through to terminating operators has proved sufficient to cover their costs and also enable a share of the call revenue to be passed to the ISP. This has enabled ISPs to fund their activities out of their share of call revenue (as well as other income sources).'[63] This fuelled concern that the NTS formula might be acting as an inhibitor of price competition. The sharp rise in Internet access was not forecast and was not, it appears, a significant factor in setting up the NTS formula – it is not essential today, for example, for Internet access always to be through local rate NTS numbers. This has generated demands from originating operators (principally BT) for a larger share of revenue from NTS calls and from terminating operators, whose share of the revenue is falling, in line with the general fall in local call prices.

There is no doubt that OFTEL's proposed change to the NTS formula is to a great extent prompted by Internet developments. OFTEL proposes to review the NTS formula as part of its overall review of price controls from 2001. The formula was, to a great extent, established with voice telephony in mind. The underlying principle was that originating operators should be able to cover their costs if they set their charges at the level determined by the formula. Terminating operators have no real power to determine what those levels will be – they simply receive the revenue left over after the originating operator has taken his share. OFTEL's primary proposal is that 'terminating operators should be able to control the retail price for calls to their NTS services by adding their required termination charge to BT's fixed retention'.[64] This would provide them with pricing flexibility to price services below local rate and encourage further competition amongst them. The proposal is that BT's retention as an originating operator should remain fixed as at present. The rest of the formula (which effectively determines the terminating operator's share) should be dropped, enabling the terminating operator to control products' retail prices by adding to BT's price the revenue they can commercially require.

In proposing that terminating operators should have a greater say over the setting of retail prices, OFTEL stresses that the originating retention set by dominant operators (effectively BT) should be non-discriminatory. All ISPs would face the same charge. Whether this effectively supports rather than discourages competition is debatable. OFTEL envisages that, under such proposed arrangements, ISPs might offer services of different quality or extent at different prices, or different methods of payment. A wider range of price points at which the level may be set does offer terminating operators far wider tariffing choice,[65] but there is potential for abuse by dominant providers, subterfuge and even more confusion among users.

There has been a steady migration from geographic to NTS numbers, fuelled primarily by the Internet, but more generally by the need to keep prices down and for customer number recognition. Originating operators' concern is that the development of effective Internet telephony might create further price distortions and, in addition to current Internet data traffic, even larger migrations of voice telephone traffic. The suggestion is that, because line rentals are below cost and the deficit is being funded through call charges, such a migration would seriously threaten 'the viability of originating operators' businesses'. OFTEL's view is that, despite the limited price competition at the originating end of the call, competition among ISPs has produced such volumes of calls that originating operators' unit costs have consequently fallen significantly. Since much of that volume is at off-peak times when the network (BT's) is generally underutilised, the general effect of the Internet is to generate significant unit cost savings. OFTEL does recognise, however, that call migration from geographic to NTS and, in two to three years, from voice to Internet telephony is potentially distortive. It intends to revisit the issue in the overall price review due to take effect in 2001, by which time operators will have a clearer view.[66]

It appears, therefore, that OFTEL is willing to champion time-based charges for Internet access. In the Consultation Paper on NTS Retail Prices,[67] and in its memorandum to the House of Commons Select Committee's Inquiry into Electronic Commerce, OFTEL presented its platform for so doing. A major argument against charging for the time that an Internet call uses the PSTN is that the costs are not caused by the duration of the call. OFTEL's view is that, at peak times, duration should be taken into account when pricing such calls. A PSTN is a circuit network. An Internet call means that the circuit between the customer and the ISP is dedicated to that call for its duration. Capacity must be capable of coping with demand at peak times, otherwise expensive additional circuits would be required to maintain quality. OFTEL's view, therefore, seems to be that the level of pricing should be such that it artificially deflates demand at peak times to such an extent that additional expenditure on extra circuitry (which would lie unused during off-peak times) is unnecessary. At off-peak times, however, very low prices and unmetered calls could increase demand to the extent that it resembles peak times. Of course, as OFTEL acknowledges, this is only partly true of Internet calls. Messages, once received by the ISPs, are conveyed by them using packet switched networks, rather than by the PSTN.

In effect, therefore, OFTEL faces a classic bottleneck problem. Because Internet customers are generally connected to the PSTN network and rely on it as their primary access to an ISP network, they are inevitably tying up circuit for the duration of their Internet connection. This is not a major problem, of course, for e-mail, where messages can be drafted off-line and be delivered quickly by going on-line, thereby tying up the circuit for a very short time. One disadvantage of this, of course, is that call rates are so designed that a significant minimum charge is generally made for every call. This is an issue that OFTEL does not appear to address, yet it is an important element of the bottleneck issue. Can an originating operator justify such a charge, when usage is so minimal? Access to the World Wide Web, on the other hand, demands on-line access. Since www access is what is driving e-commerce, the problem will get worse unless there is technological bypass, providing an effective economic alternative solution to the existing local loop for Internet access.

That bypass will come with higher bandwidth services, such as cable modems, satellite and terrestrial wireless access, third generation mobile access and, to some extent, DSL (Digital Subscriber Line) technologies (that is, technologies which facilitate the transmission of higher bandwidth services over a simple copper line). DSL provision is less of an obvious solution as it still raises bottleneck problems. If a dominant network provider, such as BT, were to offer such a service over its local loop, it would effectively foreclose the market to ISPs or other potential providers, unless they were given equal access to BT's local loop to provide such a service. Ultimately, DSL technology still relies on use of the local loop, although it will produce much higher bandwidth access over the local loop.

OFTEL's Approach: Analysis of the Case Law

The above discussion has focused on OFTEL's preoccupations with competition issues of direct relevance to Internet provision. The discussion confirms that OFTEL has made a conscious effort to define and amend regulatory principles and rules to ensure, as it sees it, maximum competition. In this it has been guided by its general view on market power in the hands of BT. More particularly, it has been preoccupied by the need to avoid or remove barriers to entry; by the effects of bundled provision by BT and the need for unbundling of service components; and, most importantly, it has been preoccupied by the pricing structures it had established in a pre-Internet environment. The result has been a constant effort to define and redefine *ante hoc* regulatory principles in the constantly shifting Internet market environment. The same preoccupations can be discerned in

OFTEL's *post hoc* competition investigations of BT's Internet activities. Although these cases are few in number, they provide useful insights into the application of the competition principles which OFTEL has attempted to establish.

Some of the earliest of BT's Internet offerings were 'BTNet', 'BT Internet' and 'Campus World'. In November 1997, OFTEL issued a statement following an investigation into the pricing of these Internet services.[68] What appeared to spur this investigation was the possibility that BT might have been acting anti-competitively and, more particularly, whether the relevant business enjoyed an unfair cross-subsidy. Under Condition 20B.15 of BT's licence, the director-general of telecommunications can issue a direction where he is satisfied that a business is receiving an 'unfair cross-subsidy' which 'could have a material effect on competition'. To do this, he must demonstrate that the business would not receive an adequate commercial return over a suitable period, and that this has or could have an adverse effect on competition. Although OFTEL found that BT had not indulged in predatory pricing or cross-subsidised these services, the methodology it employed is a useful indication of OFTEL's methodology.

BTNet, introduced in 1994, was aimed at heavy Internet business users. Access could be through either ordinary telephone connection (dial-up/modem) or a dedicated link giving permanent access to an ISP. OFTEL began this investigation into BTNet following a complaint from a competing service provider which alleged that BT was indulging in predatory conduct by differential pricing, pricing below cost and providing free introductory offers. BT Internet, BT's general Internet access service, is based on measured time usage, in line with general practice at the time. In March 1997, BT reduced its charges and this prompted OFTEL to carry out its own investigation. It found that barriers to entry to the Internet access market were so low that there was no real possibility that such costs could be a barrier to entry, and anti-competitive practices like cross-subsidy or predatory pricing were unlikely. It also saw dial-up Internet access and dedicated link access as forming part of the same market. OFTEL appears to apply the standard approach of the European Competition Directorate DG IV in determining the relevant market. In considering demand-side substitution, OFTEL regards quality of service, speed and price as the factors consumers would regard most significant in making a choice. OFTEL found that, for business users at least,

> although leased lines and modem/dial-up may not be direct substitutes for one another, the prices for these services as there is no significant difference between a 64k leased line and basic rate ISDN access can be similar. Likewise, the differences between highspeed modems utilising the PSTN and basic rate ISDN can be quite small.

> This means that, although leased lines and modem/dial-up may not be direct substitutes for one another, the prices for these services are constrained by intermediate alternatives e.g. access via leased lines.[69]

It is difficult to see how that can be generally true. ISDN provision, for example, is not a likely alternative where none is available – and that is still very often the case. It is reasonable to speculate that such demand-side substitution issues of market definition in relation to the Internet are likely to feature prominently in future investigations. Similarly, OFTEL found a significant degree of supply-side substitution among the ISPs who can, as a rule, offer leased line and dedicated links as an alternative to dial-up/modem. It is difficult to see significant supply-side issues arising in such a context in the future.

The question whether backbone provision is part of the same general Internet market, however, is less clear. The UK Internet backbone is centred on LINX, based in London and comprising 31 members: the large telecommunications and ISP providers. OFTEL recognised that, although smaller ISPs do not appear to have difficulty in renting backbone capacity, 'investment in extra backbone capacity could be an obstacle to dial-up providers in offering dedicated link Internet access'.[70] Rather cryptically, in relation to demand-side substitution, the report adds: 'It is worth noting that BTNet also operates in the wholesale Internet access market (the Internet backbone market) as a backbone provider. However the present complaint does not extend to activity in this market.'[71] Such comments suggest that OFTEL was not yet convinced that backbone provision is not a separate market, which is arguably a logical conclusion.

It is not surprising that these investigations show a marked preoccupation with market definition, but the level of analysis is peremptory. The underlying preoccupation is, however, clear: to ensure that BT's assumed position of dominance does not restrict the development of competitive structures in all aspects of Internet provision.

Conclusions

Telecommunications, in certain important respects, differs significantly from other deregulated utilities. Whereas the markets for gas, electricity and even transport have changed since privatisation and deregulation in the 1980s, they have done so gradually. Telecommunications markets have changed exponentially. The prime driver for such change has been technology. Each technological revolution has been a shift in gear.

Such driving change has transformed telecommunications from a basic utility into a fragmented, highly volatile, often very profitable and highly competitive set of markets. Yet one constant has been BT's continuing dominance of network provision. Although technology has created competitive markets in services on the periphery of BT's business, its core business – the national telecommunications network – remains intact. Early efforts to introduce competition in this core business have borne limited fruit, but continue. OFTEL's focus has shifted to regulating this dominant provider (and nascent, influential providers), so that it does not distort burgeoning service markets. OFTEL must do this in a climate of turbulent, converging and globalising telecommunications technologies, markets and regulators, and must do so without unduly hampering BT as a global competitor.

If the climate was already turbulent, Internet technology has whipped up a tempest. To pursue the analogy, navigating on uncharted waters in such conditions requires concentration, skill and, above all, minimum sail and a light touch at the tiller. The importance of the Internet to the future development of telecommunications markets – indeed, of global commerce generally – is undeniable. The British regulator has chosen light rein regulation. *Ex ante* controls appear to be kept to a minimum and are based on essentially competition law criteria. The thrust of OFTEL's approach has been to place such constraints as are necessary to encourage and maintain competition. Whether it is price regulation, network interconnection or any of the various concerns discussed in this chapter, OFTEL has avoided trying to force or dictate the pace, while at the same time keeping informed about developments. The post-deregulation era in telecommunications is replete with doomed attempts to create markets in the regulators' image.

Such turbulent times have cast OFTEL increasingly in the mould of a watchful, *ex post* competition regulator. This makes it difficult to draw general lessons valid in other, lest turbulent, regulated markets. It does, however, suggest that there is limited scope for *ex ante* regulation in such a competitive environment, other than to regulate the distortive potential of the core network provider. Certainly OFTEL's *ex post* regulation seems to be similarly constrained and, where exercised, seems designed to bolster competition.

Internet technology – not the regulator – has generated the competitive Internet markets which increasingly provide telecommunications services widely and cheaply. In a very real sense, the lesson to be learned is that technologies can define markets and, ultimately, redefine and constrain the role of the regulator. As technology drives in competition, it seems to drive out *ex ante* regulation. The regulator finds it increasingly difficult to, define, let alone regulate, the 'industry' and becomes a regulator of the competitive process.

Notes

1 See, for example, Sauter, W. (1997), *Competition Law and Industrial Policy in the EU*, Oxford: Clarendon; Long, C. (1995), *Telecommunications Law and Practice*, 2nd edn, London; Sweet & Maxwell; Noam, E. (1995), *Telecommunications in Europe*, Oxford: Oxford University Press.
2 See, for example, Baumol, W.J. and J.G. Sidak (1993), *Towards Competition in Local Telephony*, Cambridge, Mass.: MIT Press; Sidak, J.G. and D.F. Spulber (1997), *Deregulatory Takings and the Regulatory Contract: The Competitive Transformation of Network Industries in the United States*, Cambridge: Cambridge University Press; Sauter, *Competition Law* (n.1, above).
3 This was, in essence, the rationale behind the Consent Decree between AT&T and the Department of Justice, which led to the break-up of AT&T and the settlement of the antitrust action against AT&T: *US* v. *AT&T* 552 F Supp 131 (1982). The Modified Final Judgement (MFJ) sanctioning that settlement was the basis for regulation of US telecommunications until the United States Telecommunications Act 1996. The AT&T litigation *and* the 1996 Act clearly stress the important role, in the USA at least, played by competition law and competition concepts in the regulation of telecommunications for at least the last three decades. See generally Huntley, A.K. and D.C. Pitt (1990), 'The Greeneing of US Telecommunications', *International Review of Law and Economics*, 77.
4 The local loop is the generic term used to describe the connection from a trunk network to specific premises. Normally copper wires, this is often referred to as 'the last half mile'.
5 The notion of 'contestable markets', hotly debated yet influential in US antitrust in recent years, was developed largely by Baumol. For its impact on US telecommunications thinking, see Baumol and Sidak, *Towards Competition* (n.2, above); and see Huntley, A.K. and D.C. Pitt (1996), 'Dead Ends, Bottlenecks and Gridlock: Regulatory Confusion on the US Telecommunications Superhighway', in C. Scott and O. Audéoud (eds), *The Future of EC Telecommunications Law*, Köln: Bundesanzeiger, pp.75–80.
6 In March 1991, the Duopoly Review White Paper, *Competition and Choice: Telecommunications Policy for the 1990s* (Cmnd 1461), indicated that further competition would be introduced.
7 The US regulatory authorities have consistently tried to exclude computers from the regulatory domain: see Huntley and Pitt, 'The Greeneing of US Telecommunications' (n.3, above).
8 It is difficult to state when this actually happened. It is likely that it happened in the USA in 1995 (see Huntley and Pitt, 'Dead-ends' (n.5, above), footnote 35) and that BT carried more data traffic than voice for the first time in 1998.
9 The 'Performance and Innovation' Unit of the Cabinet Office has now published its report on e-commerce: *e-commerce@its.best.uk* <http://www.cabinetoffice.gov.uk/innovation/1999/ecommerce/index.htm>
10 For the most comprehensive and current bibliography, see OFTEL's convergence web page: <http://www.oftel.gov.uk/converge.htm>
11 Trade and Industry Select Committee: *Inquiry into Electronic Commerce, Memorandum by OFTEL*, (June 1999), <http://www.oftel.gov.uk/superhwy/tisc0399.htm>, p.17.
12 Department of Trade and Industry, *Review of the Internet Watch Foundation*, <http://www.dti/gov.uk/cii/iwfreview1.html>, 1.2.1.1 and references therein.
13 *Trade and Industry Select Committee Memorandum* (n.11, above), p.19.
14 The acronym 'ISP' is used throughout this chapter to indicate '*Internet* Service Provider'. ISP is also used, by OFTEL amongst others, to indicate '*Independent* Service Provider'.

15 *Promoting Competition in Services over Telecommunication Networks,* June 1996, <http://www.oftel.gov.uk/competition /pcstn.htm>, 2.13–2.15.
16 Certain corporate customers with high traffic volume who are situated in geographically appropriate positions can be accessed by competing operators by running fibre optic cables specifically to connect the operator's trunk network to the customer's premises. However, this is a very small percentage even of the corporate market.
17 A detailed review of European developments is beyond the scope of this chapter, but a penetrating analysis of the current position is to be found in Ungerer, H. 'Ensuring Efficient Access to Bottleneck Network Facilities. The Case of Telecommunications in the European Union', 1998 <http://europa.eu.int/comm/dg04/speech/eight/en/sp98056.htm>
18 *Ibid.*
19 Section 54 and sch. 10.
20 See generally Veljanovski, C. (1999), 'Market Definitions in Telecommunications: the Confusing Proliferation of Competitive Standards', *Competition and Telecommunications Law Review,* 29–34.
21 OFTEL (1999), *Draft Guidelines on the Application of the Competition Act in the Telecommunications Sector,* Draft Consultation Paper, <http://www.oftel.gov.United Kingdom/competition/cact0199.htm>, 3.3.
22 See Huntley and Pitt, 'The Greeneing of US Telecommunications' (n.3, above).
23 Such leverage may take the form of an unwillingness to 'unbundle' the components of provision, thus tying the customer to features they might not otherwise wish to take: see OFTEL, *Draft Guidelines on the Application of the Competition Act* (n.21, above), 7.48, 7.82.
24 *Ibid.,* 7.5–7.13; 7.19–7.48.
25 *Ibid.,* 3.5.
26 *Ibid.* This view has been challenged; see Veljanovski 'Market Definitions' (n.20, above).
27 OFTEL, *Effective Competition Review,* 1998 <http://www/oftel.gov.uk/competition/ecr298.htm>, 1.1.
28 *Ibid.,* 1.2.
29 *Ibid.,* 2.12.
30 Ungerer, 'Ensuring Efficient Access' (n.17, above).
31 Currently condition 44 in the BT Licence.
32 OFTEL, *Draft Guidelines on the Application of the Competition Act* (n.21, above), 4.9–4.11. See also OFTEL (1999), *Guidelines on Interconnection and Interoperability,* July, <http://www.oftel.gov.uk/competition/gii799.htm>, 1.2–1.4.
33 OFTEL, March 1997.
34 Most notably in its investigation of mobile telephony connection charges: see OFTEL (1997), *Fair Trading in the Mobile Telephony Market – Conclusions on Future Competition Policy,* London: OFTEL.
35 Veljanovski, 'Market Definitions' (n.20, above), pp.29–30.
36 OFTEL (1999), *Draft Guidelines on the Application of the Competition Act* (n.21, above), 5.17 *et seq.*
37 *Ibid.,* at 6.4–6.7.
38 OFTEL (1997), *Fair Trading in the Mobile Telephony Market,* London: OFTEL.
39 *Directive 97/13/EC on a common framework for general authorizations and individual licences in the field of telecommunications services,* OJ (L) 117 , 07/05/1997 pp.15–27.
40 Article 4.
41 OFTEL (1998), *Identification of Significant Market Power for the Purposes of the EU Interconnection Directive* (February)<http://www.oftel.gov.uk/competition/smpi298.htm>. See also *Effective Competition Review* (n.27, above), 4.22 *et seq.;*

Draft Guidelines on the Application of the Competition Act (n.21, above), 6.21, 6.22: 'Decisions about significant market power are without prejudice to an organisation's position under EU or United Kingdom competition rules'.

42 OFTEL defined a WEO as 'an operator with 25% or more of ... the relevant market' in its *Review of Cable and Wireless Communications' Status as a Well Established Operator*, Consultative Document (October 1998), Annex 1, <http://www.oftel.gov.uk/competition/weo1098.htm>. The basic definition of a WEO, however, is identical to 'market influence'.

43 OFTEL, *Draft Guidelines on Market Influence Determinations*, <http://www.oftel.gov.uk/fairtrade/mrkt499.htm>, April 1999.

44 Veljanovski, 'Market Definitions' (n.20, above).

45 OFTEL, *Promoting Competition in Services over Telecommunication Networks* (n.15, above), 2.13.

46 Ibid., 2.14.

47 Ibid., 2.15.

48 See Huntley, J. (forthcoming), 'New Directions in US Telecommunications Regulation: The Impact of the Telecommunications Act 1996 on "Local" Provision', *International Journal of Law and Information Technology*.

49 OFTEL, *Promoting Competition in Service over Telecommunications Networks* (n.15, above), 5.1.

50 *Ibid.*, 5.2.

51 *Ibid.*, 5.25–5.38.

52 'Internet Protocol', the special network arrangements required for transmitting data over the Internet. In simple terms this involves dividing the data that are to be sent into 'packets' which are sent individually (often through different routes) and often referred to as 'packet switched' rather than 'circuit switched' (which refers to the circumstances where a circuit between sender and receiver is in place for the duration of the call).

53 'Service which connects users to the Internet Protocol network, being an input to the provision of Internet services': 5.25.

54 'A data conveyance service, consisting in the conveyance of Internet Protocol datagrams across networks of routers and bearers conforming to the Internet Protocol, which is an input to the provision of Internet services': *ibid*.

55 *Ibid.*, 5.9.

56 *Ibid.*, 5.27.

57 *Ibid.*, 5.30.

58 *Ibid.*, 5.35–7. SSB services, on the other hand, need not be notified and are therefore not subject to the same regulatory controls.

59 OFTEL (1999), *Trade and Industry Select Committee, Memorandum* (n.11, above).

60 OFTEL (1999), *Trade and Industry Select Committee: Inquiry into Electronic Commerce, Additional Memorandum by OFTEL*, <http://www.oftel.gov.uk/superhwy/ecom0699.htm>.

61 *Ibid.*, p.12.

62 OFTEL (1999), *Consultation Paper on the Relationship between Retail Prices and Interconnection Charges for Number Translation Services*, <http://www.oftel.gov.uk/pricing/ints0399.htm>.

63 OFTEL, *Additional Memorandum* (n.60, above), p.14.

64 OFTEL, *Consultation Paper on the Relationship between Retail Prices and Interconnection Charges* (n.62, above), 1.10.

65 Currently, the revenue share on local calls is very much weighted in favour of the originating operator (generally BT), especially in the evening and at weekends, when the terminating operator's receipts fall to less than 0.5p per minute: *ibid.*, 3.4.

66 *Ibid.*, 4.9–12.

67 *OFTEL Consultation Paper on the Relationship between Retail Prices and Interconnection Charges for Number Translation Services*, March 1999, *http://www.oftel.gov.uk/pricing/ints0399.htm*
68 OFTEL (1997), *BT Internet Services Investigation*, <http: / /www.oftel.gov.uk/ fairtrade / net1197.htm>.
69 OFTEL, *Draft Guidelines on the Application of the Competition Act* (n.21, above), 2.5.
70 *Ibid.*, 2.6.
71 *Ibid.*, 2.7.

7 Regulation of Genetic Testing

PHILIPPA GANNON AND CHARLOTTE VILLIERS, *University of Glasgow*

Introduction

The relevance of genetic testing to the regulatory debate arises from the fact that regulation has interdependent constitutive and control features. Genetic testing is a relatively new activity that promises both benefits and risks. The role of regulation therefore is to constitute an environment in which the benefits of this activity may be achieved and the risks may be reduced or at least appropriately allocated. Given that genetic testing is still being developed, it might be thought that little regulation exists.[1] It may also be thought that such regulation that does exist must be capable of adapting to the dynamics and changes that are inevitable in a field still in its developmental stages.[2]

In this chapter we shall explore the nature of genetic testing and its potential benefits and problems. We shall also consider the nature of regulation and how it might be applied in this field. Then we shall investigate what regulatory structure exists. We shall analyse that structure with reference to its constitutive and control functions. We shall also consider how and to what extent the existing regulation might be able to adapt as the full implications of genetic testing arise. In this chapter we shall indicate that there actually exists a complex regulatory structure with both statutory and non-statutory rules implemented and applied by government and professional bodies. However, the absence of coordination between the different existing rules and regulatory bodies represents a major shortcoming of this regulatory framework.

Defining Genetic Testing

What is genetic testing?[3] This is an important question because effective regulation depends on knowledge and understanding of the activity concerned. At its most general level, genetic testing is a test to detect the presence or absence of, or change in, a particular gene or chromosome.[4] This somewhat simplified definition belies the complexity of testing. Yet regulation needs to be able to address these complexities.[5] Indeed, there exist several different categorisations of genetic tests. These categorisations include different stages of diagnosis, scientific development and context. Each such categorisation has its own requirements and objectives.

Diagnosis

In this category there are four different tests:

1 genetic testing in a symptomatic individual (an individual who already shows symptoms of a particular condition) to aid in his or her diagnosis, treatment and management;
2 presymptomatic testing primarily carried out in healthy individuals to provide information about such individuals' future health with respect to specific inherited diseases such as Huntington's Disease;
3 susceptibility testing to provide information about the genetic component in a multifactoral disorder;
4 carrier testing to detect individuals who possess a single copy of a gene which follows an autosomal pattern of inheritance (that is, the gene is not located on the X or Y chromosome). Such an individual will not normally develop any disease or disorder but may pass on the gene to his or her offspring.[6]

Scientific Development

This category includes the stages of research, investigation and clinical use. At the research stage, issues that are more generally relevant to research also arise.[7] At the investigative stage, informed consent by those being tested is necessary. At the clinical use stage there are issues of the quality of laboratories, education of those involved in testing and those being tested, as well as counselling and standards of delivery.[8]

Context

Different contexts may include pre-pregnancy, pregnancy and neonatal, as well as situations where a family relative has developed an illness that might be linked to a genetic disorder. Each such context has its own unique need for genetic screening. For example, carrier testing helps couples to learn if they carry a recessive gene for inherited disorders such as cystic fibrosis. Prenatal testing may be used to diagnose certain conditions such as Down's syndrome. Neonatal testing of blood samples might be for abnormal or missing gene products.

The complexity and broad scope of genetic testing are highlighted by this variety of purposes and situations. Genetic testing may also adopt many guises, ranging from kits sold directly to the public to services provided by genetic laboratories. Different users of genetic tests will also have their own requirements. Genetic testing raises social and economic implications. For example, sale of genetic tests directly to the public has health and consumer implications, while some laboratories and companies may be tempted to adopt anti-competitive practices, thus leading to a need for economic regulation. These facts pose a challenge for regulation and may lead to the employment of different regulatory devices.

The Potential Benefits and Problems of Genetic Testing

Genetic testing promises both benefits and problems. The potential benefits may include improved quality of life. For example, the use of genetic tests may eradicate mistaken diagnoses, and instead provide more speedy diagnoses. It may bring the possibility of early treatment or the avoidance of conception or birth of seriously affected children. Individuals might avoid the negative effects of uncertainty and escape unnecessary periodic monitoring, which is often burdensome and invasive. Genetic tests could bestow on individuals an ability to make appropriate plans with forward knowledge of a future condition. They also promise the possibility of developing more effective treatments.[9] Indeed, the financial rewards arising from patented genetic discoveries have been enormous, leading to enthusiasm for making equally lucrative discoveries.[10] These potential benefits justify encouragement of the development of genetic testing and the constitution of an environment that makes progress possible.

At the same time there are risks involved in the activity, such as public health errors, and unfair commercial practices that could impede progress in the field. Competition could lead to abuse of competitive advantage by leading companies. Some of the potential health benefits may also have correlative problems such as the psychological effect of knowing that one has a genetic disposition for an untreatable illness.[11] The results of genetic tests might also encourage exploitative or abusive conduct such as discrimination by insurance companies or employers.[12] These potential disadvantages generated by the activity of genetic testing give rise to the need for some regulatory control.

The Nature of Regulation

The introduction to this book has highlighted the fact that there exists a variety of definitions and forms of regulation. We do not wish to repeat those definitions in this chapter, but it is appropriate to reiterate the main objectives of regulation and consider how they relate to genetic testing.

Objectives

Regulation has constitutive and control objectives.[13] The constitutive role of regulation is that regulation aims to promote the public interest and to further policies with that aim. Not only may regulation help to create markets, but it may also achieve what cannot be guaranteed by the operation of market forces alone. In addition, regulation may protect against potential problems caused by the operation of market forces. For example, social regulation seeks to address the problem of lack of information with regard to quality of goods and services offered by the suppliers and the resulting adverse spillover and effects. In this respect, Ogus divides regulation into social regulation and economic regulation. Social regulation covers health and safety, environmental protection and consumer protection, while economic regulation applies to industries with monopolistic tendencies and acts as a substitute for competition.[14]

Techniques

Regulation is a mixture of control and supervision by public and private institutional bodies which may create rules and standards and seek to ensure that those covered will comply with such rules and standards. Thus they both constitute the environment by creating rules and standards and providing advice and control, and maintain that environment by supervision and enforcement. A regulatory system establishes this control through a process of accountability and transparency supported by sanctions for failure to comply. Regulation might also provide procedures for problem solving such as balancing conflicting interests by means of objective criteria and assessment.

Application to Genetic Testing

In the light of these features, how does regulation relate to the activity of genetic testing? We have already seen that genetic testing takes place at different levels and in different circumstances with a variety of objectives. It has also been observed that genetic testing has benefits and problems, falling into both economic and social categories.

Regulation should accommodate the aims and objectives of particular tests. Thus, for example, tests should be conducted in a way that takes account of the different possible consequences leading from the results obtained. Particular consequences arise in different situations. For example, the interests of a pregnant woman or couple taking pre-natal tests are likely to be different from those of an individual undergoing a pre-symptomatic test for a disease such as Huntington's or a pilot being tested for the sickle cell trait. Yet, in all these circumstances, regulation should incorporate a requirement of adequate counselling before the genetic tests and after their results have been delivered.

Publicity about genetic testing could increase demand for such tests, but there may not be a sufficient number of testers or counsellors qualified to provide an adequate testing service. Additionally, if genes are patented, that will limit the number of laboratories or companies able to provide the tests. It will also affect supply levels of the service. The laboratories or companies able to do the tests will also be in a monopoly position and thus able to demand higher prices and to limit their services to more lucrative tests. This could be reinforced by the reward structure of science that makes it desirable and responsible to report high-profile findings as soon as possible.[15] Consequently, regulation faces the challenge of protecting the public from reckless or inappropriate use of tests without stifling innovation and diffusion of new genetic testing technologies.

Regulatory Structure

How has regulation responded to genetic testing? At first glance it might be thought that genetic testing is considered still to be a developing activity and therefore not yet regulated. However, bearing in mind the potentially broad range of characteristics of regulation, it is possible to identify already a fairly extensive regulatory structure, even though not all of that has been fully developed. There are features and aspects of genetic testing that cross into other areas. For example, if sold as a product, genetic tests would need to comply with general consumer legislation. Consequently, much of what may be deployed to control activity in the genetic testing field was not designed specifically for that activity. Such regulation consists of more fully developed laws.[16] The problem of highly technical language in the field of genetic testing makes drafting of effective regulations difficult. This fact, together with the need to adapt to a dynamic and developing activity, may explain why regulations aimed specifically at genetic testing have the character more of 'soft law' and tend to have a more flexible approach based on procedure rather than substance,[17] at least in the UK. This more direct regulation is operated by a number of government-appointed agencies that have implemented self-regulatory codes of practice. Companies may also have their own policies.

Existing General Laws that Might be Applied to Genetic Testing

Legislation such as the Supply of Goods and Services Act 1982 and the Data Protection Act 1998 may be applied to genetic testing. Certain laws appear to have more specific application and objectives, but they may also apply. For example, the Employment Rights Act 1996, which includes protection for employees against unfair dismissal, could be applied in situations where genetic testing leads to dismissal.[18] Some UK provisions, such as the Medical Devices Regulations 1994, were introduced to implement European measures and in exercise of powers conferred by the Consumer Protection Act 1987.[19]

Specific Self-regulatory Measures Implemented within the Industry

Genetic tests differ from other clinical tests. They may have implications for people other than the person tested and they are also unique insofar as they have power to predict the potential future health of the individual. The complexity of implications and consequences of a genetic test also demands a different form of counselling than is needed for other clinical tests. These facts give rise to a need to have specific regulation that addresses the unique characteristics of genetic testing. This has been implemented by a combination of government appointed bodies and professional associations.

In 1995, the House of Commons Science and Technology Committee published a comprehensive report on the ambit of genetics, entitled *Human Genetics: The Science and Its Consequences*.[20] Included in the many recommendations made by the Committee was the establishment of a statutory regulatory body, a 'Human Genetics Commission' to act *inter alia* as a watchdog over the many dilemmas posed by genetic information. Whilst a body with such comprehensive powers was not been created straight away, a weaker version of the body was established.

Human Genetics Advisory Commission The Human Genetics Advisory Commission[21] is a non-statutory body that reports jointly to the Department of Trade and Industry and the Department of Health, and has a consultative role. The Commission's terms of reference are, first, to keep under review scientific progress at the frontiers of human genetics and related fields. Secondly, the Commission must report on issues arising from new developments in human genetics that have wide social, ethical and economic consequences. Finally, the Commission advises on ways to increase public understanding of genetics.

The Human Genetics Advisory Commission works in tandem with two other non-statutory bodies, the Gene Therapy Advisory Committee[22] and the Advisory Committee on Genetic Testing.[23] The responsibilities of these two bodies extend into genetic testing. Each of these bodies has published advice, guidance and codes of practice on genetic testing and related activities.

The Office of Science and Technology recently published a report[24] in which it announced that a new body, the Human Genetics Commission, would be established by the end of 1999. This new body took over the role of the previous Human Genetics Advisory Commission from 20 December 1999, with responsibility for reporting to health and science ministers, advising on human genetic technologies and their impact.

Gene Therapy Advisory Committee The role of the Gene Therapy Advisory Committee is to consider and advise on the acceptability of proposals for gene therapy research on human subjects on ethical grounds, taking account of the scientific merits of the proposals and the potential benefits and risks. The Committee must also work with other agencies that have relevant responsibilities, such as Local Research Ethics Committees, and statutory agencies such as the Medicines Control Agency, the Health and Safety Executive and the Department of the Environment. The Gene Therapy Advisory Committee also gives advice to UK health ministers on the developments and implications of gene therapy research.[25]

Advisory Committee on Genetic Testing The role of the Advisory Committee on Genetic Testing is to provide advice to ministers on developments in testing for genetic disorders. The Committee must advise on testing individuals for genetic disorders, taking account of ethical, social and scientific aspects. The Committee must also establish requirements, especially in respect of efficacy and product information, to be met by manufacturers and suppliers of genetic tests.[26]

Other professional associations have also produced their own guidelines and codes of practice. For example, the Association of British

Insurers has issued a code of practice for its members on the use of genetic information. Other bodies that have been active in this field include the Royal College of Physicians, the Royal College of Obstetricians and Gynaecologists and the Royal College of General Practitioners. In addition, the implications of genetics have been examined by specific interest groups such as the 'Genetics Interest Group' (GIG) and a comprehensive review of the impact of genetics on society by the independent Nuffield Council on Bioethics has also been of importance.[27]

International-level Regulatory Controls

Genetic testing is not just a matter of concern for the UK but is an international-level activity. Its implications are bound to extend beyond national frontiers, especially as many of the companies involved are multinational. Consequently, to restrict controls to national boundaries would be to miss the important global implications. In addition, it is possible for individuals to obtain testing kits for some conditions over the Internet,[28] so this could potentially subvert the national rules of safety towards them.

A number of European directives have been adopted that have relevance in this field. For example, there is a directive on the control of in vitro diagnostic medical devices[29] and a directive on medical devices that apply to genetic testing.[30] Additionally, there is a draft directive on the legal protection of biotechnological inventions. This draft directive aims to strike a balance between the need to protect the patentability of commercially viable products and to harmonise the law in order to assist freedom of movement of biotechnological products between EU member states.

Another international regulatory control is the Convention on Human Rights and Biomedicine. This Convention aims to protect the dignity and identity of all human beings and to guarantee them respect for their integrity and other rights and fundamental freedoms with regard to the application of biology and medicine. The Convention prohibits discrimination on the basis of genetic information.[31] However, the UK has not yet ratified this Convention.

In summary, it is possible to conclude that a regulatory structure for genetic testing already exists. This includes indirect general statutory regulation and direct industry level regulation. However, the system appears to have developed in a piecemeal and fragmented fashion without a coordinated development or application of any clear policy. This background encourages the British Medical Association to demand a 'firm and effective regulatory body which, at the same time, is sufficiently flexible to be able to respond to new challenges and dilemmas arising in a rapidly developing field of medicine'.[32] The remainder of this chapter will consider how this existing regulatory structure copes with various stages and aspects of genetic testing.

Development of Genetic Tests

The scientific development stage will be the initial stage of a genetic test and this stage raises two major issues which will be considered in turn: standards and quality of research and protection of research.

Standards and Quality of Research

All UK laboratories have to comply with general legislative regulations in relation to the environment in which scientific experiments are conducted. For example, hazardous chemicals must be used appropriately. In the UK, scientific freedom is valued and scientists are encouraged to embark upon scientific research that may have or lead to philanthropic potential. Often the ability to obtain funding, private or public, will determine the viability of scientific research. Those who fund science or who administer public scientific grants also usually take responsibility to ensure that research falls within clearly defined parameters. Such parameters in essence ensure that the scientific objectives of research are valid and are not objectionable on ethical grounds. These parameters may be influenced by the beliefs and intentions of the funding organisation and, increasingly, by decisions of ethics committees.[33]

Occasionally, legislation will specify the parameters of scientific research if the subject matter of the research is deemed to create ethical dilemmas. For example, the Human Fertilisation and Embryology Act 1990 creates a licensing structure for research in the UK involving human embryos and also stipulates the manner in which human embryos may be used for the purposes of research.[34]

In relation specifically to the scientific development of genetic tests, there has been an absence of regulation that attempts to stipulate or to limit the boundaries of scientific research into genetic tests. However, the ACGT has been active and vigilant to ensure that transparent, universal standards are attained for laboratory development of genetic tests. First, the ACGT created a Code of Practice and Guidance for suppliers of genetic testing services directly to the public.[35] This aims to facilitate genetic testing services rather than to create obstacles to the establishment of the services. The ACGT intends that customers, testing laboratories and general medical practitioners and other clinicians will also be able to use the Code of Practice and Guidance. The aspects of testing supplied directly to the public that are relevant at the developmental stage of genetic testing include standards in relation to the manufacture and maintenance of equipment, appropriate staffing and equipment of testing laboratories and storage of records. The ACGT considers that this voluntary system of compliance and monitoring of scientific and laboratory standards will create a more flexible, responsive framework than would be available to statutory schemes. However, the ACGT will also monitor the Code of Practice and Guidance in order to determine whether a statutory regime should be introduced into the UK.[36]

Additionally, in 1998, the ACGT published the *Report on Genetic Testing for Late Onset Disorders*,[37] which included a consideration of issues to be addressed by laboratories that undertake genetic testing. The report recommended that such laboratories should be accredited for the purposes of genetic testing and should participate in internal and external quality control mechanisms.[38] Secondly, the report recommended that only laboratories that are associated with other genetic services should undertake genetic testing, thus ensuring a dedicated service for genetic testing. Thirdly, there should be equal access to genetic testing services throughout the UK and, thereby, to avoid regional discrepancies.

Finally, in November 1998, the ACGT published advice to research ethics committees on points to consider in medical research involving genetic testing.[39] The advice that applies to the developmental stage of genetic testing encompasses ensuring confidentiality of research samples, separation of research specimen and use of stored specimens for further research.

Protection of Research

An additional consideration at the research and scientific development stage of genetic tests is the increasing privatisation of science and the extent to which this development is leading to research monopolies. Such monopolies cause concern because they have the potential to affect the spirit of scientific collaboration. Generally, scientific progress is perceived as being of a cumulative nature in that advances occur incrementally by the combined efforts of many. However, the commercialisation of science, which is illuminated by the increasing trend of granting patent rights over aspects of scientific advancement and the presence of private companies involved in scientific research, has the potential to diminish collaboration. For example, the desire to patent could result in clandestine scientific research as it is possible that the publication of scientific research to contemporaries could prejudice a later grant of a patent. As the commercial potential of research into genes is realised, it is possible that an increasingly commercial climate may also alienate minor players in this game who are wary, for example, of working around the patented research of a larger scientific enterprise.

Amidst controversy, the European Union has recently adopted a directive on patenting of biotechnology products and processes.[40] The directive has a protracted history as a result of the polarised views that it attracts and the emotive issues that are invoked by patenting.[41] It was intended primarily to clarify patent law between the member states and in doing so attempts to address the ethical controversies raised by the grant of patents in this area.[42] The directive clearly envisages that biotechnology products and processes should, in principle, be patented and thus it attempts explicitly to stipulate the patent criteria for such patents.[43] Whilst it can be regarded as a mechanism to support and advance the biotechnology industries, a possible outcome is that the negative implications of patenting – namely, increasing competition between rival research teams – may also become apparent. Ultimately, such rivalries could lead to restricted access to testing services or could curb the development of genetic testing.

Patenting could restrict the access or value of information to other laboratories that could make greater progress in developing both understanding and potentially treatment of the relevant genes. It may, indeed, create a disincentive for those other laboratories to continue in their research with regard to certain conditions. In addition, companies will be encouraged to search for genes and gene tests that are more likely to make profits than other genetic conditions. The end result of this process is to restrict treatment possibilities for sufferers. Furthermore, the monopoly that a company gains from patenting genes gives it considerable power in setting prices for its services as well as for making deals with its favoured drug companies for the provision of treatment of connected genetic conditions. This could reduce quality of service and increase prices for recipients of the products and services as well as creating disincentives for further progress in research.

Thus the association of private business with science may create competition between scientists that leads to the possibility of fragmentation and privatisation of the provision of healthcare. This could have the effect of restricting access to genetic testing services to those who can afford to pay for such services. However, on another level, restricted access could act as a control mechanism. Such restriction could operate to limit the range of service providers. This would ensure greater coordination of genetic testing and, it is suggested, less opportunity for abuse of a monopoly position. It is submitted that there is a specific role for regulation at this stage in the development of genetic tests to ensure that an equitable balance is struck between promoting healthy competition in the UK research market and ensuring that monopolies do not lead to abuse. For example, this might be achieved through fiscal measures such as incentives to conduct research in the UK. This could include, for example, availability of exemptions and reliefs from tax obligations or research funding.

Future Possibilities of Genetic Testing Services

At present genetic testing services are usually provided through the NHS via an initial referral by the patient's medical practitioner. The benefits of the current position are identified by the ACGT as follows. First, most genetic testing is carried out via collaboration with different components of the NHS, such as regional genetics centres and general practitioners (GPs). Secondly, links exist between laboratories and clinical genetics services including personnel who are trained to offer counselling to families and individuals. Thirdly, the current provision also incorporates a collaborative network, facilitating specialisation, and encouraging and liasing with research and development in genetics.[44]

However, an increasing possibility, given the extent of private research in the science of genetics, is that genetic tests will be developed for supply direct to the public – for example, via the Internet or by mail order. This possibility raises unique features that are not encountered in the current provision of genetic testing and may, as a result, require specific regulation in order to establish a framework within which such tests may be distributed.

Given the promise of a growing range of genetic tests, and the different guises in which they are available, it is necessary to determine the appropriate framework and standards within which the tests will be available. The key questions are, when is it appropriate to test and at what stage, if any, should tests become available directly to the public? In addition, what support in terms of counselling and education should be borne by those who manufacture, supply or administer the test? Owing to the variations between genetic conditions it is difficult to identify and to stipulate appropriate standards that can be applied without the exercise of considerable discretion. Professional bodies with some knowledge of the activity of genetic testing could exercise this discretion. Yet, since such bodies are involved in the activity, we might ask if this discretion is appropriate. However, safeguards from abuse of such discretion may be provided by the existence of a general legislative framework of sale, supply and marketing of a product or service. As a result, the specific questions and concerns regarding genetic testing may have been encountered in different contexts and may be subsumed within existing regulation.

Sale, Supply and Marketing of Tests

The manner in which a genetic test is acquired and supplied is an integral factor when considering appropriate regulation. Whilst it will be seen that the distinction between a test that is sold directly to a consumer and a test that is administered in a healthcare context is of crucial importance, consumer issues are relevant to both scenarios. Such issues include the quality of the test, accuracy of information regarding the test, price, safety of devices used and the actual testing process.

The ACGT recognises that, given the controversy surrounding genetic tests supplied direct to the public, the government has a public health and consumer protection role to encourage good practice in the provision of genetic testing.[45] The Code of Practice and Guidance published by the ACGT thus requires test suppliers to comply with its provisions and guidelines and to present their proposals regarding the provision of tests to the ACGT for comment.[46] The ACGT has set parameters in relation to the nature and purpose of tests that can be supplied directly – for example, recommending that the main purpose of tests should be to determine carrier status.[47] In addition, the ACGT has made recommendations concerning the manner in which genetic tests are distributed. For example, one recommendation is that genetic tests should include customer information pertaining to the use of the test.[48]

The existing legal framework that applies to the supply of genetic tests to individuals includes the law of contract and negligence, the general provisions of which have been enhanced by specific consumer legislation. In the UK, as in most other European countries, there exists statutory control in relation to the standards, quality and expectations with which those who place consumer products on to the market need to comply. The existence of consumer legislation acts as an incentive for manufacturers to place products on the market that comply with the standards that are enshrined in the legislation. Such legislation also levels the playing field between consumer and supplier.

A genetic test could be supplied on a sale of goods basis, between a supplier and a purchaser and also as a service, for example, if a laboratory interpretation of the test was necessary. These two possibilities will be considered in turn. The Sale of Goods Act 1979 implies terms into contracts of sale. For example, s.14 requires that goods will be of a satisfactory quality and fit for their purpose. Section 14 only operates if the seller is selling in the course of a business. The relevance of the implied contractual terms is that, if the genetic test was faulty or defective in any way – for example if the test kit was broken – then the consumer is entitled to a remedy, such as damages or a replacement test. If the genetic test were deemed to be a service then terms as to the standards of skill and care, cost and time of performance would also be implied into the contract.[49]

It is possible that attempts would be made to exclude these statutory implied contractual terms. However, in the UK, the Unfair Contract Terms Act (UCTA) 1977[50] limits the use of exclusion clauses in consumer and standard form contracts. The exclusion of liability for negligence that causes death or personal injury is always void.[51] In other circumstances, the Act grants special protection to consumer contracts.[52] In such circumstances, then, the consumer will be protected by the test of reasonableness that is stipulated in the Act. Thus an exclusion clause will only be enforced if it was 'fair and reasonable' to incorporate the term into the contract.[53] Any attempt to exclude s.14 of the Sale of Goods Act 1979 will be void in the case of consumer contracts and only applied in other contexts as long as the term is fair and reasonable.[54] The Unfair Contract Terms Act 1977 has been supplemented by the Unfair Terms in Consumer Contracts Regulations 1994. These impose upon a contractual term the test of fairness even when the term is not attempting to exclude liability.

Another legal action would be in negligence, for the supply of a faulty genetic test or genetic testing services. Any such action would have to cross hurdles of proving the existence of a duty of care, breach of that duty and damage.[55] However, the Consumer Protection Act 1987, Part 1, introduced into the UK a system of strict liability in relation to the producers of defective products. The definition of producer in s.2 is wide enough to encompass manufacturers and own-branders. A genetic test is likely to be deemed a product within the definition in s.1(2).[56] Section 3 stipulates the nature of a defect in the product which is concerned with the safety of the product. In this respect, however, safety is given a wide interpretation.[57] In reality, the Consumer Protection Act will be of little application in the absence of damage caused by a product. Scenarios where, for example, a genetic test leaked and damaged furniture would fall within the ambit of the Act. However, if use of the kit caused a reaction, such as a skin rash caused by contact with a toxic chemical when conducting a saliva swab, would damages for pain and suffering be available? More complex, and probably beyond the ambit of the Act, would be failure of a test to identify a genetic condition, leading to the onset of a genetic condition which might have been alleviated if preventative measures had been taken. According to Kelly and Attree, Article 9 of the initial EC Directive on product liability stipulates that the definition of damage is without prejudice to the national law relating to non-material damage, which, according to the recitals of the Directive, covers pain and suffering and other non-material loss arising from the law. In the opinion of those authors, the question of 'whether claims for pain and suffering are included within those for death and physical injury is unclear from the Directive'.[58] Even if damage is recognised, the existence of defences in s.4 of the Act would probably protect the manufacturer of the test from legal liability.[59] In addition, the General Product Safety Regulations 1994 govern the safety of products that are intended for consumers or are likely to be used by consumers in the event that such products are placed upon the market by producers or supplied by distributors.

Turning now to the advertising and marketing of genetic tests in the UK, advertising is controlled by the combination of statute[60] and self-regulation. Self-regulation takes the guise of the British Code of Advertising Practice which polices the use of claims made in advertising. However, with the influence of the European Union, this area is witnessing specific legislation in relation to advertising. For example, the Control of Misleading Advertisements Regulations 1988[61] prevents misleading statements that occur in any guise. The manner in which genetic tests are marketed is therefore a relevant consideration. For example, any description that is applied to a genetic test would have to comply with the provisions of the Trade Descriptions Act 1968. *Inter alia*, s.1 prohibits false trade descriptions in relation to goods and s.14 prohibits false or misleading statements about services.[62] Again, if genetic tests are supplied via mail order, the Mail Order Transactions (Information) Order 1976 entitles consumers to obtain a remedy when a trader defaults on his or her obligations. Thus any advertising and marketing of genetic tests would need to comply with these restrictions.

In addition to the above, there is a panoply of control in relation to the sale, manufacture and distribution of medicine.[63] In the UK, the principal piece of legislation is the Medicine Act 1968. This stipulates the manner in which medicines are to be controlled and criminal penalties for breach. Following European initiatives, the Medical Devices Regulations 1994[64] stipulates that medical devices, from June 1998, would not be controlled by the Medicine Act 1968 but by consumer legislation. A device is an instrument, apparatus appliance, material or other article which is to be used *inter alia* for the diagnosis, prevention, monitoring, treatment or alleviation of disease or the investigation, replacement or modification of the anatomy of any physiological process. This definition would clearly encompass genetic tests.

In addition, of crucial importance is the European In Vitro Diagnostics Directive (IVD Directive). The IVD Directive will be implemented into UK law by the In Vitro Medical Devices Regulations which will be in force by June 2000.[65] Article 1 of the Directive gives a wide definition of an in vitro device which might include a genetic testing kit or device. The aim of the Directive is to address safety and performance requirements of in vitro diagnostics and to ensure that they do not affect the health and safety of a user or a patient. The Directive requires each member state to demand that in vitro diagnostic medical devices are Conformité Européene (CE) marked in declaration of conformity with the Directive in order to be placed upon the market.

Thus it can be seen that there is a great deal of existing legislation with which genetic tests will have to comply. However, as Longley reminds us in the context of medical devices, what remains to be seen is whether

> consumer interests, in the present case patients and health care providers, are really protected when pitted against those of the medical devices industry, especially in the evolution of the alliance between standards and regulatory safety requirements where doubts must be expressed about the relative capacities of commercial and consumer interests to influence the process.[66]

In addition, notwithstanding the presence of specific and general laws in the UK, it is probable that the Internet will become a popular channel through which tests are sold and distributed. This form of sale and distribution will of course raise the additional issue of ascertaining the prevailing jurisdiction. This will have implications for private international law and will raise wider issues concerning the regulation of the Internet which are outside the scope of this chapter. In any event, it is possible to identify further issues raised by genetic testing, as will be seen in the next section.

Implications of Tests

There are two categories of third parties who are increasingly asserting a right to be informed of the results of another's genetic test. First, insurance companies and employers may seek to have access to genetic test results or may even attempt to stipulate that an individual has a genetic test for contractual purposes. Secondly, as genetics is the science of hereditary traits, blood relatives may have the same genetic history and reproductive partners may have an interest in ascertaining the genetic traits of their partner that may affect their potential offspring. For example, an individual who is a carrier of the gene for cystic fibrosis may be anxious to identify whether his or her partner is also a carrier of this gene.

The importance of the results of genetic tests to others can be problematic. The problem is manifested in the disclosure of genetic test results and may even influence the preliminary decision to participate in genetic testing. After consideration of the interests of third parties, the individual who is considering testing may come to the conclusion that a genetic test should not be entered lightly or should at least involve the participation of blood relatives. However, if such considerations only arise after the test has been performed, it may be an onerous obligation upon the individual who has been tested to disclose the test and its result to others. Consequently, the individual may be concerned that his or her decision not to disclose this vital information is respected.

It is possible that regulation can ensure that this quagmire involving the individual who has been tested and his or her obligations to others is minimised – for example, by ensuring that such tests are scientifically valid and therefore give rise to accurate results. However, regulation is also necessary to maintain a framework surrounding the participation of the individual in genetic testing and to ensure that his or her interests are acknowledged, namely in relation to consent, confidentiality and privacy of genetic information. Again, it will be seen that differences may be drawn between a test that is sold direct to the public and a test that is performed through the NHS.

The first consideration is the preliminary decision to participate in the genetic test. A decision to participate in testing requires the consent of the individual who is to be tested. To ensure that consent is valid, the individual who is to be tested must base his or her decision on information relating to the nature of the test and its implications. However, the problem arises in determining exactly the nature and scope of the information to which the individual is entitled, and is a question that continuously haunts medical law, given the vicissitudes of individuals in terms of age and mental state. Increasingly, genetic testing is provided through the NHS, such as during prenatal care, or an individual may be referred to a regional genetics centre for genetic testing. When genetic testing is provided in this context it is sufficient that the genetic test has been provided in a context which accords with general issues of consent and, as such, does not raise considerations that are not without precedent. In considering tests that are supplied direct to the public, the ACGT advocates that information be presented in a simple and assessable format, including full information about the test and any adverse consequences associated with the test.[67] The ACGT also recommends that suppliers should provide opportunities for genetic counselling by trained genetic counsellors and that, in relation to pregnancy or planning a pregnancy, a consultation should be sought with a qualified clinician prior to the genetic test.[68] In relation to the supply of genetic tests, the ACGT suggests that tests should not be supplied to under-16s or to those who are incompetent to make a medical decision.[69]

A second concern is in relation to access to genetic information. The very nature of genetic information is such that individuals are entitled to expect that the information will not be abused or disclosed to third parties. The problems here are very real, as disclosure of genetic test results might prejudice an individual's chances of obtaining health or life insurance or employment if the results were to be revealed to a third party. Disclosure of health information to employers and to insurers is not, of course, a new issue. Indeed, the sensitivity of medical information and its dangerous implications when disclosed to third parties mean that the confidentiality of such information is in fact enshrined in UK law in several ways. First, a cornerstone of the healthcare relationship is confidentiality, the preservation of which is perceived to result in the best possible medical outcomes. The patient will be confident in disclosing medical details on the understanding that such details will remain confidential.[70] Secondly, legislation enacted to ensure that information is not abused will also protect medical information. This legislation includes the Data Protection Act 1988, which deals with control of and access to stored personal information. Thirdly, and more specifically, the circumstances in which individuals have a right of access to information contained in their health records are also provided for by statute.[71] According to the ACGT, suppliers of genetic tests should keep customer data confidential and inform customers that the information will be kept confidential.[72] That this is stipulated with clarity by the ACGT is welcome, though in essence this position does not add anything new or radical to the genetics debate.

We turn now to consider the use of genetic information for employment and insurance purposes. Following the House of Commons science and technology recommendations, the insurance industry has been charged with responsibility for introducing self-regulation in relation to the fair and equitable use of genetic information for the purposes of insurance. To date, insurance companies do not require that individuals participate in genetic testing solely for the purposes of obtaining insurance. However, disclosure of the results of genetic tests may, in certain circumstances, be necessary.[73] The use of genetic testing in employment has received little coverage in the UK to date, though it was raised as a concern by the House of Commons Science and Technology Committee. As a result, protection against what may be perceived to be disclosure of or discrimination based on genetic information is encompassed within general employment legislation such as the Health and Safety at Work etc Act 1974 and the Disability Discrimination Act 1995.[74]

The Human Rights Act 1998, which will be implemented during 2000, will also have implications for the manner in which genetic tests are used in the UK and who may have access to results. According to Feldman, 'the Act initiates a fundamental constitutional change by introducing new values and an altered frame of reference to UK public law'.[75] This piece of legislation will protect and value the following individual rights: respect for private and family life and the right to have other rights secured without discrimination. It is apparent that these broad provisions will apply to genetic testing, but the impact of the Act, as in other areas, remains to be seen.

International Considerations

As noted earlier in this chapter, the science of genetics transcends jurisdictions and, as a result, there are numerous international conventions and international bodies that will influence the development of UK law in relation to genetic testing. The importance of international activities is that standards may be created which could reduce potential competition between states. International developments could also engender collaboration and consistency between states. In the context of medical law and human rights, the importance of the European Convention on Human Rights and Biomedicine, while not ratified by the UK, should not be overlooked.[76] This Convention applies within the ambit of healthcare law, but particular provisions are most applicable to the use of genetic tests. In particular, Article 12 states: 'Tests which are predictive of genetic diseases or which serve either to identify the subject as a carrier of a gene responsible for a disease or to detect a genetic predisposition or susceptibility to disease may be performed only for health purposes or for scientific research purposes, and subject to appropriate genetic counselling.' In addition, Article 11 stipulates: 'Any form of discrimination against a person on grounds of his or her genetic heritage is prohibited.' Thus, in combination and in isolation, both of these provisions protect the individual against unjustified and unauthorised use of personal genetic information. However, exceptions are made in the Convention on the grounds of public safety, crime, public health or the protection of the rights of others.[77] Whilst the UK has not ratified the Convention, its influence may be felt indirectly via the jurisprudence of the European Union. This is because other member states have ratified the Convention.

In addition, account should perhaps be taken of legislative measures that have been created in other jurisdictions that may prove to be successful and which may be emulated in the UK. That is, if such measures prove successful, as with, for example, the increasing use of privacy laws in the USA and other EU member states to protect and to control the use of genetic information,[78] they may prove influential to the UK.

Conclusion

Genetic testing is often associated with futuristic scenarios that challenge and prove insurmountable for regulation. However, this chapter has demonstrated that, contrary to popular belief, there are numerous features of genetic testing that can be addressed by regulation. Indeed, the regulation of genetics is not a study that exists in isolation. When considering genetic testing it is apparent that there are generic aspects of regulation that converge in this context. One example is provided by the increasing prevalence of consumer legislation to protect the interests of consumers and the complexity of interpreting legislation, as illustrated in the section considering the sale and supply of genetic tests. As a result, other contexts may learn from the experience of regulating genetics: perhaps, for example, from the experience encountered in juxtaposing public and private funding.

The real problem is that so many different issues converge when one considers genetic testing. Indeed, one of the prevailing aspects of the genetics debate is that there are numerous and at times conflicting demands that regulation must address. For example, there are consumer expectations of genetic tests coupled with demands that the science of genetics be controlled. Owing to the variety of issues, it is essential that regulation is flexible and adopts numerous guises. In addition, an associated benefit of this approach is that it will limit the disadvantages of genetics while as far as possible promoting the advantages. This chapter has therefore illustrated the varied nature and forms of regulation within the context of genetic testing, such as self-regulation and statutory intervention. In addition, the scope of regulation has been examined: for example, specific legislation combined with more general legislation. It is also apparent from the consideration of the implications of genetic tests that decisions have to be taken regarding whether the controls that exist are voluntary or self-regulatory, giving rise to legal implications for those who choose not to comply. However, the benefit of regulation is that it has the ability to create and to control markets by putting in place protective measures that may ultimately enable people to have confidence in participating in the market involved. One example has been provided by developments in the insurance industry in relation to genetic testing. In that context, attempts have been made by public and private bodies to protect individuals from the potential discriminatory impact of genetic testing on access to insurance cover.

The experience of genetic tests and regulation also illustrates that discretion is usually necessary in implementing regulation. In part, this may be necessary because of uncertainty regarding possible scientific advancement or because it is not possible to ascertain the ethical criteria underpinning the regulation. In this context it is the medical profession, individuals and third parties such as employers who need to exercise discretion in facing these dilemmas. Given that discretion is necessary, the question is raised as to what extent it is preferable that regulation should be entrusted to professional organisations to whom professionals are accountable if they do not adhere to the requisite professional standards.

Ultimately, the broad picture has to be scrutinised to gauge the effectiveness of the existing regulation. In order to make this assessment, the purpose and expectations of what regulation can actually achieve have to be ascertained. According to Longley, writing in the context of medical devices regulation,

> The overall aim of the present approach to harmonisation – via standards closely allied to essential, though broad, regulatory requirements – is to provide a reasonably flexible regime which will preclude any stifling of innovation in either the development of new products or modification of existing ones. As long as safety principles are adhered to – taking account of the acknowledged state of the art, solutions adopted for the design and construction of devices are for manufacturers alone.[79]

Ultimately, the issue will be whether this strategy in relation to regulation of genetic tests is sufficient. It is apparent from the regulation of genetic tests that there are many aspects of regulation and that regulation for one issue may not address others. For example, even if it is possible to regulate to ensure that genetic tests are scientifically 100 per cent accurate in the manufacturing process, that ability would not remove other problems, such as who is entitled to have access to the information contained in such tests.

Thus, whilst regulation surrounds all aspects of genetic testing, the ultimate issue is whether such regulation is achieving the purpose for which it was initially created and implemented. The genetics debate shows that regulation necessitates constant review in line with continuing scientific and technical progress and that a degree of coordination within the broad regulatory framework be maintained.

Notes

1 McGleenan, T. (1999), 'Genetic Testing and Screening: The Developing European Jurisprudence', *Human Reproduction and Genetic Ethics*, 5, 13–14 and 17.
2 *Ibid.*, 14.
3 See National Cancer Institute and National Center for Human Genome Research, *Understanding Gene Testing*, <www.accessexcellence.org/AE/AEPC/NIH/gene01>.
4 The examination of the DNA is for 'some anomaly that flags a disease or disorder'(*ibid.*, s.9).

5 'The DNA change can be relatively large: a missing or added piece of a chromosome – even an entire chromosome – that is visible under a microscope. Or it can be extremely small, as little as one extra, missing, or altered chemical base. Genes can be overexpressed (too many copies), inactivated, or lost altogether. Sometimes, pieces of chromosomes become switched, or transposed, so that a gene ends up in a location where it is permanently and inappropriately turned on or off' (*ibid.*).
6 See Advisory Committee on Genetic Testing (ACGT) (1998), *Report on Genetic Testing for Late Onset Disorders*, London: Health Departments of the UK, p.5; ACGT (1998), *Advice to Research Ethics Committees*, London: Health Departments of the UK, p.3.
7 For example, establishing scientifically valid methods, peer review and research ethics are all relevant.
8 For an overview of the issues arising from the different stages of testing see Task Force on Genetic Testing (March 1996), *Review of Genetic Testing* and *Interim Principles of the Task Force on Genetic Testing*, <www.med.jhu.edu/tffgtelsi/intro>.
9 *Ibid*. See also 'Genetic Testing', *Reuterlinkextra*, 8, Spring 1998.
10 For a discussion of the evidence for and against this claim, see Benowitz, S. (1996), 'Researchers View Genetic Testing With High Hopes, But Caution', *The Scientist* 10 (1), 6–7.
11 See *Reuterlinkextra* (n.9, above); Waalen, J. (1997), 'Genetic Testing Opens Brave New World', *Annals of Internal Medicine*, 15 June.
12 See HGAC (1997), *Report on the Implications of Genetic Testing for Insurance*, December, and *Response to the HGAC's Report* (*DTI* Department of Trade and Industry Office of Science and Technology, November 1998) and HGAC (1999), *Report on The Implications of Genetic Testing for Employment*, July. There is an extensive literature on the insurance issues: see McGleenan, 'Genetic Testing and Screening' (n.1, above), n.13 for references. On the employment issues, see Gannon, P. and Villiers, C. (1999), 'Genetic Testing and Employment', *Medical Law International*, 39–57.
13 Shearing, C.D. (1993), 'A Constitutive Conception of Regulation' in P. Grabosky and J. Braithwaite (eds), *Business Regulation and Australia's Future*, Canberra: Australian Institute of Criminology, ch.5.
14 Ogus, A. (1994), *Regulation: Legal Form and Economic Theory*, Oxford: Clarendon, pp.4–5.
15 Benowitz, 'Researchers View Genetic Testing' (n.10, above).
16 For example, the Supply of Goods and Services Act 1982.
17 See McGleenan, 'Genetic Testing and Screening' (n.1, above).
18 See Gannon and Villiers, 'Genetic Testing and Employment (n.12, above).
19 See below for discussion of European and international measures. For a discussion of the regulation of medical devices, see Longley, D. (1998), 'Who Is Calling the Piper? Is There a Tune? The New Regulatory Systems for Medical Devices in the United Kingdom and Canada', *Medical Law International*, 3, 319.
20 House of Commons Science and Technology Committee (1995), *Human Genetics: The Science and Its Consequences*, London: HMSO.
21 *First Annual Report*, London (1998): Human Genetics Advisory Commission.
22 Established in 1993, following the Committee on the Ethics of Gene Therapy Report. Its responsibilities include provision of advice upon the design and conduct of gene therapy research.
23 Established in 1995 to consider and advise on genetic testing in clinical practice and testing sold direct to the public.
24 Office of Science and Technology (1999), *The Advisory and Regulatory Framework for Biotechnology: Report from the Government's Review*, May, London.

25 Gene Therapy Advisory Committee (1998), *Fourth Annual Report: January 1997–December 1997*, Health Departments of the United Kingdom, Annex 1.
26 See Advisory Committee on Genetic Testing (1998), *First Annual Report, July 1996–December 1997*, Health Departments of the United Kingdom, March, Annex A.
27 The Nuffield Council on Bioethics was established in 1991 to consider the ethical issues arising from advances in biomedical and biological research: Nuffield Council on Bioethics (1993), *Genetic Screening: Ethical Issues*, December.
28 For example, the Michigan State University DNA Laboratory sells hereditary haemochromatosis genetic testing kits over the Internet: see Http://www.phd.msu.edu/hh/hh.html.
29 Directive 98/79/EC of the European Parliament and Council of 27 October 1998 on in vitro medical devices (OJ L 331 07.12.1998, pp.1–37) which comes into force on 7 June 2000.
30 Council Directive 93/42/EEC of 14 June 1993 on medical devices (OJ L 169, 12.07.1993, pp.1–43, amended 398 L 0079, OJ L 331, 07.12.98, p.1).
31 Articles 11 and 12. See McGleenan, 'Genetic Testing and Screening' (n.1, above).
32 British Medical Association (BMA) (1998), *Human Genetics Choice and Responsibility*, Oxford: Oxford University Press, p.192.
33 In relation to medical research, since 1991, every health authority has been required to maintain a Local Research Ethics Committee (LREC), which advises NHS bodies on research proposals. In 1997, multi-centre Research Ethics Committees (MRECs) were established to facilitate multi-centre research proposals. As a result, every designated region in the UK has an MREC to review the science and general ethics of medical research protocols: see ACGT Advisory Committee on Genetic Testing, *Advice to Research Ethics Committees*, London: Department of Health, p.1.
34 For example, s.3(3)(*a*) stipulates that a licence cannot authorise (a) keeping or using an embryo after the appearance of the primitive streak.
35 ACGT (1997), *Code of Practice and Guidance on Human Genetic Testing Services Supplied Direct to the Public*, London: Department of Health.
36 *Ibid.*, p.4.
37 ACGT, *Report on Genetic Testing for Late Onset* Disorders (n.6, above), pp.11–12.
38 These include 'registration with a National Accreditation Body and conformity with the requirements of BS EN ISO 9002 (formerly BS 5750 Part 2)'. Continued registration is dependent on satisfactory audits that are performed at prescribed intervals by the accreditation body to ensure compliance with the appropriate standards, and accreditation by Clinical Pathology Accreditation (UK) Ltd. Accreditation by this company involves external audit to standards reflecting 'best professional practice for clinical laboratories': *ibid.*, p.12.
39 ACGT, *Advice to Research Ethics Committees* (n.33, above).
40 Directive 98/44/EC of the European Parliament and of the Council of 6 July 1998 on the legal protection of biotechnological inventions.
41 Advantages of patents include acting as an incentive to embark upon scientific research.
42 Article 7. The European Group Ethics in Science and New Technologies was created in 1997 as a replacement for the former 'Group of Advisers on the Ethical Implications of Biotechnology' that had been established in 1991. There are 12 independent (political, economic and national) members of this new group appointed for a three-year period on the basis of their expertise and personal abilities. The Commission asks the group for opinions on the ethical implications of science and new technologies. The group may also examine matters on its own initiative.
43 Article 5 states that:

1. The human body, at the various stages of its formation and development, and the simple discovery of one of its elements, including the sequence of partial sequence of a gene, cannot constitute patentable inventions.
2. An element isolated from the human body or otherwise produced by means of a technical process, including the sequence or partial sequence of a gene may constitute a patentable invention, even if the structure of that element is identical to that of a natural element.

The industrial application of a sequence or a partial sequence of a gene must be disclosed in the patent application.

44 ACGT, *Code of Practice and Guidance* (n.35, above), p.9.
45 *Ibid.*, p.4.
46 *Ibid.*, p.10.
47 *Ibid.*, p.10
48 *Ibid.*, p.12.
49 In England and Wales, the Supply of Goods and Services Act 1982 , Part 2, stipulates the implied terms which are to be implied into a contract of service. In Scotland, this is governed by the common law. See Ervine, W.C.H. (1995), *Consumer Law in Scotland*, Edinburgh: W. Green/Sweet and Maxwell.
50 Parts I and III of the Unfair Contract Terms Act 1977 apply to England and Wales and Part II applies to Scotland.
51 In Scotland this is by virtue of s.16 UCTA and in England and Wales by s.2.
52 In Scotland this is by s.25(1) UCTA and in England and Wales by s.12.
53 This is deduced by looking at all the circumstances and at the guidelines that are stipulated in the Act. In Scotland this is in s.17 and in England and Wales in s.11.
54 In Scotland this is by s.20 and in England and Wales by s.6.
55 However, the problems of the negligence action would include difficulties of proving causation and the remoteness of damage that could be claimed from the breach of the duty of care.
56 Namely, 'any good or electricity and ... includes a product which is comprised in another product, whether by virtue of being a component part or raw material or otherwise'.
57 If 'the safety of the product is not such as persons generally are entitled to expect; and for those purposes "safety", in relation to a product, shall include safety with respect to products comprised in that product and safety in the context of risks of damage to property, as well as in the context of risks of death or personal injury'.
58 Kelly, P. and R. Attree (eds) (1997), *European Product Liabilities*, 2nd edn, London: Butterworths, p.13.
59 For example, the 'state of the art' defence in s.4.
60 For example, legislation exists regarding weights and measures and advertising medicinal products.
61 SI 1988 no.915.
62 These sections only apply to goods or services that are provided in the course of a business, and breach is a criminal offence.
63 For further information, see Appelbe G.E. and J. Wingfield (1997), *Dale and Appelbe's Pharmacy Law and Ethics*, 6th edn, London: The Pharmaceutical Press.
64 SI 1994 no 3017.
65 See, for example, The Medical Devices Agency (1999), *Sale and Supply of In Vitro Diagnostic Medical Devices (IVDS)*, Bulletin 12, May.
66 Longley, 'Who Is Calling The Piper?' (n.19, above), p.341.
67 ACGT, *Code of Practice and Guidance* (n.35, above), p.12.
68 *Ibid.*, p.13.

69 *Ibid.*, p.11.
70 See, for example, Montgomery, J. (1997), *Health Care Law*, Oxford: Oxford University Press.
71 Legislation includes the Access to Medical Reports Act 1988 and the Access to Health Records Act 1990. For further information see Mason J.K. and R.A. McCall Smith (1999), *Law and Medical Ethics*, 5th edn, London: Butterworths, ch.8.
72 ACGT, *Code of Practice and Guidance* (n.35, above), p.9.
73 Following the recommendation of the House of Commons Science and Technology Committee, the Association of British Insurers (ABI) published a policy statement that genetic information would not be required before insurance was offered: Association of British Insurers (1997), *ABI Policy Statement on Genetics*, February. The ABI appointed a genetics adviser and a Genetics Committee to draw up a code of practice. However, the Human Genetics Advisory Commission (HGAC) concluded in 1997 that it was not justifiable to disclose test results to the insurance companies. The HGAC recommended a two-year moratorium on asking clients for life insurance to disclose genetic test results. This will change if evidence becomes available on the superior quality of test results. See Cook, D.F. (1999), 'Genetics and the British insurance industry', *Journal of Medical Ethics*, 25, 157–62.
74 Cf Human Genetics Advisory Commission (1999), *Report on the Implications of Genetic Testing for Employment*, July, London: Department of Health. See also Gannon and Villiers, 'Genetic Testing and Employment' (n.12, above).
75 Feldman, D. (1999), 'The Human Rights Act 1998 and Constitutional Principles', *Legal Studies*, 19, 165.
76 Council of Europe (1997) 'Convention for the Protection of Human Rights and Dignity of the Human Being with Regard to the Application of Biology and Medicine: Convention on Human Rights & Biomedicine', *European Treaty Series*, vol.164, Oveido.
77 BMA, *Human Genetics Choice and Responsibility* (n.32, above), p.190.
78 See McGleenan, 'Genetic Testing and Screening' (n.1, above).
79 Longley, 'Who Is Calling the Piper?' (n.19, above), p.322.

8 Transport and Regulation

NICK McKERRELL, *Glasgow Caledonian University* **AND DUNCAN OSLER**, *Shepherd & Wedderburn*

Introduction

The concept of regulating transport may strike some readers as odd. In this age the motor car is sold as the ultimate symbol of personal freedom, regardless of how far from the truth that may be. However, in the 20th century we have witnessed the development of transport as a public service. Public transport is now synonymous with rail and bus travel. Both of these services were owned by the public sector, albeit in different forms.[1] Thus both were intrinsically tied to a model of state regulation.

However, over the last 20 years the model of regulation for public transport has been transformed, largely as a result of privatisation and deregulation of the rail and bus industries. In the two years since the election of the New Labour government there have been no fundamental framework changes to public transport structures[2] – in the words of the Rail regulator, there will be '"no going back" under the current Labour Government' to a nationalised UK railway system.[3] However, there has been a redirection of the philosophy of regulation which affects its objectives and in the longer term will have a structural impact on UK transport systems.

This chapter examines the regulatory framework in which public transport operates and explains its roots, looking at the immediate history of rail privatisation and bus deregulation. The authors contend that the rationale behind transport regulation is changing, and that these changes will alter transport infrastructure and opportunities within the UK. Now, it seems the rationale behind transport regulation is linked much more directly to an integrated transport policy model. However, it is strictly limited by the fact that each mode of transport and its accompanying regulatory structure remains separate and seems likely to remain so for the foreseeable future. Moreover, central government's decisions to allocate funds for infrastructure investment need to be linked to a regulated transport network. Trains can only run as far as the rail network extends and road transport of whatever form requires a well-maintained system of public roads. The compartmentalising of transport and the subsequent impact on regulation prevents the government's heralded policy of integration from being fully realised.

The 'free' motorist is a fictional character. The driving test,[4] licensing of roadworthy vehicles and the possible introduction of road tolls are elements of an existing regulatory framework. They are supported by the UK government's integrated transport policy, yet the absence of a regulatory body governing UK transport in an integrated way (as is the case with both rail and bus transport) cuts across the cohesion and effectiveness of the current framework.

Public Railway Transport

The UK Rail System and the Office of the Rail Regulator: The Recent Transformation

The structure of the UK rail industry was transformed in the 1990s. Rail privatisation was a unique and complex process, drawing as it did on the lessons learned in the privatisation of the UK telecommunications and electricity networks; many of the individuals within the government and the civil service, as well as the external advisers and business experts who drove rail industry privatisation, had benefited from the experience of these earlier industry transformations and this helped them to deliver its considerably more ambitious design and contractual structure. In the words of one of the key architects of the scheme, the process was a 'complex amalgam of privatisation, deregulation and incentivisation which will result in productivity gains',[5] but it has also been said that it 'fell far short of the conventional pattern of privatisation in the last decade'.[6] With the combination of awarding franchises to new train operating companies, the direct sale to the public of shares in Railtrack plc and the consequent disintegration of the formerly unified British Rail corporation, the privatisation process was difficult to follow as it developed and many key elements of the current structure remain only vaguely understood. For example, it is not universally appreciated that Railtrack plc does not run any passenger or freight train services on the UK rail network and that it has no direct control over who does.[7]

The 'new' structure of the railway was launched on 1 April 1994, when a large proportion of the assets formerly held by British Rail was vested in Railtrack plc. However, privatisation of railways was not completed until March 1997, shortly before the 1997 general election, when the last passenger rail services franchise was awarded by the Office of Passenger Rail Franchising (OPRAF).

Another aspect making rail privatisation unique was the attitude taken towards the system of regulation which should apply. Unlike the case of any other of the utilities the regulator was in place prior to the privatisation. The Office of the Rail Regulator (OPR) was established in April 1994 prior to the awarding of any passenger rail franchises. In addition, OPRAF itself carried out some regulatory functions when awarding the passenger service franchises. These functions covered the selection of franchisees and the placing of conditions on successful franchisees, effectively regulating the way in which rail franchises would be operated and, therefore, how rail services would be delivered. OPRAF's regulatory role continues, in that the licences it awards include continuing obligations which require to be met to avoid potential licence revocation.

An examination of regulation of the rail network needs to begin with the ORR, however, owing to its primary role, as set out in the Railways Act 1993. Coming into being on 1 December 1993, the office came into existence after the debate over the precise role of the utility regulators. Turning to the New Labour government's review of utility regulation after its election in 1997, the rail network was, perhaps surprisingly, excluded.[8] Yet the rail regulator has participated fully in the current debate over the philosophy of regulation.

Some of the criticisms levelled at regulators of other UK regulated industries could also be made of the rail regulator, at least at the time of his initial appointment. In the words of the first holder of the office,[9] the caricature of a regulator at this time was that of a regime 'dependent excessively on the whims of unelected individuals' giving inconsistent and unreasoned decisions.[10] In short, at the outset, there was no centrally coordinated or consistent rationale for regulation in the newly privatised sector, drawing in any formal way on the collective experience of the regulators of other industries. Although John Swift, then rail regulator, believed such characterisation was largely unfair, it held an 'element of truth'.[11]

Although perhaps hampered by these inauspicious beginnings, the Office of the Rail Regulator has sought to develop a coherent approach towards regulation. A year after taking office, John Swift stated: 'I have been appointed by Parliament to promote the public interest in the new restructured railway.'[12] This sort of statement was somewhat akin to the position taken by other regulators who received criticism on the basis that the 'public interest' is an imprecisely defined concept. However, direction is at hand, because the phrase is actually defined in the Railways Act 1993. The rail regulator is obliged to protect the interest of railway users, promote the use of the rail network, promote efficiency and economy on the part of railway providers, promote competition in the provision of railway services, promote measures which facilitate passengers making journeys over more than one passenger service, impose minimum restrictions on operators and enable railway service providers to plan their business with a degree of certainty.[13]

This statutory framework had been fleshed out as the regulator began to operate. For example, a list of the regulator's general duties was included in the Department of Transport's official report in 1995.[14] These ranged from the issuing of guidance on competition within the service and on track access charges to the involvement in negotiations over all access agreements to different rail services.

The natural tension between these, at times, contradictory duties was illustrated in the first years of the regulator's existence because he was closely involved in the awarding of franchises to make sure that the 'public interest' was upheld. Yet this affected to a great degree the introduction of competition in respect of passenger services, which is another of his statutory duties. The use of a franchising process, which required those wishing to be awarded a franchise to offer competitive terms for the delivery of franchised services, meant that potential franchisees would not welcome the advent of any additional competition for the services they were to run, in the form of a liberalised competitive market in passenger rail services in their chosen part of the UK rail network.

Their view would be that the necessary competition was contained in the franchise award process. Inevitably, one would take precedence over the other and indeed the regulator recognised this with his policy statement on competition: 'I believe it is necessary to introduce controls to limit the competition initially to enable the process of franchising to be carried out successfully.'[15] Thus the regulator was central in determining the nature of the privatised passenger services, and the price of ensuring that franchising was successful (in other words, that those awarded franchises were able profitably to provide passenger rail services in accordance with the terms of their franchise agreements) as was the reduction of the scope for effective competition between franchisees, at least in the short term after award.

The Scope of Railway Privatisation

During privatisation the railway industry was broken up, from a unified network into a number of different industries. This fragmentation went much further in the railway industry than any other utility privatisation. Initially, it was felt that the controller of the railway infrastructure – Railtrack plc – would remain in the public sector at least until all franchises had been transferred from the public to the private sector. This would have created a situation whereby the dominant supplier in this privatised network would have been publicly owned, which would have been a unique experience for any regulator in Britain.

However, this did not take place because, following a parliamentary statement by the secretary of state for transport in 1994, the flotation of Railtrack plc on the London and New York Stock Exchanges[16] was accelerated[17] and preceded the awarding of the majority of the franchises. So, like his counterparts at OFTEL and OFGAS, the rail regulator has had to contend with a dominant privatised supplier – albeit that Railtrack plc is only responsible for the rail network and infrastructure and only has a role in the running of passenger services to the extent of its role in relation to rail safety. But this hasty sell-off to ensure that an incoming New Labour government could not easily unwind rail privatisation created another role for the rail regulator as watchdog for Railtrack plc. As is explained later, this has taken on a new dimension since Railtrack plc has consistently failed to meet investment targets for infrastructure developments.[18]

Thus the rail regulator has developed a number of roles in the 'new' railway system, some of which are unique in the area of UK regulation and some of which share similarities with the regulators of the large utilities. ORR publications and speeches made by the regulator are important in developing roles for the regulators and creating a philosophical structure in which they can work.[19] Speaking to a law conference in 1998, the first rail regulator used the watchwords of 'Transparency, Consistency and Predictability' as key regulatory objectives.[20] These were not his own creation but had been proposed by the government at the time of its review of utilities' regulation.[21] John Swift has argued that his office carried this out and, moreover, that this approach is shared by other regulators.[22] For him the approach of the regulator in all fields should emulate the economic philosophy of one of the chancellor of the exchequer's main economic advisers, Ed Balls: 'stability through constrained discretion'.[23] The purpose of this approach is to 'protect and promote the interests of customers of the regulated markets',[24] implying that it is not possible to leave this to 'the operation of the competitive market'[25] in the rail context.

This seems to suggest that the first rail regulator believed himself to be a 'customer's advocate' in the new railway. This may be because of the competitive framework which, in the passenger rail network, is determined by the franchise. Franchisees compete with each other for custom and profit only indirectly. Therefore they provide the 'competitive' environment the customer wishes to travel in, enjoying low-price, reliable and comfortable journeys. This is far from an open free-for-all competitive market between different operators on the same route. In a sense it is 'yardstick' competition, although there is an element of direct competition as well – for example, on journeys between Scotland and London where there are two different routes. Following the logic of the 'free market', this is not a purely competitive approach, so additional protection is needed for the consumer. In a sense this echoes the argument put forward by Professor Stephen Littlechild in the early 1980s in his examination of a regulatory structure for telecommunications: 'Regulation is essentially a means of preventing the worst excesses of monopoly; it is not a substitute for competition.'[26] The major difference between this model and a model where competition is less indirect is that the regulatory structures for rail are not to be a temporary measure until complete competition is introduced.[27]

It could be argued that the ORR fitted into the model of a perfect regulator for the New Labour government. The rail regulator echoes the government's views on the philosophy of regulation and aims to become a protection for consumers. Yet the regulatory model for rail is to undergo further change, with a new incumbent of the office and the proposed statutory introduction of a Strategic Rail Authority (SRA).

Further Changes in Perceptions of the Regulatory Role

The New Labour government undertook a review of rail regulation immediately after taking office in May 1997. The first consequence of this was a Concordat between the transport minister and the rail regulator signed on 6 November 1997.[28] This was to mark a time of cooperation between central government and the regulator which did not require legislative authority. In John Swift's words, it marked 'an important step in the development of the railways as a partnership between the public and private sectors'.[29]

Yet this was only an interim measure and the conclusion of the review of railway regulation came on 16 September 1998.[30] The purpose was to review the 'shortcomings' of the present system and to see how a 'Strategic Rail Authority could rectify them'.[31] The government's main criticisms lay in the lack of 'focus' within the new railway. The 'independence' of the regulator was also a problem, particularly as he had control over sensitive areas like open access competition; that is, he was under no obligation to take into account government policy. The administration also mentioned the lack of sanctions available, the inadequacy of the regulation of the rolling stock companies (ROSCOs), the need to ensure that investment was carried out by

Railtrack and, perhaps surprisingly given Swift's assurances, the need to involve the 'views of rail users' more.[32] It seems that, although, in the first period of his existence, the regulator may have fitted into the governmental paradigm of regulation in procedural terms at least the substantive role needed to be altered.

This view is reinforced by the first major speech given by Tom Winsor, the current rail regulator, who took office on 5 July 1999.[33] He argued that the railway is emerging from a period of 'regulatory uncertainty',[34] again underlining his commitment to the government's view that there needs to be 'tougher and more effective regulation'.[35] He even criticises the underlying structure of rail regulation as having 'significant shortcomings' which 'were built into the regulatory system for railways'.[36] These words would have been unlikely to be spoken by the previous regulator, although Winsor's comments on public involvement follow similar lines to his predecessor's. 'I want the public to know that I am on their side. To date the public has been short-changed.'[37]

Thus the rail regulator is seeking to build his role as an advocate for the public who will not ask but 'demand'[38] that standards be met by both Railtrack and the train operating companies. As if to underline his new 'hard-line' attitude, he finished his address to the Railway Forum with an old-fashioned schoolmaster approach, saying there is an 'easy way or hard way' to improve railway services: 'It's your choice, but we are going to do it.'[39] The overall tone of these words suggests that a new era for rail regulation may be opening up.[40] Perhaps these words could be dismissed as the over-enthusiasm of a new regulator, but it could be something more significant: a redrawing of the boundaries of transport regulation. Rather than having a confusing mix of responsibilities, the rail regulator wants to build a larger, distinctive niche for himself.

This is underlined by the current statutory intervention in the railways. The Railways Bill[41] was introduced into the House of Commons on 7 July 1999.[42] The primary purpose of this legislation is to create a Strategic Rail Authority while abolishing the Office of the Franchising Director and the residual British Rail Board. This initiative has been well sign-posted and a shadow Strategic Rail Authority was established in September 1998.[43] The authority is meant to fill the gap identified by the government in their post-election review of rail regulation. That is to say, it will provide a 'a necessary focus for strategic planning, a means of supporting integrated transport initiatives and of supervising the disbursment of public funds'.[44] By taking on these roles it seems to make the rail regulator's job more precise. In the Bill the power of the regulator over consumer protection is transferred to the new authority. The regulator's existing duties are also to be redefined. Significantly, the promotion of competition[45] has been altered to be 'for the benefit of railway users'.[46] Further, the power to impose sanctions on breaches of licensing conditions by train operators is expanded and the sum enlarged to be without limit.[47] The Regulator also becomes much closer to central government, as he is given a new duty to 'have regard to general guidance from the Secretary of State about railway services'.[48] This essentially returns the regulator to the role he performed during the process of privatisation, as the 1993 Railways Act allowed the secretary of state to give guidance. This only lasted until 31 December 1996.[49] In a sense, then, the Office of the Rail Regulator was only really independent of government for three years. The notes to the Transport Bill state that independence is being achieved as the 'Secretary of State is now no longer exercising privatisation functions under the1993 Act'.[50]

Thus in the five years of its existence the Office of the Rail Regulator has undergone some major changes. Its early creation in the cycle of privatisation set it apart from other utility regulators. However, it meant that the regulator had to make decisions that would be critical in ensuring that the 'new' railway would be created at all: that the passenger franchises would be awarded and Railtrack directly sold. Further, the regulator had to protect the 'public interest' as defined in the Railways Act 1993 as well as promoting competition on the railways.[51] These multiple and sometimes contradictory roles made it difficult to discern the precise position of the regulator within the privatised industry. This is changing, as shown by the proposed Railways Bill and the review of regulation undertaken by New Labour. The role of the regulator will be both more focused and more linked to central government. This will raise the questions of how 'independent' the regulator will be from the administration and how the regulator will relate to the new Strategic Railway Authority.

In a sense the multiple tasks of rail regulation are now going to be shared between the regulator, the government and the SRA. The tensions that exist between distinct rationales of regulation more often confined to one institution may now exist in interorganisational disputes. Yet it must also be remembered that this is only one mode of public transport and these new structures are confined to an examination of these issues. However welcome the introduction of a strategic authority and the creation of a more precise role for the rail regulator is for the railways, it does not aid the policy aim of an integrated transport network. It has split the regulatory roles for the railway but it seems also to have separated rail from other modes of transport.

Public Bus Transport

The obvious partner to rail in an integrated transport system is the bus network, since it offers increased routes to the rail network and the possibility of service flexibility. Indeed, many of the successful bidders for the rail franchises come from privatised bus companies which had consolidated after deregulation in the 1980s. Unlike the rail system, the bus industry was never centrally controlled by a public corporation. Bus companies tended to be controlled by local authorities, although not all of them were publicly owned. However, the publicly owned companies totally dominated the provision of bus services: prior to Thatcher's election in 1979, 101 public operators provided 92 per cent of stage carriage mileage.[52] This was true for both local and national 'inter-city' services.

The Conservative government was not slow in altering the regulatory structure for bus services. These had been in place more or less unaltered since the Transport Act, 1930. This predated the nationalisation of the major utilities by the post war Labour government and it utilised a very different model of regulation from the public corporation norm used by these industries. The 1930 Act divided the country into seven areas in which the licensing of bus routes was carried out by an official: the traffic commissioner. Thus the planning of bus routes was centrally controlled by a government official. For the reforming Thatcher administration this symbolised public sector obstruction of the 'market' place and entrepreneurial skill in running bus services.

The transformation of the role of the traffic commissioners – in essence the deregulation of the buses – occurred in two stages through the 1980s. Firstly, the Transport Act 1980 ended the regulation of express services: that is, longer services between cities and towns. The onus of proof was also changed for new entrants to local bus services. The commissioner had to show that any new service was not in the public interest, rather than the entrant having to prove that the service was needed. This 'limbo' in which the regulatory regime of the buses was put lasted only for five years as the Transport Act 1985 ended any role for the traffic commissioner in licensing and removed all quantity restrictions for local services. This radical deregulatory move took place at the same time as the first major utility privatisations of the Thatcher era. The initial buses White Paper[53] was met with an avalanche of objections. There were eight thousand responses, the great majority of which were opposed to the plans.[54] Thus this area of public transport became the first to be removed from any regulatory boundaries.

These regulatory changes were coupled with a move to privatise the publicly owned National Bus Company. Although operating across England and Wales,[55] the NBC devolved a lot of power to its local operators. This was because the company grew by stealth, acquiring local bus companies. Thus the scheme to privatise took the form of selling each subsidiary. Local authorities ran other significant publicly owned services. Although the 1985 Act did not privatise these, it did require the local authorities to form separate companies, which paved the way to their eventual sell-off. The absence of any clear regulatory structure[56] was meant to allow new entrants into the bus market. Yet during the decade following deregulation there was an intense consolidation in the industry. By the mid-1990s a few 'giant' operators dominated the provision of bus services. In 1994, nine bus companies controlled 56 per cent of the bus market throughout Britain. Largely these companies came from privatised public operators – both National Bus Company and local authorities – who used their strong local position to expand into other areas by buying up other bus companies: a kind of 'bus imperialism'. The expected emergence of new entrants into the deregulated market did not occur to any great extent even though there was a large independent sector of bus and coach operators prior to deregulation. The notable exception to this was Stagecoach, which emerged from a mini-bus rental service in the 1970s to become an international transport company.[57]

The reason these developments are significant from a regulatory perspective is that they illustrate the difficulty of completely removing regulation from the delivery of public transport. Although the model for the bus industry was of its complete liberalisation from regulatory 'obstacles', the reality was that, because of the tendency to consolidate in the industry, there was significant intervention from the competition authorities. As noted earlier, the mid-1990s was the high point of the period of consolidation in the industry. This was illustrated by a number of 'turf wars' between different operators. Between 1987 and 1994, the Office of Fair Trading received 541 representations regarding the bus industry. Further, the Monopolies and Mergers Commission had to rule in a number of cases: between 1989 and 1995, the MMC published 16 reports on bus services. Thus these authorities had to carry out reactive regulation, responding to the worst excesses of unbridled competition in the industry. Perhaps unsurprisingly, they were at the forefront of the argument for the reregulation of the industry. Sir Brian Carsberg, the former director-general of the OFT, bluntly stated to the Transport Select Committee's investigation of bus deregulation that 'the regulatory system is not strong enough'.[58] Significantly, that particular report,[59] published in 1995, came out in favour of creating a specialist regulator for the bus industry. This would not be a resurrection of the old role of the traffic commissioners;[60] rather, the regulator would have 'a specialist expertise in the bus industry and act as a referee, quickly on the spot, able to settle disputes in a firm and fair manner'.[61]

The Conservative government of that time rejected these recommendations, falling back on its original justification for deregulation in their official response: 'The present regime of deregulated bus services run almost entirely by private sector operators provides the best means of delivering effectively the services people want.'[62] Yet this obscures the fact that in the preceding period the Conservative government had made some changes to the bus industry. Notably, in 1995, regulations were introduced to give the traffic commissioners more power to deal with traffic congestion.[63] This was actually denounced by the Confederation of Passenger Transport as an attempt to 're-regulate the industry by the back door'.[64] In a sense this illustrates the quandary which the Conservative government found itself in as regards the regulation of bus transport. After introducing complete liberalisation this created its own problems in the haphazard nature of service delivery and the eventual consolidation of the industry. This necessarily involved the competition authorities in a form of regulation which they felt ill-equipped to deal with. So the deregulatory ethos contradicted the concrete reality of running public services. This contradiction never arose in any other industry as the utility privatisations created regulators, although arguably their role was not clearly defined. This *de facto* absence of regulation is in marked distinction to the broad regulation present in the rail industry, at least in the early stages of the privatisation.

So did the election of the New Labour government mark a return to a regulated bus service or a review, as in the context of rail regulation? Clearly, if the policy preferences were to be believed, the support for an integrated transport service requires buses to play a prominent role. On issuing a discussion document on the role of buses, the deputy prime minister and the head of the Department of Environment, Transport and the Regions (DETR), John Prescott, said, 'We need to secure greater accountability to the wider travelling community and give elected local authorities powers – and resources – to *promote* higher quality bus services'(emphasis added).[65] This illustrates the extent and the limits of elements of the current government's policy on transport. Quality bus services will be promoted rather than directly operated by local authorities; thus there is no question of reversing the process of privatisation. Moreover, there is no mention of reregulating entry to the bus market. This is confirmed by the proposals on quality partnerships (QPs).[66] At present, these involve a voluntary agreement between local authorities and bus operators to invest in services. Local authorities may introduce traffic management services, while bus operators may invest in new, more 'passenger-friendly' vehicles. However, as this is only voluntary, it does not stop smaller operators using the same facilities without investing in its own services. In short, this method of regulation could only really work where one dominant operator ran the majority of bus services. The government senses this and believes that 'QPs would be more effective, and more widely adopted, if they had statutory force'.[67] This could work by setting minimum standards which had to be met by all bus operators on the specified routes and which could be enforced by the traffic commissioners. In essence, this incorporates a type of franchising while allowing many bus services to run the same routes. Thus regulation continues to give priority to quality over quantity of actual services. This is very different from the method of regulation adopted prior to the 1985 Transport Act. It also leaves the private sector intact to make profits very much in line with New Labour philosophy. This move to promote statutory QPs is at a very early stage and only at the discussion paper level.

The discussion document also raises the possibility of further enhancing the traffic commissioners' role. This would include raising the financial standards needed to enter the bus market, the varying of their powers of sanctions and increasing the power to intervene when traffic conditions demand it. Thus, as well as reducing traffic congestion, environmental reasons could also be taken into account.[68] The paper also hints at increasing the role of the traffic commissioners in hearing consumer complaints along with the Bus Appeals Body,[69] which means that the commissioners would combine enforcing quality on the roads with hearing customer complaints. This again emphasises the importance of quality rather than quantity regulation.

But how does this fit in with the new structures for rail, as seems vital, given the commitment to an integrated policy? This is underlined by the dominance of bus operators in operating rail franchises and the continual existence of passenger transport authorities[70] which, in certain metropolitan areas, used to run bus services in close coordination with their local rail services. It has already been noted that the rail regulatory model is very much focused solely on rail services. The only real mention of intermodal transport in the buses discussion paper comes in the examination of quality contracts and local transport plans. Quality contracts are an extension of the quality partnerships into sole franchises for bus routes. The government's support for this franchising scheme is much less enthusiastic than previously thought. Quality contracts would only be supported in local areas, 'where a case can be made in the light of special local circumstances'.[71] The examination of local transport plans notes that bus deregulation has 'significantly reduced the scope for local authorities to influence bus services in their areas'.[72] However, there is no mention of how bus services could be integrated into rail services. This illustrates again the lack of a comprehensive transport consciousness in regulating transport.

An examination of current developments in bus and rail regulation shows that, although these modes of public transport are closely linked, institutionally they remain separate. The two regulatory structures will operate largely independently of each other. Moreover, the types of regulation are not similar. There will be no bus regulator akin to the Office of the Rail Regulator; equally, no Strategic Bus Authority will be in place. The method of bus regulation is much 'lighter' than the potential power that the rail regulator has in fining operators and Railtrack. It could be argued that the government has deliberately avoided a stronger regulatory model and in fact has never used the phrase 'reregulation' for the bus industry. These differences in regulatory powers underline the lack of cross-transport cooperation, which will pose problems in introducing an integrated transport policy.

Integrated Transport and Investment Decisions on Infrastructure Projects

Although there has been a tendency to separate regulation of different modes of transport – notably road, rail, air and sea – the existence of a Department of Transport (now amalgamated into the Department of Environment, Transport and the Regions, DETR) has provided the opportunity to legislate across transport modes. The failure to take up such an opportunity is perhaps not surprising, however, given that the idea of an integrated transport policy is a relatively recent one. Since the launch of the government's White Papers and its integrated transport policy,[73] a more coherent, cross-modal strategy might be hoped for. To date, this has not been the case and the recent announcement of a Strategic Rail Authority[74] is distinctly lacking in any integrated elements, as noted above.

The important role of light rail systems, such as the London and Glasgow Undergrounds, the Newcastle Metro, the Croydon Tramlink and Manchester's new transport infrastructure, must not be underestimated. Their importance in achieving efficient transport within and between our cities[75] deserves close and dedicated review. In addition, there are numerous proposed schemes across Britain in various stages of development. These should all be taken forward in a way which enhances, rather than conflicts with or disadvantages, existing transport provision, subject to overriding social policy concerns such as the environment and social exclusion.

In fact, rather than focusing on integrated elements of the transport policy, the prevailing emphasis seems to be on the merits of public transport versus private transport. This focus is exemplified by the heated debate over user-paid tolls for roads and workplace parking charges, promoted by the government and the environmental lobby as a disincentive to ever-increasing car use but challenged by motoring organisations as an attack on the basic freedoms of the private motorist.

The rationale behind the use of these 'carrot and stick' policies is that to reduce road traffic there is a need to penalise the private motorist.[76] In conjunction with this, it is usually assumed that some form of 'carrot' will be created in the form of improved public transport, although this is not always immediately evident. Transport advisers appreciate that it is not enough to price against the car: improved and enhanced public transport services must also be developed and delivered.

However, any analysis looking at public or private transport as straight alternatives is over-simplistic, given the dominance of car use and the more fractured position of public transport. A better approach is for any geographical area to analyse the alternative modes of transport, their respective advantages and the costs of delivering improvements, regardless of any prior existing modal preferences. Only in this way, with an integrated approach to the regulation of transport, can the regulation of transport in the UK deliver optimum economic and social benefits.

That is not to say that there are not clear and widely accepted benefits in, for instance, developing greatly increased public passenger transport services, and, for cost and flexibility, investing in a mode of transport (or in combinations) for a particular area where the demographics and economic activities support it. One example, as outlined in the *Travel Choices for Scotland* White Paper, is the use of bus passenger services in Scotland, which is encouraged to a greater degree than the use of buses under the UK White Paper. Perhaps understandably, this focuses on the different concerns for England, exemplified and dominated by the south east, namely over-congestion and environmental pollution.

Nonetheless, despite the well-intentioned policy objectives set out in the integrated transport White Papers, there are few prospects for a truly integrated transport system in the UK unless some form of integrated (which would ideally be dynamic cross-modal) regulation also takes place, if this is not achieved by the establishment of a Strategic Rail Authority which, however well-empowered to regulate the rail industry, cannot adjudicate or moderate between competing claims for improvement of road and rail infrastructure.[77]

The next best solution might be to develop systems and procedures at least to ensure that there is some discussion of the implications for one mode of transport of a particular investment decision, not unlike a planning inquiry where submissions from interested parties are intended to facilitate consideration of all relevant issues. Thus an element of direct participation is introduced into the delivery of transport services, at least indirectly.

Turning to decision making as regards transport infrastructure investment, this has links to two disconnected administrative areas, namely the UK planning process (which is administered on a local basis by local authorities, except where responsibility for decision making is taken over by the secretary of state) and financial controls and holding of the purse strings for provision of the additional public sector funding which is usually required, given the high costs of infrastructure investment.

Whilst this is the case in relation to many road projects, the picture in the rail sector is clouded by investment in infrastructure being controlled by Railtrack – itself regulated by the Office of the Rail Regulator – and, shortly, the Strategic Rail Authority, and, as regards the extent and nature of rail services, by OPRAF. Neither of these bodies is required to have regard to the planning or other implications of any proposed investment outside the rail sphere and neither is required to have regard to the implications for other modes of transport. Again, this lack of overall coherence and integration is an unfortunate limitation which shows every sign of remaining in place under the current government.

Conclusions

It may be naive to suppose that there would ever be a single integrated UK transport regulator. Under the British parliamentary system, this role is really one for a government minister, spanning as it does so many facets of political life, and it would never be ceded to a non-elected body. It is important, nevertheless, to understand the fundamental limitations of the present disparate regulatory structures and for the 'transport debate' to move on from the present public versus private arguments.

In one sense, this puts the regulatory travails of transport in context. As explored above, there has been significant change in regulation since the 1997 general election. This has occurred both in structural terms with the creation of the Strategic Rail Authority and in changing the nature and, perhaps, to a degree the philosophy of the Office of the Rail Regulator. Perhaps this could be seen as part of the moves towards 'better regulation' on the part of the government since 1997.

Markets have been both constituted and restrained by transport regulation. In rail the role of regulation was extremely diverse as it had a role both in creating the privatised industry and in holding back its worse excesses. For bus transport, although there was deregulation with the alteration of the role of the traffic commissioners, the increased workload of the competition authorities illustrated that there could not be an elimination of this aspect of regulation. Thus the different definitions of regulation found institutional form in the field of transport.

By examining each regulatory structure currently used in the field of public transport, this chapter has aimed to show how each has its own specific history but, more importantly, each is an independent organisation with no history of cooperation. This is significant from a regulatory standpoint because transport regulation is not viewed in a holistic way. The disparate nature of regulation in this area means that the different rationales for regulating public services are separated by different institutions. For example, the role of the traffic commissioner is qualitatively different from the role of the rail regulator. Equally, the Strategic Rail Authority will perform a different task than the local authorities with their local transport plans. Perhaps these distinctions are inevitable in a complex system of transport regulation, particularly one which combines the private and public sectors. Yet it must be accepted that a broader policy aim of an integrated transport system will be difficult to achieve when such a distinct system of regulation remains in place.

Notes

1 Rail owned as a nationalised 'public corporation' and bus services controlled largely by local authorities.
2 That is, there has been no process of renationalisation in the industries.
3 ORR, speech, 26 January 1999, 'Regulating a Privatised Rail Industry: Lessons from the UK Experience', para. 5.
4 Which was made more difficult on 4 May 1999: Press Release from Driving Standards Agency, 2/99.
5 Foster, Sir Christopher (1994), 'The Economics of Rail Privatisation', unpublished, p.1.
6 *Financial Times*, 7 March 1994.
7 The director of passenger rail franchising has a statutory duty to award rail franchises and a licence from the rail regulator is also required.
8 Although, significantly, the ORR did make a submission to the committee: ORR (1997), *Review of Utility Regulation*, London: HMSO, doc. 51.
9 John Swift QC, a competition lawyer.
10 ORR, speech, 25 March 1998, 'Transparency, Consistency and Predictability as Regulatory Objectives', para. 2.
11 *Ibid*, para. 3.
12 *Financial Times*, 12 January 1995.
13 These duties are listed in s.4(1) (*a*)–(*g*).
14 Cm 2806, 1994–5.
15 ORR (1994), *Competition for Railway Passenger Services*, London: HMSO, doc. 17, p.1.
16 Shares in Railtrack plc were offered to the public as 'stapled stock' capable of

being traded on the London and New York Stock Exchanges, to ensure sufficient initial appetite for the flotation.

17 *Hansard*, vol. 250, 24 November 1994, 759.

18 And on 19 August 1999, Tom Winsor, newly appointed as rail regulator, announced the first ever 'enforcement order' requiring Railtrack plc to deliver improved passenger rail service levels of punctuality in the following months at the risk of a fine of up to £40 million if it failed to do so.

19 This is one of the reasons that the regulator contributed to the government review of regulation. See n.7, above.

20 ORR, 'Transparency' (n.10, above).

21 *Ibid.*, para. 1.

22 They met four times a year to discuss issues of regulatory importance.

23 'Transparency' (n.10, above), para. 24.

24 *Ibid.*, para. 36.

25 *Ibid.*

26 Littlechild, Stephen (1983), *Regulation of British Telecom's Profitability*, London: HMSO, p.7.

27 Admittedly, Littlechild himself wrote of a more permanent form of regulation when examining the water industry: Littlechild, Stephen (1987), *Economic Regulation of Privatised Water Authorities*, London: HMSO.

28 Press release of ORR, 97/31.

29 *Ibid.*

30 DOETR (1998), *A New Deal for the Railways*, London: Department of the Environment, Transport and the Regions.

31 *Ibid.*, para. 5.

32 *Ibid.*, para. 6.

33 ORR, speech, 9 July 1999, 'The New Regulatory Agenda'.

34 *Ibid*, para. 1

35 *Ibid*, para. 2.

36 *Ibid.*, para. 14.

37 *Ibid.*, para. 19

38 *Ibid.*, para. 15.

39 *Ibid.*, para. 34.

40 Emphasised by the speech's title.

41 Bill 133 of 1998–9.

42 This followed the White Paper (Cmnd 3897) on transport, published in July 1998.

43 Sir Alastair Morton, ex-Euro Tunnel chief was appointed chair of the British Rail Board in April 1999; part of the responsibility of this was to act as part-time chairman of the shadow authority.

44 HC Research Paper 99/72, p.14.

45 See above.

46 Clause 18.

47 Although it has to be a 'reasonable amount' (clause 19).

48 Clause 18.

49 1993 Act.

50 HC (1998–9), para. 44.

51 Which in part was in conflict with the franchising scheme.

52 Savage, I. (1985), *The Deregulation of Bus Services*, Aldershot: Gower, p.7.

53 Cm 9300, 1983–4.

54 Savage, *The Deregulation of Bus Services* (n.52, above), p.12.

55 The Scottish Bus Group had a similar structure. This was not privatised until the Transport (Scotland) Act 1989.

56 Although the commissioners remained, with extremely limited powers.

57 Stagecoach was also heavily involved in the rail privatisation process.
58 HC 54, II (1995–6), p.23.
59 HC 54 (1995–6).
60 Although they would retain their power over inspecting the quality of buses entering the market.
61 HC 54, p.liv.
62 HC 392 (1995–6), p.ix.
63 SI 1994/3724.
64 *Financial Times*, 2 February 1995.
65 DETR (1999), 'Foreword', *From Workhorse to Thoroughbred: A Better Role for Bus Travel*, London: DOETR.
66 *Ibid.*, s.4.
67 *Ibid.*, s.4.3.
68 Although the government claims that this would need primary legislation: *ibid.*, s.10.9.
69 A new body established by the Confederation of Public Transport.
70 Created by the Transport Act 1968.
71 DETR, *From Workhorse to Thoroughbred* (n.65, above), s.6.7.
72 *Ibid.*, s.3.6.
73 *A New Deal for Transport*, the UK White Paper issued by the Department of Environment, Transport and the Regions, and *Travel Choices for Scotland*, the Scottish Integrated Transport White Paper, The Scottish Office. They were published on consecutive days, 21 and 22 July 1998.
74 Announcement (23 July) of the Railways Bill launching a Strategic Rail Authority. (See above.)
75 As well as sensible commuter solutions which will be taken up, and not ignored in favour of the car.
76 It is also seen as creating financial benefits for the public purse.
77 Nor, indeed, can the regulatory bodies below or in parallel with it do so.

9 Environmental Law in the United Kingdom

FRANCIS McMANUS, ***University of Edinburgh Napier*** **AND COLIN INNES,** ***Shepherd & Wedderburn***

Introduction

Of fundamental importance to modern commercial practice is the requirement of businesses to comply with the various laws relating to environmental pollution. The need for firms in the UK to comply with environmental law steadily increases with the passage of time. After very briefly looking at the historical development of the law, this chapter examines the main areas of environmental law, together with the public agencies responsible for enforcing the law.

During the 19th century, responsibility for the enforcement of environmental law rested very much at local level with the police commissions,[1] local authorities and, to a much lesser extent, parochial boards. The fact that responsibility for implementing environmental law was shared amongst a number of public bodies had an undoubtedly detrimental effect on the implementation of the law. It also confused the general public as to which body was responsible for enforcing the law.[2] This is a theme to which we will return later in this chapter.

The 20th century witnessed a reduction in the number of local authorities. However, since the Second World War ad hoc bodies charged with regulatory control over both pollution of the atmosphere and water have come into being.

The European Union and Environmental Regulation

As will be evident from much of the contents of this chapter, the EU plays an increasingly significant role in environmental regulation in the UK. Although the original Treaty of Rome[3] did not make any specific reference to the environment, objectives such as the improvement of living and working conditions,[4] equality between Member States in respect of the regulation of business[5] and the harmonisation of market regulation have resulted in a considerable body of environmental regulation through a series of Directives.

The Single European Act 1986 enacted new Treaty Articles which dealt specifically with environmental matters[6] and ensured that environmental considerations were given high priority when considering economic matters.[7] The development of European environmental policy continued with the Maastricht Treaty,[8] which increased standards of environmental protection, introduced the concept of sustainability to the Treaty of Rome and embraced the precautionary principle. In addition, title XVI now sets out four principal objectives of environmental policy:

1 to preserve, protect and improve the quality of the environment;
2 to contribute towards the protection of human health;
3 to ensure prudent and rational utilisation of national resources; and
4 promotion of measures at an international level to deal with regional or worldwide environmental problems.

The primary legislative instruments of the EU in this context have been Directives, which require implementation by Member States, and Regulations, which become directly applicable in Member States. Particularly important in the environmental context is the stage at which an individual can rely on a Directive. European jurisprudence has created the doctrine of 'direct effect'. This provides that, if a directive is sufficiently precise and clear, an individual can rely on the provisions of the Directive where the individual Member State has not implemented it into national law within the time limit specified in the Directive.

Increasingly, UK environmental legislation is being directly influenced by the EU. Recent important examples include the IPPC Directive,[9] the Urban Waste Water Treatment Directive[10] and the Landfill Directive.[11] In addition, the EU is working towards the Water Framework Directive, which will have radical implications for the management of the water resources in the UK, and continues to examine the question of civil liability for environmental damage. It would appear that the EU will have an ever-increasing role in developing environmental regulation.

Air Pollution

The London Smog disaster of 1952 made clear the fact that air pollution had a pronounced detrimental effect on human health and the Beaver Committee was established to investigate the problem. Its report[12] was almost entirely accepted by the government and the recommendations of the Committee were incorporated in the Clean Air Act, 1956.

The fundamental problem which had to be tackled was that atmospheric pollution was generated not only by industry but also by domestic premises. For the first time since the cholera epidemics of the 1830s and 1840s, the government had to take positive action in relation to domestic activities. Traditionally, British governments have found great difficulty in interfering with domestic activities. Indeed, Vogel has argued that there is a fundamental principle in British politics that British governments should make every effort to avoid coercing its own citizenry.[13]

Another major obstacle which had to be addressed was the issue of funding – that is, it was obvious that vast sums of money would be required for providing the means necessary to reduce pollution of the atmosphere from both industrial and domestic sources. Another more nebulous but nonetheless formidable hurdle which the government faced in reforming the law relating to air pollution was the attitude which prevailed at the time (and had done so since Victorian times) to the effect that atmospheric pollution was indicative of economic prosperity. While the sentiment expressed in the apothegm, 'where there's dirt, there's money', may have been less pronounced after the London Smog disaster, it did to some extent persist in the mind both of the public and of industry. It would therefore have to be replaced as the principal means of combating air pollution. However, almost equally clear was the fact that a legal regime which would be heavily dependent on fixed standards was probably inappropriate on the grounds of inflexibility. The 1956 Act, which was heavily amended by the Clean Air Act 1968, was repealed and re-enacted by the Clean Air Act 1993.

The Clean Air Act 1993

The Clean Air Act, 1956 (now the 1993 Act) in effect instituted a completely new regime as far as the control of industrial pollution was concerned. The Act divides roughly into three separate parts – namely, general, industrial and domestic provisions.

Smoke, grit and dust In summary, the Act makes it an offence to emit dark smoke[14] from a chimney of any building. The Act makes further provision for reducing pollution from furnaces *inter alia* by regulating the capacity of furnaces to produce smoke, grit and dust. Furthermore, chimney heights are regulated to ensure that they are of a sufficient height to disperse effluvium.

Smoke control areas It was beyond peradventure that domestic premises which were heavily dependent on bituminous fuels as a source of heat were partly responsible for the London Smog disaster. The status quo was not an option. Something had to be done quickly to remedy the situation. So-called 'command and control' legislation would need to be employed to secure the necessary improvements. It was also equally clear that the requisite legislative measures would have to interfere with individual liberty. The Englishman's castle, replete with its traditional fireplace and chimney, was no longer to be sacrosanct. In the last analysis the government opted for the concept of smoke control areas.[15] In essence, the 1956 Act (now contained in Part 3 of the Clean Air Act 1993) empowered local authorities to set up smoke control areas. After such an area came into existence it was an offence, subject to certain defences, for the occupier of premises to emit smoke from the chimney of a building to which the relevant order related,[16] on pain of penalty.[17]

The above measures indeed had a profound effect on individual liberty. The other notable feature in the concept of smoke control areas was that their inauguration and operation was to be the concern of local authorities in Great Britain.[18] The conferring of such a responsibility on local authorities in the UK ranked, in effect, as an endorsement of the confidence central government had in local government, which did not possess particularly high status in the minds of the public in the immediate post-war years.[19]

The concept of smoke control areas was embraced with great enthusiasm by local authorities in the UK. The 1960s and 1970s saw large areas of urban Britain being designated smoke control areas. The effect of the smoke control area policy had a profoundly beneficial effect on the external environment.

Environmental Protection Act 1990

The 1980s witnessed an increased awareness of the harm being done to the environment, especially by industry. There was also a realisation that the existing legislation, mainly in the form of the Clean Air Acts 1956 and 1968 and the Alkali Acts which simply addressed a single medium, namely the atmosphere, were rather myopic in outlook. In other words, a more holistic approach was required.

Integrated pollution control and local authority air pollution control Part 1 of the Environmental Protection Act 1990 (EPA) introduced the concept of integrated pollution control (IPC) into UK air pollution control. It was the intention of the EPA to make industries which posed a substantial threat to the environment in general subject to integrated pollution control, and industries which possessed the capacity to pollute simply the air subject to local authority air pollution control (LAPC). The EPA represents a continuing trend in the law of the UK towards a more holistic approach to pollution control. Section 2 of the EPA gives the Secretary of State power to prescribe by regulations any description of process for which authorisation is required.[20] The Environmental Protection (Prescribed Processes and Substances) Regulations 1991[21] designate a number of processes which require to be authorised for the purposes of Part 1 of the EPA. Schedule 1 to the Regulations divides the various processes into two categories, Part A and Part B processes. Part A processes relate to activities and the like which have the capacity to pollute more than one environmental medium and are therefore subject to integrated pollution control,[22] whereas Part B processes are likely simply to affect the atmosphere. As far as England and Wales are concerned, Part A processes are currently regulated by the Environment Agency, whereas Part B processes are regulated by local authorities. In Scotland, however, since 1996, both Part A and Part B processes are regulated by the Scottish Environmental Protection Agency (SEPA).

Enforcement The EPA establishes its own machinery for the enforcement of its provisions. The devices employed are similar in nature to those found in other legal regimes, including the Health and Safety at Work Act 1974 and the Food Safety Act 1990. Under s.13, the Environment Agency or SEPA is empowered to serve an enforcement notice if it is of the opinion that the person carrying on the prescribed process under an authorisation is contravening any condition. Under s.14, if the enforcing authority is of the opinion that the carrying on of a prescribed process, or the carrying on in a particular manner, under an authorisation involves an imminent risk of serious pollution to the environment, the authority is required to serve a prohibition notice on the person carrying on the process. The significance of a prohibition notice is that it is more draconian than the enforcement notice, in that the former can direct that the authorisation in question ceases to have effect until the notice is withdrawn. Except where the relevant notice implements a direction of the Secretary of State, an appeal lies to him against either an enforcement or a prohibition notice.

Integrated Pollution Prevention and Control (IPPC)

As outlined above, Great Britain has had a form of integrated pollution control since the passing of the EPA. The European Community has also considered the question of environmental regulation and decided that Europe-wide standards should apply. The result was the adoption of a Directive in 1996 concerning integrated pollution prevention and control which was implemented in Great Britain by the Pollution Prevention and Control (PCC) Act 1999. Whilst IPC and IPPC are relatively similar, IPPC covers a far greater number of installations including not only end processes but also input processes, looking at issues such as energy efficiency, noise and vibration and accident prevention. As with the IPC regime, SEPA will regulate all processes in Scotland. In England and Wales, local authorities will retain responsibility for the bulk of the 1500 or so IPPC installations which they currently regulate under the LAPC, with the Environment Agency having responsibility for the balance. New applications for prescribed processes will need to comply with the Act and guidance issued under it. Existing installations must be IPPC-compliant by 2007 at the latest, although there will be a staged process to ensure that in practice most sectors are governed by the regime prior to the official date.

The government intends to issue sectoral guidance containing clear indicative performance standards for plant and, in setting emission standards, the regulator must have regard to the guidance and ensure that processes conform to the indicative standards set out therein. The regulator will have to explain why he or she agreed to any departure from the standards. To assist the regulator, Government Guidance Notes[23] will be issued indicating when a departure might be appropriate, although it is clear that the standards set in the Guidance Notes are minimum requirements and that, when environmental conditions merit it, stricter conditions should apply.

When an operator applies for a new permit under IPPC, he will be obliged to provide a site report identifying any pre-existing contamination and a further report at the time of closure of the installation. Pollution appearing in the second report but not the first will be deemed to have been caused by the operator and the onus will be on him to prove that he is not responsible for it. Any contamination identified at closure of the installation will need to be remedied to the standard prior to commencement of the IPPC process rather than the standard of suitability for use set out in Part IIA of the EPA (the New Contaminated Land Regime).

The consultation papers specifically point out that negotiated agreements in relation to energy efficiency matters might offer an alternative to site-specific conditions being imposed in a permit by the regulator.

Such agreements would, however, have to deliver a level of energy efficiency at least equal to that which would have been delivered had the requirement been set through separate permit conditions. There is no mandatory period at present in which the regulator has to review IPPC permits, although the draft Regulations[24] do set out criteria for setting review periods, including the expected rate of technological advance in a sector and the sectoral investment cycles themselves, the risk and level of environmental impacts associated with a sector and the likelihood of operators in a sector undertaking improvements on their own account. The draft Regulations also acknowledge that, where there is a review/monitoring function contained in other regulatory regimes,[25] the review period under IPPC can be staggered accordingly.

The review periods set by the regulator indicate the maximum length of time between permit reviews, although in practice reviews will occur, for example, where pollution caused by an installation is of such significance that the permit emission limits need to be revised or where substantial changes in best available technique make it possible to reduce an installation's emissions without imposing excessive costs. One point which does emerge from the consultation papers is that industries which can be seen as comparatively clean and willing to undertake changes in technology where appropriate will encounter more infrequent permit reviews than those which require prompting. However, at the end of the day, there does seem to be an opportunity for all sectors of industry to put their case to the regulator and influence his or her decision in setting the applicable permit review period.

The concept of IPPC is broader than IPC and illustrates a growing belief that environmental objectives can be reached through a number of different sources.[26] It is noteworthy, however, that the government received considerable criticism in relation to the way in which the PPC Act (which contains only six sections and a number of schedules) was drafted. The Act is very short. Given the importance of IPPC in the context of environmental regulation, it was suggested that the government should not devolve the implementation of the legislation to subsequent Regulations. Ultimately, however, the government's view prevailed and the PPC Act is now law.[27]

Air Quality

UK air pollution law has tended to concentrate on controlling pollution from specific sources, in contradistinction to dealing with air pollution on a more global basis. Part IV of the Environment Act 1995 introduces an innovatory approach to air pollution control. Under s.80 a duty is placed on the Secretary of State to prepare and publish a national air quality strategy which contains policies with respect to the assessment or management of the quality of the air. The strategy may also contain policies for implementing EU obligations or international agreements to which the UK is party. A duty is placed on the Secretary of State to keep the strategy under review. The strategy may also be modified. In preparing the new strategy, the Secretary of State is required to consult both the Environment Agency and the SEPA. In discharging their pollution control functions both these agencies are required to have regard to the strategy. The United Kingdom National Air Quality Strategy was published in 1997.[28]

Under s.82 of the 1995 Act, a local authority is required to carry out a review of both the current and the future air quality within its area. The local authority is required to assess whether the national air quality standards and objectives[29] are being achieved or are likely to be achieved. Under s.83, if it appears that any air quality standards or objectives are not being achieved or are not likely to be achieved within the relevant period,[30] the local authority is required to designate the area a 'designated area'. Under s.84, the local authority is required to prepare an action plan in relation to any part of the area where either the relevant objectives are not being met or the objectives are not likely to be achieved within the relevant period.

Part IV of the 1995 Act represents a more holistic approach to UK environmental control and the move towards quantitative environmental standards. The existence of such standards is conducive to local authorities being more publicly accountable as far as their stewardship of the environment is concerned. The 1995 Act is also significant in that it reaffirms the government's confidence in local authorities in such a role. Arguably, it would have been more logical to confer the duties placed on local authorities by the Act on either the Environment Agency or SEPA.

Noise

The development of substantive noise law in the United Kingdom has been piecemeal and can be described as a veritable hotchpotch.[31] A variety of unrelated statutes govern various forms of noise pollution. There has never been any coherent noise policy in the UK. Indeed, Lowe and Ward argue that UK environmental law as a whole has no guiding principles.[32] The authors go on to argue that environmental policy in the UK occupies a position of 'low politics' which has resulted in a pragmatic, piecemeal and incremental development of environmental law. Some authors have argued that British environmental policy as a whole is prone to ad hoc improvisational and piecemeal responses. This state of affairs has led to a lack of direction and a confusing medley of institutions and laws.[33] In the present authors' opinion, British noise law would seem to square comfortably with this description. Furthermore, the substantive law, with the possible exception of the Noise Act 1996, has never been prefaced by either widespread public or parliamentary debate. Noise pollution control, therefore, occupies a position of low politics.

As far as noise law is concerned, there has also been difficulty not only in formulating appropriate substantive law but also in providing appropriate enforcement machinery. Indeed, Howarth argues that the task of translating broadly, and often imprecisely, formulated environmental goals into the precise detail for effective regulatory law and also providing for appropriately constituted regulatory authorities, properly empowered to oversee its adherence, remains a fundamental challenge to law and legal systems.[34] It is suggested that this view is particularly apposite as far as UK noise law and policy is concerned. In the limited space available in this chapter, we must confine our discussion to the law relating to neighbourhood noise, which is currently attracting increasing attention, not least in terms of the popular media coverage.

The Environmental Protection Act 1990

The main corpus of substantive law dealing with neighbourhood noise pollution is now contained in Part III of the Environmental Protection Act 1990 (EPA) which places a duty on a local authority to abate statutory nuisances occurring within its area. The statutory nuisance removal provisions of EPA have generated a plethora of complicated case law, with the outcome of a particular case depending upon somewhat fine distinctions.[35]

Statutory nuisance and Scots law The courts have assimilated the concept of nuisance as used in statute with that at common law. This may pose problems as far as Scotland is concerned since, there, one needs to prove *culpa* (or fault) on the part of the defender for liability to exist.[36]

Advantages and disadvantages of nuisance While one of the present authors has discussed the advantages and disadvantages of the law of nuisance as an instrument of environmental improvement elsewhere,[37] it would be useful briefly to summarise the merits and demerits of nuisance law in this context.

One of the main advantages of the law of nuisance is that it is sufficiently flexible to allow new factors to be taken into account when determining whether a given state of affairs is capable of ranking as a nuisance. The list of the various factors is not closed. However, the courts have not displayed a great deal of imagination in developing this aspect of the law of nuisance.[38] The law of nuisance can also be invoked to deal with noise from a variety of sources.

As far as the disadvantages of the law of nuisance is concerned, the main disadvantage in the view of the authors is that the law of nuisance is really based on the protection of the rights of proprietors of land from external interference.[39] The courts, in ascertaining if a given state of affairs is an unreasonable use of land on the part of the defendant and, therefore, constitutes a nuisance in law, essentially carries out a crude balancing exercise between the defendant's proprietary rights and those of the plaintiff.[40] In so doing, however, the courts have set little, if any, store on the effect that the adverse state of affairs has on the general environment.[41] In the present authors' view, this somewhat myopic approach to nuisance law fundamentally detracts from the efficiency of nuisance as an instrument of pollution control.

The second main disadvantage is that nuisance is reactive in nature; that is to say, the relevant authority needs to wait until a noise nuisance comes into existence before it can take the relevant corrective action. Thirdly, the law of nuisance is very technical in nature and over-complicated.[42] The upshot of the law being so complicated is that in order to command public support the relevant law needs to be made transparent and readily understood by the public. Therefore it is suggested that nuisance as the main instrument of environmental control for noise is fairly limited.

However, notwithstanding the fact that the substantive law of nuisance is complicated in nature, it is, from the evidence available,[43] supported by local authority environmental health officers who are responsible for enforcing the law. There are possibly a number of reasons why environmental health officers are so supportive of the concept of nuisance. Given the esoteric nature of nuisance, the officer investigating complaints about neighbourhood noise would, in practice, seem to be capable of enjoying the position of both judge and jury as to whether a given noise source amounts to a nuisance. In the words of Rowan-Robinson and Watchman, the officer, as far as enforcement of noise law is concerned, operates in a localised system of enforcement where he or she has wide discretion to decide what action to take when a breach is discovered. Of significance here is that enforcing officers are not subject to effective scrutiny from elected members. Officers are, therefore, less accountable in the area of noise control than in respect of other forms of pollution. Furthermore, a nuisance-based noise regime, as opposed to one based on fixed standards, has the tendency to facilitate the process of negotiation and persuasion (especially as far as industry-generated noise is concerned) which is deeply ingrained in British environmental control.[44] This is the case because the various factors which need to be taken into account are diverse.[45] In other words, there are, in theory as well as in practice, a number of ways in which a noise nuisance could be abated. For example, in response to a complaint about noise from a printworks, the enforcing officer could come to an agreement with the occupier that the 'offending' machinery be adequately insulated to reduce the noise, certain windows of the premises be blocked off to reduce the transmission of the noise and, also, that certain noisy equipment not be used after a certain hour of the day. Another separate factor is that the complicated state of the law of nuisance lends itself to negotiation in a situation where, perforce, the officer is in a more advantageous position than the author of the nuisance.

The enforcement of noise law One of the outstanding features of the enforcement of noise law in the UK is the disparity of the manner in which the law is enforced.[46] The way in which noise law is enforced would seem to indicate that there is not as strong a commitment on the part of local authorities to combat neighbourhood noise. It would seem logical to place the enforcement of noise law in the hands of the Environment Agency or SEPA. One advantage of doing this would be that, under the new integrated pollution prevention control regime which will be instituted under the Pollution Prevention and Control Act 1999, both the Environment Agency and SEPA will require to take into account noise pollution when considering whether to grant a permit.

Conclusions By way of general conclusion, as far as noise law is concerned, the UK provides a good example of how the law can develop if it is not driven by clearly focused objectives on the part of the government. Noise law in its current state also illustrates the general principle to the effect that a lack of policy focus produces poor-quality law, the main characteristic of which is lack of overall coherence.

Waste

The foundations of modern waste law derive from the nuisance removal legislation of the 1840s, during which period it was believed that waste matter, especially organic waste, could generate disease. The nuisance removal legislation which was set in place[47] was largely aimed at giving municipal authorities and ad hoc boards powers to remove offensive refuse from premises and so on. The modern law concerning waste is now contained in Part II of the EPA, the main provisions of which are now briefly discussed.

Waste Disposal

Under s.33 of the EPA it is made illegal to deposit controlled waste[48] unless there is in force a waste management licence authorising the deposit. A waste management licence is also required in order to treat, keep or dispose of controlled waste. In essence, the effect of s.33 is that, in order to deal lawfully with waste on a commercial basis, a waste management licence is required. Since 1996, the responsibility for granting waste management licences falls either on the Environment Agency or on SEPA. Section 35 makes specific provision relating to the conditions which may be attached to a site licence. In essence, the Environment Agency and SEPA have wide powers as to the conditions which can be attached to a site licence.

Section 36(3) provides that an application for a waste management licence may not be rejected unless either the Environment Agency or SEPA are satisfied that the rejection is necessary to prevent (a) pollution of the environment, (b) harm to human health, or (c) serious detriment to the amenities of the locality. It is also mandatory that the applicant be a 'fit and proper person', an expression which is defined in s.74 of the Act.

Duty of Care

Perhaps the most revolutionary feature of the new legal regime under the EPA governing waste is the concept of the duty of care, a phrase borrowed from the law of tort or delict. Section 34 provides that any person who either imports, produces, carries, keeps, treats or disposes of controlled waste is placed under an obligation to take all reasonable measures in the circumstances (a) to prevent any contravention by any other person of s.33, above, and (b) to prevent the escape of the waste from his control or that of any other person. Furthermore, the importer, producer and so on of waste must ensure that, on the transfer of the waste, such transfer is only to an authorised person.[49] The duties imposed by s.34 are innovative for a number of reasons, the main one being that no longer does the producer and so on of waste absolve himself of any legal obligation simply by relinquishing physical possession of the waste in question. The person who transfers waste is placed under a continuing legal obligation to ensure that the waste is lawfully dealt with. Another reason why the concept of duty of care is important is that it is, in theory at least, corrective of the notion that the state is mainly responsible for ensuring that waste, once it leaves the possession of the producer, is dealt with lawfully. The law would seem to fit four-square with the paradigm presented by Robinson and Dunkley to the effect that, not only should the law facilitate effective enforcement to secure a pre-determined objective, but the relevant body of statutory law should be dynamic, as it were, and be capable of influencing human behaviour.[50] The objectives contained in s.34 seem sufficiently clear to allow the law to be effective. Of further significance is the fact that the new regime established under s.34 represents a further step away from the dominance of the law of nuisance as the main instrument of controlling waste. Of wider import is the fact that the new regime also encourages more self-regulation by commerce in relation to the waste it produces. The regime is also more prophylactic than the traditional nuisance-based regime, in that the prudent waste producer will only allow his waste to be dealt with by competent contractors in the first place.

Current Government Policy on Waste

Current government policy as far as waste is concerned is expressed in the National Waste Strategy.[51] The Strategy recognises five key principles to underpin UK waste management: the principles of proximity, self-sufficiency, the precautionary principle, the polluter pays and the best practicable environmental option. In order to attain these objectives a variety of instruments are to be used, including the traditional 'command and control' technique which for more than a century and a half has characterised the UK approach to waste. Education and economic instruments are recognised as having an important role to play.

Contaminated Land

Prior to the enactment of Part IIA of the EPA,[52] the regulatory regime dealing with aspects of pollution resulting from contaminated land was extremely disjointed. In addition to the rights of regulators under various pieces of legislation, individuals could utilise common law remedies where their rights had been adversely affected. The 1990 Act as amended represents an attempt to put in place a comprehensive regime dealing with contaminated land.

It was originally proposed in the EPA[53] that there should be a Register of Contaminated Land. At the time this proposal was widely criticised as potentially having a blighting effect on contaminated land without providing any effective policy for remediation. Many commentators believed that a Contaminated Land Register was likely to discourage remediation and, as a consequence, it was never brought into force.

An increasing feature of planning guidance in Great Britain through the 1990s has been a desire to encourage the regeneration of brownfield sites. Planning policies have actively promoted the re-use of such sites, at the same time discouraging the use of greenfield sites,[54] with the result that many developers are now well experienced in dealing with contaminated sites. It was recognised, however, that redevelopment of land has not dealt with some of the most complex and difficult sites and as a result the government brought forward measures in the 1995 Act to introduce a new regime to deal with the most seriously contaminated sites.

Part IIA of the EPA gives local authorities powers in relation to the remediation of contaminated land and, indeed, obliges them to identify such land and secure its remediation. The legislative provisions are relatively complex although, in general terms, they are based on the polluter pays principle. However, Part IIA cannot come into force until the government Guidance is approved. The Guidance is still in draft form, although a final draft is expected shortly and the government has recently renewed its commitment to introduce the regime by April 2000. Under the Guidance, local authorities must put in place a strategy for identifying contaminated land in their area which should be rational, ordered and efficient, proportionate to the seriousness of the actual or potential risks and should ensure that resources are concentrated on investigating areas where the authority is most likely to identify contaminated land. The Guidance goes on to point out that, given the statutory duties of other bodies, including the Health and Safety Executive and nature conservation bodies, it is likely that local authorities will have to take the initiative and identify risks in relation to human health, particularly where land is used for housing or schools.

In order for a local authority to identify land as being 'contaminated' it has to be satisfied that a pollutant linkage exists. A pollutant linkage comprises a contaminant, a pathway and a receptor and all three elements must be present in order for there to be 'contamination'. In theory it would be possible for an owner of contaminated land to break the linkage by simply removing the receptor – for example, by excluding human beings from the site. In that event, no further action would be required in relation to the removal of the pollution unless some other receptor was present. The authority must be satisfied that the land is in such a condition, by reason of substances in, on or under the land, that significant harm is being caused or there is a significant possibility of such harm being caused or pollution of controlled waters is being or is likely to be caused. The Guidance contains detailed definitions of significant harm, and the significant possibility of significant harm, which concentrate on matters such as injuries to human health, the environment or property.

Once the authority has determined that land should be identified as 'contaminated', it must give notice to the relevant environment agency, the owner of the land, anyone who appears to be the owner or occupier of all or part of the land and any person who appears to be the 'Appropriate Person' (that is, the person who has caused or knowingly permitted the land to be contaminated). The Guidance makes it quite clear that, prior to serving any notices requiring anyone to carry out work to the land in question, the local authority must consult those on whom a notice has been served. Anything which is determined to be required in the way of remediation must be reasonable taking account of the nature of the seriousness of the harm. The authorities are obliged to look at each part of the pollutant linkage separately and should then produce a suitable remediation package which should seek to strike a balance between practical ability, effectiveness, durability in maintaining effectiveness and efficiency. This part of the Guidance (and indeed the Guidance in general) is framed in such a way that there must be discussions and negotiations between the authority and the appropriate person. It therefore seems clear that, despite the complex terms of the legislation and Guidance, a consensual approach is preferred.

The Guidance subdivides 'Appropriate Persons' into Class A and Class B persons: Class A being a person who has caused or knowingly permitted pollution and Class B being a person who is the owner or occupier of contaminated land. The Guidance reiterates the statutory position by apportioning liability in the first instance to Class A persons, with no liability being apportioned to Class B persons unless no Class A person can be found. However, where a number of Class A persons are responsible for the pollution, the Guidance states that it is not possible to prescribe detailed rules for the apportionment of liability between those persons which will be fair and appropriate in all cases, given the history and circumstances of different areas of contaminated land. The Guidance does, however, contain six tests which set out criteria for determining whether a person who has otherwise been a Class A person should be excluded from that liability group.

In a situation where no Class A person can be found after reasonable enquiry, liability will ultimately fall on the Class B person. There is an exclusion from Class B liability for persons who do not have an interest in the capital value of the land in question. To satisfy the test, a party must pay a rent equivalent to the full market or rack rent for the land and hold no interest in the land other than the tenancy; alternatively, the party must occupy the land under a licence or other agreement which has no marketable value or which cannot be assigned or transferred to another person.

The new contaminated land regime will not apply to all sites which are 'contaminated' in a non-statutory sense. Only where the three elements of the pollutant linkage are present will the regime come into effect. The impact on sites which are 'contaminated' in a statutory sense could, however, be significant and may result in a stagnation of the rejuvenation process, since the extensive liabilities under the regime may unsettle property investors and, indeed, public authorities who have traditionally taken on such sites. However, developers and environmental consultants do now have a good deal of experience in this field, bolstered by newer technologies which reduce the costs of remediation. Finally, given the costs involved in inspecting and policing the regime, one might reasonably expect local authorities to focus only on the most serious cases of contamination, securing the remediation of less contaminated 'developer friendly' sites through the imposition of specific conditions in planning consents.

Water Regulation

The importance of controlling pollution to the water environment has long been recognised, although it was not until the 1950s that the initial control regimes were introduced. More sophisticated control regimes were introduced in the 1970s and these included national laws and also obligations imposed by the European Community. These have continued to evolve. The control of the quality of water is influenced by a number of regulatory regimes, ranging from the general scheme preventing the entry of matter into water to specific controls dealing with the quality of water for drinking.

The European Union and the Regulation of Water

Europe has historically placed considerable importance on water quality and numerous Directives have been issued regulating discharges to the water environment and setting identifiable standards.[55] The European Union has also been active in setting quality objectives for water, including the Bathing Water Directive[56] and the Drinking Water Directive.[57] The former Directive is perhaps one of the best-known Directives in the water pollution field as considerable publicity has been given to the fact that many UK beaches fail to meet the standards which the Directive sets. In addition, steps have been taken to outlaw certain activities: for example, through the Directive relating to Municipal Waste Water Treatment.[58] The consequences of this Directive have been enormous, since it effectively prohibits the dumping at sea of sewerage sludge. The privatised water utilities in England and Wales have had to invest heavily in new treatment plant and in Scotland the water authorities have entered into a number of major PFI projects or contracts with the private sector.

By and large, most of the Directives have been implemented in the UK through existing legislation. Perhaps the most radical measure to be proposed by the EU is the European Framework Directive for Community Action on Water Pollution. The Directive has yet to be finalised, but drafts have been developed over a number of years and it is anticipated that these will ultimately result in a Directive. The nature of the Directive is fundamental and it is likely to result in a radical overhaul to the way in which water resources are managed. The EU identifies four main objectives of a sustainable water policy. These are the provision of drinking water, the provision of water for other economic requirements, protection of the environment and the alleviation of the impact of floods and droughts. The key element of the Water Framework Directive is the attempt to bring an integrated and coherent water policy to member states and national and regional authorities. The initial objective of the Directive will be to ensure that there is an adequate assessment of the water resource and an important element of this process will be to ensure that a standardised approach is developed in relation to such an assessment. The assessment having been carried out, waters will be classified into various categories: high status, good status and fair status. The ultimate aim of the Directive is for waters to achieve good status as a base minimum prior to specified dates.

The Framework Directive will result in a major overhaul of aquatic environment regulation although the fact that the majority of environmental regulation has been consolidated within the environmental agencies in Great Britain will greatly assist in the implementation of this complex Directive. SEPA has recently produced a comprehensive report on the present status of water quality in Scotland and has also identified the major sources of pollution. It has also advised that it has identified the actions necessary to improve water quality where problems are present. It would therefore appear that the regulators are trying to put themselves in a position of being able to implement the Framework Directive prior to the mandatory requirement to do so.[59]

Water Pollution in Great Britain

Water pollution in Great Britain is controlled by the Environment Agency in England and Wales and SEPA in Scotland. The primary statutory regimes are contained within the Water Resources Act 1991 and the Water Industry Act 1991 ('the 1991 Act') for England and Wales and the Control of Pollution Act 1974 ('the 1974 Act') for Scotland. In terms of the 1991 Act and the 1974 Act, the secretary of state in England and Wales and Scottish ministers are able to prescribe the classification of waters and also set water quality objectives.

A statutory duty is imposed on the Secretary of State and Scottish ministers and the environmental regulators to exercise the powers conferred upon them in terms of the legislation to achieve and maintain those objectives.

The statutory regimes rely on a general criminal offence prohibiting a person from causing or knowingly permitting any 'poisonous, noxious or polluting matter or any solid waste matter to enter any controlled waters'. Controlled waters are widely defined and include territorial waters up to three miles, coastal waters, inland fresh waters and ground waters. One of the key defences to the general prohibition on the entry of a polluting matter to controlled waters is that the discharge was specifically consented to in terms of the 1974 or 1991 Acts or under alternative control regimes. Formerly, discharges caused by abandoned mines were also excluded, although this defence is in the process of being removed in respect of mines abandoned after the year 2000. In addition to the general statutory offence, there are other provisions which prevent deposits of vegetation in rivers.

A key part of the regime for controlling water pollution is the consent to discharge provisions contained in both statutory regimes. This allows a person to apply for a consent to discharge from the relevant environmental agency which may grant consent unconditionally, or subject to conditions, or refuse it.[60] The Secretary of State and Scottish ministers in Scotland have powers in terms of the legislation to call in applications which they consider are more appropriately dealt with by them. In addition, where an applicant considers that the regulator has unreasonably withheld consent or refused it, or granted it subject to conditions which are unreasonable, he may appeal to the Secretary of State or, in Scotland, Scottish ministers.

In addition to the criminal sanctions contained in the legislation, the regulators are empowered to take direct action to prevent matter entering controlled waters or, where such matter has entered waters, to clean up and potentially recover costs from those who have caused or knowingly permitted the situation to occur.[61] These powers have not been widely used. The difficulty with such powers is that the regulator in question may be unwilling to incur substantial expenditure without a guarantee that he or she will recover the costs. In England and Wales, further measures have been introduced which allow the Environment Agency to serve a Works Notice requiring the party who has caused or knowingly permitted the matter either to be present in, or likely to enter, controlled waters to carry out operations or works either to prevent it or to remedy or mitigate the pollution and also to restore the waters, including any flora or fauna.[62] It is likely that the environmental agencies will use these new powers as opposed to the ones which involve them in carrying out direct action. There are appeal procedures against the serving of a Works

Notice. Similar provisions exist in terms of the Control of Pollution Act, but have yet to be brought into force in Scotland. It is anticipated that they will be brought into force in the course of 2000.

The water pollution regime outlined above has been in force for almost three decades. The inherent weakness in the initial system was the limited sanction of criminal penalties. While the courts had increasingly recognised the importance of environmental crimes, they had generally applied very low fines. During the last decade the courts' attitude has altered and now significant fines are being imposed. Recent examples include the £4 million fine for the Harbour Authority over the *Sea Empress* disaster at Milford Haven. The Works Notice procedure is a significant addition to the powers of the Environment Agency and it could have significant implications for major pollution incidents.

Sewerage

The sewerage and water industry in England and Wales has been privatised and is now governed by the 1991 Act, whereas in Scotland the industry remains in the public sector via the water authorities.[63] In general terms, the discharge of trade effluent into sewers is controlled by a regime similar to that outlined above in respect of water pollution. In order to discharge into the sewer it is necessary to have a consent which may be subject to conditions and it is a criminal offence to do so without a consent or in breach of those conditions.

Water Abstraction

In England and Wales there are fairly extensive powers dealing with and licensing the abstraction and impounding of water contained within the 1991 Act. There are also powers to impose Drought Orders which control the use of water and location from which water may be taken. In Scotland, perhaps reflecting the higher rainfall and the lesser concern relating to the use of water, there are less stringent controls. There are, however, Control Orders which can be issued; these control the abstraction of water for irrigation.

Overlapping Regimes

As previously highlighted in this chapter, where industrial processes are regulated under IPC or IPPC, the regulator will deal with all matters in terms of that authorisation including discharges to water. In addition there are provisions within the New Contaminated Land Regime which deal with the potential for pollution of water. It is anticipated that the Contaminated Land Regime will be used if those provisions are applicable, although in certain circumstances the regulators may have a choice of action.

Conclusion

The regulatory regime is essentially one of prohibition unless a discharge to water is specifically consented to. The regime has recently been enhanced by the Works Notice Procedure in England which is likely also to be introduced in Scotland. These measures provide the regulators with wide powers not only to prevent pollution but also to ensure that, where it occurs, the polluter will ultimately pay for it. In a recent document the Scottish Environmental Protection Agency stated that the protection of the aquatic environment required information on water quality, water quantity and habitat quality. To date the primary focus of environmental regulation has been on the chemical purity of water. In England and Wales, the question of the quantity of water has to a degree been controlled via abstraction control measures, although in Scotland there are very few controls apart from limited controls on irrigation. It is evident that the primary aim of the regulatory system has been to ensure that the chemical quality of water is 'good' since this would ultimately lead to good habitat quality. It is increasingly recognised that this is not always the case and this issue is likely to be brought into focus once the EU Water Framework Directive has been adopted. The Directive will probably result in a regulatory regime which aims to look at the water environment in its widest context and involve closer scrutiny of land uses such as forestry and agriculture, which are at present largely unregulated.

Human Rights and Environmental Regulation

The impact of environmental regulation on human rights has been recognised by the European Court of Human Rights on a number of occasions. This has particular relevance in the UK since the passing of the Human Rights Act 1998, which enables courts to give effect to the European Convention on Human Rights. In addition, in terms of the Scotland Act 1998, it is beyond the competence of the Scottish Parliament to pass legislation which is incompatible with Convention rights. There is no express right in the European Convention on Human Rights relating to the environment, but some of the articles have been construed in the context of environmental matters.

Article 8 of the Convention includes the right to respect of a person's private and family life and home. It was successfully invoked in the case of *Guarra and Others* v. *Italy*,[64] where the individuals' rights under Article 8 had been violated by the failure to provide information on the pollution hazards associated with a chemical works. Similarly, in the case of *Lopez Ostra* v. *Spain*,[65] the Spanish government was held to have breached an individual's human rights by failing to regulate a waste treatment plant which was causing emissions which were potentially harmful to health. These cases illustrate that the European Court of Human Rights is prepared to step in to find that states, by failing to provide adequate environmental protection, have not protected individuals' human rights. While it is not anticipated that there are numerous gaps in the existing UK regulation, as further health risks are identified this may have implications both in terms of Article 8 in respect of property and also in the context of the right to life in terms of Article 2 of the Convention.

Access to Environmental Information

Access to environmental information is necessary for those who wish to monitor the effectiveness of a regulatory regime. Historically, in the UK, certain statutory environmental regimes provided for the keeping of registers which were open to public access, whilst others have not. In America, environmental groups identified the importance of information obtained under the Freedom of Information legislation. The ad hoc system adopted in the UK was substantially altered as a result of an EC Directive on Freedom of Access to Information on the Environment.[66] This was implemented in the UK by the Environmental Information Regulations 1992.[67] The Regulations give individuals very broad rights to obtain information from public authorities, subject to a number of defences including international relations, national defence, public security, information relating to legal proceedings, commercially confidential information and documents which are yet to be completed.

Conclusion

By way of general conclusion, one can discern a fundamental change in UK environmental law and policy over the last ten years. The law is moving away from a medium-by-medium approach to pollution control and is becoming more holistic. The law is also more prophylactic in nature. Of fundamental significance in UK environmental law is the fact that Europe continues to tighten its grip on UK national law. However, many years will no doubt pass before the latter loses its national character, which is predicated on more than a century and a half's development. In the more immediate future, it will be interesting to observe the extent to which the principle of subsidiarity acts as a brake on the advance of European law on our national system. The line between that which may legitimately be dealt with under EU law and that which is the sole preserve of national governments may, indeed, be fine, not least in the realms of noise pollution, in respect of which Europe is becoming increasingly active and in relation to which the UK government has, thus far, looked askance at some of Europe's attempts to interfere.

As far as the regulators of the environment are concerned, the move to a more integrated approach to pollution control will, in the authors' view, strengthen the case for environmental enforcement to be placed in the hands of large agencies such as the Environment Agency and SEPA, at the expense of local authorities who have accumulated pollution control powers largely by way of default, rather than as a result of serious reflection by parliament. The principle of sustainability which is now well ingrained in UK environmental policy will, no doubt, act as a further stimulus to the transfer of responsibility for environmental enforcement to ad hoc agencies, since having one regulatory agency responsible for enforcing regulatory environmental control over commercial activities would facilitate a more comprehensive overview of the impact of all the activities of that industry on the environment as a whole. In the same context, another factor which requires to be addressed as far as domestic environmental law is concerned is the role of central government in terms of its relationship with local enforcing bodies. In certain areas such as planning law (which lack of space precluded us from discussing in this chapter) central government control is fairly strong, whereas, at the other end of the spectrum, in the area of noise pollution, central government influence over local authorities is fairly weak. The system as a whole palpably lacks coherence, one of the upshots of which is confusion, not least on the part of the public. The situation is further obfuscated by the advent of the Environment Agency and SEPA in the equation. For example, in certain areas of the law relating to air pollution and contaminated land, there is an ugly amalgam of powers and duties possessed by different authorities. This situation would, of course, be greatly clarified if the number of regulators were reduced. The most obvious way of doing this would be simply to transfer local authority responsibility for environmental control to the new agencies.

However, one can say that any wholesale transfer of enforcement functions from local authorities to agencies would require the latter to command greater public support and confidence than at present. The new agencies need to serve a lengthier apprenticeship, as it were, before their present responsibilities are increased. Therefore it may be somewhat premature for parliament to deprive local authorities of their long-established environmental control functions.

Notes

1 Police commissions had been established in various towns in Scotland towards the end of the 18th century to oversee the police forces operating there. However, as the 19th century progressed, police commissions tended to merge with town councils.
2 During the 19th century, there was a proliferation of administrative public bodies at local level.
3 Treaty establishing the European Economic Community, 1957.
4 *Ibid.*, para. 4 of the preamble.
5 *Ibid.*, Art. 100.
6 *Ibid.*, 130 R to 130 T.
7 *Ibid.*, Art. 100 A.
8 Treaty on European Union 1992.
9 Council Directive 96/61/EC.
10 Council Directive 91/271/EEC as amended by Commission Directive 98/15/EC.
11 Council Directive 1999/31/EC.
12 The Committee reported in 1954. See the *Report of the Committee on Air Pollution*, Cmnd 9322, London: HMSO.
13 Vogel, D. (1983), 'Comparing Policy Styles: Environmental Protection in the US and Britain', *Public Administration Bulletin*, 42, 75.
14 Section 3(1) defines the expression,'dark smoke' as being as dark or darker than shade 2 on the Ringlemann Chart.
15 The idea of 'smokeless zones' originated in Manchester in 1935: Clapp, B.W. (1994), *An Environmental History of Britain*, London: Longman, p.48.
16 Under s.18 of the Clean Air Act 1993 a local authority is given discretion as to which classes of building the relevant smoke control order should apply.
17 Section 20(4) makes provision for a defence.
18 Central government is given the power to require the creation of a smoke control area in the face of failure on the part of a local authority to declare such an area if it would be expedient to do so.
19 Local authorities, as a result of the policy of nationalisation, had lost their responsibilities for electricity and gas supply when these were taken over by electricity and gas boards in 1947–8. Many local authorities had also lost their responsibility for water supply. Local authorities had also failed to attract responsibility for new functions. For example, under the New Towns Act 1946 the development of new towns was placed in the hands of appointed boards in contradistinction to local authorities. See Byrne, T. (1992), *Local Government in Britain*, London: Penguin, pp.18–19.
20 A wide meaning is given to the expression 'process', which is defined by s.1(5) as 'any activities carried on in Great Britain, whether on premises or by means of mobile plant which are capable of causing pollution of the environment'.
21 SI 1991 no.472.
22 See (1993), *Integrated Pollution Control: A Practical Guide*, London: HMSO.
23 Based on Best Available Technology Documents (BREF Notes) to be produced by the European Commission. This will obviously reinforce Europe's influence on environmental regulation.

24 See August 1999 Consultation Papers.
25 For example, under The Control of Major Accident Hazards Regulations 1999, SI 1999 no. 743.
26 Such as the inclusion in IPPC of energy efficiency and noise.
27 Examples of the broad powers which are to be delegated include the powers to introduce schemes for the trading or transfer of quotas relating to emissions.
28 (1997) Cmnd 3587, London: HMSO.
29 Ibid., p.20.
30 That is, by the year 2005. (*Ibid.*, p.22).
31 See Adams, M. and F. McManus (1994), *Noise and Noise Law*, London: Wiley Chancery, p.151.
32 See Lowe, P. and S. Ward (eds) (1998), *British Environmental Policy and Europe*, London: Routledge, p.8.
33 See McCormick, J. (1991), *British Politics and the Environment*, London: Earthscan, p.10.
34 Howarth, W. (1993), 'Poisonous, Noxious or Polluting: Contrasting Approaches to Environmental Regulation', *Modern Law Review*, 56, 172.
35 Much case law has centred on how detailed and specific the abatement notice requires to be in order to be valid. See, for example, *East Staffordshire Borough Council* v. *Fairless, The Times*, 26 October 1998; *Kirklees Metropolitan Council* v. *Field* [1998] Env.LR 337; *Lowe* v. *South Somerset District Council* [1998] JPL 458. See also *Budd* v. *Colchester BC, The Times*, 14 April 1999.
36 See, for example, *RHM Bakeries Ltd.* v. *Strathclyde Regional Council* 1985 SC (HL) 17; *Kennedy* v. *Glenbelle* 1996 SCLR 411. For a discussion of the concept of *culpa* and the law of nuisance, see McManus, F. (1997), 'Culpa and the Law of Nuisance', *Juridical Review*, 259.
37 See McManus, F. (1999), 'The EC Green Paper on Future Noise Policy and its Impact on the United Kingdom', *European Public Law*, 5, 125, 139–40.
38 For example, in *Hunter* v. *Canary Wharf Ltd*[1997] Env.LR 488 the Court of Appeal, in determining whether the interference with the reception of television signals amounted to a nuisance, was prepared to take into account the fact that tall buildings of a kind which caused the interference in question were now fairly common.
39 *Hunter* v. *Canary Wharf Ltd* [1997] 2 WLR 684.
40 For a more detailed discussion of this issue, see Penner, F.E. (1993), 'Nuisance and the Character of the Neighbourhood', *Journal of Environmental Law*, 5, 1.
41 See McManus, G. and E. Russell (1998), *Delict*, Chichester: Wiley, pp.214–15. For a contrary view, see McLaren, J. (1972), 'The Common Law Nuisance Actions and the Environmental Battle – Well Tempered Swords or Broken Reeds?', *Osgoode Hall Law Journal*, 10, 505. The author argues that, as far as Canadian law is concerned, the law of private nuisance is sufficiently malleable to allow the courts to take into account wider environmental factors in determining nuisance cases.
42 See Hawke, N. (1995), *Environmental Law*, London: Sweet and Maxwell, pp.426–46; Wignall, G. (1998), *Nuisances*, London: Sweet and Maxwell, ch.3; Ormandy, D. (1997), *Law of Statutory Nuisances*, London: Chadwick House Group.
43 The 1998 National Society for Clean Air and Environmental Protection survey found that only 18 per cent of local authorities in England and Wales considered that nuisance was no longer an appropriate standard to use. See the National Society for Clean Air (NSCA) Noise Survey, 1998, p.14. In the 1999 Survey, only 13 per cent of local authorities considered that nuisance was no longer an appropriate standard (see p.12). Furthermore, one of the authors recently interviewed environmental health officers in several London boroughs. Those interviewed were generally supportive of the law of nuisance as a con-

trol device for noise. The officials were of the opinion that nuisance gave them 'discretion' when dealing with noise problems. It allowed them to act in a 'reasonable' way. See Rowan-Robinson, J. and P. Watchman (1990), *Crime and Regulation*, Edinburgh: T&T Clark, p.221.

44 See Richardson, G., A. Ogus and P. Burrows (1982), *Policing Pollution – A Study of Regulation and Enforcement*, Oxford: Clarendon, p.63.

45 See, for example, W.V.H.Rogers (ed.) (1998), *Winfield and Jolowicz on Tort*, 15th edn, London: Sweet and Maxwell, pp.496–512; McManus and Russell, pp.214–23; Stewart, W. (1998), *Delict*, 3rd edn, Edinburgh: W.Green/Sweet and Maxwell, 2-12–2-19.

46 The National Society for Clean Air (NSCA) Environmental Protection Survey for the year 1999 revealed that only 21 per cent of the total local authorities responding to its questionnaire had officers dedicated to enforcing noise law (Brighton: NSCA, 1999, p.8.) Furthermore, there were only 28 per cent of local authorities which had a 7-day, 24-hour cover as far as noise was concerned (*ibid*. p.9).

47 Namely, the Nuisance Removal Acts, 1846, 1848 and 1856.

48 The expression 'controlled waste' is defined as including household, industrial and commercial waste. The Environment Act 1995 (sch. 22, para. 88) and the Waste Management Licensing Regulations 1994 (SI 1994 no.1056) amend the definition of controlled waste in the EPA to bring UK law into line with EU law as contained in the Framework Directive EC 75/442/EEC (as amended by 91/156/EEC).

49 Section 34(3) includes a list of classes of persons authorised for the purposes of s.34. Included in the various categories are waste collection authorities as well as those registered as carriers of controlled waste in terms of s.2 of the Control of Pollution (Amendment) Act 1989.

50 See Robinson, D. and J. Dunkley (1994), 'Public Interest and Environmental Law – Community and Analysis', in D. Robinson and J. Dunkley (eds), *Public Interest Perspectives in Environmental Law*, Chichester: Wiley, p.204.

51 See 'National Waste Strategy – Scotland' (Consultation Draft) Executive Summary, Stirling: SEPA, 1999.

52 Environmental Protection Act 1990 as amended by the Environment Act 1995.

53 Environmental Protection Act 1990, s.143

54 For example, targets are now being set at a national level in relation to new housing sites.

55 For example, the Dangerous Substances (76/769/EEC) and the Ground Water Directive (80/68/EEC).

56 Directive 76/160/EEC.

57 Directive 80/778/EEC.

58 Council Directive 91/271.

59 SEPA (1999), *Improving Scotland's Water Environment*, Part 2, July, p.10.

60 It should be noted that discharge consents could be subsequently reviewed.

61 Section 46 of the Control of Pollution Act 1974 and s.161 of the Water Resources Act 1991.

62 The Anti-Pollution Works Regulations 1999 (SI 1006/1999).

63 The Local Government etc. (Scotland) Act 1994.

64 *Guarra and Others* v. *Italy* (116/1996/735/932) judgment 19 February 1998.

65 *Lopez Ostra* v. *Spain* (Application no. 16798/90) (1995) 20 EHRR 277.

66 Access to Environmental Information, EC Directive 90/313.

67 Access to Environmental Information Regulations 1992 (SI 3240/1992).

10 Tax as a Regulatory Tool: The Case of the Proposed Climate Change Levy

ROBERT DUNBAR, ***University of Glasgow****

Introduction

Over the last two decades or more, environmental problems have become a major concern for voters in many countries, particularly in the industrialised west, and, as a result, have taken on considerable importance as political issues. Amongst the most hotly debated environmental issues over the last several years has been that of climate change, or 'global warming', which an increasing body of scientific evidence is suggesting is the result of emissions of certain pollutants, in particular 'greenhouse gases', the most important of which are carbon dioxide (CO^2), methane (CH^4) and nitrous oxide (N^2O).[1]

The international community has responded to the threat of global warming by negotiating an international agreement under the aegis of the United Nations, the United Nations Framework Convention on Climate Change (the 'Framework Convention') of 1992.[2] The Framework Convention set an ultimate objective of stabilising 'greenhouse gas concentrations in the atmosphere at a level that would prevent dangerous anthropogenic [human-induced] interference with the climate system', but did not specify what those levels should be. Following protracted negotiations, however, broad targets for the reduction of greenhouse gases were set in the Kyoto Protocol to the

* The author would like to thank Jamie Apold of Shepherd & Wedderburn, solicitors, Edinburgh, for his invaluable comments on this chapter. The opinions expressed herein and any errors or omissions are, however, solely the responsibility of the author.

United Nations Framework Convention on Climate Change (the 'Kyoto Protocol') of 1997.[3]

Under Article 3 of the Kyoto Protocol, developed countries agreed to targets for reducing their emissions of six greenhouse gases by 2008–12.[4] The European Union agreed to a reduction of 8 per cent below 1990 levels, in June 1998; the UK took on a legal target of a 12.5 per cent reduction as its share of the EU commitment. The Kyoto Protocol does not specify the means by which states should meet their targets, although under paragraph 2 of Article 2 parties agree to 'strive to implement policies and measures ... in such a way as to minimize [*sic*] adverse effects, including the adverse effects of climate change, effects on international trade, and social, environmental and economic impacts on other Parties'. The UK has set its own domestic aim of a 20 per cent reduction from 1990 levels in emissions of one greenhouse gas, carbon dioxide, by the year 2010.[5]

In March 1998, the chancellor of the exchequer established a task force, headed by Sir Colin Marshall and comprising senior civil servants from HM Treasury, the Department of the Environment, Transport and the Regions, the Department of Trade and Industry and HM Customs & Excise, to consider whether economic instruments such as an 'energy tax' had a role to play in meeting the government's commitments under the Kyoto Protocol. The task force issued a consultation paper in March, 1998 and, after a period of consultation, its final report was issued on 9 November 1998, at the time of the chancellor's autumn pre-budget statement.[6]

The chancellor announced in his 9 March 1999 budget statement that the government would, in response to the recommendations contained in the Marshall Task Force Report, introduce a climate change levy on business use of energy from April 2001; the chancellor did not table draft legislation, however. The same day, HM Customs & Excise released a consultation document entitled 'Consultation on a Climate Change Levy' (the 'Consultation Document') and a Draft Regulatory Impact Assessment, and invited responses to be submitted by 28 May 1999. The Consultation Document gives a clear and relatively detailed picture of the structure and scope of the proposed levy, as well as relieving provisions and administrative mechanisms.

The proposed climate change levy is not the first British experiment with what are broadly referred to as 'green' taxes, but it nonetheless represents, if passed into law, perhaps the most significant attempt to date by a British government to use the tax system to achieve environmental objectives. While the Consultation Document has met with what the Select Committee on Trade and Industry has described as a scale of adverse reaction that is 'unprecedented',[7] the government seems determined to introduce a levy based essentially on the proposals contained therein. At the same time, the same committee found widespread acceptance that the UK must meet its targets under the Kyoto Protocol.[8] Likewise, there has developed a broad consensus among academics and policy makers, explored in the next section of this chapter, that economic instruments such as the proposed levy are generally a preferable mechanism for environmental and other forms of regulation.

It would be easy to dismiss the views reported by the Select Committee on Trade and Industry as the usual reaction of industry to a proposed tax measure. This would, however, be unjustified. For, in spite of the undoubted benefits of economic instruments as regulatory tools in general, and those of 'green' tax measures in particular, the government proposals illustrate a number of serious design and implementation problems to which such measures can give rise – problems which are exacerbated when the environmental objectives behind the tax measure come into conflict with other legitimate objectives of the tax system. This chapter will begin with a discussion of the theoretical case for economic instruments such as 'green' taxes, together with an exploration of their limitations. We shall then turn to the proposed climate change levy, and analyse it in the context of this theoretical discussion.

The Theoretical Basis for 'Green' or Environmental Taxes

The terms 'green' tax or 'environmental' tax are not terms of art, and it is important to distinguish them from other phrases which appear in the literature, such as the 'greening of the tax system', a term of much broader import. A useful definition of a 'green' or 'environmental' tax is as follows: 'A tax falls into the category environmental if the tax base [that is, the thing that is subject to the tax] is a physical unit (or a proxy for it) of something that has a proven specific negative impact on the environment, when used or released.'[9] As we shall see, the proposed climate change levy is clearly such a tax. The 'greening of the tax system' simply refers to a process whereby states include environmental objectives in the formulation and implementation of tax policy. Thus the 'greening of the tax system' would include not only the imposition of 'green' or 'environmental' taxes of the sort just described, but also the removal or modification of existing environmentally distorting subsidies and tax provisions and the restructuring of existing taxes.[10]

Examples of environmentally distorting tax provisions in the British tax system are numerous, and would include the exemption from the rules on employees' taxable benefits given in respect of car parking space at or near the workplace,[11] which exception could encourage employees to drive their cars to work rather than taking more 'environmentally friendly' alternatives, such as public transport. Britain has not yet addressed these sorts of measure in any systematic way. By contrast, Britain has sought to restructure some existing taxes so as to make them more environmentally friendly, and therefore can be said to have started on the process of 'greening the tax system'. For example, the Major government announced in the March 1993 budget that it was going to impose value added tax ('VAT') on domestic energy consumption, first at a rate of 8 per cent from 1 April 1994, then at the standard rate of 17.5 per cent, from 1 April 1995; previously, domestic energy had been zero-rated and therefore effectively free of VAT. While the measure was primarily motivated to raise revenues, the government noted environmental benefits which would also flow from the change.[12] Owing to strong public opposition to the imposition of VAT, based on the regressive nature of the imposition,[13] the government did not implement the second stage of this reform, and VAT on domestic energy consumption remains taxable at a lower rate.[14] The current government has proposed a reduction in the vehicle excise duty of £50 for the cleanest and smallest cars; this proposal was justified primarily by reference to environmental objectives, in particular the reduction of greenhouse gas emissions and of local air pollutants.[15] In spite of this and other recent initiatives of the Labour government, including the introduced climate change levy, the UK is still a long way from developing a coherent strategy of 'greening the tax system'.

The idea of using a tax or other charge as a means of environmental regulation is well established, and rests on the characterisation of environmental pollution as a 'negative externality' of the process of producing goods or services;[16] that is, pollution represents a cost to society at large which is not reflected in the market price of the good or service. The resultant under-pricing results in a relative over-consumption of the polluting good or service. There is a growing agreement among economists that a 'corrective' tax – that is, one which effectively increases the market price of the good or service – is a more economically efficient and effective means of dealing with pollution than other forms of regulation, such as more traditional forms of 'command and control' regulation or the imposition of criminal or quasi-criminal sanctions.[17] Indeed, this emerging consensus has been embraced by the OECD and domestic policy makers of a growing number of OECD member states.[18]

The economic arguments for green taxes, as opposed to more traditional forms of regulation, are based on two sorts of efficiencies identified by economists: 'static' efficiency and 'dynamic' efficiency. The optimal level of pollution abatement will be achieved where the marginal cost to polluters of reducing pollution is the same as the marginal benefit to society of any such further reduction in levels of pollution. The 'static' efficiency argument is that this intersection is, in general, accomplished more efficiently through the imposition of a tax than through more direct forms of regulation. For some polluters, the opportunities for, and costs of, reducing pollution will be different. The most efficient reduction in levels of pollution is accomplished by demanding greater reductions from those polluters for whom the costs of reducing polluting are low, and lesser reductions from those for whom the costs of pollution abatement are high. Even if a regulatory agency possessed the potentially significant amounts of information that would be required to calibrate the levels of pollution abatement to the particular cost structures of each polluter, the same result might be achievable at much lower cost by simply imposing a tax or other charge which was related to the amount of pollution being produced. In this way, polluters will be forced to decide for themselves on their appropriate level of pollution abatement: polluters whose costs of abatement are lower than the potential tax payable will be expected to reduce emissions, while those for whom costs of abatement are higher will be expected to pay the tax.[19]

The 'dynamic' efficiency argument relates to the incentive which the continued existence of the tax creates for polluters to find relatively less costly ways of reducing emissions. If a polluter can reduce its costs of abatement by an amount greater than the tax being imposed, it is in a position to make savings. Thus there is an incentive to engage in research and development that may lead to the development of pollution abatement technologies. By contrast, those polluters facing a regulatory regime will generally have fewer incentives to engage in the search for methods of reducing emissions by amounts greater than those specified by the regulatory regime.[20]

Advocates of green taxes point to a number of other advantages that such measures have over other regulatory mechanisms. They are, it is argued, easier to administer and enforce. The tax sets a price signal to which polluters themselves will respond; there is no need for what can become a large governmental bureaucracy to design and monitor the implementation of regulatory controls, nor do such taxes generally need to involve the creation of a complex statutory regime.[21] And, because of this, tax mechanisms are less prone to regulatory 'failure' – the ability of the regulated polluter to affect the way that regulations are applied because of the greater information that the regulated party has concerning the regulated activity[22] – and regulatory 'capture': the ability of the regulated party in effect to control the regulator through the provision of information and personnel to the regulatory body. Finally, green taxes have the potential to raise revenues, and, it is argued, the use of such revenues to reduce other taxes which have potentially distorting effects on the economy can give rise to additional efficiency gains: this is the so-called 'double dividend' which can arise from environmental taxes, although there is, as we shall see below, much debate as to the real potential for such additional gains.

While green taxes have a number of advantages over other regulatory tools, they are also subject to a number of limitations,[23] and even advocates of such measures recognise that they raise a very wide variety of issues, ranging from design to enforcement.[24] The most fundamental issues relate to the nature and rate of the tax imposition itself: if the tax does not, by virtue of faults in its design, effectively encourage a reduction in the emission of the particular pollutant in question, any theoretical advantage over other regulatory mechanisms is lost. The first issue here is 'linkage', the degree to which the tax measure is closely linked to the pollution that it is supposed to control,[25] and involves a close consideration of the 'tax base', or the thing to be taxed:

> A direct and clear link between the tax and the environmental damage is key to the widespread acceptability of the tax and to proper market signals. The effectiveness of an environmental tax in achieving an efficient reduction in environmental damage depends on the degree to which the tax is closely linked to the environmental damage which it aims to control. . . .
>
> Where the linkage between the tax base and the environmental damage is weak, the tax may fail to induce polluters to change their behaviour, and the tax may simply become the cause of more market distortions.[26]

The most direct link is created where the charge is imposed on the emission itself; in this case, the tax is often referred to as a levy rather than a tax. Such charges create incentives not only for the polluter to reduce emissions through decreased use of the pollutant but to search for 'end-of-pipe' technology; that is, technology which reduces the emission of pollutants per given unit of input.

In many cases, however, this direct link through an emission-oriented tax or levy is not possible; this is the case, for example, where emissions are difficult to measure for technical reasons or because of the large number of sources of the pollution.[27] In such cases, the charge will have to be imposed indirectly, either on products which are inputs in the production process or on the goods and services which come out of the process. Given the importance of linkage, indirect taxes on inputs are to be preferred to those on the products or services themselves, the prices of which will reflect all inputs in the production process, not merely those inputs which cause the pollution.[28]

There are a number of difficulties in determining the appropriate rate of the tax. As noted earlier, the optimal rate of tax is that which equates the marginal cost of reducing emissions and the marginal social damage arising from the pollution. If the rate of tax is set too low, it will encourage insufficient abatement; if too high, it will produce excessive reductions.[29] However, most analysts recognise that setting an appropriate rate is extremely difficult, because it requires a large amount of information, and the estimation of social costs is, in itself, an extremely difficult task to accomplish.[30] There are further complications if the tax is imposed indirectly, on products associated with the pollution, rather than directly on the pollution itself. In setting the appropriate tax rate, the government will in this case also have to consider demand elasticities[31] for the product. Thus, among products which can be substituted for each other, for example, the tax should be differentiated according to the polluting content of the product.[32] Because of these various uncertainties, it is likely that the rate or rates of the green tax will have to be adjusted over time, in accordance with experience. While tax regimes may be more amenable to this sort of 'fine-tuning' than other regulatory models, this characteristic also reduces the purported administrative and compliance benefits of such measures somewhat, because market actors will have less certainty with respect to the level of the tax, and the government will have to incur costs of monitoring the impact of the tax.[33]

The revenue-raising nature of green taxes is also not without its problems. There is, for example, considerable debate as to how such revenues should be used. As noted above, the use of green tax revenues to reduce other distorting taxes, thereby producing an economic 'double dividend', has been the subject of much debate.[34] Economists are particularly hopeful about the possibility of enhancing employment through the use of green tax revenues to reduce 'labour taxes' on business, such as social security contributions like National Insurance Contributions paid by employers. Recent empirical research in OECD member countries suggests, however, that only a significant reduction in such taxes on labour could have an appreciable effect on levels of employment, and that states have thus far been reluctant to impose green taxes that would be sufficiently large to generate such revenues. At best, the evidence for a double dividend has been mixed; where there has been a positive effect on employment, it seems to have been small, and is not in any case likely to provide a long-term structural solution to employment problems in OECD countries.[35]

Other potential applications of green taxes have provoked even more controversy, most notably the 'earmarking' of such revenues for things like specific environmental projects, special environmental funds to finance various environmental projects, or redistribution among those that pay the tax.[36] First, if the tax is itself set at a level meant to produce the optimal amount of pollution abatement, earmarking revenues to subsidise the adoption by polluters of further pollution-abatement measures will lead to excessive abatement, and is therefore an inefficient use of the revenue.[37] Further, earmarking means that the amounts available for the particular expenditure programme will be dependent on the level of green tax revenue produced; this, however, may result in either too much or too little being spent on the particular programme.[38] There is, of course, a wider debate in tax theory about the use of the tax system to encourage particular types of investments, for example through tax credits or enhanced capital allowances, and these sorts of 'tax expenditures' raise significant problems.[39] Finally, revenues can be used to offset some of the negative consequences which green taxes may have on particular groups of consumers – the so-called 'distributional' issues, discussed next – and on particular producers, such as those which bear a particularly heavy burden owing to a relative inability to take steps to mitigate the burden of the green tax, or those, like exporters, who may suffer a competitive disadvantage, and we shall return to these issues below.

One difficulty with green taxes is their potential 'regressivity'; that is, the tendency of such taxes to absorb a proportionately larger share of the total income of the less well-off. This is the so-called 'distributional' issue referred to earlier, and is common to many excise taxes imposed on particular goods and services.[40] Excise taxes can have both a direct and indirect impact on such taxpayers: if imposed directly on products which the consumer purchases for his or her use, the consumer will bear the green tax; and if imposed on goods which are used in the process of producing consumer goods, the consumer may still end up bearing the cost imposed by the tax.[41] Recent research by the OECD has uncovered little empirical evidence on the distributional impact of green taxes, although it must be said that the experience of OECD countries in this regard is limited.[42] There is a considerable body of research which suggests that taxes on energy and/or carbon use tend to be regressive; this is not surprising, given that heating bills tend to form a larger percentage of household expenditure and consume a larger share of household income in less well-off households.[43] However, it is not clear that such taxes would necessarily impinge very heavily on even the poorest households; a recent OECD report concluded, for example, that 'The distributional issues and concerns that arise with environmental taxes are greater than with economic instruments which do not raise revenues and have no fiscal character, but they are nevertheless largely overstated.'[44] Still, even the OECD report just quoted concluded that the distributional impact of such taxes should nonetheless be addressed; the debate revolves around the most efficient way of doing so.

One method of addressing the distributional impact would be to mitigate the effects of any green tax, perhaps by effectively exempting certain consumers or producers from the tax. The obvious problem with this type of solution is that it compromises the effectiveness of the tax by removing the incentives that such consumers or producers have to alter their behaviour.[45] Thus analysts tend to favour other methods of compensating those who bear a disproportionate burden of the green tax, such as a reduction in another tax or taxes which are also regressive, a tax credit against income tax liability, or an increase in transfer payments which such households are already receiving.[46]

There are problems associated with the imposition of the green tax measure in only one jurisdiction, or in a small number of jurisdictions. First, there is the impact of such an imposition on not only exporters, but other producers whose goods and services reflect the tax and who must compete in the domestic market against imported goods and services which have not borne the tax; this is the 'competitiveness' issue. Second, there is the problem of 'leakage' of pollution; where other states have not taken measures of similar effect, producers in the jurisdiction may be encouraged to relocate their production in those other states, with the result that jobs are lost in that state without any necessary reduction in global levels of pollution. Where the pollution has primarily a local effect, this is a loss which the state may feel is worth paying; but where the pollution in question recognises no boundaries and is global in its impact, as is the case with the pollution caused by emissions of greenhouse gases, both domestic producers and, more particularly, those they employ will be rightly concerned with this 'leakage' issue.

The impact of an environmental tax on the competitiveness of domestic industries will depend on a number of variables, not least of which is the elasticity of demand for the producers' output and the use which is made of the revenues raised by the tax. Again, a recent OECD study has concluded that, thus far, there is little strong evidence that differences in environmental standards are a major source of competitive advantage.[47] Such taxes may, however, have more dramatic effects on particular firms, or even industries, and any proposals are likely to spark sharp opposition from those companies and industries potentially affected.

Similarly, there is no clear consensus on the extent of the leakage problem, although it is clear that, like the issue of competitiveness, it is a potential problem, and that the greater the number of countries which implement similar policies, the more the scope for 'leakage' (and indeed the potential negative impact on competitiveness) is reduced.[48]

In spite of a lack of solid consensus on the extent of either of these problems, there will almost certainly be the need to address them, owing to political pressure from potentially affected groups. Thus the debate here centres on the most appropriate response to these potential problems. One solution mirrors that which is occasionally suggested for the distributional problem: by effectively exempting or simply compensating those producers likely to be most adversely affected by the imposition of the green tax. This is not, however, a particularly effective solution, for the same reasons as were discussed above: namely, that it compromises the effectiveness of the tax by removing the incentives that such producers have to alter their behaviour.[49] A potentially more appealing solution is the use of 'border tax adjustments', provisions within the green tax which allow for the imposition of the green tax at the border on imports of products that would be subject to the tax or of goods and services in which tax products would be used as an input, and the provision of tax relief to exporters of products which have been subject to the tax or of goods and services whose inputs have borne the green tax. While theoretically appealing, such adjustments can be difficult to implement, particularly in their application to goods and services in the cost of which the taxable input is buried. Such adjustments also have implications under the multilateral trade rules of the World Trade Organisation (WTO), and careful attention must be paid to such rules.[50]

A final issue relates to the enforcement of green taxes. As noted above, green taxes are usually easier to apply than other regulatory instruments, as they tend to involve less detailed legislation and less complex regulations. Nonetheless, taxes must still be interpreted, and taxing statutes are subject to the same interpretive difficulties – perhaps greater difficulties – as any other enactment.[51] These problems can be reduced, however, where the green tax can be integrated fully or in part into an existing excise tax, or where appropriate statutory constructions can be borrowed from such other taxes. The taxpayer, tax advisor and revenue official will, in these circumstances, be working with more familiar terminology, resulting in less room for uncertainty.

Therefore, while green taxes are an attractive regulatory tool in principle, there are a number of very significant issues which the government must bear in mind. Added to these are issues of broader government tax and industrial policy, to say nothing of those relating to political expedience, which any government must bear in mind, and which have obvious implications for the effectiveness of the green tax. The government has, in its Statement of Intent on Environmental Taxation, recognised the importance of subjecting any proposed climate change levy to the standards demanded of any tax measure:

> Environmental taxation must meet the general tests of good taxation. It must be well designed, to meet objectives without undesirable side effects; it must keep deadweight compliance costs to a minimum; distributional impact must be acceptable; and care must be had to implications for international competitiveness.[52]

As we shall see, the proposals for a climate change levy contain a number of provisions which appear to be driven by broader policy and political concerns. At issue is whether the compromises which the government has sought to make have, as a result, fundamentally compromised the levy as an effective regulatory mechanism. In the next section of the chapter, we shall briefly describe the proposals, and then in the subsequent, and final, section, we shall critically appraise them, on the basis of the foregoing discussion.

The Customs and Excise Consultation Document

The government's proposals for the climate change levy are contained in the Consultation Document.[53] Both the language of the Consultation Document and the limited scope of the consultation suggest, however, that the government does not intend to depart very dramatically from the provisions of the Consultation Document with respect to the fundamental aspects of the climate change levy.[54]

With respect to the tax base and structure of the proposed levy, it will be imposed on the supply of certain forms of energy to a certain class of user. The levy will be imposed at an amount which will differ for the various sources of energy covered by the levy but which is specified for each nominal unit of energy content supplied. As with the VAT, while the liability to pay the levy falls on the user, or the person to whom the energy is supplied, the obligation to collect and remit the levy to the government is on the supplier of the energy; it is the suppliers of energy who will have to register with and pay to the Customs any levy that is due.[55]

The levy will apply to supplies of the following forms of energy: electricity, coal, coal and hydrocarbon derivatives such as orimulsion and petcoke, and natural gas (including compressed natural gas, 'CNG', other than that used in road vehicles) and liquid petroleum gas ('LPG'; again, other than LPG used in road vehicles).[56] The levy will not apply, however, to mineral oils (gas oil, fuel oil and kerosene), renewable sources of energy or waste materials, or by-products used for heating purposes such as coke oven and blast furnace gases,[57] on the basis that such sources are already within the scope of existing excise duties.[58] Likewise, the levy will not be imposed on supplies of road fuels such as petrol and diesel, as well as CNG and LPG when sold as road fuels (as just noted above), nor on aviation fuels such as aviation kerosene ('AVTUR') or AVGAS, on the basis that the government already has a fiscal strategy in place for reducing emissions from road transport through proposed future changes in road fuel duties.[59]

The levy is to be charged only on 'industrial and commercial use' of the energy sources described above. Although the Consultation Document indicates that this will cover energy use for lighting, heating, motive power and power for appliances in industry (including fuel industries), commerce, agriculture, public administration and other services (including certain transport services),[60] it appears that the way the levy will accomplish this result is simply by excluding certain types of supplies from the levy, with the result that all supplies of covered energy products not so excluded will be subject to the levy.

The government does not, for example, intend to impose the levy on domestic use of fuel and power for social policy reasons,[61] presumably because of concerns that such an imposition would be regressive and therefore have negative distributional consequences. The government proposes instead to provide in the levy that the energy producers who are to charge and collect the tax will not be required to do so in respect of supplies of energy for domestic use. Under the Value Added Tax Act 1994[62] ('VATA 1994'), VAT is charged, as was noted above, at a reduced rate of 5 per cent in respect of supplies of fuel and power for a 'qualifying use',[63] which use includes 'domestic use', defined as use in a house, flat or other dwelling, some types of communal residential accommodation,[64] self-catering holiday accommodation, a caravan or a houseboat.[65] A 'qualifying use' within the meaning of the VATA 1994 provisions also includes certain non-domestic uses, principally supplies of fuel and power to charities for use in their non-business activities, and so the government is also exempting such supplies from the levy. Presumably, the government decided simply to adopt, for reasons of administrative convenience and simplicity, the existing VAT provision in its entirety, on the basis that those who will be charging and collecting the levy, the suppliers of energy (see below), will already be familiar with this definition.

Similarly, the government does not intend to impose the levy in respect of supplies of energy to be used in public transport;[66] the reason for this is that the government is, as part of its broader transport policy, set out in the Integrated Transport White Paper,[67] seeking to encourage the use of public transport. The government is proposing to define the availability of this exemption once again by reference to the VATA 1994: public transport for the purposes of the levy will be any form of transport the supply of which is zero-rated for VAT purposes.[68]

Furthermore, in order to avoid double taxation, or the indirect imposition of the levy on domestic or other exempt uses of energy, the levy will not be charged on supplies of energy where such energy is to be used as an input to the production of another levyable energy product. Examples given include supplies of gas and coal for use in generating electricity, coal used to make coke, and energy used to crack crude oil in the oil refining process.[69] This proposal will, however, introduce some administrative difficulties, because suppliers of such energy will not necessarily know the uses to which the energy will be put, and therefore presumably the purchaser will have to be made liable to provide some form of representation or other evidence of use to the supplier who is meant under the proposals to charge and collect the levy (see below, regarding administration).

As noted above, the government is seeking to impose the levy only on energy used for lighting, heating, motive power and power for appliances in industry, commerce, agriculture, public administration and other services. Therefore the levy will not be imposed on supplies of fuels used for other purposes, such as use as a lubricant or raw material, perhaps in a chemical process.[70] The Consultation Document proposes to refer to these other uses as 'non-energy' purposes, and while it recognises that 'it will be important to define what is meant by ... "non-energy" use', the Consultation Document does not do so.[71]

The Consultation Document also makes clear that the government intends to set substantially lower rates of the levy 'for those energy-intensive sectors which can come forward with proposals which meet the government's criteria'. The government has not, however, made clear what its criteria are, nor how much of a reduction in rates can be expected.[72] The government has indicated, however, that it will not be taking 'a blanket "across the board" approach to setting the appropriate level of the new levy'.[73]

The government has not yet determined the rates at which the levy will be charged, but has indicated that it will be applied as a specific rate per nominal unit of energy.[74] This is surprising, given that the levy is meant to address the emission of greenhouse gases, and that each energy source has a different carbon content (carbon being the most important generator of greenhouse gases) and therefore a different marginal impact on the production of such greenhouse gases. This is a limitation which the Consultation Document itself recognises,[75] and will be discussed further, in the next section, below. The chancellor announced in his 1999 budget statement that the levy will raise approximately £1.75 billion in the fiscal year 2001/2, its first year of operation.[76] The Consultation Document shows, for illustrative purposes only, the rates which would apply to different energy sources, based on the chancellor's revenue expectations: supplies of coal would be chargeable at a rate of £0.21 per kilowatt-hour (kWh), gas also at a rate of £0.21 per kWh, and electricity at a rate of £0.60 per kWh.[77]

The Consultation Document provides that energy imported will generally be subject to the levy when the user of the imported energy itself either supplies the imported energy or supplies energy generated by the imported energy, and therefore energy imports generally present no particular problems. However, the Consultation Document does recognise that, when energy is imported by industrial and commercial users themselves for their own use, it should be subject to the levy, and contemplates that those users will account for such use through some unspecified self-supply mechanism.[78] The Consultation Document also provides that the levy will not be charged on exports of energy, but that exporters will have to keep records to show that the energy has, in fact, been exported.[79]

As noted above, although the levy will be charged on industrial and commercial users of certain sorts of energy, it will be the suppliers of the energy which will have to collect and remit the levy to the Customs authorities. To this end, suppliers of energy products will be the ones who must register with the Customs.[80] The Consultation Document indicates that the type of businesses which should expect to register and account for the levy are electricity supply companies, gas supply companies and other energy suppliers (although such suppliers who make only supplies to domestic consumers may be entitled to special treatment).[81] The government estimates that there will be fewer than 1000 businesses that will be required to register for the levy, and that it is likely that all will already be registered with the Customs and Excise for VAT purposes.[82] Therefore the government has decided to adopt the VAT model for dealing with returns and payments, and so the standard accounting period will be three months, with returns to be rendered and any levy due to be paid no later than one month after the end of the accounting period.[83] The Consultation Document also provides that registered persons will have to keep records, and that there will be a system of penalties, interest and appeals that is similar for other indirect taxes such as the VAT, but gives no further particulars.[84] The Consultation Document also provides that the chargeable event (the event which gives rise to a liability to pay the levy) occurs when energy is supplied to the final consumer (in this case, the commercial or industrial user) and indicates that, in determining the time of supply for these purposes, the levy will follow the relevant VAT rules.[85]

Finally, the chancellor has indicated that he intends to recycle the revenues generated by the levy (again, estimated to be about £1.75 billion in 2001/2) in full to business, primarily by way of a cut of 0.5 percentage points in the main rate of employer National Insurance Contributions ('NICs') and by schemes to promote energy efficiency.[86]

Critical Analysis

The proposed carbon change levy provides many clear examples of some of the pitfalls to which green taxes can succumb. Nowhere is this clearer than in terms of the most basic aspects of its design, notably the choice of tax base and the setting of the rate. It also, however, provides clear examples of the sorts of definitional and, therefore, administrative problems that can afflict any tax measure, as well as some of the difficulties that are thrown up in trying to accommodate concerns about the distributional impact of such taxes, and their potential effect on competitiveness.

The most fundamental problem is that the levy will be a tax on energy use, rather than on carbon use, with the result that the fundamentally important linkage between the thing taxed and the pollutant to be reduced has been fatally weakened. The underlying aim of the levy is to reduce British emissions of six greenhouse gases, the most important, by far, being CO^2, which accounts for some 84 per cent of all such gases. Levels of CO^2 emissions are directly related to the combustion of carbon-rich fuels. Simply put, not all forms of energy have the same carbon content, and therefore a levy based on the energy content, rather than the carbon content, of fuels is in danger of breaking the linkage that is necessary for any effective green tax, with the result that the appropriate substitution of less carbon-rich fuels for more carbon-rich fuels is less likely to occur quickly and efficiently, if at all. As an OECD study pithily notes: 'Among substitutes, the taxes should be differentiated according to the polluting content of the product, in a similar way as a carbon tax would be based on the carbon content of different fossil fuels.'[87] There is little debate about this in the literature.

Why, then, has the government opted for what is, in essence, a tax on energy rather than carbon? Part of the reason is the government's decision to exempt domestic consumers completely from the scope of the levy, for social policy reasons presumably relating to the supposed adverse distributional impact which would otherwise occur. In the Marshall Task Force Report, for example, Lord Marshall acknowledges this:

> I can see that this [that is, the idea that the tax should be directed at carbon dioxide emissions by business and domestic users of energy] is an attractive option in principle. It would target carbon dioxide emissions directly and, if applied 'upstream' to the use of primary fuels by industry and commerce (including fuels used by electricity generators in the generation of electricity), could encourage fuel switching on the part of those businesses towards low carbon fuels.
>
> However, an 'upstream' tax could conflict with other objectives of Government policy. For social policy reasons, it is the Government's

> intention not to introduce new taxes on *domestic* consumption of fuel and power. An 'upstream' tax could impact directly on domestic customers if the electricity generators attempted to pass on the higher costs in the form of higher prices. Even with a complex system of rebates, there would be no way of guaranteeing an exemption for domestic customers.[88]

Yet, as we saw above, there are other means of addressing distributional concerns than simply the reliance on rebates. Thus, owing to this constraint imposed by the government itself, the government was forced towards an energy tax which Lord Marshall acknowledged would be less effective in environmental terms, because it fails to encourage fuel switching.[89]

Another possible motive for the choice of tax base was disclosed in the course of the hearings of the Select Committee on Trade and Industry, and is the government's desire to protect the domestic coal industry. The concern is that a carbon tax would impinge most heavily on coal, a carbon-rich fuel, with very serious consequences for demand for coal.[90] A recent report by an Oxford-based energy consultancy has noted that, even under an energy rather than a carbon tax, 'the economic despatch of generation within the electricity market is likely to lead to coal plant bearing the brunt of reduced demand'. The report notes that 'Both energy and carbon taxes are therefore likely to lead to a reduced coal burn, but an energy tax will do so at greater cost to the consumer than would a carbon-based tax.'[91]

Similarly, it does not appear that the rates which the government is proposing for the levy bear any necessary relationship to rates that would be required to have the optimal effect in terms of emissions abatement. As noted above, ideally, the rate of the tax should be set so that it equates the marginal cost of reducing emissions and the marginal social damage arising from the pollution. There does not appear to have been any consideration of this fundamental issue. By the government's own estimates, the effect of the levy on greenhouse gas emissions will be minimal: the government estimates that it will result in an annual reduction of approximately 1.5 million tons of carbon emissions,[92] which is less than 1 per cent of total current levels of carbon emission in the UK.[93] One may be forgiven for concluding that the rate was set more with a view to financing the reduction of employer NICs than meeting the UK's Kyoto commitments.[94] And, indeed, there will be some curious distributional effects which result from this method of revenue recycling: while energy-intensive businesses may be adversely affected by the combination of the climate change levy and the reduction in employer NICs, the service industry as a whole may be a beneficiary.[95]

The decision to recycle revenues from the levy by way of such cuts to employer NICs is broadly in keeping with the approach suggested by proponents of the 'double dividend' theory, described previously. It is an approach which seems to have been taken by other OECD members which have experimented with carbon taxes.[96] While the government has said that some of the revenues would also be used to fund schemes to promote energy efficiency, the details of such uses are still not clear. A number of witnesses before the Select Committee on Trade and Industry proposed alternative means of recycling, such as the use of tax credits or capital allowances for investments in energy-efficient equipment, although, as noted above, there are difficulties with this sort of recycling as well.[97] On the whole, however, there seems to have been insufficient consideration of the complex issues relating to recycling.

Similarly, the government's approach to the issue of international competitiveness is unclear. As noted, the Consultation Document does make limited provision for the imposition of the levy on certain imports of energy and the remission of levy on exports of energy. Of more concern to commercial and industrial users of energy, however, will be the impact of the levy on their cost structures, and therefore the competitive position of their output in both British and foreign markets. The Consultation Document does not address this issue in its limited proposals for a sort of system of border tax adjustments. As noted above, the government is proposing to respond to the concerns of energy-intensive industries to the potential impact of the levy by providing for the setting of substantially lower rates of the levy for those energy-intensive sectors 'which can come forward with proposals which meet the Government's criteria'.[98] Even accepting that some form of relief may be appropriate, which may not be the case, it is questionable whether the approach intended by the government is the best one. The government has stated, for example, that sectors will be able to enter into the agreements if they meet the qualifying criterion of coverage by the EU Integrated Pollution and Prevention Control ('IPPC') Directive.[99] The Marshall Task Force Report concluded, however, that IPPC coverage is not a good way of identifying energy-intensive users, because some sites covered by the IPPC are not energy-intensive sites, and some energy-intensive users are not covered by the IPPC.[100] Furthermore, the Select Committee on Trade and Industry has raised serious concerns about the way in which the government is planning to negotiate these agreements.[101] Indeed, the concept of negotiating emissions and other standards on an industry or enterprise basis begins to look suspiciously like the 'command and control' form of regulation which green taxes are meant to replace in appropriate circumstances, and may result in additional compliance costs for both industry and the government. A related issue is the fate of carbon trading permits as an alternative economic instrument to a green tax. The government is proceeding with a pilot programme to test the feasibility of a carbon trading regime, but on the basis of the Marshall Task Force Report, has chosen a tax rather than a trading regime in the first instance. Space does not permit the analysis of the way a trading regime may work, but negotiations are proceeding at a European level towards the development of such a regime in response to the Kyoto Protocol. ILEX has recently issued a report that indicates that such a regime could be highly beneficial to UK industry, largely because it is already fairly well advanced in terms of emissions reduction strategies.[102] It is not clear that the government has given sufficient consideration as to how the proposed levy could most easily and efficiently be integrated into some future European or wider carbon permit trading scheme.

Finally, the proposals for the levy, as disclosed in the Consultation Document, point up the fact that the use of economic instruments such as green taxes can still be prone to definitional, and therefore administrative, difficulties. Sensibly, the government has sought to model the levy as much as possible on existing excise taxes, in particular, the VAT. And the use of appropriate VAT definitions is also laudable. Energy producers who will have to charge, collect and remit the tax will be more familiar with existing VAT definitions, and will already have systems in place to implement the new levy. Indeed, this approach can only promote the government's goal of reducing administrative costs for businesses.[103]

However, definitional problems remain. Take, for example, one of the proposed exemptions from the levy, that for energy used for public transport. As noted, the government is proposing to define the availability of this exemption by reference to the VATA 1994: public transport for the purposes of the levy will be any form of transport the supply of which is zero-rated for VAT purposes.[104] However, the definition to which the Consultation Document is making reference is not altogether clear. Supplies which are zero-rated are set out in Schedule 8 to the VATA 1994, and zero-rated supplies relating to transport are set out in Group 8 of this Schedule. There is not, however, a clear reference to 'public transport' in this group, although paragraph 4 of Group 8 does provide that the transport of passengers in any vehicle, ship or aircraft designed or adapted to carry not less than 12 passengers, or the transport of passengers on any scheduled flight, are zero-rated. This reference is not, therefore, as clear as one might have hoped. Even if this is the definition which the government had in mind, though, it is not one with which energy suppliers are likely to be familiar. It is, after all, a provision relevant to the exemption from VAT on supplies of certain transport services, and will therefore be familiar to the suppliers of those services. It will not be familiar, or even useful, to energy suppliers who provide energy to such businesses. Therefore it will presumably be up to the provider of such public transport services to identify for the energy supplier which purchases of energy will be for public transport services and which are for other purposes.

As noted earlier, a potentially even larger definitional problem surrounds the exemption which the government proposes to give in respect of so-called 'non-energy' uses of energy. The government is seeking to impose the levy only on energy used for lighting, heating, motive power and power for appliances in industry, commerce, agriculture, public administration and other services. Therefore the levy will not be imposed on supplies of fuels used for other purposes, such as use as a lubricant or raw material, perhaps in a chemical process.[105] There is, of course, some justification for this; the use of petroleum for lubrication, rather than combustion, or the use of coal in a filter, rather than for combustion, does not seem to result in the production of greenhouse gases, and therefore should not be taxed. However, defining such uses will be very difficult, because, as the Consultation Document itself recognises, the dividing line here between uses which should and should not be taxed is thin.[106] Furthermore, the supplier of the fuel, again, the party responsible for charging and collecting the levy, will be in a poor position to identify such use, and will have to rely on representations made by the user. Policing compliance in this area may be difficult.

Conclusions

As has been illustrated elsewhere in this volume, there has been a rapid change in recent years from direct regulation by government departments to other forms of regulation. Indeed, there has been a growing recognition that for certain purposes – for example, the control and reduction of 'negative externalities' such as environmental pollution, the use of taxes and other charges may be the most economically efficient and effective means of regulation. The proposals for a climate change levy as a means of achieving reductions in the levels of emissions of certain greenhouse gases may be offered as an example of this trend; however, they also illustrate some of the difficulties which confront such measures. The legislation by which the proposed levy will be implemented has not yet been released: as illustrated above, however, the proposed climate change levy suffers from a number of fundamental design problems, and as it is anticipated that the legislation will not differ in any significant way from the proposals that have been outlined in this chapter, it is unlikely that these problems will be addressed.

These problems have in part resulted from the competition between environmental policy goals and other concerns, such as broader energy policy, transport policy, employment and social policy and industrial strategy. Indeed, concerns about the impact of the proposed levy on the competitiveness of energy-intensive industries has caused the government to return to what looks suspiciously like direct regulation by government departments in the form of the current negotiations between the Department of the Environment, Transport and the Regions with these industries concerning reductions in the rate of the levy in return for agreed targets for improvements in energy efficiency. Such concerns, however, derive from the fact that the levy represents a British response to what is an international problem, and this illustrates another theme which runs through this volume: the importance of regulatory measures being taken at the appropriate jurisdictional level. National regulation of activities which have international consequences is, in the absence of effective international mechanisms, necessarily going to be compromised. The shortcomings of the proposed climate change levy do not, however, weaken the case for the use of tax and other similar measures as regulatory tools; they merely provide a good illustration of the many complexities which such tools must work upon.

Notes

1 See, for example, UNEP Information Unit for Conventions, (January 1997), 'Understanding Climate Change: A Beginner's Guide to the UN Framework Convention', <http://www.unfcc.de/resource/beginner.html>. There is now a massive literature on the issue of global warming, and there is much debate about the existence, extent and reasons for the problem. Similarly, there is no scientific certainty as to the extent of the danger that these emissions cause.

2 http://www.unfccc.de/resource/conv. The Framework Convention was adopted at the United Nations Headquarters (the 'UNHQ') in New York on 9 May 1992, and was open for signature at the Rio de Janeiro conference on Climate Change, 4–14 June 1992 and thereafter at the UNHQ from 20 June 1992 to 19 June 1993, at which date it had been signed by 166 states. It took effect on 21 March 1994 and by 14 June 1999 had been ratified by 179 states.

3 <http://www.unfccc.de/resource/docs/convkp/kpeng.html>. The text of the Kyoto Protocol was adopted in Kyoto, Japan, on 11 December 1997, and was open for signature from 16 March 1998 to 15 March 1999 at the UNHQ. As of 16 July 1999, the Kyoto Protocol had been signed by 84 states, but only ratified by 12, and has not yet come into force. Britain signed the Kyoto Protocol on 29 April 1998, but has yet to ratify it.

4 The six greenhouse gases are carbon dioxide (CO^2), methane (CH^4), nitrous oxide (N^2O), hydrofluorocarbons (HFCs), perfluorocarbons (PFCs) and sulphur hexafluoride (SF^6): Kyoto Protocol, Annex A.

5 See *Economic Instruments and the Business Use of Energy: A Consultation Paper*, Government Task Force on the Industrial Use of Energy, chaired by Sir Colin Marshall, March 1998 (the 'Marshall Task Force Consultation Paper'), 'Fore-

word', and *Economic Instruments and the Business Use of Energy: A Report by Lord Marshall*, November 1998 (the 'Marshall Task Force Report'), para. 3.

6 *Ibid.*

7 Select Committee on Trade and Industry, Ninth Report, 'Impact on Industry of the Climate Change Levy', 19 July 1999, para. (f), 'Summary of Conclusions and Recommendations'.

8 *Ibid.*, para. (a).

9 'Manual: Statistics on Environmental Taxes', ATW-Research (1996), commissioned by the European Commission, and quoted in Organisation for Economic Co-operation and Development, (1997) *Environmental Taxes and Green Tax Reform*, Paris: OECD (hereinafter referred to as 'OECD, 1997'), p.18.

10 See, for example, *Environmental Taxes and Green Tax Reform* (note 9, above), pp.19 *et seq.*

11 Income and Corporation Taxes Act 1988 ('ICTA 1988'), subsection 155(1A).

12 See, for example, Smith, S. (1995), *'Green' Taxes and Charges: Policy and Practice in Britain and Germany*, London: The Institute for Fiscal Studies, pp.85–8. The imposition of VAT would encourage reductions in demand for fuels, including carbon-intensive fuels, and would help redress the 'perverse incentives' under VAT whereby domestic energy consumption was untaxed but products which encouraged energy efficiency, such as insulation and double glazing, were taxed at standard rates.

13 Expenditure on domestic energy tends to take up a larger portion of the income of lower-income than higher-income taxpayers in Britain, and therefore the VAT would fall proportionately more heavily on such taxpayers.

14 Subsection 2(1A), Value Added Tax Act 1994 ('VATA 1994'). The rate has been reduced from 8 per cent to 5 per cent on supplies made after 1 September, 1997: section 6, Finance Act (No. 2) 1997.

15 See, for example, the HM Treasury consultation paper, 'Consultation on reform of Vehicle Excise Duty to ensure a cleaner environment', (HM Treasury, 1998); the proposals were announced in the chancellor's March 1998 budget.

16 See, for example, Ogus, A. (1998), 'Corrective Taxes and Financial Impositions as Regulatory Instruments' *Modern Law Review*, 61(6), 768–9, and references there at notes 6, 8 and 9.

17 See, for example, Smith, *'Green' Taxes and Changes* (n.12, above) and the sources referred to therein, and Satya Poddar, 'Taxation and Regulation' and Michael J. Trebilcock, 'Comment: Regulation by Taxation', in R.M. Bird and J.M. Mintz (eds) (1992), *Taxation to 2000 and Beyond*, Toronto: Canadian Tax Foundation, Toronto, pp.71 and 97, respectively.

18 See, for example, *Environmental Taxes and Green Tax Reform* (n.9, above), pp.15–16; Smith, *'Green' Taxes and Changes* (n.12, above), pp.1–7.

19 See Smith, *'Green' Taxes and Changes* (n.12, above), pp.11–12; Poddar, 'Taxation and Regulation' (n.17, above), pp.92–3. Often, of course, regulatory agencies do not have sufficient information to allow them to tailor pollution reduction requirements to the cost structures of firms, and the requirements are applied uniformly, which results in inefficiencies, as those polluters with low abatement costs will reduce emissions by too small an amount while those with high abatement costs will face unnecessarily – and comparatively – high costs for achieving similar amounts of reductions.

20 Smith, *'Green' Taxes and Changes* (n.12, above), pp.12–13.

21 Ogus, 'Corrective Taxes and Financial Impositions' (n.16, above), p.776; Poddar, 'Taxation and Regulation' (n.17, above), pp.92–3.

22 Smith, *'Green' Taxes and Changes* (n.12, above), p.13.

23 Ogus (n.16, above), pp.769, 787–8.

24 See, for example, Organisation for Economic Co-operation and Development

(1996) *Implementation Strategies for Environmental Taxes*, Paris: OECD (hereinafter referred to as 'OECD, 1996'), and OECD, 1997 (n.9, above).

25 Smith, *'Green' Taxes and Changes* (n.12, above), p.21.

26 OECD, 1996 (n.24, above), p.20.

27 *Ibid.*, p.19.

28 As is noted in *ibid.*, when pollution is associated with the consumption, taxes on products will likely be efficient, but direct taxes on emissions at the producer level will be more efficient. Here the reference is to products used as inputs, not the outputs of the production process, though the same could hold in respect of the outputs if they themselves cause the pollution.

29 *Ibid.*, pp.23–4; Ogus, 'Corrective Taxes and Financial Impositions' (n.16, above), p.778.

30 OECD, 1996 (n.24, above, p.24; Ogus, 'Corrective Taxes and Financial Impositions' (n.16, above), p.778, who notes that measuring the social costs (or externalities) involves the quantification of things such as the value of life, health and the environment, which have no ready market values, the discounting for effects which happen over time, and the resolution of scientific uncertainty as to what effects will accrue.

31 Demand elasticity measures the amount by which demand for a product will respond to a change in its market price; demand for a product is said to be inelastic if it is relatively unresponsive to a change in price, while demand is elastic where it changes more markedly in response to a change in price. This has implications for the appropriate level of tax, for if the tax is being imposed on a product the demand for which is elastic, a relatively smaller tax increase (and hence, price increase) will result in a relatively large reduction in demand and, if there is good linkage between the product and the emissions, a relatively large reduction in emissions.

32 OECD, 1996, (n.24, above), p.25.

33 Ogus, 'Corrective Taxes and Financial Impositions' (n.16, above), p.779.

34 See, for example, the essays in O'Riordan, T. (1997), *Ecotaxation*, London: Earthscan, Part II: 'The Double Dividend Debate', pp.77–216.

35 OECD, *Environmental Taxes and Green Tax Reform* (n.9, above), pp.33–6.

36 *Ibid.*, pp.31–2.

37 OECD, 1996 (n.24, above), p.30.

38 *Ibid.* Given that green taxes are meant to create an incentive to reduce emissions over time, if successful, they are also likely to produce less revenue over time. The restrictions which this potentially imposes on the related expenditure programme are clear.

39 See, for example, Surrey, S.S. and P.R. McDaniel (1985), *Tax Expenditures*, Cambridge, Mass.: Harvard University Press; Surrey, S.S. (1979), 'Tax Expenditure Analysis: The Concept and Its Uses', *Canadian Taxation*, Summer Issue, p.3, Surrey, S.S. (1970), 'Tax Incentives as a Device for Implementing Government Policy: A Comparison with Direct Government Expenditures', *Harvard Law Review*, 83(4), 705; Poddar 'Taxation and Regulation' (n.17, above), pp.87–8.

40 Excise taxes are, generally, taxes laid on the manufacture, sale or consumption of goods or services, or upon licences to pursue certain occupations or enjoy certain privileges. VAT is the most obvious example of an excise tax in the UK. Most green taxes and, in particular, any of the taxes referred to earlier that are imposed indirectly, on products which bear some relation to the pollution produced, are excise taxes.

41 This refers to the 'incidence' of the tax: that is, the identity of the person who ultimately bears the cost imposed by the tax. The incidence of a tax imposed on an input in the production process will depend on a number of variables,

including the existence of products the production of which has not been subject to the tax and which may act as substitutes for the product in question.

42 OECD, 1997 (n.9, above), pp.38–40.

43 Smith, *'Green Taxes and Changes'* (n.12, above), pp.83–6, reviews the distributional impact of the imposition of VAT on domestic energy consumption in Britain; Poterba, J. (1991), 'Tax Policy to Combat Global Warming: On Designing a Carbon Tax', in R. Dornbusch and J. Poterba (eds), *Global Warming: Economic Policy Responses*, Cambridge, Mass.: MIT Press, pp.82–3.

44 OECD, 1997 (n.9, above), p.44.

45 *Ibid.*, pp.41–2.

46 *Ibid.*, pp.43–4; and Poterba, 'Tax Policy to Combat Global Warming' (n.43, above), pp.82–3.

47 OECD, 1997 (n.9, above), pp.45–6.

48 Ibid., pp.46–8. This report cites another recent OECD study, Adams, J. (1997), *Environmental Policy and Competitiveness in a Global Economy: Conceptual Issues and a Review of the Empirical Evidence*, Paris: OECD, which concluded that 'neither the investment data nor the evidence on location decisions show evidence of industrial migration or pollution havens in response to differential environmental standards'.

49 OECD, 1997 (n.9, above), pp.48–9.

50 See, for example, Jackson, J.H. (1997), *The World Trading System: Law and Policy of International Economic Relations*, 2nd edn, London: MIT, pp.218–21.

51 See, for example, Ogus, 'Corrective Taxes and Financial Imposition' (n.16, above), pp.781–2.

52 HM Customs & Excise (1999), *Consultation on a Climate Change Levy*, London: HMSO, available at <http://www.hmce.gov.uk/notices/cc-levy.htm> (the 'Consultation Document'), para. 1.4, and Annex A, 'Government Policy on Environmental Taxation'.

53 Consultation Document, para. 1.2, and discussions with Philip Wood of the HM Customs & Excise Environmental Taxes Team, 30 July 1999.

54 *Ibid.* Para. 1.2 provides, for example, that Customs has been asked by the government 'to consult on *practical issues* which will affect the way the levy *is administered*' (emphasis added).

55 *Ibid.*, para. 4.1.

56 *Ibid.*, para. 4.2.

57 *Ibid.*, para. 4.3; it is noted in the Consultation Document that, while the levy does not apply to such sources directly, it will, perversely, apply to electricity generated from such sources, because of the decision to tax electricity.

58 *Ibid.*, para. 2.5.

59 *Ibid.*, para. 2.4.

60 *Ibid.*, paras 2.1 and 2.2.

61 *Ibid.*, para. 2.3.

62 1994, c. 23.

63 Subsection 2(1A), VATA 1994, and subsection 1(1), Schedule A1 thereto.

64 Set out in subsection 3(2) of Schedule A1, VATA 1994.

65 See subsection 3(1) of Schedule A1, VATA 1994. Section 2 of Schedule A1 provides that supplies of relatively small quantities of fuel and power will be considered to be for domestic use regardless of the actual use to which such supplies are put.

66 Consultation Document, paras 4.4 and 8.1.

67 Department of the Environment, Transport and the Regions (1999), *A New Deal for Transport: Better for Everyone*, <http://www.detr.gov.uk/itwp/paper/>.

68 Consultation Document, para. 8.1.

69 *Ibid.*, paras 4.4 and 9.1.
70 *Ibid.*, at para. 10.1. The Consultation Document gives examples such as the use of natural gas in the production of acetic acid, methanol and ammonia, the use of petroleum coke to manufacture electrodes, and the use of coal to manufacture carbon filters. The Consultation Document notes, however, that the levy would not apply to electricity used for such purposes – for example, in electrolysis – because the production of the electricity itself gives rise to emissions of greenhouse gases.
71 *Ibid.*, para. 10.2.
72 *Ibid.*, paras 1.3 and 11.1. The Consultation Document does not contain details of these schemes, and the chancellor offered little more guidance in his budget statement: see *Economic and Fiscal Strategy Report and Financial and Budget Statement Report 1999*, March 1999, at para. 5.65: <http://www.official-documents.co.uk/document/hmt/budget99/fsbrhome.htm>.
73 HM Treasury Press Office, Press Release HMT6, 9 March 1999.
74 *Ibid.*, para. 5.1.
75 *Ibid.*, para. 5.2: 'The Government is aware of the attractions, in principle, of structuring the levy so that it reflects the *carbon content* of different fuels.'
76 *Ibid.*, para. 6.3.
77 *Ibid.* The Consultation Document provides that the rates which apply to electricity will have to be determined by special rules, because 'a considerable proportion of the energy content of fossil fuels used in electricity generation is lost in combustion, transmission and distribution', and so 'Calculating the rate for electricity based on the metered energy content of electricity supplied to the consumer would result in undertaxation' (para. 6.1).
78 *Ibid.*, paras 18.1 and 18.2.
79 *Ibid.*, para. 18.3.
80 *Ibid.*, para. 4.1.
81 *Ibid.*, para. 21.2. Importers of energy for their own commercial or industrial consumption, energy producers using their own produced energy and community heating schemes (generally exempt from the levy) who supply surplus heat to industrial and commercial customers will also likely have to register and account for the levy.
82 Draft Regulatory Impact Assessment, para. 29, and Consultation Document, para. 21.1.
83 Consultation Document, para. 22.1.
84 *Ibid.*, paras 23 and 24.
85 *Ibid.*, para. 19.
86 *Ibid.*, para. 1.3, and Draft Regulatory Impact Assessment, para. 30. The main rate of Employers' National Insurance Contribution is currently 12.2 per cent and shall be lowered to 11.7 per cent as a result of these proposals.
87 OECD, 1996 (n.24, above), p.25.
88 Marshall Task Force Report, paras 105 and 106.
89 *Ibid.*, para. 117.
90 Select Committee on Trade and Industry, Ninth Report (n.7, above), para. 34. The Hon. Michael Meacher, Minister for the Environment, acknowledged in testimony to the Committee that a carbon tax would have 'a very disproportionate impact' on coal use, and witness noted that a carbon tax would 'run contrary to the thrust of Government energy policy which is to protect the coal industry and restrict the expansion of electricity generation by gas'.
91 ILEX (April 1999), 'Is Brown Really Green?', para. 3.7.
92 Draft Regulatory Impact Assessment, para. 26.
93 ILEX, 'Is Brown Really Green?' (n.92, above), para. 1.3.
94 Select Committee Report (n.7, above), para. 47: 'We remain to be convinced

that the Treasury has not seen the Climate Change Levy as an opportunity for the Chancellor to offer the majority of the business and commercial sectors a significant tax cut, by reducing employers' NICs, in his next Budget.'

95 See, for example, *ibid.*, para. 25.

96 For example, the Netherlands, Finland, Sweden and Norway all have such taxes, and have experimented with reductions in social security contributions. See OECD, 1997 (n.9, above), Box 8, p.35, and Organisation for Economic Co-operation and Development (1992), *Climate Change: Designing a Practical Tax System*, Paris: OECD, ch. 2, pp.25–54.

97 Select Committee Report (n.7, above), para. 30.

98 The Marshall Task Force Report offered two justifications for this special treatment: that the additional costs of energy attributable to the tax could form a significant part of the total costs of certain firms, and that there may be limited scope for energy-intensive firms, which already strive to minimise their energy costs, to improve significantly their energy efficiency: para. 134.

99 Select Committee Report (n.7, above), para. 41.

100 Marshall Task Force Report, Annex D, para. D4. This has been confirmed in testimony before the Select Committee on Trade and Industry, and by research done by the Institute for Public Policy Research: Select Committee Report (n.7, above), para. 41.

101 Select Committee Report (n.7, above), paras 43 and 44. Voluntary agreements on energy efficiency are being negotiated by the Department of the Environment, Transport and the Regions, apparently without input from the Treasury, while it will be the Treasury which will have a role in determining the nature and extent of any reductions in the rate of the levy.

102 ILEX (July 1999), 'Carbon Trading: Putting Britain in the Black?'

103 Draft Regulatory Impact Assessment, para. 25.2.

104 Consultation Document, para. 8.1.

105 *Ibid.*, para. 10.1. See note 70 above.

106 Consultation Document, para. 10.3: 'As far as "non-energy" use is concerned there are a number of potentially borderline cases, for example, where fuel is burnt in an industrial process with heat as a by-product, or where there is dual use of fuels. To help in determining the rules for this relief, we need to be aware of as many non-energy and dual uses of energy products as possible.'

11 Corporate Governance and the Approach to Regulation

CHARLOTTE VILLIERS, *University of Glasgow*, AND GEORGE BOYLE, *Shepherd & Wedderburn*

Introduction

Corporate governance is concerned with the relationship between the structure of rules, laws and conventional practices within which companies operate and their style of management and the decisions that they make.[1] This concern is clearly close to that of participants in the regulatory debate. In the UK, the corporate governance system has been defined as predominantly 'self-regulatory' in nature insofar as members of the regulated sector create the rules, supervise activity and operate enforcement mechanisms.[2] This is also relevant since regulation may not just consist of public interventions but also may be delegated through use of 'self-regulation'.[3]

Despite the predominance of self-regulation, the corporate governance system in the UK may more accurately be described as a combination of three broad regulatory techniques: voluntary, self-regulatory and regulatory control. Voluntary controls are created internally in the company: for example, company policies and strategies, company codes, rule books and internal monitoring procedures. Self-regulatory controls include industry codes of practice, rules established by commercial or business associations such as the Stock Exchange Listing Rules (which clearly have no direct effect, in terms of perceived 'sanctions' for breach on the majority of companies in the UK – it is well recognised that over 99 per cent of companies are private companies, and that these account for the vast majority of trade and business carried on within the UK), and rules created by professional bodies such as the Institutes of Chartered Accountants.

Regulatory controls include statutory rules backed up by sanctions for non-compliance. For example, the Companies Act 1985 contains a broad range of obligations such as requirements of financial disclosure, access to company information and procedural requirements designed to ensure fairness to shareholders, protection for creditors and so on, with civil and sometimes criminal, penalties for failure to comply with those requirements. In short, governmental and statutory interventions as well as informal, behind-the-scenes relationships between boards of directors and institutional shareholders[4] support the self-regulatory corporate governance framework.

In this chapter we shall explore the corporate governance system in the UK in the light of the regulatory debate. We shall consider the need for corporate governance and the definition adopted in the UK. We shall also consider the regulatory techniques adopted before describing some of the rules or principles of corporate governance. Then we shall consider the system from the point of view of its constitutive function and to what extent it addresses issues of public interest in the activities of public companies in the UK. A brief comparison with systems adopted outside the UK to see if any light can be cast on the future development of corporate governance in the UK and to consider whether fresh ideas can be introduced into the debate will complete our review.

The Need for Corporate Governance

Company directors and managers have an important role in running the company. They enjoy considerable power within the company because they have discretion in how the company is operated arising from the effective delegation to them of the power of overall direction and management of the company's affairs. Such discretion and power must be viewed from the point of view of the relationship of directors to the company, the shareholders, in certain cases its employees and, finally, its creditors. This 'pluralist' approach has tended to be the continental/Japanese emphasis, as contrasted to the Anglo-American tradition which effectively sets up shareholder interests as the principal, if not exclusive, determinant of how a company should be run.

Company law regards directors effectively as agents who act on behalf of the company. However, the company is, in essence, an entity without the ability to make its own decisions, created as a legally convenient vehicle for trade. Its interests have to be represented somehow by human actors: even in the case of corporate directors the ultimate decision-making responsibility will inevitably rest at some stage with individuals. Historically, in a deed-of-settlement company, the members were the company. Thus the company's interests have traditionally been equated with the interests of the shareholders.[5] Even after the introduction of the legal process of incorporation, entailing the substitution of a metaphysical entity with a new, separate legal persona for a collective organism or group, the shareholder's interests were and continue to be regarded broadly as the measure of the interests of the company.[6] In this way, the distinction between the corporation and its shareholders may be regarded as elusive, so that not to act for the economic advantage of the corporate entity would amount to disregarding the interests of the members.[7]

From this perspective the directors have traditionally been regarded as agents acting on behalf of and for the benefit of the shareholders. This approach has shaped the legal duties of directors. However, the practical position of directors and managers altered as companies grew in size and the number of shareholders increased. This corporate demographic change led shareholders to delegate their powers of 'ownership' of the company to the controlling management, leading to what is generally known as the separation of ownership and control. Berle and Means described the new position of the shareholder in the 1930s:

> His power to participate in management has, in large measure, been lost to him, and has become vested in the 'control'. He becomes simply a supplier of capital on terms less definite than those customarily given or demanded by bondholders; and the thinking about his position must be qualified by the realization that he is, in a highly modified sense, not dissimilar in kind from the bondholder or lender of money.[8]

Berle and Means were describing the corporate environment of the USA in the early 20th century, but their description might equally accurately describe the corporate environment of the UK. There has been a growing dominance of institutional shareholders on both sides of the Atlantic during the 1980s and 1990s,[9] which casts some doubt on the apparent weakness of the shareholders' position in the company. Nevertheless, the basic corporate structure that separates the managers from the shareholders *ex facie* provides the managers with an opportunity to pursue their own interests rather than act in the interests of the shareholders or even the company. This corporate structure gives rise to 'positional conflicts' between top corporate managers and shareholders[10] and thus creates a need to control the activities of the managers in order to ensure that they behave in accordance with rather than against the interests of the shareholders. Without such control managers might be able to distort the constitution of the company in pursuit of their own interests such as to maintain and enhance their position in the company. These might be regarded as 'internal reasons' for the need for corporate governance.

Potential 'external reasons' for corporate governance also exist. These rest in the fact that a company has a relationship with the wider community in which it is situated and that community may be affected by the company's activities. These effects could be very local but they could also spread out to an international scale. For example, a company could provide employment for a local community, thus having an influence on that community's economy. A locally based company may have extremely important ties with other local businesses in terms of trading relationships which, if the company relocates, or indeed expands, may have serious positive or negative economic and social repercussions. Failure to control a company's activities could also result in damage to the environment or risk to the safety of consumers or employees. Without adequate controls, public confidence in the commercial activities of companies might diminish. This could reduce a company's, and in turn the nation's, prosperity. It is from this perspective that some commentators have advocated a more 'inclusive' approach to corporate governance. This more holistic approach is promulgated by certain 'progressive' organisations, such as the 'Tomorrow's Company' group of the Royal Society of Arts.[11] Indeed, statistics have been presented which show that this general approach in encouraging worker and community links and involvement produces not only a better and more productive operational environment but in the long term more secure and 'successful' financial performance.[12]

Corporate governance promises to be a mechanism by which the management of corporate activities may be controlled. As was stated by the Department of Trade and Industry (DTI), corporate governance 'can have a major impact on the overall direction of the company and thus its commercial prospects'.[13] However, the shape and the effectiveness of corporate governance are largely determined by how it is defined. In the UK, a narrow definition tends to have been adopted, focusing on the 'internal' reasons for corporate governance.

Defining Corporate Governance

There are many available definitions of what constitutes corporate governance. We shall focus on what has been accepted as the most authoritative definition of corporate governance in the UK. The Cadbury Committee, reporting in December 1992 on the financial aspects of corporate governance, provided this definition, which is that corporate governance is 'the system by which companies are directed and controlled'.[14] This is a vague and not entirely helpful definition. However, the rest of the paragraph in the Report in which this definition appears offers some light on the definition:

> Boards of directors are responsible for the governance of their companies. The shareholders' role in governance is to appoint the directors and the auditors and to satisfy themselves that an appropriate governance structure is in place. The responsibilities of the board include setting the company's strategic aims, providing the leadership to put them into effect, supervising the management of the business and reporting to shareholders on their stewardship. The board's actions are subject to laws, regulations and the shareholders in general meeting.

From this definition and explanation it is clear that the company is to be directed and controlled from within the company. Indeed, corporate governance in the UK has emphasised the structure of the company and its internal processes.[15] In particular, the central focus is the relationship between the shareholders and directors/management. Responsibility rests with directors to establish the company's policies and to supervise how the company is managed. The directors are, in turn, accountable to the shareholders. This focus on the internal relationships gives rise to what Sheikh and Chatterjee describe as a 'tripartite' system in which are involved the directors, shareholders and auditors.[16]

In this tripartite system the directors manage the company with a view to maximisation of the company's profits. Indeed, the *Hampel Report on Corporate Governance,* published in 1998, claims that the single overriding objective shared by all listed companies, whatever their size or type of business, is the preservation and the greatest practicable enhancement over time of their shareholders' investment.[17] Thus the shareholders seek to ensure that the directors will maximise the profits on their behalf and the auditors guard against financial irregularities and aim for the directors to provide a 'true and fair view' of the company's performance.

Corporate Governance via Best Practice

The tripartite system of corporate governance purports to operate as a means of checks and balances to ensure that managers do not abuse their powers within the corporation. The preferred approach of industry and government for making this system effective has been to establish principles of best practice. This strategy has been implemented through codes of best practice. These have been issued by all three of the committees (Cadbury, 1992; Greenbury, 1995; Hampel, 1998) that have reported on corporate governance during the 1990s, culminating in a Combined Code of Best Practice, implemented by the London Stock Exchange.[18]

The Combined Code comprises principles of corporate governance and a code of best practice. These focus on structural issues, including the membership of the board of directors, directors' remuneration and relations between the board and shareholders, as well as accountability issues, including financial reporting, internal control and the relationship between the board and the company's auditors. The aim of the Combined Code is to allow companies to create and establish their own governance policies in the light of the principles set out in the Code. This seeks to offer flexibility for companies but within a broad framework of requirements. Listed companies must make a disclosure statement in two parts. In the first part of the statement the company must report on how it applies the Code's principles. It is for the companies to define and explain their own governance policies and for their shareholders and others to evaluate this part of the company's statement. In the second part of the statement the company must confirm that it complies with the Code provisions or explain why it does not. Again the shareholders and others must evaluate such explanations. The role of institutional investors is also addressed, although the Code states that this aspect is not appropriate for the Listing Rules to include within the disclosure requirement. Instead, the provisions relating to the role of institutional investors are recommendations only.

It is clear that the Code aims to provide flexibility to companies in order to take account of their diversity. The Code reflects the Hampel Committee's objective which was 'to restrict the regulatory burden on companies e.g. by substituting principles for detail wherever possible'.[19]

The Limits of the UK's Approach to Corporate Governance

The reliance on a combination of internal relationships being conducted in accordance with principles of best practice published in codes of practice is problematic. First, there are problems inherent in a company's internal relationships that make effective checks and balances difficult to accomplish. Secondly, codes of practice alone are insufficient to guarantee the establishment of good or best practice and indeed, given that these tend to affect, like the Combined Code, only listed companies and not the vast majority of the UK's companies, it can easily be argued that they have little practical application and influence. This easy argument, however, perhaps ignores the need for, and importance of, creating 'examples' in the more high-profile case of listed plcs, which by their nature clearly tend to have more ability to comply with regulations, interact with the public on a much more widespread basis and generally be more capable of being, and recognising the need to be, regulated than a typical owner-managed small private company. These points will be dealt with in turn.

The Problems of Internal Relationships in the Company

In reality, reliance purely on the internal control mechanisms is unlikely to be sufficient for ensuring openness, integrity and accountability of those managing companies. The limits of these internal controls arise from the fact that shareholders are generally disadvantaged in their position in comparison with the managers. First, they have restricted access to information about the activities of managers. For example, the annual report and financial reports are not always particularly informative or helpful for monitoring purposes. According to Brown, financial statements concentrate on legal form rather than economic substance, on past events rather than the future, on cost rather than value and on profit rather than wealth.[20] These legal requirements are regularly supplemented in practice. Invariably, corporate lawyers will include in legal documentation, such as shareholders' agreements, rights for their clients to obtain, and obligations on the investee company to provide, detailed financial information (such as monthly management accounts, cash-flow reports and budgetary forecasts usually only available to the board, not shareholders) where there is an intention to become involved in, or invest in, a company as a shareholder.

The financial information delivered to shareholders is sometimes too detailed and not within an easily comprehensible context, with the result that (individual) shareholders do not read the statements properly or cannot necessarily appreciate the implications of the information provided.[21] Further, at least for individual shareholders, channels of communication with directors and managers are notoriously ineffective. The weakness of the Annual General Meeting has been well documented.[22] The directors are easily able to manipulate decisions taken in the Annual General Meeting by methods such as control or influence of proxy votes and information provided in circulars in advance of the meetings.[23] Thirdly, individual shareholders have little incentive to monitor the activities of the directors. The costs and energy involved in doing so may outweigh significantly the value of their individual investments.[24] Indeed, shareholders who seek to challenge directors' actions in the courts[25] face procedural barriers and judicial reluctance to intervene in commercial decisions.[26]

For these reasons greater attention has been focused on institutional shareholders as more effective monitors of the activities of directors.[27]

This is understandable since approximately 80 per cent of investors in listed companies in the UK are institutional investors.[28] Thus the Hampel Committee stated that institutional shareholders have a responsibility to make considered use of their vote.[29] However, focus upon institutional shareholders has generally concentrated more on their informal means of influence. Clearly, one problem with this approach is that there is no regulation of their behaviour at an informal level.[30] Furthermore, institutional investors offer no guarantee of effective control of managers' behaviour. Despite their potential power, they have not always been prepared to intervene, and where they have this has allegedly been with an emphasis on short-term earnings, it being recognised that institutional investors' interests are not always in accord with those of individual shareholders.[31]

Other potential 'internal' watchdogs who have received attention are non-executive directors and auditors. However, the level of independence of the non-executive directors and auditors is open to doubt. The independence of auditors has continued to be a major source of controversy in the auditing profession.[32] Similarly, surveys have continued to reveal a lack of independence of non-executive directors. For example, Cosh and Hughes provide empirical data that corroborate a long-held belief in the lack of independence of non-executive directors. In this respect, Cosh and Hughes suggest that the presence of significant numbers of 'insider' non-executives does not seem consistent with independent outsider judgments.[33] Although, particularly in relation to listed companies, remuneration committees tend to consist of independent non-executive directors,[34] suspicions of 'cronyism' have tended to persist.

In conclusion, the problems with the structural positions of actors in the company's 'internal' relationships indicate that internal checks and balances are unlikely to achieve an adequate system of control of corporate activity. Arguably, this emphasis on the internal aspects is too restrictive an approach and one that does not take into account the reality of its limitations.

The Problems of Self-regulatory Codes of Best Practice

The principles for best practice adopted in the self-regulatory codes have also been subjected to considerable criticism. As is stated by Dignan, the codes are 'at the very loose end of any regulatory control system'.[35] The flexibility that they offer may allow directors to abuse the system. Other difficulties include potential bias, insufficient coordination of government policy and enforcement problems.[36] Heavy reliance on self-regulation could result in a fragmentation of responsibility with what Cheffins reports as allegations of 'too many cooks in the regulatory kitchen'.[37] A clear example of this problem is the approach to length of appointment of service of directors. The existing statutory provision on this issue requires shareholder approval for appointments of more than five years.[38] The Cadbury Committee stated that directors' service contracts should not exceed three years without shareholders' approval.[39] The Greenbury Committee indicated a preference for notice or contract periods of one year or less.[40] The Hampel Committee supported Greenbury's proposal but recognised that one-year notice or contract periods could not be achieved immediately.[41] This view was possibly a response to the potential problems caused by appointments that might have been considered too short. The Combined Code adopts a flexible approach to the issue, stating that there is a strong case for setting notice or contract periods at, or reducing them to, one year or less. It adds that boards 'should set this as an objective, but they should recognise that it may not be possible to achieve it immediately'.[42] It states further that 'if it is necessary to offer longer notice or contract periods to new directors recruited from outside, such periods should reduce after the initial period'.[43] Thus Cheffins' prediction of insufficient coordination of government policy appears to be confirmed by these provisions. The self-regulatory codes have culminated in aspirations far stricter than the statutory requirements but effectively with an equivocal stance that leaves considerable discretion to the companies themselves. Whilst some would argue that this is preferable, allowing a pragmatic application by companies within their commercial context, perceptions of inconsistency and 'fudge' may be difficult to refute. Enforcement problems are bound to arise when companies are given so much flexibility. Nor are the courts likely to intervene where the codes have no statutory or common law backing.

It is possible to conclude from these observations that effective corporate governance cannot be guaranteed by reference to private relations and arrangements alone. At the least the system requires the involvement of professional or industry-associated institutions the existence of which is known to the public, open to comment if not scrutiny. Moreover, although these institutions are privately constituted their quasi-public status cannot be denied. For example, the Takeover Panel is technically a self-regulatory body. However, Lord Donaldson, in the case of *R* v. *Panel on Take-overs and Mergers, ex parte Datafin plc*,[44] describing self-regulation as an 'emotive' and 'ambiguous' term, stated that the Takeover Panel had a role as part legislator, part judge and so on. This description, supporting the arguments for judicial review of the Panel's decisions, recognises the public impact of the activities and decisions of such organisations. This indicates that it is difficult to confer purely self-regulatory status even on arrangements that are left to private organisations. Indeed, a thin line exists between self-regulation and formal intervention. This is evidenced by the fact that the DTI was closely attached to the work of the Cadbury Committee, going so far as to provide staff, including the Committee's secretary.[45] The Cadbury Committee itself stated that, if the standards of financial reporting and business conduct are not seen to be raised, a greater reliance on statutory regulation 'may be inevitable'.[46]

These observations are not new. There were similar experiences in the context of financial services more than a decade ago.[47] Despite a preference for self-regulation in financial services, it cannot be denied that developments have led to a sector that is increasingly regulated by statute.

A Three-tiered Corporate Governance System

In reality, despite the predominance of an industry-associated self-regulatory system, corporate governance in the UK may be more accurately described as a three-tiered system comprising (a) common law and statutory rules, (b) guidance principles and (c) company-level measures and structures. The common law rules relevant to corporate governance consist mainly of fiduciary duties incumbent on directors and other officers of a company aimed at promoting honesty and disclosure, and combating conflicts of interest.

These include a duty to act bona fide in the interests of the company and not to exercise their powers for any collateral purpose; a duty not to make a secret profit by use of their position; and a duty to avoid a conflict between their duty to the company and their personal interests.[48] Fiduciary duties alone would be regarded as weak mechanisms for protecting companies and their constituent interests against pursuit of self-interest by corporate managers. Indeed, fiduciary duties cannot be prescribed in detail because they are fact-specific[49] and therefore unpredictable. Furthermore, the courts' policy of non-interference means that they will only intervene in *Wednesbury*-type situations such as when a decision has been made that is so unreasonable that no reasonable person or body could have made it.[50]

Fiduciary duties are backed by a myriad of statutory provisions that guard against self-dealing by directors. In particular, Part X of the Companies Act 1985 contains obligations such as disclosure of interest in relevant transactions. Criminal and civil sanctions apply against breach of many of the provisions in Part X. There are also detailed financial disclosure provisions and obligations with regard to disclosure of remuneration. Many of these disclosure obligations are supplemented by requirements and standards set by City institutions such as the London Stock Exchange and relevant professional bodies such as the Institutes of Chartered Accountants. The London Stock Exchange implements the Combined Code. Thus it is possible to see that the corporate governance system opens out beyond strictly legal requirements to include supporting industry or professionally associated requirements. Some of these 'self-regulatory' aspects may involve stringent sanctions for non-compliance, such as denial of listing status, initiated by the Takeover Panel, for example.

Alongside the Combined Code and association requirements, many companies have also created their own codes of conduct. Bodies such as the Organisation for Economic Co-operation and Development[51] and the International Labour Office have also published codes and guidelines. Such codes have many virtues. For example, they may improve bottom-line results, or provide overall strategic direction, or nurture open communication in the business environment.[52] However, as with the Combined Code, a number of problems exist with regard to these voluntary codes. Often they are restricted to specific issues such as employment conditions and they tend to be vague, inconsistent and lacking in legal force.[53] Another problem is that they lack the support of staff training and are not widely publicised.[54]

Ultimately, the UK corporate governance system illustrates the 'merits and disadvantages' of the different possible forms of regulation. Thus, according to the DTI's Steering Committee, statutory regulation has the advantages of democratic legitimacy, accountability of ministers and open and independent enforcement through the courts. The disadvantages of statutory regulation include the failure to be able to respond adequately to the changes inherent in commercial practice and complexity. The nature of 'hard-and-fast' rules may also be to encourage a box ticking approach that applies with the letter rather than with the spirit of the law.[55] Another problem is that regulations may create burdens on companies such as time and monetary costs of compliance. Indeed, the recent spate of 'public to private' transactions whereby companies have de-listed from the London Stock Exchange has, at least in relation to some of the smaller capitalisation companies, been due to some extent to the disproportionately high costs (measured against the 'benefits' of listing which have sometimes not been as apparent) in complying with the various regulatory standards imposed. Against statutory regulations self-regulation has the benefits of expertise, flexibility and dynamism as well as greater sensitivity to specific circumstances.[56] The disadvantages of self-regulation, however, are lack of precision and lack of transparency and potential bias. These observations are familiar to the broader regulatory debate[57] for which the benefits and disadvantages of different regulatory forms are of central concern. Even in combination it is possible to observe strengths and weaknesses. For example, the Cadbury Code gained legitimacy both because of its governmental support and because it existed against the threat of more formal regulation. The provisions relating to length of contracts service for directors, however, have shown the potential complexities and uncertainty involved in a combined structure.

The last observation leads us to consider another aspect of the regulatory debate: whether regulation should be facilitative or directive. This is also an issue for company lawyers. This consideration could in fact provide a yardstick against which the merits of the corporate governance system might be measured.

Facilitation or Obligation?

For more than a decade corporate lawyers have been concerned with the nature of the rules applicable in company regulation. To what extent should the rules be mandatory and to what extent should they be facilitative?[58] Before exploring the arguments it is appropriate to explain these terms. Generally, facilitative or enabling rules may be divided into two categories: permissive rules or presumptive rules. Permissive rules are rules that would legitimise operations that might otherwise not be valid. Generally, they require the participants to opt in. Presumptive rules are default rules that apply automatically unless the parties decide to opt out. Ramsay states that enabling rules promote private arrangements between corporate participants since they are in a better position to understand and contract for their own needs rather than the government. Thus individuals are also prominent in enforcing such rules. Mandatory rules are coercive in nature and apply automatically without opportunity to vary or opt out by the participants. The state is prominent in enforcing mandatory obligations.[59]

The DTI criticised the Companies Act 1985 as 'essentially backward looking – seeking to deal with problems that have arisen in the past rather than to facilitate modern practices'.[60] This suggests that the DTI would prefer a company law system with a facilitative approach rather than a directive focus.

This connection between the facilitative function of law and regulation for effective operation of the market coincides with the views of certain commentators in both the company law and the regulation fields. Ramsay, for example, regards mandatory or directive obligations as a response to market failure. This implies some opposition between regulation and market control. Similarly, in the regulatory arena, Ogus distinguishes between 'market systems' and 'collectivist systems'. He suggests that, generally, a market system will be facilitative and a collectivist system will be directive.[61] If one agrees with Ramsay and Ogus and if it is accepted that companies have a role in the operation of markets, one might expect a greater emphasis on facilitative rules, with a move away from public intervention towards more reliance on private arrangements. Indeed, deregulatory steps have been taken in company law since the 1980s, in particular for smaller and private limited companies. For example, smaller companies have less onerous accounting obligations. Private companies may also elect to adopt written resolutions rather than proceed with general meetings.

However, this deregulatory approach does not appear to have been applied to larger public limited companies, in particular those with a listing on a stock market. For these companies it is possible to witness a greater emphasis on directive or mandatory rules. This difference in treatment may be explained by reference to Eisenberg's analysis.

Eisenberg advocates, for both public and private companies, a mixture of enabling and mandatory rules but with different emphasis in each type of company. Thus in private companies the structural and distributive issues should contain at their core enabling or default rules with mandatory rules at the periphery to avoid oppression. For example, financial assistance rules (prohibiting a company to utilise its own assets in connection with a purchase of its shares) should be default rules and the elective resolution an enabling rule. The long-term aspects that cannot be predicted or addressed in advance should be subject to mandatory provisions. The core of fiduciary rules such as the directors' duty to act in good faith on behalf of the company should be mandatory. Default or enabling provisions should apply at their periphery. Thus some specific situations could be left to the private agreement of the company participants, such as when the director has the opportunity of making a profit.

In public companies bureaucratic ordering and direction by managers is predominant. There is a possibility of self-interest of top managers and of positional conflicts between the top managers and other participants. Large public companies in particular are powerful institutions with a potential to affect the national economy and to have an impact on social and environmental conditions. Furthermore,[62] bargaining possibilities among participants in large public companies are considerably more limited than in small companies because the participants are more likely to be dispersed and to have more diverse constituents. This background makes it necessary to have mandatory rules for the core aspects of structural and fiduciary matters such as appointment of directors and financial disclosure. Where top managers may be affected by arrangements they should not have power to make those arrangements because this would involve conflict of interests and a danger of coerced consent by shareholders because of limitations in the voting system. On the other hand, matters concerning lower-level participants could be left to enabling or default rules.

Eisenberg's constitutive framework focuses on the ability of companies to operate. In order to function properly, they require strong structural foundations that do not allow positional conflicts to hinder them. His view suggests that the purpose of mandatory rules is to redress the weaknesses of bargaining. These are particularly strong in public companies. These issues are relevant not only in and for each company but also between companies. Thus the recent introduction of the Late Payment of Commercial Debts (Interest) Act 1998 may be criticised from a practical perspective. Many smaller companies would be unlikely, it is thought, to risk incurring the wrath of larger more powerful customers by invoking the Act, as this may prejudice the relationship which is often 'one-sided' to start with.

In conclusion, mandatory rules are not in fact in opposition to the market-place but they should rather work in conjunction with markets and morals to curb traditional and positional conflicts. Eisenberg is suggesting that markets are *not* able to eradicate inefficiency or to guarantee a correspondence between managers' pay and company performance. Thus the purpose of regulation is to *assist* markets with these objectives.

In fact if we view companies as key market actors it could be argued that the continued existence of the market-place actually depends upon the ability of companies to function. From this point of view it could also be argued that Eisenberg's constitutive rules go beyond constituting the internal structures and processes of companies but contribute to constituting the market-place too. This argument would coincide with Shearing's suggestion that market ordering cannot occur by itself but needs to be constituted by regulation.[63] Indeed, the functions of company law go beyond profit maximisation to include also the reduction of risks, fairness and justice, the definition of boundaries in order to gain cooperation and the maintenance of stability.[64] All of these functions are of crucial importance to a successful market-place. As Shearing observes, markets are dependent on trust and trust is at the heart of regulation.[65] These points therefore take the debate beyond the arguments for and against mandatory or enabling rules but towards judgments about whether the system of company law and corporate governance, including both mandatory and enabling rules, is conducive to a successful market-place. The important questions then become: does company law allow companies to operate effectively by eliminating internal conflicts and creating efficiency and trust, and is there trust in the market-place? The answer to these questions determines the quality of the UK's corporate governance system.

Directors' Remuneration: A Case Study

A key aspect of the corporate governance debate in the UK has been that of directors' remuneration. This aspect has been the exclusive subject of the Greenbury Report and has been a favourite subject of the media for most of the 1990s.

Directors' remuneration illustrates our observation that corporate governance is not simply a self-regulatory arena. Rather, remuneration makes clear that corporate governance has utilised a variety of regulatory techniques, including statutory rules, industry-associated codes of practice and internal control mechanisms such as remuneration committees. Thus Section 232 and Schedule 6 of the Companies Act 1985, as well as secondary legislation,[66] direct the disclosure of directors' emoluments and other benefits. The Combined Code contains principles and more detailed provisions on the level and make-up of directors' remuneration, including policy and service contracts and compensation, procedure for developing policy and fixing remuneration packages, and disclosure of policy and details of the remuneration of each director.[67] Listed companies have remuneration committees and within the guidelines of the Combined Code are free to create their own remuneration policies. Failure to comply with the guidelines, however, must be reported on by listed companies, thus ensuring a degree of accountability, adverse publicity often being the major sanction and therefore acting to a substantial extent as an incentive to compliance.

Within this network of controls there are mandatory, presumptive and permissive rules. The rules in the Combined Code in fact illustrate the possible overlap between mandatory and enabling rules. For example, the requirement that a proportion of executive directors' remuneration should be structured so as to link rewards to corporate and individual performance appears to be a mandatory provision. However, the difficulty of proving this and the ease with which a link between pay and performance can be broken or created means that the rule is effectively no more than a presumptive rule that can be opted out of. It could be argued that in order for mandatory rules to be effective they require the backing of sanctions and enforcement mechanisms.

More importantly, the effectiveness of the rules is connected to the way they fit into the structure of the company. If the rules do not eliminate the positional conflicts that exist between the top managers and other corporate participants, their effectiveness is bound to be limited. Indeed, a key problem in the area of directors' pay has been the inability of shareholders to curb the discretion of top managers. Remuneration committees, for example, currently are not directly accountable to shareholders, although their members must be named in the annual report. Nor do institutional shareholders make sufficient use of their votes, despite the fact that these appear to be in the best position to influence managers. Thus from this point of view it appears that effective structures are necessary to enable other rules to succeed. If company law rules fail, trust in the system diminishes. This creates a lack of trust in the market-place itself.

The Narrow Framework of Corporate Governance in the UK

One limitation is the narrow perspective of corporate governance in the UK. The Hampel Committee, accepting the Cadbury definition of corporate governance, also conceded that it is a restrictive definition that 'excludes many activities involved in managing a company which may nevertheless be vital to the success of the business'. Indeed, it is limited by the fact that it concentrates only on the internal factors. This fact limits the definition from the perspective of justifications for mandatory rules and the constitution of the market-place.

The market-place requires companies to attract investment, not only in terms of purchase of shares but also in terms of obtaining credit for the supply of goods and services as well as in terms of purchase of goods and services offered by companies. However, the participants in these aspects, creditors and suppliers, are normally viewed as outside the company and are not therefore in a position to bargain so effectively with regard to positional conflicts with the company or its managers. The theory of mandatory rules would suggest that these groups in particular require the protection offered by such rules: for example, being able to obtain payment of interest where debts remain outstanding beyond reasonable limits. That would also help to build trust in the market-place. Yet the UK's corporate governance system, framed by Cadbury's definition that concentrates on the internal processes, does not adequately address these needs.

Sheridan and Kendall provide a broader definition of corporate governance that recognises the relationship between the company and the community and goes beyond the notion that profit maximisation is the only relevant objective of the enterprise. They argue that good corporate governance consists of a 'system of structuring, operating and controlling a company' such as to achieve the following:

> (i) Fulfil the long-term strategic goal of the owners, which, after survival may consist of building shareholder value or establishing a dominant market share or maintaining a technical lead in a chosen sphere, or something else, but will certainly not be the same for all organisations.

(ii) Consider and care for the interests of employees, past, present and future, which we take to comprise the whole life-cycle including planning future needs, recruitment, training, working environment, severance and retirement procedures, through to looking after pensioners.

(iii) Take account of the needs of the environment and the local community, both in terms of the physical effects of the company's operations on the surroundings and the economic and cultural interaction with the local population.

(iv) Work to maintain excellent relations with both customers and suppliers, in terms of such matters as quality of service provided, considerate ordering and account settlement procedures, etc.

(v) Maintain proper compliance with all the applicable legal and regulatory requirements under which the company is carrying out its activities.[68]

Immediately it is possible to observe that Sheridan and Kendall's approach is much broader and addresses the 'external' as well as the 'internal' aspects of corporate activity. This definition indicates that the shareholders' profit-oriented interest is not the only relevant goal of the company but that other constituent interests are also relevant to the company. Such other constituent interests must influence how that company is run as well as the control structure that seeks to ensure that the company's activities are managed properly. In order for these other groups to have an effective influence mandatory rules will be required because they have less bargaining power and market forces alone are unlikely to protect them adequately.[69] Obviously fundamental changes to the current system and corporate law framework are necessary to achieve these goals. At the very least, the mandatory rules would have to be enforceable and backed up by sanctions in order for them to be effective.

Corporate Governance outside the UK

As mentioned above, a seminal debate in relation to corporate governance is whether a company should be run on behalf of its owners, the shareholders, and exclusively for their benefit or whether a company is more akin to a social institution, not really 'owned' in that sense, to be run to further the interests of its business. In the former case the board is regarded as agent of the shareholders, and in the latter as trustee for 'stakeholders'. The agency model has its roots in Anglo-American corporate culture, with the maximisation of shareholder value as its principal objective. One argument the agency model supporters took forward against the differing continental European and Japanese approach is that the board risks being accountable to nobody if it attempts to look after the interests of too many disparate stakeholders. However, this 'stakeholder' approach argues that the agency model prioritises short-term results at the expense of long-term development, although the continued success of UK and US corporations seems to militate against this argument.

The 'stakeholder' approach promulgated by Japanese and continental corporate culture has tended to emphasise the wider role of companies in society. The Peters Report in the Netherlands[70] contains an opening statement that 'Companies and the enterprise connected therewith play an important role in society' and 'They must seek a good balance between the interests of the providers of risk capital (investors) and the other stakeholders'. In France, the Vienot Report[71] emphasised that 'the interests of the company may be understood as an overriding claim of the company as a separate economic agent, pursuing its own objectives which are distinct from those of shareholders, employees, creditors including the internal revenue authorities, suppliers and customers. It nonetheless represents the common interest of all these persons which is for the company to remain in business and prosper.' In Japan, the objective to be pursued is the general welfare of the company based on continued growth, guaranteed employment, favourable business relationships with creditors, suppliers and distributors, and shareholders' interests have traditionally not been such a primary concern. Under German law, a management board is required to run the company in the interests of the company as a whole, shareholders being seen as only a part of the differing groups of 'stakeholders'. Despite some differing views, opposition to the supposedly short-term objectives of Anglo-American companies may be appeased to an extent by their continuing success and profitability on a worldwide scale. Finding the balance between shareholders and other stakeholders, according to the Dutch Peters Report which says that 'in the long term, this should not mean a conflict of interests', is difficult, but not impossible.

To an extent the equity ownership pattern in listed companies throughout the world does seem to give some broad overviews. For example, in the USA and the UK pension funds account for around 70 per cent of total pension funds assets in the western world, and Canada, Australia and the Netherlands have also built up sizable pension funds over the years. It is in these countries with more developed pension fund equity ownership that the stock exchanges play a more important role. Recent developments in Germany seem to suggest that two-thirds of new German investments may be going into equity funds, whereas until as late as 1996 most German savings went into bond funds.

The question therefore is where the trends of the future will be. Will they tend to take more account of the 'holistic' approach to corporate governance advocates on the continent, often with the need to be backed up by mandatory regulation, or will the financial strength of Anglo-American corporations continue to ensure that the shareholder interest is the paramount 'approach', focusing more on 'enabling' provisions where possible and emphasising self-regulation and voluntary codes, and is maintained with minor concessions to wider stakeholder involvement?

Conclusion

What has been observed in this chapter is that the corporate governance system in the UK illustrates a range of different regulatory techniques, all of which have both merits and disadvantages. It is unlikely that the use of only one regulatory form would achieve an effective system. However, even a mixture of such regulatory techniques is not guaranteed to be effective.

The objectives of regulation must be made clear. Otherwise the debate about the use of enabling or regulatory rules becomes sterile. It is also necessary to recognise the link between the different functions of regulation and the different regulatory techniques. Thus by seeing corporate governance as a purely internal matter for companies to address is likely to lead to a greater emphasis on a self-regulatory framework. However, the impact of corporate activities beyond the internal relations of companies, together with a perceived imbalance of power between the different participants, calls for a framework that not only makes stronger demands but ultimately provides clear protections for those that most need them. That might bring about a need for governance by external bodies as well as by those within the industries concerned.

Perhaps more important is the goal of constituting a market in which the public has trust and which recognises a broad range of interests, while equally being sufficiently flexible to adapt to the overall commercial and political context. The structure and operation of companies is a key aspect of the effectiveness of the market-place. If there is a lack of internal trust within the company then trust is unlikely to be achieved in the market-place itself. The 'external' interest groups which have a role in achieving the success of the company must also be accommodated by the market-place and it is the challenge of formulating new means by which this can be achieved which will determine the success in taking corporate

governance into the third millennium. Mandatory rules appear to be particularly relevant to those interests. Ultimately, it is the interaction of markets and rules and the extent to which trust is achieved that will determine the quality of the regulatory system.

Notes

1 Kay, J. and A. Silberston (1995), 'Corporate Governance', *National Institute Economic Review*, 153, 85.
2 See, for example, Dignan, A. (1998), 'A Principled Approach to Self-regulation? The Report of the Hampel Committee on Corporate Governance', *Company Lawyer*, 19, 140; Cheffins, B.R. (1997), *Company Law: Theory, Structure and Operation*, Oxford: Clarendon, refers to the self-regulatory characteristics of the Cadbury Committee and the Greenbury Committee (p.373).
3 Prosser, T. (1997), *Law and the Regulators*, Oxford: Clarendon, p.4.
4 For a detailed account of the 'behind the scenes' relations between boards and institutional investors see Holland, J. (1996), 'Self Regulation and the Financial Aspects of Corporate Governance', *Journal of Business Law*, 127. Note also the very strong influence of the Association of British Insurers and the National Association of Pension Funds (NAPF) in terms of guidelines issued from time to time on a variety of issues relating to listed plcs: departure from guidelines issued by the ABI/NAPF would be considered very carefully by the board of any major plc because of the negative ramifications which could ensue.
5 Sealy, L.S. (1967), 'The Director as Trustee', *Cambridge Law Journal*, 88–9.
6 Grantham, R. (1991), 'The Judicial Extension of Directors' Duties to Creditors', *Journal of Business Law*, 5–6.
7 This view is expressed by Gower in Paul Davies (ed.) (1997), *Principles of Modern Company Law*, 6th edn, London: Sweet & Maxwell, p.602.
8 Berle, A.A. and G.C. Means (1991), *The Modern Corporation and Private Property*, New Brunswick; Transaction Publishers, p.245, originally published 1932.
9 The Hampel Report notes that approximately 80 per cent of shares in listed UK companies are held by institutions: *The Hampel Report on Corporate Governance* (1998), London: Gee, para 5.1, p.40.
10 Eisenberg, M.A. (1989), 'The Structure of Corporation Law', *Columbia Law Review*, 89, 1461.
11 RSA (1995), *Tomorrow's Company*, London: RSA, and see <www. tomorrowscompany.com>
12 *Ibid.*
13 DTI (1998), *Modern Company Law for a Competitive Economy*, Consultation Paper, March, London: DTI, para 3.5, p.9.
14 Cadbury Committee (1992), *Report on the Financial Aspects of Corporate Governance*, London: Gee, para 2.5. The DTI adopted this definition (1998), *Modern Company Law* (n.13, above), para 3.5 at p.9. See also *Hampel Report* (n.9, above), para 1.16.
15 Watson, M. 'Defining Corporate Governance', Institute of Directors, Professional Development, <http://www.iod.co.uk/profdev/defgov.html> - undated.
16 Sheikh, S. and S.K. Chatterjee (1995), 'Perspectives on Corporate Governance', in S. Sheikh and W. Rees (eds), *Corporate Governance & Corporate Control*, London: Cavendish, p.1.
17 *Hampel Report* (n.9, above), para 1.16.
18 Committee on Corporate Governance and the London Stock Exchange (1998),

The Combined Code, London: Gee Publishing. This was updated in 1999 to incorporate the Turnbull Committees *Report on International Control: Guidance for Directors on the Combined Code* (London: ICAEW, 1999) – see *The Combined Code; A Practical Guide,* London: Gee Publishing, 1999.

19 *Hampel Report* (n.9, above), Annex B, at p.66.

20 Brown, Ewan (1991) *Who Runs Companies? – Some thoughts on the Corporate Governance of Quoted Companies,* Working Paper No. 7, Edinburgh: Heriot-Watt University Business School, p.3.

21 Institute of Chartered Accountants in England and Wales (1996), 'Summary Financial Statements: The Way Forward'.

22 See Butcher, Donald (1995), 'Reform of the General Meetings', in Sheikh and Rees (n.16, above), ch.11, p.221. See also Sheridan, T. and N. Kendall (1992), *Corporate Governance: An Action Plan for Profitability and Business Success,* London: Pitman, p.83.

23 Butcher, 'Reform of the General Meetings' (n.22, above), ch.11, p.221. But see recent developments following a joint seminar on 19 July 1999 of the ABI/NAPF, when Stephen Byers, Secretary of State for Industry, outlined his views on enfranchising shareholders in respect of executive remuneration policy: two of the five possible approaches identified involve changes being made to AGM resolutions and voting: *Practical Law for Companies,* August 1999, pp.7–8.

24 See Finch, Vanessa (1992), 'Company Directors: Who Cares About Skill and Care?', *Modern Law Review,* 55, 179.

25 All UK company lawyers are familiar with the difficulties caused by *Foss* v. *Harbottle* (1843) 2 Hare 461.

26 See, for example, Lord Greene MR, stating in *Re Smith & Fawcett Ltd* [1942] Ch304 (CA) that directors are bound to exercise the powers conferred upon them 'bona fide in what they consider – not what a court may consider – is in the interests of the company' (p.306).

27 See Myners, P. *et al.* (1996), *Developing a Winning Partnership: How Companies and Institutional Investors are Working Together,* London: DTI; Holland, (n.4, above).

28 *Hampel Report,* para. 5.1, at p.40.

29 *Ibid.,* para 5.7, p.41.

30 Holland, 'Self-regulation' (n.4, above), p.148.

31 *Ibid.,* p.148.

32 For an overview, see Macgregor, L. and C. Villiers (1998), 'Independence of Auditors', *European Business Law Review,* 9, 318.

33 Cosh, A. and A. Hughes (1997), 'The Changing Anatomy of Corporate Control and the Market for Executives in the United Kingdom', *Journal of Law and Society,* 24, 111 and 121.

34 Combined Code, Section 1, B.2.2.

35 See Dignan (n.2 above).

36 Cheffins, *Company Law* (n.2, above), pp.397–418.

37 *Ibid.,* p.406, referring to 'Too Many Cooks in Regulatory Kitchen', *Financial Times,* 6 July 1995 (quoting Christopher Sharples, then chairman of SFA).

38 Section 319, Companies Act 1985.

39 Cadbury Committee, *Report* (n.14, above), 3.1.

40 Greenbury Code of Best Practice, D2 and see section 7 of the 1995 *Report on Directors' Remuneration,* London: Gee.

41 *Hampel Report,* (n.9, above), para 4.9, p.34.

42 Combined Code, Provision B.1.7.

43 Combined Code, Provision B.1.8.

44 [1987] 1 QB 815.

45 Cheffins, *Company Law* (n.2, above), p.374.

46 Para. 3.5.

47 See Page, A.C. (1987), 'Financial Services: The Self-Regulatory Alternative?', in Robert Baldwin and Christopher McCrudden (eds), *Regulation and Public Law*, London: Weidenfeld and Nicolson, p.298.
48 See *Company Directors: Regulating Conflicts of Interests and Formulating a Statement of Duties*, Law Commission Consultation paper No. 153 and Scottish Law Commission Discussion paper No. 105, London: Stationery Office, 1998.
49 Mitchell, L. (1990), 'The Death of Fiduciary Duty in Close Corporations' *University of Pennsylvania Law Review*, 138, 1677.
50 *Associated Provincial Picture Houses Ltd* v. *Wednesbury Corporation* [1948] 1 KB 223. Similar reasoning was given in *Shuttleworth* v. *Cox Bros & Co (Maidenhead) Ltd* [1927] 2 KB 9 (CA); see also *Howard Smith* v. *Ampol Petroleum Ltd* [1974] AC 821, (PC) especially p.835; *Re a Company ex parte Glossop* [1988] BCLC 570.
51 On 22 June 1999; the text can be downloaded from <www.oecd.org>.
52 See Sheikh, S. and S.K. Chatterjee (1995), 'Codes of Conduct and Their Impact on Corporate Governance', in Sheikh and Rees (n.16, above), ch.12, p.241.
53 See Griseri, P. (1995), 'Ethical Codes of Conduct: Developing an Ethical Framework for Corporate Governance', in Sheikh and Rees (n.16, above), ch.13, p.269.
54 See News Brief, 'Codes of Business Conduct – Companies Surveyed' (1999), *Practical Law for Companies*, January/February, 10.
55 See *Hampel Report* (n.9 above), paras 1.11–1.14, pp.10–11.
56 See Cheffins, *Company Law* (n.2, above), pp.378–97.
57 See Baldwin, R. (1995), *Rules and Government*, Oxford: Clarendon; Black, J. (1997), *Rules and Regulators*, Oxford: Clarendon.
58 See especially Eisenberg, 'The Structure of Corporation Law' (n.10, above); Cheffins *Company Law* (n.2, above), ch.5, p.217; Ramsay, I.M. (1998), 'Models of Corporate Regulation: The Mandatory/Enabling Debate', in Grantham, R. and C. Rickett (eds), *Corporate Personality in the 20th Century*, Oxford: Hart, ch.12, p.215.
59 It is not always easy to classify rules in this way, especially as they tend to operate in tandem. Sometimes what might appear to be a mandatory rule may effectively operate as an opt-out rule because, for example, it can be avoided or bypassed.
60 DTI, *Modern Company Law* (n.13, above), para 3.4, p.8.
61 Ogus, A. (1994), *Regulation*, Oxford: Clarendon, pp.2–3.
62 See Kaysen, C. (1959), 'The Corporation: How Much Power? What Scope?', in Mason, E.S. (ed.), *The Corporation in Modern Society*, Cambridge, Mass: Harvard, p.85.
63 Shearing, C.D. (1993), 'A Constitutive Conception of Regulation', in Grabosky, P. and J. Braithwaite (eds), *Business Regulation and Australia's Future*, Canberra: Australian Institute of Criminology, pp.70–71.
64 Ramsay, 'Models of Corporate Regulation' (n.57, above), p.219.
65 Shearing, 'A Constitutive Concept of Regulation' (n.62, above), p.76.
66 Company Accounts (Disclosure of Directors' Emoluments) Regulations 1997, SI 1997/570.
67 See Principles B1 to B3 and their corresponding provisions.
68 Sheridan and Kendall, *Corporate Governance* (n.22, above), pp.27–8. See also <www.tomorrowscompany.com> for a similar approach.
69 See also Department of Trade and Industry (1999), *Modern Company Law for a Competitive Economy: The Strategic Framework*, A Consultation Document from the Company Law Review Steering Committee, London: DTI, which suggests two alternatives, the 'enlightened shareholder value' approach and the 'pluralist' approach.
70 *Corporate Governance in the Netherlands: Forty Recommendations* (25 June 1997).
71 *The Boards of Directors of Listed Companies in France*, Report of the 'Vienot Committee' (July 1995).

12 Regulation of Financial Services

JENNY HAMILTON, *University of Strathclyde*

Introduction

As explained in the chapter 1 to this book, it is no longer feasible to speak of regulation in the modern state in terms of an undifferentiated and external source of interference in the operation of the markets. The institutions of regulation take one of a number of different and sometimes complex forms and this is never better illustrated than in relation to the regulation of financial services. Prior to the introduction in 1986 of the current regulatory structure, regulation of the industry was piecemeal and ad hoc, involving elements of self-regulation, statutory regulation and, in some cases, no regulation at all.[1] This situation was subject to reform in 1986 and replaced, for investment business, by a system of 'self-regulation under a statutory umbrella'. However, this has not proved to be the optimum form of regulatory structure. Regulation has, in some cases, been insufficiently robust, insufficiently flexible to cope with a rapidly changing market-place, and the division of responsibilities between a number of regulators has proved inefficient and costly. This structure is being reformed via the Financial Services and Markets Bill, which was introduced in June 1999. It will, when passed, replace the system of 'self-regulation' with one of statutory regulation and will merge the functions of a number of current regulatory bodies into one 'super-regulator'.

This new regulatory structure will retain some of the 'best features' of the previous system: the regulator will be (largely) independent of government; it will operate close to the markets; and there will continue to be practitioner involvement. At the same time the regulator will have extensive powers to legislate (and legislate quickly) across the financial services industry, backed up by statutory enforcement powers, including the power to impose unlimited fines.

Despite the championing in the 1980s of 'self-regulation' as the most appropriate form of regulation for the financial services sector, industry objection to its demise under the Financial Services and Markets Bill (FSM Bill) has been surprisingly muted. No doubt this is partly because of the negative public image of self-regulation, which has been generated rightly or wrongly by the recent 'scandals' such as pension mis-selling and the Maxwell raid on employee pension funds. It may also be because the current regulatory system introduced in 1986 has never truly been one of 'self-regulation' at all. Rather, the Securities and Investment Board (SIB) is itself a statutory creation with statutory powers and has exercised considerable direct and indirect control over regulation by the self-regulatory organisations (SROs) recognised pursuant to the Financial Services Act 1986. The current reforms therefore represent an incremental development of the regulatory system rather than wholesale reform.

The purpose of this chapter is to trace the development of what has been (and will continue to be) an unusual regulatory structure and to highlight some of the difficulties which have arisen in practice as a result of this structure. It will also focus on certain aspects of the new regime which have attracted particular comment and criticism, namely the new regulatory objectives and the related, but additional, issue of regulatory accountability.

The Current Regulatory Structure

The present regulatory regime, encompassed in the 1986 Financial Services Act, arose out of a report prepared by Professor Gower in 1984 into investor protection in the UK. In the 1980s a series of scandals involving the collapse of two major firms of investment managers had prompted the government to appoint Professor Gower to consider what statutory protection was required by investors, and to advise on the need for new legislation.[2] The clear implication of the government action was that the collapses were the result of a decline in the moral standards of the market-place, over which there was inadequate regulation.[3]

Gower identified a number of defects in the existing rather piecemeal and ad hoc system of regulation – defects which stemmed from the diversity of regulations and regulators, inflexibility, failure to treat like alike, delays and lax enforcement.[4] He concluded that if investors were to be adequately protected it would be necessary to rationalise and reform the regulatory structure.

Gower considered a number of options for reform, including the introduction of comprehensive securities legislation, and the introduction of statutory regulatory agencies along the lines of the US Securities and Exchange Commission (SEC). He rejected the introduction of securities legislation on the basis that it would be likely to suffer from the same drawbacks as existing statutory regulation.[5] In other words, it would be characterised by inflexibility and lack of discretion, with decisions being taken by low-level civil servants remote from the scene of action, thus leading to a voluminous rule book which would be followed more or less slavishly, thus stifling the industry.[6] He rejected an SEC style of statutory regulatory agency with executive, judicial and legislative powers (which he was inclined to favour) on the pragmatic ground that it would be unacceptable to the government (with its dislike of QUANGOs) and to the industry, fearful of the creation of a 'bureaucratic juggernaut'.[7]

Instead, he proposed a system in which there would be an adjusted balance between governmental regulation and self-regulation. Gower regarded these two types of regulation as complementary, not antithetical, and he believed they could be welded together into a harmonious structure, each doing what it did best.[8] Self-regulation had certain advantages, including flexibility, expertise, speed and reduced cost to the taxpayer.[9] However, it required supervision. Otherwise there was the risk that self-interest would outweigh public interest. Therefore self-regulation required government supervision. In addition, he believed that government should decide matters of public policy.

Although Gower's focus was on investor protection, he was also concerned to balance that protection with market efficiency. He believed that regulation should be kept to a minimum. Investment products inevitably carry an element of risk and regulation should not seek to 'protect fools from their own folly'.[10] For Gower, regulation was necessary not only to protect the investor, but also to ensure a healthy financial market. Confidence in the market-place is a vital ingredient of the financial services market. Without such confidence investors will invest elsewhere (either in other markets such as property or in other countries where the sector has a better reputation). A good regulatory system provides that confidence, but at the same time should not be so heavy-handed as to drive markets overseas. Unless investors and market participants believed that the system was safe they would not participate. The task facing Gower was to design a regulatory system which would deliver the right balance.

The system ultimately introduced under the Financial Services Act 1986 (FSA) was based upon Gower's model. Briefly, under this system no one is permitted to carry on investment business in the UK unless authorised (or exempted). Authority is delegated by the Secretary of State to the Securities and Investment Board to provide such authorisation and to impose rules and regulations upon those so authorised. SIB is also given the power to 'recognise' self-regulatory organisations (SROs) (and practitioner bodies) whose rules and procedures provide similar levels of protection for the investor to its own.[11] Membership of a recognised SRO (and practitioner body) also confers authorisation. These bodies in turn are responsible for the admission and conduct of their own members, under the supervision of SIB.

SIB itself is a private company limited by guarantee rather than a government department or a self-standing statutory commission as recommended by Gower. While the reasons for preferring a private company structure are not clear,[12] as Gower subsequently acknowledged, it has certain advantages in that it does not have to be paid for out of the public purse (it is financed through a levy on the industry) and is not constrained by civil service conditions of employment or salaries. It therefore has a better chance of recruiting staff from industry.[13]

Ultimately, the shape of the regulatory structure put in place as a result of the Gower proposals is one which has sought to build upon the existing tradition of self-regulation in the city. At the same time, it put self-regulatory organisations under the supervision of SIB, a private company run by its members, but one which nevertheless exercises significant public authority and which has legislative power to determine its own policy, principles and rules, independent of government.

The government retains only a residual role in the regulatory structure given that it, together with the Bank of England, appoints the chairman and board of SIB. In addition, the Office of Fair Trading and HM Treasury have a continuing responsibility for scrutinising the rules and practices of SIB and the SROs for anti-competitiveness and the Treasury can direct rule changes should substantial anti-competitiveness result.[14] SIB is accountable to the government via its annual report. However, in other respects, the opportunity for political interference in SIB is very limited. The government has no power to order SIB to alter any of its rules (other than for reasons of anti-competitiveness). If SIB is not carrying out any of its functions adequately or is failing to provide adequate investor protection, the only option available to the government is to remove the board, or to resume SIB's functions in whole or part (the 'nuclear deterrent').[15]

The government believed that this particular structure would produce a number of advantages. Such advantages include the fact that it would combine adequate investor protection with a competitive and innovative market, it would be run by those familiar with the market with the necessary expertise, because it was regulated by the market it was more likely to achieve high standards of regulation 'as a matter of integrity and principle' than through imposing compliance from outside, and, as a private sector body SIB would have more flexibility than a legislative body to change its rules quickly. This latter factor is important in a quick-changing industry.[16] In other words, this structure was intended to have all the advantages traditionally associated with self-regulation, while at the same time providing regulatory supervision by a body both independent of government and sufficiently independent of industry not to suffer the potential for 'regulatory capture'.

However, this structure was described shortly after its implementation as 'almost a confidence trick'. In the words of Gower: 'The White Paper described its proposals as "self-regulation within a statutory framework" but in fact a more accurate description of what has emerged is "statutory regulation monitored by self-regulatory organisations recognised by, and under the surveillance of, a self-standing Commission."'[17]

The System in Practice

One of the difficulties which quickly emerged was the nature of the relationship between SIB and the SROs. It was clearly expected by the industry that it would be the SROs who would be the 'hands on' regulators of their respective sectors, 'hands on' in the sense that they would devise and enforce the rules appropriate for their particular sectors. The SIB's role, on the other hand, was anticipated to be primarily that of the supervisor of the SROs, establishing the rules by which they would obtain recognition from SIB, and monitoring their rules but otherwise having little direct impact upon firms regulated by the SROs.

In practice the role exercised by SIB was quite different. Instead of SIB exercising a monitoring and supervisory function over the SROs, it operated as the primary rule maker, devising rules for the entire industry which the SROs were then required to enforce. There were several reasons for this development, including political pressure to be seen to be a tough regulator.[18] However, it was the failure either of the White Paper or of the legislation to clarify their respective roles that resulted in considerable tension between these two tiers of regulation. The SROs became highly critical of the failure of SIB to establish a formal supervisory role and its overly interventionist approach in relation to rule making. Despite attempts by the SIB to clarify what it believed to be its objectives – that is, to reposition itself as a 'supervisor' (regulator of regulators) and to step back from the role of direct regulator[19] – tensions in the system remained. These tensions existed not only over the respective roles of the various regulators but also over the purpose of regulation and the most appropriate means of providing investor protection (including the weight which should be given to the 'traditional' contractual principle of *caveat emptor*).

In its report into the regulation of financial services of 1995,[20] the Treasury and Civil Service Committee identified that the current regulatory regime was facing criticisms from a number of quarters (many of which had in fact already been acknowledged by SIB[21]). Such criticisms stemmed in part from problems caused by the division of regulatory responsibility amongst different regulators,[22] but also from the perceived inadequacy of regulation in certain sectors (particularly the retail sector[23]) and inadequate enforcement. The Committee recognised a clear need to make the regime more effective, not simply in order to provide better protection for the investor, but also in order to protect the industry:

> Good regulation is good for the City ... Clean, transparent markets are ... also a key objective and benefit not only the actual investor but also, by inspiring confidence, attract greater numbers of market participants. In this way competent and effective regulation can be of benefit to the 'City of London' as well as providing investor protection. Accordingly the efficacy of the regulatory structure, as well as the efficacy of the regulatory community are key factors in helping to maintain and enhance London's position as the pre-eminent European financial centre.[24]

For the Committee, therefore, regulation performed not just a protective, control function, it also performed an important constitutive function, the importance of which was underscored by the considerable drop in life insurance as well as pension sales in the aftermath of the pensions mis-sellings scandal.[25] As one writer has noted, without regulation to give consumers some independent assurance about the terms on which contracts are offered, the safety of assets which underpin them, and the quality of advice received, saving and investment may be discouraged, again with damaging economic consequences.[26]

The Committee made a number of recommendations to improve the effectiveness of the regime, not simply to provide greater protection for the investor but also to protect and enhance the industry itself. It concluded, however, that constant tweaking of the existing structure by the regulators might not be sufficient, and that the government should give consideration to new legislation. Evidence given before the Committee suggested that elements of the government (particularly HM Treasury) were also critical of the profusion of regulatory bodies and would welcome more streamlining of the system.

The Reasons for Reform

The scene was thus set for reform of the system, and such reform was foreshadowed in the Labour Party's Business Manifesto of April 1997 in which it pledged to transfer direct regulatory responsibilities under the 1986 Act to SIB.[27] In May 1997, shortly after winning the election, the new government announced the demise of the two-tier system of regulation and its replacement by one statutory 'super-regulator'.[28] The existing system, said Gordon Brown, was 'not delivering the standard of supervision and investor protection that the industry and the public has the right to expect', as evidenced by the various scandals that had engulfed the industry in recent years. As Howard Davies (the chairman of the Financial Services Authority) has commented, there existed a perception that the regulators had been 'captured' by the industry they were supposed to be regulating.[29] It is also clear, however, that, in addition to wanting to improve investor protection, the government was also concerned to protect the market given its immense importance to the UK economy. In announcing a reform of the regulatory regime, the government wanted to restore that vital ingredient of public confidence in the financial services sector (including the banking sector, itself hit by recent high-profile scandals) and so protect the pre-eminent position of the UK as a leading financial centre.[30]

At the same time, Brown cited other motivations for reform (factors already identified in the 1995 Report), including the inefficiencies of, and confusion caused to investors by, the existence of a number of different regulators, the lack of clear lines of accountability and responsibility within the existing two-tier system and the breakdown of the traditional distinctions between different types of institution (and the products they offered) which made the existing demarcation of regulatory responsibility between the individual SROs, the Bank of England (responsible for banking supervision) and so on seem increasingly irrelevant, costly and inefficient. In other words, the market-place was changing and the traditional demarcation of products sold by banks, insurance companies and securities firms was breaking down. The regulatory regime needed to accommodate these changes.

For Gordon Brown it was time to replace the existing system with a statutory regime which would 'put the public interest first'.[31] It is clear, therefore, that the 'formal' motivations for reform were broadly twofold: at the 'micro' level to improve investor protection and thereby reduce the chances of pension mis-selling occurring again; and at the 'macro' level to make the structure more appropriate for, and responsive to, the structural changes occurring in the industry, including the increasingly integrated and often international character of financial services. At the same time Brown nevertheless made it clear that he wanted to preserve the best features of the existing system, such as practitioner involvement.[32] It is also clear that he wanted to keep such involvement firmly in check by providing various checks and balances against any possibility of regulatory capture (see further below).

It has also been suggested that the real motivating factor behind the decision to reform the structure had rather more to do with the decision to grant the Bank of England monetary policy independence and the consequent need to find a new 'home' for banking supervision. Wholesale reform of the FSA regulatory structure was more of an afterthought, rather than part of any grand plan, and justifications for the creation of a 'super regulator' were supplied 'after the fact'.[33] This would explain why details of the new regime were so slow to emerge.

The New Regime

The Financial Services and Markets Bill was presented to parliament on 17 June 1999 and it is anticipated that it will receive Royal Assent in 2000. Under the new regime, the Financial Services Authority (formerly SIB) will take over the existing regulatory functions of a number of bodies including the existing SROs, the Recognised Professional Bodies, the Insurance Directorate of the Treasury and the Supervision and Surveillance Division of the Bank of England.[34] In addition, there will be one Ombudsman scheme and one compensation scheme. The aim of this new structure is primarily to rationalise the existing regulatory structure, rather than to introduce regulation where none has previously existed.[35] Thus, while regulation of deposit taking and general insurance are brought into this structure, they will continue to be subject only to authorisation requirements and prudential supervision, but not to conduct of business rules.[36]

The legal status of the FSA (the 'Authority') will be largely inherited from SIB. It will be a private company limited by guarantee, its chairman and board will be appointed by HM Treasury, it will be funded by a levy on industry and, like SIB (and the SROs[37]), it will have statutory immunity from liability in damages except for acts or omissions in bad faith.[38] As was previously the case with SIB, while the government retains some important residual powers,[39] it will have little opportunity to exercise political interference over the exercise of regulatory functions and powers. The Treasury will, however, have the power to alter any legislation made by the FSA which it and the Director General of Fair Trading (DGFT) believe has a significantly anti-competitive effect.[40]

When asked to explain the reason for this particular status, Howard Davies, current chairman of the Authority, commented that the reason was largely historical, but it seems that:

> Parliament concluded that, because it wanted a regulatory scheme which was as far as possible rooted in the markets that it regulated and funded by those markets, it should be constructed as a private company operating within these markets with private company-type corporate governance procedures and funding direct from institutions with public powers given to it. That would allow it to relate to the market place, and would allow it to employ people on broadly speaking private sector terms.[41]

So while the government wanted to remove the self-regulatory element of the regime, it remained committed to a regime which remained close to the markets, able to draw on staff from industry. To this end, in order to maintain industry links, the Bill makes provision for the establishment of a Practitioner Panel (a practice already instituted by SIB) consisting of industry representatives, with whom the Authority has a general duty to consult.[42] In addition, the board must contain a majority of non-executive members and clearly some these members will be from industry (though unlike the position under the existing legislation, the Bill itself does not require the board to contain a 'proper balance' of industry and public interest members). The functions of the non-executive members specifically include determining the remuneration of the chairman and monitoring the Authority's financial affairs. Thus in continuing with the private company model of regulator the government has sought to ensure that the Authority will be subject to some, but not all,[43] of the principles of corporate governance which it has been so keen to encourage in relation to trading companies.

On the other hand, the Bill also makes provision for the creation of a consumer panel[44] with whom the Authority must also consult and for public consultation in respect of all proposed new rules. In this way the regulated community is not accorded any superior status under the legislation and its influence is counterbalanced (in theory) by input from other constituents.

The functions of the Authority under the new Act can be broadly summarised as follows: authorisation,[45] prudential regulation and conduct of business regulation of investment business; prudential supervision of deposit taking and insurance (including a supervisory role over Lloyd's); and the supervision of markets and exchanges.[46] The Authority is also given significant legislative and enforcement powers. However, other than in the case of the new civil powers in relation to market abuse, these powers are basically a consolidation of existing statutory powers and the contractual powers currently exercised by the SROs. Thus the Authority has legislative powers to make rules and regulations (including the issuing of statements of principle, codes of practice, and guidance) for authorised persons in relation to various matters including conduct of business,[47] as well as powers to issue statements of principle and codes of practice for 'approved persons'[48] (in line with the current practice of the SROs to concentrate upon the responsibilities of senior managers).

As with its rule-making powers, the disciplinary and enforcement powers of the Authority are extensive, but again represent a consolidation of the powers exercised by the existing regulators. These powers will include public censure, fines, restitution or disgorgement, withdrawal of authorisation, withdrawal of approval to carry on a regulated activity, or, in the case of approved persons, public censure, fines, and withdrawal of approval.[49] The power to impose fines will be new to the Authority. Under the current regime the Authority has only limited disciplinary powers. In addition it will be given new powers of prosecution (except in Scotland) in relation to insider dealing under Part V of the Criminal Justice Act 1993, money laundering under prescribed regulations, as well as for various offences created under the FSM Bill.[50]

Problematic Issues: The Regulatory Objectives, Regulatory Accountability

The existence of one regulator for the financial services industry is not novel. Sweden, Denmark, Norway, Japan, Korea and Iceland all have one regulator, and Australia has two: one for prudential regulation and one for supervision of securities firms and conduct of business requirements. In addition, Ireland, Israel, Mexico and South Africa are also considering moving to a single regulator.[51] The concentration of so much power in the hands of one UK regulator has led to much concern about the creation of a 'mega-regulator with potentially excessive powers'.[52] These concerns have been reflected in the recent Joint Parliamentary Scrutiny Committee Reports into the draft Bill[53]and have centred on the need for clear objectives of the regulatory regime, issues concerning discipline and enforcement, and accountability of the Authority generally.

One of the key criticisms of the existing regulatory regime has been the lack of clear regulatory objectives, leading to tensions within the 'regulatory space' over the purpose of regulation. Without clear objectives there is real difficulty in holding regulators accountable. The government has responded by setting out four specific regulatory objectives in the Bill: market confidence, public awareness, protection of consumers and the reduction of financial crime.[54] In addition, underpinning these objectives are six statutory principles to which the Authority must have regard: the need to use its resources efficiently and economically; the responsibilities of the managers of authorised firms; the principle that the burdens of regulation should be proportionate to the expected benefits; the need for industry innovation; maintaining the UK's competitive position internationally; and no unnecessary distortion of competition.[55]

While the provision of specific objectives for regulation has generally been welcomed, some criticism has been expressed that, as currently articulated, they are vague and potentially inconsistent. This can be seen most clearly in the objectives of market confidence. Market participants might argue that this demands a light regulatory touch, and that consumer protection might demand a heavier touch. The danger lies in the fact that this may result in inconsistent and weak regulation. Taylor argues that there are three primary goals for financial services regulation: stability, consumer protection and ensuring that markets are fair and orderly. He further argues that the difficulty of holding these goals in balance requires that they be pursued by different regulators, with different objectives.[56] Others have argued that significant differences between institutions and types of business demand different regulatory approaches and, therefore, different regulators.[57] However, having separate regulators with separate objectives will not of itself remove the potential for conflicts between those objectives. Trade-offs may still be necessary and the issue then becomes one of who should determine which trade-off. Nor is multiple regulation likely to prove efficient. Those firms which engage in more than one type of business will still require to be regulated by more than one regulator.[58] Instead, one regulator can potentially offer significant efficiencies (in terms of costs, resource allocation and conflict resolution) and can provide consistent regulation across product markets, for example. At the same time, the flexibility inherent in the new system will allow the Authority the scope to introduce differentiation between, for example, different types of consumer and different types of market where appropriate.[59] However, the fact that the new regime can offer significant efficiencies and flexibility does not resolve the issue of how tensions between regulatory objectives, should they arise, are to be resolved.

There is an argument that regulators should properly only be concerned with one objective. This would provide for consistent regulation and also a clear standard against which regulatory action can be assessed and regulators held accountable. An analogy is sometimes drawn with utilities regulation which, it is said, is concerned with one primary objective of the rate of return earned by monopolistic (or semi-monopolistic) providers of utilities, telecommunications and other essential services. However this view of the existence of one, overriding (economic) objective has been rejected. Regulation of utilities and telecommunications also involves regulating for the 'social' goal of universal service and regulation of broadcasting for the goal of diversity.[60] As Prosser has commented in relation to utility regulators, regulators have come to resemble 'governments in miniature' and this therefore requires a pluralist approach to regulation: 'no single logic can or should form a basis for their decision making'.[61] Nor would the existence of a single regulatory objective necessarily provide the answer to the question of how a regulator should act in any given situation. Consumer protection, for example, can take many forms from, at one extreme, direct intervention by way of product regulation, through to indirect intervention by promoting greater competition. The answer lies (in part at least) in the regulator's view about the nature of the problem and the knowledge and experience of the consumer. This is shown by the current divergence of view between the OFT and the Authority about the continued need for polarisation rules[62] introduced to ensure that consumers were clear about the status of the adviser and the independence of his/her advice. The OFT believes that the polarisation rules are anti-competitive and operate to the detriment of the consumer by restricting consumer choice, while the Authority believes that the consumer benefit of polarisation (in terms of ensuring that the consumer is clear about the independence of advice received) outweighs its anti-competitive effects.

Competition as a Regulatory Objective

The possibility for conflict between objectives, however, is recognised by the Authority.[63] It has stated that, in pursuing them, it will be guided, not just by the underlying six principles, but also by what it believes to be the two principal rationales for regulation of financial markets, namely systemic risk (the risk that failures in one sector could seriously disrupt other sectors of the economy) and asymmetries of information which make it difficult for consumers to make rational choices in competitive markets.[64]

The rationale for regulation to be adopted by the Authority is, in other words, one of market failure.[65] As Llewellyn explains:[66]

> If financial services were conducted in perfectly competitive markets ... there would be no case for regulation, and any regulation that was imposed would be a net cost to the consumers. *Per contra,* if there are market imperfections and failures but no regulation, the consumer pays a cost because the unregulated market is sub-optimum.
>
> The purpose of regulation is not to replace competition but to enhance it and make it effective in the market place by offsetting market imperfections which potentially compromise consumer welfare.

This view that the purpose of regulation is to enhance competition has led some to argue that competition should be elevated from a guiding principle to a specific objective. The Joint Committee and the government, however, have rejected this suggestion on the basis that it would both confuse the roles of the OFT and the Authority and potentially impede cooperation with overseas regulators. They further argued that competition and competitiveness were already sufficiently pervasive influences by virtue of being underlying principles.[67]

More recently in the consultation document into banking services in the UK,[68] Cruikshank (the former telecommunications regulator) has recommended that the FSM Bill be amended to give greater emphasis to competition. He concludes that, while regulation of banking and the financial services sector is important to ensure public confidence and to close information gaps, regulation has a high potential to distort competition. Consumers, he believes, are best served by competition but 'a competition objective that is weak relative to the regulator's other objectives is unlikely to be delivered effectively'.[69] He therefore recommends removing the 'principle' that competition between authorised persons should not be impeded or distorted unnecessarily and replacing it with a fifth 'objective'. This is 'to minimise the anti-competitive effects of requirements placed on authorised persons by the Authority'.[70] He further recommends that anyone disadvantaged by Authority rules should have the right to seek a review by the Competition Commission, which would be the final arbiter of whether the FSA rule has an unnecessarily significant anti-competitive effect (and would presumably have the power currently proposed for the Treasury to direct the Authority to change its rule).

There are a number of difficulties with this proposal. It would inevitably tip the balance in favour of the 'competition' objective. The risk of any member of the regulatory community (estimated to be over 30,000 firms) triggering a competition review of any new rule would force the Authority to give priority to competition issues above all else, or face potential regulatory paralysis. It is also very questionable whether competition should be the guiding principle for regulation in a sector where there is a recognised risk of systemic failure, where the nature of the products sold make it difficult for investors (retail investors in particular) to judge at the time of purchase the likely quality and suitability of products and where, as the Treasury and Civil Service Committee noted in their Report in 1995, 'sellers of financial services are competing less on price and quality, as in traditional markets, but more on the methods of sale and promotion'.[71] In addition, giving the right of review to the regulatory community will inevitably add to an increase in costs and delays in the regulatory process (and will provide a cheap alternative to judicial review proceedings, but only in relation to that objective, and only for the regulatory community).

While Cruikshank admits that regulation does not always produce negative results but can also benefit competition, his basic premise is that regulation is primarily anti-competitive. However, some would argue that disclosure requirements are anti-competitive because they represent an entry barrier, or because they give larger companies a competitive advantage over smaller companies (which are unable to absorb the costs so easily). Such regulation also has the potential to enhance competition by, for example, widening the dimension in which competition operates (to include competition over contract terms, for instance) and by enabling advisers to focus on the different terms offered by various suppliers. It can also lead to the unbundling of contracts and could result in the development of better compliance standards.[72] Regulation and competition are therefore not in conflict. On the contrary, regulation performs an important constitutive function by supporting the market. The same sorts of argument can be made for prudential regulation. On a narrow view such regulation can be regarded as anti-competitive in imposing entry barriers, increasing costs to the consumer and so on. However, taking a broader view, such regulation can operate to enhance confidence in the market (particularly when it is remembered that, unlike the situation in other markets, the value of financial investment products, and hence of product provider, to the investor increases rather than decreases after purchase) hence leading to greater investor participation.

In addition, making the Competition Authority, which (unlike the government) has no historical or current connections with regulation of the financial services sector, the final arbiter of the anti-competitiveness of Authority rules runs the risk of destroying the balance of interests which has developed and is continuing to develop within the regulatory framework. Pursuit of better competition may in fact serve to undermine the broad interest groups represented within the Authority. This may, for example, operate to disenfranchise consumer interests by subordinating the more subtle balancing of consumer protection measures to the rather blunt goal of competition. Competition should therefore be a by-product of good regulation which addresses specific market failures and specific market conditions. Requiring a regulator to focus on the anti-competitive effects of regulation as an independent objective is both unnecessary, and in terms of the Cruikshank proposal, undesirable.

Regulatory Legitimacy

By way of summary, the existence of multiple objectives for regulators is not a new phenomenon. Ultimately, regulators will always have to carry out a balancing act, not just between different objectives but also between the demands of different interest groups. Regulators will have choices to make about what course of action to pursue in any given situation. Regulators, like governments, are appointed not just to police communities but to manage them, albeit within boundaries which may be set externally. Tying a regulator to a specific objective rather than multiple objectives may not produce any greater certainty of regulatory outcome. Much will depend upon the balance of interests and values represented in the particular regulatory space, the Authority's understanding of the sector and of the appropriateness of various alternative courses of action which may present themselves in order to achieve particular objective(s). However, if we accept that regulators function in a sense as 'government in miniature' but at the same time function outside the usual democratic structures of government, the issue then becomes by what means the Authority is to be secured to those democratic structures in order to enable it to be held accountable.

Despite the considerable importance of regulatory bodies in the UK, it is probably true to say that the assumption persists that by being independent of the government and of electors, regulators lack accountability and, therefore, democratic legitimacy. However, in fact, the independence of the Financial Services Authority is relative. It is given its powers by statute. The board and chair are appointed (and removed) by government, the regulatory objectives and principles are prescribed in the statute, its rule making is subject to procedures designed to open it up to public input and scrutiny, its decisions are open to judicial review and, in some cases, to *de novo* review by the new and independent Financial Services and Markets Tribunal. Arguably, the Authority is no less accountable than government, particularly if we accept that accountability is achieved not only through the ballot box but also through transparent decision making according to specified objectives,[73] with an opportunity for independent review.[74]

Rule Making

Nevertheless, accountability issues for the Authority have arisen in at least two specific contexts: in relation to the exercise of its rule-making power, and in relation to discipline and enforcement. The degree of independent power given to the Authority in these areas has raised concerns about the extent of parliamentary control over its exercise. The initial draft Bill provided for only limited parliamentary scrutiny of regulatory rule making; as the Parliamentary Delegated Powers and Deregulation Committee has noted:

> The FSAs' 'legislation' will not be set out in statutory instruments and so is not intended to be subject to direct Parliamentary control yet it is of far greater practical importance than the statutory instruments which ministers are empowered to make under the draft Bill and which are rightly to be subject to Parliamentary control. If powers of this kind were to be vested in Ministers, we would undoubtedly advise that there should be a measure of Parliamentary control.[75]

The explanation for this absence of direct parliamentary control lies in the desire to make the Authority independent of political control, to allow it to operate close to the market, and to enable it to act quickly and decisively in response to particular market conditions. Instead of parliamentary scrutiny of individual rule making, the Authority will be required to submit an annual report to the Treasury containing at least information on the discharge of its functions generally and on the extent to which regulatory objectives have been met. That report (which must also contain a report from the non-executive committee about its activities) is then laid before parliament, where it is likely to receive scrutiny at Parliamentary Committee level.[76] While there is also a statutory requirement that all exercises of law making by the Authority are notified to the Treasury,[77] no power is given to the government to direct rule changes (other than in the case of anti-competitive effects). In addition, there is no power given to the government to issue guidance to the Authority to clarify the statutory objectives or principles. The result is that, while the government has established a general policy framework for the Authority, the interpretation of that framework remains firmly with the Authority. It is for the Authority therefore to interpret the rather vague objective of 'maintaining market confidence', when, for the purposes of accountability if nothing else, clarification of statutory policy should more properly be a matter for the government. The Treasury will also have the power to commission independent reviews into the way in which the Authority has used its resources, and to commission inquiries into suspected regulatory failures and to make recommendations accordingly.[78]

In addition to government scrutiny, Authority law making is also subject to public scrutiny. Whenever it intends to exercise its legislative powers, the Authority will be required *inter alia* to consult widely on any proposed rule[79] and to undertake a cost–benefit analysis of the proposal. Presumably the purpose of such an analysis would be to provide a discipline for the Authority when devising rules.

If ultimately the rule differs from the draft, the Authority must publish a statement of the difference and provide a further cost–benefit analysis.[80] Also the Authority is required to 'have regard to' any representations made to it by the Practitioner Panel,[81] but the government stopped short of requiring the Authority to consult the panel prior to proposing legislation. The Practitioner Panel is not therefore given any enhanced status with respect the Authority's legislative powers, so reducing the possibility of 'regulatory capture' by the industry[82] (and also the risk of regulatory paralysis).

The result is that, while not subject to the same type of accountability measures traditionally associated with democratic law making, nevertheless this particular regulator is subject to significant formal transparency requirements which open up the decision-making process to public scrutiny and which arguably provide for greater transparency and accountability in decision making than occurs in reality at Westminster level. Ultimately, if the government does not believe that the Authority has carried out its functions appropriately, it has the sanction of removing the chairman and the board.

Disciplinary Powers and Authorisation

Accountability issues in relation to the Authority's proposed disciplinary powers have been, and may yet prove to be, more problematic. One major issue to have surrounded the draft Bill has been the relationship between the exercise of regulatory power, particularly disciplinary power, and other external accountability mechanisms, but particularly that to be imposed under the Human Rights Act 1998. This Act, when it comes into effect (2000), will incorporate the European Convention on Human Rights (ECHR) into domestic law and provide a right of action where that Convention is breached. Although the full implications of the ECHR for the Authority (and for other regulators[83]) are not yet certain, what is certain is that the Convention requires that any determination of a person's civil or criminal rights and obligations be before an independent and impartial tribunal.[84] In addition, where the proceedings are criminal in nature, the Convention imposes additional safeguards for the 'accused', such as the right to a presumption of innocence (including the right against self-incrimination)[85] and the right to legal aid in appropriate circumstances.[86] The Convention also requires that any criminal offence must be clearly defined in law (at least to the extent that the form of behaviour required to constitute the offence must be reasonably foreseeable).[87]

A breach of the Convention by a public authority will entitle a court to grant such relief as it finds necessary, including an award of damages if this would be necessary to afford satisfaction to the victim of the breach. 'Public authority' is widely defined to include courts and tribunals and also those whose functions are of a public nature, and this, it is clearly anticipated, would include the Financial Services Authority.[88] These requirements have a potential impact in a number of areas, particularly in relation to the disciplinary and enforcement regime. For this reason, the government made certain amendments to the draft Bill, but there is still some doubt as to whether those amendments will go far enough.

As regards the fair trial 'requirement', it was initially proposed that the Authority would have the power to make rules, investigate breaches and take disciplinary action against those in breach. However, a concern that the Authority would find itself in breach of the Convention in acting as prosecutor, judge and jury in respect of regulatory breaches prompted the government to amend the draft Bill. The Bill presented to parliament provides that, where the Authority proposes to take disciplinary action against a regulatee, that regulatee will have the right to have the matter referred to a Financial Services and Markets Tribunal for adjudication. However, if the regulatee does not exercise that right, a 'decision notice' will be published by the Authority.[89] That Tribunal (which will be a part of the court service) will be independent of the Authority and will have the power to hear referrals *de novo* and on the merits and the power to determine the appropriate penalty. This change should be sufficient to ensure no breach of the 'fair trial' requirement.

The implications of the Convention may go even further. One issue which has taxed both the Joint Committee, academics and commentators since the publication of the draft Bill is the extent to which the disciplinary powers of the Authority constitute criminal rather than civil proceedings, and therefore demand the more extensive procedural safeguards provided in the Convention (such as the privilege against self-incrimination, the right to legal aid[90] and the demand that criminal offences be clearly defined in law[91]). The government has accepted that the new, civil, 'market abuse' regime[92] (introduced in order to 'plug the gaps' in the criminal law on insider dealing and market manipulation) may constitute a criminal proceedings for the purposes of the Convention (on the grounds that the penalties at stake are criminal in nature and the regime is intended to punish and deter). It has therefore taken steps to implement the ECHR safeguards (including that evidence obtained under compulsion under the Authority's information-gathering and investigations powers will not be admissible in market abuse proceedings and that legal aid will be available in appropriate circumstances).[93]

However, it has not extended the same safeguards to disciplinary action for breach of rules made under the Authority's general legislative powers in relation to authorised persons and approved persons.[94] It has been suggested that the government is over-confident in its assessment that this disciplinary regime is 'civil' in nature, particularly given that the penalties for breach include the power to impose unlimited fines.[95] Any successful challenge to the nature of the disciplinary regime may mean that the Authority could yet be required to introduce such safeguards generally. The wider implications of the Human Rights Act are that the entire regulatory regime might subsequently become much more adversarial, expensive, slow and uncertain. This would be a disastrous consequence for a regulatory regime intended to be flexible and able to respond quickly to a rapidly changing market-place.

It is not only in the area of discipline that the ECHR may have an impact. The Authority could be exposed to potentially substantial damages claims in the area of authorisation. Article 6 of the Convention provides for the right of a fair and public hearing in relation to a determination of a civil right. It seems clear from existing European case law that a refusal, modification or revocation of a licence would constitute a civil right for the purposes of the Convention.[96] In order to obtain authorisation under the FSM Bill a person must be granted permission to carry on regulated activities. That permission can be granted subject to such limitations as the Authority deems appropriate, or can be refused, or can be varied subsequently. While a refusal or variation is subject to the right to have the matter referred to the Tribunal for an independent hearing, the granting of permission subject to limitations is not. The imposition of limitations in permission is also arguably a civil right and a breach of the Convention will occur unless the applicant is provided with a 'fair and public hearing' by an independent tribunal. While the regulatee might have a right to bring an application for judicial review to challenge the imposition of limitations, the current reluctance of the courts to entertain issues of merit would mean that such a review would not constitute a fair hearing for the purposes of the Convention.[97]

The implications of the Human Rights Act 1998 remain uncertain in relation to regulation under the new Bill. The implementation of the Convention introduces another layer of accountability against which regulatory actions will be judged. This layer is rather more opaque than others at this particular moment, but has serious implications for the effectiveness and efficiency of the new regime if it is subject to attack under the Human Rights Act. As others have noted, it is perhaps unfortunate that the government has not adopted a cautious approach to the potential application of the Convention in order to avoid such attacks. At the same time, there appears to be a real potential for the ECHR to slow down the regulatory process.

Conclusion

The reforms to the regulatory structure contained in the 1999 Bill represent the latest instalment in the evolution of financial services regulation in the UK. The structure has moved from the diverse and piecemeal regulation which existed prior to 1986, through the more comprehensive 'self-regulatory' regime under the Financial Services Act, to the yet more comprehensive statutory regime about to be introduced.

In devising this new regulatory structure there has been an attempt to preserve the best features of the 'self-regulatory' regime identified by Gower in his Report: regulation by a body close to the market, with powers to act flexibly and quickly in response to changing market conditions and with practitioner input. At the same time, the government has attempted to rationalise the structure to remove the inefficiencies and inconsistencies caused by having multiple regulators, and to provide for better investor protection. Instead of multiple regulators (and multiple ombudsmen and multiple compensation schemes) there will be one central regulator (with certain exceptions) with a clear set of objectives and comprehensive statutory legislative and enforcement powers over an industry which generates 7 per cent of British gross domestic product. This regulator will be accountable for its actions via a number of diverse mechanisms ranging from internal scrutiny (such as via independent internal investigation of complaints) through to Treasury inquiries, public meetings to discuss the Annual Report, and parliamentary scrutiny of the Annual Report. In addition, as with its predecessors, it will be subject to judicial review by the courts.

Undoubtedly, the new regime will have advantages over the previous system, such as economies of scale, a greater range of expertise and the opportunity for greater consistency in regulation across particular sectors. It will be able to formulate a more comprehensive view of the industry as a whole, and it will provide a point of contact in the development of international regulatory systems. In addition it has specific objectives and clear lines of accountability.

It remains doubtful whether it will be any more successful in achieving those objectives than the previous regime. The government clearly believes that the replacement of 'self-regulation' with statutory regulation will have benefits for the investor. However, the likelihood is that the ability of the regulator to achieve its particular objectives will depend upon a number of factors which have little to do with the particular form of regulation. A simple reconstitution of the form of regulation – putting on a statutory basis regulatory powers which have previously existed on a contractual basis – is, of itself, unlikely to have a significant impact upon the effectiveness of the new regulatory structure.

In carrying out its functions the regulator will need to balance the demands of its various constituents, including the practitioner and consumer panels, the non-executive board members, industry generally, the media and the government. These constituents, however, may or may not share similar agendas at any one time. The method by which, for example, the practitioner and consumer fora are integrated into the regulatory process will be crucial not only in terms of their ability to influence regulation but also in terms of establishing the legitimacy of the regulator within the broader community, particularly the industry. Without such legitimacy it will be more difficult for the regulator to establish an appropriate 'regulatory culture' within the industry, or to maintain the confidence of consumers of financial services. Because the legislative functions of the Authority can only be exercised by the board and not delegated, the constitution of the board (which must contain a majority of non-executive members, appointed by the Authority) may also be significant for the way in which the Authority carries out its functions. A strong industry presence on the board has advantages (in terms of expertise and knowledge) but also disadvantages (the possibility of 'regulatory capture'). The board is in a powerful position to influence the way in which the Authority approaches each of its four objectives.

Other 'external' factors such as the ability of the government (or the competition authorities) to intervene under their competition powers to direct rule changes, and the approach to be adopted by the courts to the European Convention on Human Rights, may also turn out to be very significant.

As referred to in chapter 1, existing literature suggests that the more familiar views of the way regulation works may be subject to doubt. Regulation cannot be reduced to a single dimensional issue about the battle to impose the public interest over private interests. To do so is to ignore the extent to which political, legal and cultural factors have shaped the 'regulatory space' in which the particular regulator operates and which operate to inform and limit the regulatory process, irrespective of 'form'.[98] Other writers have stressed the importance of rule choice[99] and enforcement strategies:[100] in other words, the importance of method for achieving regulatory objectives.

The government has attempted to create a statutory regime with strong, flexible regulatory powers but also with strong accountability measures, including the right of constituents other than the regulated community to participate in the regulatory process. In this sense it is an incremental, rather than radical, development of the regime currently in place. Nevertheless, there are a number of dangers ahead for the new regime, not least of which is that the combined banking, insurance and securities sector is simply too big for one regulator to manage effectively. Perhaps the greatest danger facing the Authority is that of just one more major scandal. Whereas in the past it was the self-regulatory organisations (or the Bank of England) which were blamed for such scandals, leaving the reputation of SIB, the statutory regulator, relatively unscathed, just one new significant collapse may be all that is required to undermine fatally the credibility of, and confidence in, the new regime. Whether this new form of regulation stands the test of time remains to be seen.

Notes

1 There existed no regulation (for example, some investment managers, members of some 'recognised associations'), tight statutory regulation (for example, authorised unit trusts), self-regulation (for example, the Stock Exchange, the Council for the Securities Industry, the Association of Licensed Dealers in Securities, the Association of Futures, Brokers and Dealers) or loose government regulation (for example, insurance companies). For discussion of the existing system, see Gower, L.C.B. (1982), *Review of Investor Protection: A Discussion Document*, London: HMSO; Wilson Report, *Report of the Committee to review the Functioning of Financial Institutions*, Cm 7937, London: HMSO 1980.

2 Gower, *Review of Investor Protection* (n.1, above). For the final report, see Gower, J., *Review of Investor Protection*, 1984, Cm 9125.

3 For an alternative explanation for the occurrence of the 'fraud crisis' in the City of London, see Moran, M. (1989), 'Investor Protection and the Culture of Capitalism', in L. Hancher and M. Moran (eds), *Capitalism, Culture and Economic Regulation*, Oxford: Clarendon, pp.49–75.

4 Gower, *Review of Investor Protection* (n.1, above), ch.5.

5 *Ibid.*, para. 7.04.

6 *Ibid.*, para. 5.06.

7 *Ibid.*, para. 7.08.

8 *Ibid.*, para. 6.02.

9 *Ibid.*, para. 6.01.

10 *Ibid.*, para. 1.15.

11 FSA 1986, s.10 and sch. 2, para. 3, as amended by s.203(1) of the Companies Act 1989.

12 See further Pimlott, G.F. (1985), 'The Reform of Investor Protection in the UK – An Examination of the Proposals of the Gower Report and the UK Government's White Paper of January 1985', *Journal of Comparative Business and Capital Market Law*, 7, 141–72.

13 Gower, L.C.B. (1988), '"Big Bang" and the City Revolution', *Modern Law Review*, 51, 1–22.

14 Section 121(2). See Black, J. (1997), *Rules and Regulations*, Oxford: Clarendon, for a discussion of the impact of this provision upon SIB rule making, particularly in the early period.

15 FSA 1986, sch. 7, para. 1; s.115. The Treasury does retain some residual functions under the FSA 1986; for example, functions relating to the certification of persons authorised in another EU member state and the scope of the category of exempted persons; see further, s.114.

16 DTI White Paper, *Financial Services in the United Kingdom*, Cm 9432, London: HMSO, 1985, para. 3.1.

17 Gower, *Review of Investor Protection* (n.13, above), 11.

18 Black, *Rules and Regulations* (n.14, above), ch.3.

19 For example, in the wake of a report by Andrew Large, Chairman of SIB (1993), *Financial Services Regulation: Making the Two Tier System Work*, ('the Large Report').
20 Treasury and Civil Service Select Committee, Sixth Report (1995/6), *The Regulation of Financial Services in the UK*, Vol. 1, HC Paper 332–I.
21 For example in the Large Report, 1993 (n.19, above).
22 Such as the problem of enforcement where different regulators have interlinking or overlapping responsibilities, and the difficulty of regulating new products which fell between regulators and where no lead regulator is identified (such as occurred in relation to the regulation of bank derivatives trading – an issue brought into sharp focus with the collapse of Barings Bank).
23 As evidenced by the home income plan and pension mis-selling scandals.
24 Select Committee Sixth Report (n.20, above), para. 22.
25 Ibid., para. 27.
26 Davies, H. (1999), 'Financial Regulation: Why Bother?', Society of Business Economists Lecture, January, FSA *mimeo*.
27 *Labour's Business Manifesto – Equipping Britain for the Future*, 1997, p.15.
28 Chancellor of the Exchequer (Gordon Brown), HC 20 May 1997, 508.
29 Reported in Geeson, S. (1998), 'Financial Services: The New Face of Regulation', *Amicus Curiae*, 5, 27–30.
30 Government documents issued at the time of, and since, the decision to reform the sector are littered with references to the importance of this sector to the UK economy; see, for example, *Labour's Business Manifesto*, p.15; Foreword by Rt Hon Gordon Brown MP, Chancellor of the Exchequer, HM Treasury, *Financial Services and Markets Bill: A Consultation Document, Part 1*, HM Treasury, July 1998; Mr Alan Milburn, Chief Secretary to the Treasury, HC Deb. 28 June 1998, col. 34.
31 HC 20 May 1997, col. 510.
32 The Chancellor's letter to Sir A. Large, chairman, SIB, 20 May 1997.
33 Taylor, M. (1997), *Regulatory Leviathan: Will Super-SIB Work?*, London: CTA Financial Publishing.
34 Some of this transfer has already occurred under the Bank of England Act 1998.
35 An important extension of the scope of regulation under the Act is that the Authority will have greater supervision over Lloyd's. Additionally, it has recently been announced that the Authority will take over the role of the London Stock Exchange as the competent authority for listing (*The Guardian*, 5 October, 1999).
36 While certain areas of what many would consider to constitute financial services will remain outside this regulatory structure (for example, mortgages, long-term care insurance, conduct of deposit takers and conduct of general insurers), power for their subsequent inclusion will exist. Thus, despite government rhetoric, there will not, in fact, be a 'one stop' regulatory system, at least in the initial stages.
37 FSA 1986, s.187(1) & (3).
38 FSM Bill 121, sch. 1, para.19. This immunity will not apply in respect of breach of s.6(1) of the Human Rights Act 1998. See also *Three Rivers District Council & Ors* v. *Bank of England* [1999] 7 Lloyd's Law Reports, 283, where, in the context of the BCCI collapse, the Council tried to circumvent statutory immunity by suing the Bank for the tort of misfeasance of public office. The action ultimately failed on the facts because the plaintiffs could not prove the existence of the requisite dishonest state of mind.

39 For example, in relation to exempt persons, and prescribing regulated activities, FSM Bill, cl. 34 & cl. 20.
40 FSM Bill, cl. 132.
41 Evidence given to the Joint Committee on Financial Services and Markets, *First Report*, 1999, HC 328–I, para. 104.
42 FSM Bill, cl. 7. This panel has already been constituted and is referred to as the Practitioner Forum.
43 There is no requirement at present for the separation of the function of chairman and chief executive.
44 FSM Bill, cl. 8.
45 Offences include carrying on a 'regulated activity' (that is, deposit taking, insurance or investment business) unless authorised or exempt. FSM Bill, cl. 21.
46 In addition to the existing power of 'recognition', the Authority is given new powers to issue 'directions' (FSM Bill, cl. 267).
47 In addition to financial resources, client money, cancellation, price stabilisation and financial promotion, compensation, the ombudsman scheme (FSM Bill, cls 110–18, 184 and 198).
48 FSM Bill, cl. 61. An 'approved person' is approved by the FSA for the purposes of engaging in one of three types of 'controlled functions' (cl. 56). Such functions give the person significant control over the authorised person, involve the person dealing directly with customers and involve him/her dealing directly with customer property.
49 FSM Bill, cls 176,177,334,30,40, 63 & 60, respectively.
50 Ibid., cls 341–5.
51 Briault, C. (1999), *The Rationale for a Single National Financial Services Regulator*, FSA Occasional Paper Series.
52 Goodhart, C. and D. Llewellyn (1997), 'A Blurred Outlook', *Financial Times*, 30 May.
53 Joint Committee on Financial Services and Markets, *First Report*, HC 328–I & 328–II, 1999; *Second Report*, HC 465, 1999.
54 FSM Bill, cl. 2(2).
55 Ibid., cl. 2(3).
56 Taylor, *Regulatory Leviathan* (n.33, above).
57 Goodhart, C.A.E *et al.* (1998), *Financial Regulation*, London: Routledge.
58 Briault, *The Rationale* (n.51, above).
59 See FSA (1998), *Meeting Our Responsibilities*, (1998), London, para. 32, in which the Authority states that its regulatory approach will, in practice, reflect such differentiation.
60 Prosser, T. (1999), 'Theorising Utility Regulation', *Modern Law Review*, 62, 196–217; Prosser, T. (1997), *Law and the Regulators*, Oxford: Clarendon, chs 1 and 9.
61 Prosser, 'Theorising Utility Regulation' (n.60, above), p.200.
62 Such rules cover the situation where an adviser must be either tied to one product provider or be fully independent and able to offer 'best advice'.
63 See Briault, *The Rationale* (n.51, above).
64 See the speech by Howard Davies, Chairman, FSA, 'Why Regulate?', Henry Thornton Lecture, City University Business School, 4 November 1998.
65 The ability of the Authority to insulate itself from regulating for social or distributive objectives such as access to financial services might remain a moot point after the introduction of stakeholder pensions.
66 Llewellyn, D. (1999),*The Economic Rationale for Financial Regulation*, FSA Occasional Paper.
67 HM Treasury Joint Committee, First Report, paras 47–51; *Financial Services and Markets Bill – Progress Report*, March 1999, para. 4.16.

68 Cruikshank, D. (1999), 'Competition and Regulation: An Interim', 22 July 1999, available at <www.bankreview.org.uk>.
69 *Ibid.*, para. 49 conclusion.
70 *Ibid.*, Annex 3. The Report also recommends that there be no unnecessary exclusions from UK competition law, and that the Competition Commission rather than the Treasury be the final arbiter of whether the FSA rules operate against the public interest.
71 Select Committee, Sixth Report (n.20, above), para. 20.
72 Llewellyn, *The Economic Rationale* (n.66 above), 47–8.
73 The objectives must be clearly specified. The objective of market confidence in particular lacks clarity (whose confidence?) and therefore as a mechanism of accountability may prove less than satisfactory. Similarly, the objective of reducing financial crime may prove problematic for accountability owing to the overlap between the Authority's role and the role of other enforcement agencies such as the Serious Fraud Office, the Crown Prosecution Service and the DTI. Will the Authority be able to pass the buck and so avoid accountability? The Authority has announced it is working with these other bodies to produce a memorandum of understanding between them to clarify their relationships (FSA, *A Short Guide to our Preparations for the New Regulatory Regime*, July 1999).
74 For further discussion of regulatory accountability and legitimacy (including issues of both procedural and substantive legitimacy), see Majone, G. (1996), *Regulating Europe*, London: Routledge; Black, J. (1996), 'Constitutionalising Self Regulation', *Modern Law Review*, 59, 24; Prosser, T. (1999), 'Theorising Utility Regulation' (n.60, above), 62, 196.
75 Joint Committee, *First Report*, 1999, Annex B, Submission from the Delegated Powers & Deregulation Committee, para. 8.
76 HM Treasury, *Financial Services and Markets Bill: Government Response to the Reports of the Joint Committee on Financial Services and Markets*, London: HMSO, 17 June 1999.
77 For example, FSM Bill, cls 122, 128 and 62(7).
78 FSM Bill, cls 10 and 12.
79 On the FSA's approach to consultation, see FSA, *The Open Approach to Regulation*, July 1998, and FSA, *A Short Guide*, (n.73, above). As part of the consultation process the Authority plans to hold informal discussions with those likely to be directly affected, to produce formal consultation proposals, conduct open hearings 'where appropriate', make all formal (but not informal) responses available for public inspection and, in relation to major policy issues, publish feedback.
80 FSM Bill, cl. 125. These requirements are relaxed in certain situations, such as 'emergency' (cl. 125(6)).
81 *Ibid.*, cl. 8(4).
82 In reality, the possibility of 'regulatory capture' must be reduced by the sheer number and diversity of regulatees.
83 See, for example, Hamilton, S. (1999), 'The Human Rights Act and the Regulation of Utilities', *Utilities Law Review*, 10(3), 115–24.
84 ECHR, Art. 6(1).
85 *Ibid.*, Art. 6(2).
86 *Ibid.*, Art. 6(3).
87 *Ibid.*, Art. 7(1).
88 HM Treasury, *Government Response to the First Report*, (n.76, above).
89 If the regulatee does not exercise the right of referral to the Tribunal, the Authority's 'decision notice' (including penalty) will stand. Provided proper procedures have been followed and the regulatee has been informed of its

right to a referral, it would seem unlikely that the regulatee could complain of breach of the Convention in circumstances where the regulatee declines to refer.

90 ECHR, Art. 6(3).

91 *Ibid.*, Art. 7(1).

92 This was introduced under Part VII of the FSM Bill.

93 It has not, however, acted to tighten the very broad definition of 'market abuse' contained in cl. 95, a definition which arguably would not satisfy the Convention requirement of 'certainty'. For a discussion of this issue, see, for example, Joint Committee, *First Report* (n.41, above), paras 260–63 and Annex D, and the 'Government Response to the First Report', (n. section 6. However, if the Code of Practice to be issued by the Authority to supplement the statutory provision is sufficiently precise, this may satisfy the Convention requirement.

94 FSM Bill, Parts IX and V, respectively.

95 See Annexes C and D to the Joint Committee *First Report* (n.41, above); see also the *Second Report*, 1999, HC 463, HL 66.

96 *Tre Traktorer Aktiebalag* v. *Sweden*, (1991) 13 EHRR 309; see also the Commission Decisions in *APB* v. *IMRO* (Appln 30552/96, 15 January 1998), *X* v. *UK* (Appln 28530/95, 18 January 1998).

97 On the other hand, it may be that the Authority is not liable at all in this circumstance, given that, at the stage when the Authority takes the decision, the independent review process is not complete, only becoming so after judicial review. The court might therefore find that it is not the Authority which is in breach, but the process itself. See further Hamilton (n.83, above).

98 Hancher, L. and M. Moran (1998), 'Organising Regulatory Space', in R. Baldwin, C. Scott and C. Hood (eds), *A Reader on Regulation*, Oxford: Oxford University Press.

99 Diver, C.S. (1983), 'The Optimal Precision of Administrative Rules', *Yale Law Journal*, 93, 65; Baldwin, R. (1991), 'Why Rules Don't Work', *Modern Law Review*, 53, 321; Black, J. (1997), *Rules and Regulators*, Oxford: Clarendon.

100 Baldwin, 'Why Rules Don't Work' (n.99, above) and Baldwin, R. (1995), *Rules and Government*, Oxford: Oxford University Press.

13 Regulating Public Procurement in the Single European Market: Past, Present and Future

ROBIN G. MILNE, *University of Glasgow*
AND DUNCAN OSLER, *Shepherd & Wedderburn*[1]

Introduction

One of the main goals of the European Union (EU) and its predecessors has been the free movement of labour, capital, goods and services within its boundaries. Earlier in the life of the Community, two directives, in 1971 and 1977, were issued in respect of the public procurement of works and supplies, respectively, with this goal in mind.

Tariff barriers had largely been eliminated by the mid-1980s, but non-tariff barriers were perceived to be a problem, to which the practice of public procurement was a contributory factor. The issue was given greater urgency because European firms faced serious competition in their domestic and world markets from America, Japan and the newly industrialised countries. The Single European Act of 1987 established a programme of some 300 directives,[2] of which a set related to public procurement. Public procurement, of course, was and still is important. In 1986, it was valued at some 15 per cent of the Community's gross domestic product.[3] Currently it is 11 per cent.[4] In March 1998, the European Commission proposed further changes to the directives for beyond the year 2000.

In this chapter we describe some of the legislative changes introduced since 1987. We then evaluate these changes in terms of compliance and economic impact. Finally, we describe some of the European Commission's proposals, and assess their significance for the year 2000 and beyond.

EC Procurement Directives: the Current Legislative Framework

The aim of this section is to introduce the public procurement directives which established the framework of the European Community procurement regime, and to explain their significance.

Historic Development of the Procurement Directives

Various EC directives have been made by the EC Council with the aim of furthering the fundamental principles of EC Law contained in The Treaty of Rome, 1957 (the 'EC Treaty'), namely the principles of free movement of goods, services, labour and capital. Many Treaty provisions are relevant to a degree, but in brief the most pertinent provisions are the following:

1 Article 12, EC Treaty, prohibiting discrimination on grounds of nationality.
2 Article 28, EC Treaty and subsequent provisions, prohibiting quantitative restrictions on imports and exports and all measures having equivalent effect between member states; that is, the 'free movement of goods'.
3 Article 43, EC Treaty and subsequent provisions, prohibiting restrictions on freedom to provide services within the Community in respect of nationals of member states; that is, the 'right of establishment'.
4 Article 49, EC Treaty and subsequent provisions, prohibiting restrictions on freedom to provide services within the Community in respect of nationals of member states; that is, the 'free movement of services'.

In general terms, the regime implemented by the procurement directives is intended to ensure that competition for public procurement takes place on a 'level playing field' as between nationals of all member states.

Community legislation to ensure non-discriminatory treatment of competing suppliers in the field of public procurement has been introduced piecemeal. First, Council directives on public works[5] and on public supplies[6] were enacted, based on the principles of non-discrimination and transparency. They did not cover contracts for services, or procurement in relation to energy, water, transport and telecommunications; moreover, their lack of any harmonised procedures for the enforcement of remedies increased the difficulties for aggrieved suppliers in seeking redress, whether by challenging procurement decisions or by claiming damages. This limited scope contributed to the minimal impact they had in relation to public procurement in the Community at that time.

As the legal framework of the EU developed, and as part of the 1985 Internal Market White Paper[7] programme, the public works and public supplies directives were separately updated in 1988[8] and in 1989.[9] The principal changes to both directives addressed (a) advertising, provision of information and statistics (to improve transparency), (b) technical specifications (to accord with Community objectives on harmonisation), (c) widening the scope for using negotiation in contract awards, (d) increasing notification and tendering time limits, and (e) developing and improving definitions. In addition, the 1988 Works Directive increased the contract value threshold (over which the directive would apply) from ECU 1 million to ECU 5 million.

In 1993, the amended public works and public supplies directives were consolidated by Works Directive 93/37 and, with some additional amendments to align certain provisions, by Supplies Directive 93/36. A directive on supplies and works procurement by utilities in the water, energy, transport and telecommunications sectors was adopted in 1990.[10] This applied both to public undertakings and to those undertakings granted special or exclusive rights by member states, in respect of contracts for works and supplies (with effect from 1 January 1993).

Coverage spread to the procurement of service contracts with Directive 92/50, which came into force on 1 July 1993, and as regards the utilities sector, a consolidated version of the Utilities Directive including service contracts (Directive 93/38) came into force on 1 July 1994, thus completing the level of coverage envisaged by the Commission in the Internal Market White Paper programme.

In addition to these directives extending the coverage of the procurement regime, the Community legislation on remedies was supplemented. The Remedies Directive covering the 'traditional' procurement sectors[11] was amended[12] and an additional directive for the utilities sector was introduced.[13] As a result, member states are required to ensure that administrative or legal remedies are available to suppliers in the event of non-compliance with the substantive rules on fair and open procurement.

Transposition of the Directives and Implementation into UK Law

The procurement directives need to be transposed[14] into national law by implementing legislation to be enacted by each member state. The

Commission recognises the fundamental importance of this to delivering the public procurement regime, and it is unfortunate that the extent of implementation to date has been well below the Commission's expectation.[15] As regards the UK, the Commission has initiated infringement proceedings in respect of a failure to complete implementing measures in respect of the Utilities Remedies Directive.[16]

The UK government passed the Services Regulations,[17] the Supply Regulations,[18] the Works Regulations[19] and the Utilities Regulations[20] (collectively the 'Procurement Regulations'). These implement the corresponding EC directives in the UK for relevant services, supplies and works contracts, and for procurement contracts entered into by utilities in relation to the activity for which they are a specified utility. The wording of these regulations largely tracks the English translation of the corresponding provision in the relevant directive and to this extent implementation generally accords with the corresponding Community provision it is intended to implement.

Beyond the EU

A limitation of the EU procurement regime is that it applies only to contracts being awarded by EC public bodies and offers protection only to nationals (including legal and natural persons) of a member state. It does not provide any protection for EU nationals in tendering for contracts outside the EU, nor (subject to comments below) does it offer protection to non-nationals tendering in the EU, except to the extent that they incorporate a tendering vehicle in the EU for this purpose.

There are global trends towards the extension of the EC public procurement regime beyond the borders of the EU. Three key initiatives are highlighted below, but there are others at differing stages of development and implementation. It is in the nature of these developments that they will evolve in line with political and social change.

First, the European Economic Area Agreement was signed by the European Free Trade Association (EFTA) states[21] and required the EC procurement rules, with modifications, to be implemented into domestic legislation. Second, the Community and its member states have entered into a number of 'Europe Agreements' with certain states of Central and Eastern Europe, recognising the possibility of their becoming members of the EU at some point in the future.[22] These agreements provide for access by undertakings of the relevant state to Community contracts on terms not less favourable than those applied to Community companies.[23]

Third, and finally, the Government Procurement Agreement (GPA), signed in Marrakesh on 15 April 1994 and embodying the results of the Uruguay Round of World Trade Organisation negotiations, has coverage in parallel with the EU procurement provisions.[24] As well as giving rights to non-EU tenderers, it applies to public contracting authorities outside the EU, thereby affording EU and non-EU tenderers protections outside the EU as well as within.

A review of the non-EU aspects of the GPA is outside the scope of this chapter, but it should be noted that the GPA contains differences as regards the EU and non-EU protections it delivers, both in terms of the threshold for application and as regards the types of contracts and contracting authorities which it covers. There are also differences in the non-EU coverage, notably as regards the financial thresholds which apply in the USA and Japan. Certain provisions of the GPA (such as the financial thresholds) are more stringent than those set out in the procurement directives, and the procurement directives have been amended (by the Amending Directive 97/52) to ensure compliance within the EU. The UK Procurement Regulations are currently at variance with the corresponding procurement directives since the provisions of Amending Directive 97/52 have not yet been implemented in the UK.

Financial Thresholds

The directives and regulations only apply if the estimated value of the contract is above an agreed threshold. The thresholds are set at levels to ensure the competitive procurement rules apply to contracts likely to interest suppliers from other member states, but low enough to avoid disproportionate administrative and procedural costs on lower value contracts. These thresholds are generally fixed in ECUs and SDRs.[25] The equivalent amount in sterling and other currencies is calculated every two years, and the current levels apply for the period from 1 January 1998 to 31 December 1999. The current thresholds under the UK Regulations are as follows:

- *Services Regulations* – for most services being procured by non-central government bodies (to which the GPA does not apply) the threshold is SDR 200 000.[26]
- *Supply Regulations* – for most supplies being procured by non-central government bodies the threshold is SDR 200 000;[27] for specified central government departments and other bodies subject to the GPA, the threshold is SDR 130 000.
- *Works Regulations* – for works being procured by both local and central government the threshold is SDR 5 million[28] except in respect of subsidised contracts under regulation 23 of the Works Regulations, which have a threshold of ECU 5 million.[29]
- *Utilities Regulations* – the thresholds are split according to the types of contract being awarded and the sectors in which the

utility is operating. For works contracts in the energy, water, transport and telecommunications sectors, the threshold is ECU 5 million.[30] For supplies and services contracts in the energy, water and transport sectors the threshold is ECU 400 000,[31] but in the telecommunications sector the threshold for supplies and services is ECU 600 000.[32]

Classification of Contracts: A Common Procurement Vocabulary

By a Recommendation of 30 July 1996,[33] and with a view to achieving greater standardisation, transparency and harmonisation in OJEC Notices, the Commission has recommended that the Common Procurement Vocabulary 1996 (CPV) should be used for categorising contracts.[34] The principal benefit of using the CPV classifications is that, regardless of the language in which the OJEC is published, the subject matter of the OJEC Notice can be easily determined using these classifications, allowing potential bidders for contracts more easily to consider whether or not they should respond to the OJEC Notice.[35]

Conclusions

In recent years the public procurement of utilities and services has become subject to EU legislation. Whilst there have been delays in its transposition into national legislation, some impact on openness and transparency in public procurement is expected. Openness and transparency will be further enhanced by improvements in the classification of contracts. These changes, together with the extension of legislation outside the EU, can be expected to increase competition in the supply of public procurement.

Some Key Features of EC Procurement Procedures

The aim of this section is to set out some of the key features of the Community's procurement regime.

Introduction

It is outside the scope of this chapter to explain in detail all the procurement procedures set out in each of the procurement directives (as implemented into the UK by the Procurement Regulations) but there are basic similarities between the procedures laid down in the Works, Supplies and Services Directives and Regulations, and (with modifications) in the Utilities Directive and Regulations. The scope of the Services Regulations, and salient features of their procedures, are outlined in part below. Services are selected so as to inform the evaluation contained in this chapter.

Scope, Exclusions and the Description of Technical Specifications

The Regulations specify what is a contracting authority, but in outline this includes central government bodies, local authorities and bodies governed by public law.[36] There are extensive categories of general exclusions from the application of the Regulations,[37] though the contracting authority may choose to comply with the Regulations. The Services Regulations[38] specify the grounds upon which any technical specifications in a contract can be described *other than* by reference to European specifications. But unless these grounds apply, European specifications must be used.

Award Procedures

Broadly, there are three possible procedures a contracting authority can use: the open, restricted and negotiated procedures.[39] The open procedure allows all interested persons to tender. In contrast, under the restricted procedure, only persons selected by the contracting authority may submit tenders for the contract; this may be particularly useful where the contract requires suppliers with particular expertise. Neither of these procedures permits any negotiation.[40]

The negotiated procedure allows the contracting authority to negotiate both contractual terms and price with bidders. It may only be used in certain circumstances,[41] largely to minimise the opportunities for contracting authorities to take advantage of its less transparent nature – although being able to negotiate can be of great benefit to the public sector. For instance, contracts under the Private Finance Initiative are customarily awarded under the negotiated procedure.

OJEC Notices

An important part of the EU procurement procedures is the publication of notices using a specified format, to ensure key information is available. There are three main categories. First, each of the Procurement Regulations provides[42] that a contracting authority must, as soon as possible after the commencement of each of its financial years, send a notice to the *Official Journal* of the procurement contracts (in excess of specified thresholds) in relation to which it expects to seek offers during the course of that year. Where such a 'Prior Information Notice' (PIN) is issued, this has a bearing on the notice periods which apply in respect of the open and restricted procedures.[43] PINs are therefore a prior indication of forthcoming procurement but do not contain adequate information to allow interested parties to tender. Secondly, under the open, restricted and negotiated procedures, an 'OJEC Notice' must be published in relation to each specific contract,[44] inviting interested parties to respond. Finally, no more than 48 days after contract award, a contract award notice must be published in the *Official Journal*: this assists bidders, the Commission and others to monitor contract awards.

Selection of Services, Works and Supplies Providers

Under the negotiated procedure and the restricted procedure, the next stage for a contracting authority is to select a number of parties to negotiate or tender for the contract as the case may be. At least three parties must be selected to negotiate[45] and, for the restricted procedure, if the range of number of persons to be invited to tender is stated in the notice, this must be between five and 20.[46]

Certain grounds must be used for the evaluation and selection of services, works or supplies providers, such as a person being insolvent or a company having a receiver appointed, which automatically entitle a contracting authority to treat a provider as ineligible. Evaluation can be on the basis of economic and financial standing, ability and technical capacity as well as supplementary related information.[47] Importantly, this information is to be used by the contracting authority to make its selection as to whom it will invite to negotiate (under the negotiated procedure). No prices may be asked for at this stage, and these criteria do not apply to the *award* of a public services contract; the criteria for contract award itself are as set out in the following section.

Criteria for the Award of a Public Services Contract

According to Regulation 21, a contracting authority shall award a public services contract[48] on the basis of the offer which (a) is the most economically advantageous to the contracting authority, or (b) offers the lowest price. The Procurement Regulations specify the criteria to be used by contracting authorities, and that contracting authorities should indicate their order of importance. The criteria *include* period for completion or delivery, quality, aesthetic and functional characteristics, technical merit, after sales service, technical assistance and price.[49]

The use of the lowest price criteria would not allow an authority to choose a higher-priced tender even if it offered advantages – for example, in technical merit. For this reason the most economically advantageous basis will often be used, and in these circumstances the criteria upon which the authority intends to base its decision must be stated, in descending order of importance if possible. This will limit the authority's scope for tender evaluation and this is appropriate because tenderers will tend to tailor their bids according to criteria given. As an example, tenderers might provide higher levels of quality if that is stated to be of high importance, probably increasing prices beyond the minimum. In contrast, if price is of high importance then tenderers will tend to bid as low a price as possible, perhaps reducing quality levels where technically possible. This illustrates the importance to tenderers of correctly assessing how tenders are to be evaluated, and of fairness and transparency in the evaluation process.

Evaluating the Impact of the Directives: Review of Previous Studies

The aim of this section is to identify the economic impact of the directives since the mid-1980s, based on published sources.

Methodology

The first step in the implementation of the directives is the publication of notices in the OJEC Supplement, inviting firms to express their interest in tendering. The extent of publication is a key measure of compliance, and of openness when contracts are put out to tender. Further, there is evidence that businesses, especially larger ones, find it a useful source of information, and this may lead to the award of contracts, not only domestically but also in other EU countries.[50]

The requirement to publish is a response to the European Commission's perception that the award of public sector contracts is biased toward domestic firms, as indicated by the limited extent of import penetration in the public sector vis-à-vis the private sector.[51]

The economic purpose of the directives is not merely to correct national bias in the award of contracts, but to achieve economic benefit. The requirements for 'openness' through the publication of notices, and 'fairness' through the appropriate use of selection and award criteria, are expected to increase (international) competitiveness. Increased competitiveness can be measured in terms of the number and national spread of firms expressing an interest in tendering, and given the opportunity to do so. Increased competitiveness in turn is expected to reduce prices and price disparities to consumers and producers in the short to medium term, and to increase supplier concentration in the EU in the long term.

Ideally, the above parameters of performance should be analysed in *comparative* terms: for example, comparing outcomes before and after the directives were introduced, or comparing public with private sector to reflect their coverage/non-coverage by the directives. Even when such comparisons are possible, correction for extraneous factors affecting compliance and performance is necessary to isolate the specific impact of the directives.

Evidence

Published evidence is presented on the various parameters identified above. A key source is the EuroStrategy study, one of a set of reports prepared for the European Commission to review the Single Market.[52] Most of its evidence covers the period from 1987 to 1994, ending only a year or two after the Utilities and Services Directives came into force.

Notices published in the OJEC Supplement This measure is probably the least subject to the influence of extraneous factors. Martin and Hartley use the TED (Tenders Electronic Daily) archive to cover the period 1992 to 1996.[53] They find an increase in notices inviting tenders for supplies, works and services, and that all EU-15 countries experienced this growth. Part of the increase reflects the extension of directives to utilities and services that came into force during this period; the remainder is due to the increasing compliance with the previously existing Supplies and Works Directives.[54] Further, supplies from ten industries, identified as nationally protected, increased more or less in line with the increase in supplies for all industries.[55] It is clear, therefore, that there has been compliance with the directives, though its extent is not known.

Import penetration in the public sector The EuroStrategy study[56] is the only source known to us with comparative data. The difficulties of obtaining reliable data are acknowledged. Nevertheless, clear changes are indicated. For the EU-15 group of countries the proportion increased from 6 per cent in 1987 to 10 per cent in 1994. The corresponding data for the UK are 4 and 12 per cent. The study also distinguishes between 'direct' imports, where there is transfer of goods and services across national boundaries, and 'indirect' imports where the supply is made domestically but by a foreign-owned company or is supplied by a domestic importer. Thus, comparing the situation in 1987 with 1994 at the EU-15 level, direct imports from member states increased from 0.6 to 2.5 per cent. The corresponding proportions for indirect imports are 4.7 and 7.2 per cent.

Competitiveness The EuroStrategy study[57] also provides some comparative information on the number and national origin of firms interested in tendering, based on a survey in 1996 of contracting authorities. Significantly the survey includes questions on their perception of changes. A common perception was an increase in the number of firms submitting bids, in the nationality of firms particularly from the EU, and that this experience was shared by utilities and not restricted to central and sub-central government. No distinction is made between contracts for supplies, works and services.

Prices and price disparities The EuroStrategy 1996 survey of contracting authorities also contained some information on prices for contracts. A significant minority of contracting authorities perceived a fall in contract prices, and in the majority of cases they attributed this 'in part' to the legislation.[58] Utilities shared this perception with central and sub-central government. The utilities covered were water, energy, transport and telecommunications, and sub-central government included regional and local government bodies, uniformed services, purchasing consortia and health bodies. Again no distinction is made between contracts for supplies, works and services.

Limited information on price convergence of supplies is available from the EuroStrategy study,[59] and covers the periods from 1987 to 1994 and from 1990 to 1994 for five and seven member states, respectively. Thirteen products are differentiated according to whether they would be 'procurement-sensitive' and according to their technical sophistication. The study concludes: 'In general, no conclusive evidence exists for a measurable degree of price convergence between member states for products bought by the public sector. There are some exceptions, pertaining to high-tech products.'

Industrial structure The issue here is a long-term one, affecting market concentration through the realisation of economies of scale at the EU level that the directives are intended to facilitate. The EuroStrategy study[60] examines the experience of ten 'procurement-sensitive' sectors over the period 1987 to 1994, using such industry data as are available. Three of the sectors would seem to have been covered by the Utilities Directive, one by the Works Directive (with a sub-set covered by the Services Directive), and the remainder by the Supplies Directive. In almost all cases these sectors experienced increased supplier concentration. Five of these sectors, selected as those most likely to be affected by the directives, were subject to more detailed analysis. For all but one sector, for which no conclusions were reached, the impact of the Single European Market was found to be marginal.

Conclusions

Analyses covering the period up to 1996, when the extension of the legislation to include utilities and services had at least two to three years for its implementation, are generally positive in their assessment in terms of the openness of public procurement to competition and in the perceived impact on prices.

Analyses which cover the period up to only 1994 also suggest an impact in respect of import penetration. However, this would have been largely confined to central and sub-central government, and to supplies and works. Over the same period industrial production became more concentrated, but the single market legislative programme is thought to have had a modest contributory impact at most.

Evaluating the Impact of the Directives: Description of Current Sample

The aim of this section is to define the sample to be studied and to put it into the context of the public procurement directives.

It is an admitted shortcoming of the EuroStrategy study that most of its evaluation ends at 1994, when the Utilities Directive, and also notably the Services Directive, had been in force for only a short period. The material below attempts to fill this gap. The sample studied are contracts for *hotel* services – in the sense that at least one service is domestic, catering or laundry services – for National Health Services (NHS) hospitals in Scotland. Until 1983, these services were usually provided in-house by direct service organisations (DSOs). What happened in the NHS was part of a larger picture also affecting central and local government.

The public policy issue for the UK Conservative Government at that time was whether identified support services should continue to be provided by DSOs, or whether contractors are employed. The chosen criterion was to test the cost-effectiveness of the incumbent (typically a DSO) by putting these services out to competitive tender. DSOs tended to win the majority of contracts when given the opportunity to tender, whether in central government,[61] local government[62] or the NHS.[63]

The purpose of the procurement directives is not that particular activities be put out to competitive tender. Rather it is that, once the decision to market test has been made, the *process* of tendering be 'open' and 'fair'. The directives have been grounded in the Single Market Programme for the European Community, and 'openness' and 'fairness' are tested on the basis that there be no discrimination against foreign firms. The public policy issue for the European Commission has been to prevent discrimination against non-national contractors.

The relevant EC procurement legislation for hotel service contracts is the Services Procurement Directive, which came into operation on 1

July 1993. The corresponding British enabling legislation came into force on 13 January 1994. The Services Directive distinguishes between 'priority' and 'non-priority' services. In the case of priority services, notices inviting expressions of interest in tendering have to be published in the OJEC Supplement when the value of the contract exceeds a defined threshold; there is no such requirement to publish for non-priority services. Martin and Hartley,[64] and Cox[65] have suggested that the priority/non-priority distinction be based on the extent to which the particular service is subject to significant cross-border trade.

Domestic services come within the category 'Building-cleaning and property management services' and are a priority service. Catering and hotel services are explicitly identified as non-priority services. Laundry/linen services are not named and would come within the category 'Other services' and be a non-priority service.

The period studied is from 1995 to 1998. Contracts starting in 1995 are sufficiently recent to be covered by the EC Services Directive for their full tendering process. The most recent year for which data are available nationally is 1998. The Scottish NHS Management Executive provided information on contracts starting in this period, and 17 separate tendering exercises are identified, drawn from 15 separate NHS Trusts and health boards. Eight of the 17 exercises comprised full sets of hotel services, in the sense that domestic, catering (including the preparation as well as the serving of meals), portering and often other services as well were put out to tender for award to a single entity. A further seven include a sub-set of these services, only three of which were predominantly for domestic services and therefore could be considered a 'priority' service. Two tendering exercises were exclusively for laundry/linen services. The analysis will tend to concentrate on the so-called 'hotel service contracts'.

Evaluating the Impact of the Directives: Publication of Invitations to Tender in the OJEC Supplement

The aim of this section is to examine the notices published in OJEC to indicate what opportunity this medium gave contractors to tender for public contracts, and the criteria used to select among those expressing an interest in tendering. The sample studied is the 17 NHS contracts for various hotel-type services.

The EuroStrategy study indicated the *perceptions* of contracting authorities. In this section we have more firmly based evidence of compliance. In addition, we assess the value of the information contained in the published notices.

All but about three of the 17 identified tendering exercises comprised non-priority services, for which there was no requirement to publish a notice inviting expressions of interest in tendering. Two tendering exercises, both for laundry services and hence non-priority, are known not to have had notices published in the OJEC Supplement. However, of the other 15, notices have been found in the Supplement for ten. We have *unpublished* information for another two, but have no information on the format in which they appeared in the Supplement. We have no information on the content for the remaining three. Even with this limited information it is clear that the NHS trusts and health boards overwhelmingly published notices in the Supplement although there was no requirement for them to do so. The information contained in this section refers to these 12 tendering exercises on which we have some information.

The Opportunity to Tender

The use of OJEC as an opportunity for firms to tender is based on five pieces of information: what services are put out to tender and where they are to be provided; what is the award procedure (that is, open, restricted or negotiated); what are the qualifications to tender; the possibility of dividing the contract into lots; and how many invitations to tender will be issued. It is our judgment that the information contained on the 10 published notices, though brief, gave a clear idea to firms with experience in the market for NHS hotel services what services were required and where they were wanted.

The contracting authority's choice of award procedure has some significance for a firm's ability to tender. As noted above, the possibilities are open, restricted and negotiated. All but two of the ten tendering exercises with published notices indicated that the restricted procedure would be used. One exception was the open procedure, for a contract much like several of the others using the restricted procedure. Significantly, the notice added: 'The Trust is not bound to accept the lowest or any tender' – a statement hardly consistent with the use of the open procedure but nevertheless often included in notices to ensure that the contracting authority is not contractually bound by the mere submission of the lowest tender. The other exception was a negotiated procedure. This one differed from similar contracts using the restricted procedure, in that a Private Finance Initiative (PFI) funding arrangement was involved.

Finally, in the case of one tendering exercise, the OJEC notice was re-published six weeks later. The original intention to use the restricted procedure was changed to use of the negotiated procedure. There are some other changes to the notice: for example, the estates element could now be tendered separately from the hotel services, for what was essentially a full-blooded facilities management contract.

The dominance of the restricted procedure in our sample of the ten tendering exercises means that the qualification to tender assumes some importance in drawing up the shortlist of those who will be invited to tender. No statement of qualification was given for the single tendering exercise using the open procedure, and this is consistent with what one might expect with this procedure. All but one of the other tendering exercises had some sort of statement. In four cases explicit reference was made to particular articles in the Services Directive or in its UK statutory counterpart. In other cases, similar information was sought on the firm's financial viability and technical competence. In three cases firms were expected to complete a pre-tender questionnaire. All in all, these qualification requirements were little different in spirit from what had been required of tendering exercises when the UK government introduced competitive tendering in the NHS in 1983.

The opportunity to tender for parts of a contract as well as for the contract as a whole can be attractive to some firms, and a deterrent to others. For all but two (subsequently three, on the re-publication of the notice – see above) of the 12 contracts on which we have information, contracts were not divisible into lots.

Some contracts were for a single facility, such as a district general hospital, and for quite a limited range of services, such as for only domestic and portering. In these cases, requiring a single contractor is hardly surprising. Where *several* services were put out to tender, as is the case for the hotel services, subcontracting would have been a solution to the problem of divisibility if the main contractor did not have the full range of skills or did not wish to supply them. Subcontracting allows contracting authorities to look to a *single* supplier for a number of subcontracted services, not to the subcontractors themselves. Having several contractors on a single hospital site is probably an unattractive alternative.

Two of the exceptions that allowed division into lots were for hotel services at *several* facilities. In both cases divisibility by service mix *and* by geography was encouraged. Even so, there would have been at most only two or three main contractors on a single site. The third exception was for the only full facilities management contract. The indicated division suggested a concern whether a single contractor could handle successfully two major sets of services, hotel services and estates management. In the end, a single contractor was awarded the contract in each of the three cases. In terms of the contracts awarded, few firms would have been sufficiently viable financially and competent technically to tender.

Finally, the number of contractors invited to tender is clearly important, but only applies in cases where the restricted and negotiated procedures are used. In the case of restricted procedures the number permitted by UK legislation lies between five and 20,[66] and in the case of negotiated procedures it is not less than three.[67] Of the eight notices published using the restricted procedure, the numbers are indicated in only four cases, being two cases each of 'Minimum 3' and '5–8'. The two published notices for negotiated procedures indicated 'Minimum of 5' and '3–6'.

Award Criteria

Information is given below for the ten tendering exercises for which notices were published.[68] The award procedure – open, restricted and negotiated – is expected to have a bearing on the published award criteria: lowest cost and most economically advantageous. It will be remembered that the open procedure was used for one notice, the restricted procedure for eight and the negotiated procedure for two.

The sole notice for the open procedure provides less than precise guidance to contractors. The procedure implies the contract be awarded on the basis of the lowest bid. Yet the obligation to accept the lowest bid was explicitly rejected, nor was an alternative basis indicated.

A mixed set of results was obtained in the eight notices using the restricted procedure. In four cases the basis of the award was quite straightforward: it was the most economically advantageous. Several criteria were indicated in all four cases, but all included 'price'. Other criteria were 'quality, technical merit, technical back-up and other methods of work', 'period of delivery, and reliability in meeting quality, technical and performance standards specified' and 'quality and compliance with specification'.

The four other cases were far less straightforward. In two cases no information was provided in the notice, and contractors had to wait for the invitation to tender. In the remaining two cases the basis was 'lowest price' *and* 'economically most advantageous', with an almost exhaustively complete list of the possible criteria indicated in the notice from which to decide which was the economically most advantageous tender.

Two notices involved negotiated procedures. In one case no basis or criteria are indicated. In the other the basis is the economically most advantageous, but information on the criteria is to be found in the contract documents, not in the OJEC notice.

Conclusion

In this sample of hotel services for the NHS in Scotland, contracting authorities were far more 'open' than the Service Directive required them to be, in the sense that there was a readiness to publish notices in the OJEC issuing invitations to tender. The restricted procedure was commonly used, so that the qualifying and award criteria assume some importance. However, information on the criteria was often unclear, and so the process was less 'fair' than it might have been.

Evaluating the Impact of the Directives: Comparison with pre-EC Procurement Directives

The aim of this section is to compare two sets of similar contracts put out to tender, one set before and the other after the Services Procurement Directive was in force.

Background

As noted above, the majority of the 17 tendering exercises for contracts that started between 1995 and 1998 combined services. This was not typical when NHS domestic, catering and laundry services contracts were first put out to tender in the mid-1980s. At that time services were put out to tender on an individual service basis. This reflected the current industrial structure, in the sense that there were established contract cleaners, established contract caterers and established commercial laundries, each of which could be invited to tender for their particular service speciality.

In Scotland, as elsewhere in the UK, contract cleaners were keen to enter the NHS hospital market; contract caterers were not. Commercial laundries were keen to enter the NHS market in England, but not in Scotland, partly at least because they had limited spare laundry capacity. The response in Scotland was for the government to waive the requirement to put laundry services out to tender, and for health boards to combine other hotel-type services to form multi-service contracts not very different from seven of the 17 identified tendering exercises for domestic catering including the preparation of meals and other services. Not included among these seven hotel service contracts is the one that also included estates management. The first multi-services contracts contract started in 1989 and, in the period up to and including 1992, 26 such contracts had started. The evaluation of the directive is based on the comparison of these two groups of 26 and seven contracts.

Although the two groups are very similar in terms of their mix of services, it is important to look at other dimensions that might affect contractor interest in tendering which are unconnected with the directive. Two such dimensions are the size of the contract and the identity of the incumbent. As noted above, contract size influences which firms are likely to be financially viable and technically competent. Other studies suggest that size also influences non-domestic contractor interest: the larger the contract, the greater the non-domestic interest. Incumbency is important, possibly for substantive reasons, but also for contractors' perceptions of their ability to win contracts. Contractors are more confident of winning a contract when the incumbent is a(nother) contractor rather than a DSO.

Information on contract size is given in Table 13.1 below. The smallest size group reflects the financial threshold for the Services directive, being ECU 200 000 when it came into force. The other size groups are chosen arbitrarily. It will be apparent that the post-directive group of contracts tended to be very much larger, though there were some contracts in the pre-directive group which were just as large. Both groups would have been/were covered by the directive in terms of the financial threshold.

Table 13.1 Distribution of contracts by first year value (£000s)

Value[1] (£k)	Pre-directive	Post-directive[2]
Less than 140	2	0
Between 140 and 500	10	0
Between 500 and 1000	4	2
1000 and over	10	5
All values	26	7

Notes:
1 Based on current prices.
2 The data refer to tendering exercises, two of which allowed the contract to be divided into lots. In both cases a single contract was awarded to all lots, and the data given refer to the aggregate of lots.

There is a similar difference in respect of incumbency. As one might expect, the pre-directive period is one when most of the contracts were often put out to tender for the first time, and were intended to test the cost-effectiveness of the DSOs. But there were some other contracts that were put out to tender for a second time. Less predictably, the incumbents were also all DSOs. In the post-directive period the situation was quite different, partly because some multi-service contracts came from putting together contracts that had previously been put out to tender as single services. The incumbents were exclusively DSOs for only two of the seven tendering exercises. For three others the incumbents were exclusively contractors. The remaining two incumbents were a mixture of DSOs and contractors. Thus on grounds of incumbency, and possibly size as well, one would expect greater contractor interest in the post-directive period, including non-domestic suppliers.

Evaluation

Evaluation of the impact of the directive is done in terms of the numbers of firms invited to tender, the numbers submitting bids and the nationality of the firms. The data presented are firmly based, in contrast with the EuroStategy survey that asked contracting authorities what were their *perceptions*.

The extent of contractor interest in tendering is given in Table 13.2. Direct comparisons are made slightly difficult between the pre- and post-directive groups because of the divisibility of contracts into lots. We assume this was not possible for the 26 pre-directive group of contracts. On the other hand, notices in the OJEC Supplement make it clear that it was a possibility for at least two of the seven post-directive contracts, and our own research indicates that use was made of this possibility in both cases. Our estimates for the post-directive group include all firms, those with an interest in part of the contract as well as those for the contract as a whole.

The numbers of invitations and bids varied widely. In addition, the post-directive group on which information is available is also very small. The information in Table 13.2 therefore does not allow

Table 13.2 Contractor interest in tendering

Number of firms (includes DSOs)	Invitations to tender		Bids submitted	
	Pre-directive	Post-directive[1]	Pre-directive	Post-directive[1]
1	0	0	6	1
2	1	0	15	1
3	3	0	1	1
4	2	2	3	1
5	6	1	1	1
6	9	0	0	1
7 and over	5	3	0	0
Not known	0	1	0	1
All contracts	26	7	26	7

Note:
1 Includes firms invited/tendered for part of contract.

obvious conclusions from comparing the two groups. Comparing *group averages*, however, is suggestive both of an increase in invitations, from 5.5 to 7.3, and of an increase in bids, from 2.2 to 3.5.

We have given reasons already to explain an increase in tendering unrelated to the Services Directive. The contracts increased in size and, possibly more significantly, contractors were less likely to be competing against incumbent DSOs. If the directive had an additional impact of its own, we might expect more non-domestic firms to be invited to tender, and possibly even to win contracts. An examination of the identities of those invited to tender and those winning contracts does indeed indicate marked changes in these ways. Of the 26 pre-directive contracts, only seven were one or more of three non-British owned firms invited to bid, being from firms that were French, American and Australian owned. At that time the French and American firms had hardly any NHS support services contracts, and the Australian had no NHS catering contracts. All three, therefore, lacked the requisite experience to tender successfully. Of these 26 contracts, only three were won by contractors, all British.

The experience of the seven post-directive contracts is in marked contrast. Of the six contracts on which we have information, all but one invited one or more of five non-British owned companies with an identified interest in tendering. One was the same French company. By this time its British based operations were well-established, achieved partly through organic growth but also through a major acquisition of a British owned company with experience in this market. A second was Danish owned. It seems to have made an unprofitable entry in the early period of competitive tendering, but by 1995 it had also acquired a British company with experience in this market. The other three were firms that were American owned. One entered the NHS on its own account with almost no track record in the UK. The second, like the French and Danish companies, entered this market by acquisition. The third had already had some slight experience on its own account of the NHS market; this time round it was as a joint venture with a British owned facilities management contractor. Contractors won five of the seven contracts. Two were won by the French company, the other three by British owned companies.

The evidence allows the directive some influence in reducing discrimination against non-domestic firms when it came to issuing invitations to tender. What is perhaps more striking is the use of acquisitions to enter an established market.

Conclusions

The directive could have increased contractor interest in tendering and import penetration. However, other changes would have led to similar developments in these two respects. Our conclusions for these hotel *services* are therefore little different from those found in the EuroStrategy study largely based on the experience of works and supplies, though we find reasons other than the directives to explain what has happened.

Experience of the local market is shown to be important if firms are to tender successfully, especially when the market is well established. Arguably the easiest route for foreign owned firms to gain entry into this services market is through acquisition. This inevitably limits import penetration to only the largest firms.

The above conclusions, however, are subject to two reservations. First, the contracts studied would normally be within the non-priority group of services, identified as such because of the limited scope for their cross-border trading. And second, although tight definitions were used for service type, that very decision limited the number of contracts that could be compared.

The Way Forward: Proposals for Reform

A Commission Communication of 11 March 1998[69] sets out the areas for improvement on which the Commission intends to concentrate. The aim of this section is to put some of its key proposals in context.

Introduction

One fundamental problem is the incomplete transposition of directives into national law, with only 55.6 per cent of the directives being correctly implemented in all member states.[70] The Commission also recognises the need for adaptation to accommodate changes in the prevailing economic environment, remembering that the public procurement legislative regime was enacted a quarter of a century ago. The Commission suggests it is the information revolution, and the privatisation and liberalisation of utilities – and not the directives – that have had the greatest impact, and illustrate the complexity and rigidity of present procedures.

With these concerns in mind, we identify three sets of proposals put forward by the Commission in its 1998 communication. The first addresses the issue of non-compliance; the second, the need for flexibility; and the third identifies the benefits of e-commerce with its obvious links to the publication of notices to tender and so on.

Improving Implementation

Not only is the deficit in transposition into national legislation a problem, so also is the lack of compliance when transposition has occurred. In response, the following proposals were made:

1 The European Parliament should strengthen the investigative powers of the Commission[71] and the Commission should accelerate and streamline its infringement procedures.
2 The Commission should encourage member states to designate existing bodies as independent authorities to deal with most disputes, identify interpretation problems and act as a contact point for the notification and resolution of problems.
3 Statistical requirements should to be scaled down but compliance, notably the publication of contract award notices, should be enforced in parallel with current studies and surveys as necessary.

Developing a Favourable Environment

There has been a low rate of response to procurement opportunities, particularly from small and medium-sized enterprises (SMEs). To address this, the Commission intends to introduce electronic (Internet) procurement, in place of the current paper-based system of publication of tender notices. This would allow contractors access to essential purchaser profile and market-monitoring information and would itself, to a degree, drive reform in other areas of the regime. In addition, measures (as yet unspecified) intended to help SMEs participate in the procurement process are to be introduced.

Contracting authorities often lack the confidence to deal with unknown suppliers especially from another member state. Mutual recognition of national qualification systems for potential bidders should therefore be promoted. It is suggested that dealing with this issue effectively may deliver the largest single improvement in the impact of the public procurement regime as a whole.

Legal Framework to be Simplified and Made More Flexible

There will be some clarification[72] of existing rules, predominantly those which are obscure or complex. The Commission has also stated its intention to bring forward a legislative package covering areas where flexibility needs to be increased (such as to take account of changing practices or market realities).[73] Elements of this legislative package are indicated below:

1 The Commission proposes an adjustment of the scope of the Utili-

ties Directive so as to exclude services or sectors in a particular member state which, because they have been opened up to competition, operate in an effectively competitive environment. It is recognised that there are few benefits – and indeed increased costs and delays in procurement – in continuing to apply the procurement procedures to sectors which are forced to operate (and hence procure) as efficiently as possible by the conditions under which they operate.

2 The introduction of a new 'competitive dialogue' procedure to facilitate technical dialogue between suppliers and the procurement entity is to be introduced to replace the negotiated procedure and to be based in part on the principles of transparency and equal treatment. The rationale for this is that suppliers are often well aware of purchasers' needs but not of the best technical solution to meet these needs.

3 The adoption of uniform rules for all types of concessions. This is important since Service Concessions are increasingly used for public–private partnerships and a new framework for such partnerships is anticipated.

4 The consolidation of the Works, Supplies and Services Directives into a single directive. This may lead to some simplification of the procedures, and would be a welcome development for many involved in public procurement.

Electronic Commerce Future

The Commission is embracing, at least in principle, the opportunities of electronic commerce as it applies to public procurement. It believes there would be cost and time savings and increased information exchange through the use of e-mail and the Internet (in part to publish notices). It accepts that promoting electronic procurement is not its direct responsibility. Nevertheless, it has set an objective of 25 per cent of all procurement transactions taking place electronically by 2003. For this to be delivered in practice would require still more amendments to the procurement directives as well as modifications to the GPA and the Europe Agreements, but would open up and extend competition in public procurement still further.[74]

Conclusions

Great progress in openness and transparency in public procurement in the Community has been achieved since the first directive was published in 1971. Nevertheless, there is a problem of a significant deficit in transposition and non-compliance, exacerbated by a constantly evolving market situation. The Commission's 1998 communication addresses these issues, with a set of proposals to be implemented up to the year 2000 and beyond.

Overall Conclusions

The development of the Community public procurement regime echoes the development of the Community itself, with a series of improvements in effectiveness introduced as the Single European Market was created. In this concluding section we bring out points of significance to this book on regulation and markets beyond 2000. In particular, we focus on the issues of compliance, effectiveness and market making.

Legislative compliance is most likely to be achieved when the benefits to participants from compliance exceed the costs incurred by them. The original aim of procurement legislation, to correct import bias by national governments, hardly encouraged compliance. The European Community and those who saw an advantage from the Single European Market were the chief beneficiaries, but the costs were partly if not largely borne by the constituent national governments.

A major achievement of the Cecchini Report was to show the *national* economic benefits which compliance could deliver. It is, therefore, hardly surprising that notices inviting tenders were increasingly published in the OJEC Supplement. It is also hardly surprising how few contract award notices are published, and what little information they contain beyond the identity of the successful bidder. Delays in the transposition of EU legislation by many member states indicate that non-compliance is still a major problem, which the Commission intends to tackle head on.

It is much more difficult to assess the extent of compliance by purchasing agencies in member states that have adopted the EU legislation. Little is known of the effectiveness of the Remedies Directives. On the one hand, their mere existence could act as a deterrent to non-compliance. On the other, there is a real concern that contractors are reluctant to complain since they believe this may make success in tendering for other public sector contracts more elusive. Nevertheless, if the experience of hotel services in the Scottish NHS is at all typical, this concern will have been exaggerated. Again the issue of incentives is important. Arguably, the contracting authorities in the Scottish NHS considered the OJEC Supplement a cheap and effective means of securing contractor interest, and in the 1990s this is what they wanted.

The effectiveness of the legislation has been mixed. It has been most effective in terms of 'openness' and 'fairness': the number of published invitations to tender and import penetration have both increased, and more than just marginally. The picture is much less favourable in economic terms. Competition has undoubtedly increased, but the effect on prices and industrial structure is thought to have been marginal at best. Small improvements can be worthwhile when public procurement accounts for such a significant proportion of EU expenditure and output, but only so long as the costs of compliance do not exceed the benefits obtained. Sometimes the cost seems to have been greater, and contracting authorities have questioned the value of the process.[75]

Finally, what future for legislation on public procurement and market making? EU legislation, of course, is not directly responsible for market making in public procurement: that depends on the willingness of national governments to put activities out to tender. The achievement of the EU legislation has been to develop an information system to make effective use of what market opportunities are available, and to realise the potential for economies of scale which go beyond national markets. This market for *contractual information* promises to develop further. On the supply side, the adoption of e-commerce through the use of Tenders Electronic Daily (TED) will go a long way towards solving the technological constraints of hard copy publication in the OJEC Supplement. On the demand side, it will be important both that national governments are convinced that competition is economically efficient, and that contractors see the legislation as securing an open and fair market in the contracts advertised. So long as the EU sees national discrimination as a potential problem, it is likely to continue to underwrite part of the cost of compliance.

Notes

1 Acknowledgments: unpublished information was supplied by the Department of Health at the Scottish Office, and health boards and NHS trusts throughout Scotland, without which it would not have been possible to do the analysis in the fifth, sixth and seventh sections above. The views expressed, however, are our own.
2 EuroStrategy Consultants (1997), *Public Procurement*, The Single Market Review, Subseries lll: Dismantling of Barriers, Office for Official Publications of the European Commission, London: Earthscan, p.41.
3 Cecchini, P. (1988), *The European Challenge 1992: The Benefits of a Single Market*, Aldershot: Wildwood House, p.16.
4 Commission of the European Communities (1998), *Public Procurement in the European Union*, COM(98)143, Brussels: Commission of the European Communities, p.1.
5 71/305/EC of 26 July 1971.
6 77/62/EC of 21 December 1976.

7 European Commission (1985), *Completing the Internal Market,* COM(85) 310 final of 14 June 1985. (Brussels: Commission of the European Communities).
8 Directive 88/295/EEC.
9 Directive 89/440/EEC.
10 Directive 90/531/EEC.
11 Directive 89/665.
12 By the Services Directive 92/50.
13 Directive 92/13.
14 That is, incorporated.
15 Commission of the European Communities, *Public Procurements* (n.4, above).
16 *Ibid.*, Annex 1.
17 The Public Services Contracts Regulations 1993 (1993/3228).
18 The Public Supply Contracts Regulations 1995 (1995/201)).
19 The Public Works Contracts Regulations 1991 (1991/2680).
20 The Utilities Contracts Regulations 1996 (1996/2911).
21 The EFTA States are Austria, Sweden, Finland, Norway, Iceland and Liechtenstein, but since the EEA Agreement came into force on 1 January 1994, Austria, Sweden and Finland have become full members of the European Union.
22 There are currently Europe Agreements between Hungary (OJ No L347, 31.12.93), Poland (OJ No L348, 31.12.93), Romania (OJ No L357, 31.12.94), Bulgaria (OJ No L358, 31.12.94), Slovakia (OJ No L359, 31.12.94), Czech Republic (OJ No L360, 31.12.94), Latvia, Lithuania and Estonia (COM (95) 207) and Slovenia (COM (95) 341).
23 See, for example, Article 68 of the Europe Agreement between the Czech Republic, the Community and its Member States (OJ L360, 31.12.94).
24 See COM(94) 143 final (15.4.94).
25 SDRs are Special Drawing Rights, the currency of the GPA.
26 The sterling equivalent is £160 670. For certain services (Part B ('residual') services, Research and Development services, certain telecoms services and subsidised contracts) there is a different threshold of ECU 200 000 (£155 973). For specified central government departments and other bodies (listed in Schedule 1 to the Supply Regulations), which are subject to GPA, the threshold was lowered by the GPA to SDR 130 000 (£104 435).
27 £160 670.
28 £4 016 744.
29 £3 899 337.
30 £3 899 337.
31 £311 947.
32 £467 920.
33 Commission Recommendation 96/527/EC.
34 This replaced an earlier recommendation that a Common Procurement Classification (CPC) should be used.
35 There are also clear advantages to the Commission and others in their review of procurement statistics and trends.
36 Regulation 3 of the Services Regulations. There is considerably more to be said about what constitutes a contracting authority, but this is outside the scope of this chapter.
37 Set out in Regulation 6 of the Services Regulations and ranging from the acquisition of land, broadcasting, central banking and financial services to the essential interests of a member state's security.
38 Regulation 9 of the Services Regulations.
39 Regulation 10(6) of the Services Regulations.
40 For the open and restricted procedures, except for minor clarifications and the possibility of allowing bidders to re-tender in limited circumstances (with

delay and cost implications), the contracting authority must choose between tenders as bid.

41 Set out in Regulation 10 of the Services Regulations, including where (exceptionally) an open or restricted procedure was discontinued because of irregular tenders, when the nature of the services to be provided, or the risks attaching thereto, are such as not to permit overall pricing; or for reasons of extreme urgency (only if strictly necessary).

42 Regulation 9.

43 The Utilities Regulations require the issue of a 'Periodic Indicative Notice' in very similar terms and circumstances.

44 See Regulations 11, 12 and 13 of the Services Regulations, Supplies Regulations and Works Regulations, the provisions in the Utilities Regulations being slightly different.

45 Regulation 13(6) of the Services Regulations and Regulation 13(5) of the Works Regulations and the Supplies Regulations.

46 Regulation 12(6) of the Services Regulations, Works Regulations and Supply Regulations.

47 Regulation 14(1) of the Services Regulations, Works Regulations and Supply Regulations.

48 Note that these criteria also apply as regards works and supply contracts.

49 Regulation 21(2).

50 EuroStrategy, *Public Procurement* (n. 2, above), ch.13.

51 Cox, A. and P. Long (1996), 'The Jury is Still Out for Utilities Procurement: The Impact of the EU Procurement Directives on the Location of Utility Contract Awards in the 'Twelve' Member States', *Public Procurement Law Review,* 5(5), 57–8.

52 EuroStrategy, *Public Procurement* (n. 2, above).

53 Martin, S. and K. Hartley (1997), 'Public Procurement in the European Union: Issues and Policies', *Public Procurement Law Review,* 6(2), 92–113.

54 EuroStrategy, *Public Procurement* (n. 2, above), ch.11.

55 Martin and Hartley, *Public Procurement* (n. 53, above), table 6.

56 EuroStrategy, *Public Procurement* (n. 2, above), ch.14.

57 *Ibid.,* sections 12.4 and 12.5.

58 *Ibid.,* table 12.50.

59 *Ibid.,* ch.15.

60 *Ibid.,* chs 16 to 22.

61 United Kingdom, Efficiency Unit of the Cabinet Office (1996), *Competing for Quality Policy Review,* London: Her Majesty's Stationery Office, Annex F.

62 Local Government Management Board (1996), *CCT Information Service,* Survey report no. 13, London: Local Government Management Board, p.11.

63 National Audit Office (1987), *Competitive Tendering for Support Services in the National Health Service,* HC 318, London: Her Majesty's Stationery Office, table 3.

64 Martin and Hartley, 'Public Procurement' (n. 53, above), p.97.

65 Cox, A. (1993), *The Single Market Rules and the Enforcement Regime after 1992,* Humberside: Earlsgate Press, p.201.

66 See note 46 and corresponding text.

67 Articles 12(6)(*a*) and 13(5) UK legislation, respectively.

68 It will be recalled that one tendering exercise had two notices.

69 Commission of the European Communities, 1998. Public Procurement Commission Communication in the European Union, Com (98) 143, Brussels, 11 March 1998.

70 *Ibid.,* p.2.

71 Article 169.

72 This clarification will take the form of changing or clarifying the interpretation of the (numerous) areas where interpretation is uncertain or unclear.
73 Although the Commission acknowledges that redressing the failures of member states to implement the existing proposals is another crucial part of the improvement process.
74 It is also worth noting that the Commission's Communication addresses the means by which the developing public procurement policy will complement other policy areas, notably defence, environmental protection, social policy, consumer protection and international aspects of Community policy.
75 See Lundendorf and Trost (1997), 'Effects of the European Community Directives on Public Procurement – Status Quo, Experience and Outlook from the Perspective of Public Utilities', *Public Procurement Law Review*, 6(1), 35–48.

14 Governing Information

CLAIRE JOHNSON, ***University of Glasgow***
AND ALISON WHITE, ***Shepherd & Wedderburn***

> Government intervenes more and more in our society, whatever its political hue. Different roles require different sorts and amounts of information. The administrative regulatory state is the most acquisitive. In addition, the sophistication of information technology has made the collection, storage and retrieval of information not simply a national and corporate preoccupation, but a global one.[1]

Introduction

It is well accepted that business operation is governed by an array of legislation and part of that governance requires particular records to be created and stored as evidence of appropriate and legitimate transactions by companies and other business entities.[2] These existing statutory requirements largely assume that records are maintained in paper-based format. However, as will be seen, organisations are currently moving from an era of entirely paper-based text records to one that is paper-free. We are currently experiencing a time of profound change for information creators in regard to IT choices and information management. This chapter will look at the regulatory and organisational culture implications of these changes.

The growing reliance on digital methods of information storage has resulted in an increasing number of decisions that need to be made about records and information management. The outcomes of these decisions are largely driven by two concerns, security and authenticity. As indicated, there are many operational areas in which organisations have to retain information, to comply with the legal framework as well as the organisation's own operational procedures, and this is done by using a variety of media. These requirements not affect only the content and structure of corporate information but also require that *processes* of business transactions are documented, not just *outcomes*: for example, the board minutes of a company which show whether or not transactions have been properly authorised.

The main focus of this chapter will be the implications for business of the Data Protection Act 1984 and the implementation of the Data Protection Act 1998, as well as looking to the proposed legislation on freedom of information and its implications for information transfer and storage by government. Given the increased emphasis on authenticity and security, it is also appropriate to look at the current discussions regarding the regulation of encryption technology, which is one of the main issues addressed by the draft Electronic Communications Bill published in 1999.

Regulation of Underlying Technological Change

Rapid technological change means that hardware and software regularly become obsolete and require constant updating and upgrading. This has obvious impact for systems managers, not least from a technical perspective. Guidance for technical problems encountered as a result of system changes is readily available from official sources and in many cases this guidance also addresses the ensuing requirements of document migration. For example, the European Union (EU) through the DLM-Forum has produced guidelines on best practice for using electronic information, and another example of such guidance is the certification scheme launched by the government in May 1998 for BS7799, the British Standard for Information Security. This initiative is part of the government's commitment to encourage the use of electronic commerce and to ensure that the UK offers the best environment possible for electronic trading. The certification scheme, known as 'c:cure', was referred to by Barbara Roche, former minister for small businesses, as the means by which companies of all sizes could demonstrate the effectiveness of their information security. Regulation will be achieved through voluntary approaches by organisations to BSI that will lead on to certification. 'C:cure' requires independent assessors to review the information security arrangements in an organisation to assess the possible risks.

BS7799 is an industry-developed standard that is now being adopted in the public sector. The 1999 edition addresses recent technological development and offers some advice in relation to protecting against viruses, hackers, data loss and fraud. It also responds to the changes of organisational culture and working practice brought about through developments in e-commerce, mobile computing, teleworking and outsourcing. The protection and security of information is of prime importance for many aspects of an organisation's business – not least to ensure continued customer confidence. As BSI emphasises, it is important that an organisation should not only implement a set of controls and procedures for information security but also manage and maintain them.[3]

The guidance given in BS7799 provides a single reference point for identifying the range of controls needed for most situations where information systems are used. As there is an increasing amount of electronic networking between organisations, there is a clear benefit to having a common reference document for information security management. A common reference standard should enable trust to be established between networked systems and trading partners at an early stage and provide a basis for management of these systems between users and service providers.

Organisational Risks

The Audit Commission Update Report (1998)[4] shows that fraud or cases of IT abuse often occur as a result of the absence of basic controls, with 50 per cent of all frauds found by accident:

> The survey of 900 public and private sector companies reveals that in the UK the incidents of IT fraud and abuse in 1997 rose to 45% from 36% in 1994. The Internet exposes organisations to an increased risk that networks will be accessed improperly, data corrupted and viruses introduced. The percentage of organisations reporting hacking incidents has trebled.

Not all breaches are the result of crime, inadvertent use and human error also play their part. Virus infections are the most prevalent form of abuse. More commonplace, and just as destructive, are threats like fire, system crashes and power cuts. Poor supervision of staff and lack of proper authorisation procedures are frequently mentioned as the main causes of security incidents.

Companies exhibit varied responses to the threat of security breaches: some restrict access to all types of information, making the execution of basic administrative tasks across their organisations cumbersome, whilst others expose themselves to a high degree of risk through lax procedures, and permit access by all to all.

E-mail is a particular example of a major contributor to the communications revolution which has created new avenues for abuse,[5] loss of control over official records and vast increases in trivial or duplicated information. In many organisations e-mail has replaced the paper memorandum as the main form of internal communication.

One of the greatest challenges of managing e-mail effectively is to ensure that all records that originate in or are transmitted through an organisation's system are identified and only retained if operationally necessary. As Microsoft has discovered, e-mails can return to haunt the sender and the contents can be taken to mean radically different things from their original intention.

E-mail highlights the issue that the volume of records a human must appraise for enduring value to either themselves (or successors) or their organisation has increased dramatically. It is not, however, the only medium which raises questions. At some point a decision must be taken as to whether any document, fax, e-mail, drawing or note should be defined as a record. What developments in technology do mean is that the number of such decisions requiring to be made has been vastly increased.

Given this fundamental premise, an issue that rapidly becomes apparent is *who* should make the decision. The problem that electronic media present is that, generally speaking, the decision is devolved to the recipient and an organisational policy may not contain enough detail to provide guidance on the criteria for retention. Unless such decisions are taken, for all record types, effective business will be compromised under the volume of records. The issue is not necessarily the treatment of electronic records but how we ensure that the decision taker is sufficiently trained to make sound decisions and that they have the right tools to allow them to do so.

Increasingly, records retained by organisations will be held in digital medium and it is not appropriate just to print the records on to paper for long-term retention; the records should be retained, as far as possible, in the original medium.[6] This will preserve the contextual evidence of their creation and document their use. It is necessary to integrate information management strategies with information technology planning so that content and structure are addressed concurrently.

The recent US Federal Court case of *Public Citizen* v. *Carlin*[7] can be looked to for guidance as to how information is required to be stored electronically. In this case it was held that preservation of the paper printout of an e-mail was not enough and that metadata (the data about the data) must also be preserved as part of the record. However, rather unhelpfully, the case does not explore just what metadata would mean in this context.

Specific Statutory Regulation

The issues already discussed apply equally in the public as well as the private sphere. Document retention and storage are equally important issues for government agencies and this is reflected in the extension of BS7799 into use by public bodies as their recognised standard. However, document retention and having appropriate policies and procedures in place are only part of the issue, and it is also necessary to consider in what circumstances records/information can be accessed and by whom, and how the integrity of the information accessed can be relied upon.

As we will discuss later, it is not in the nature of successive UK governments to offer open access to government information; however, the attitude is somewhat different where the concern is the access of government agencies to information. The freedom of information proposals to be addressed later can be contrasted with the approach taken by the government on the topic of licensing of cryptography service providers as outlined in the draft Electronic Communications Bill.[8]

However, one of the few areas in which there is existing statutory regulation focused purely on the holding and provision of information in digital media and which is largely well developed and accepted is the existing data protection legislation: the Data Protection Act 1984. This legislation was brought into force in 1985; however, it is soon to be updated with the implementation of the new Data Protection Act 1998. The Data Protection Act 1998 was enacted in response to the European directive on the protection of individuals with regard to the processing of personal data and on the free movement of such data.[9] Although it was enacted in the first session of the new parliament, the UK government has not fully complied with its international obligations, as the 1998 Act has yet to be brought into force. It has recently been indicated, in reply to a parliamentary question,[10] that the 1998 Act will be brought into force on 1 March 2000, over 16 months after the date set in terms of the directive.

Data Protection

A Brief History

We have had data protection legislation in the UK since the coming into force of the Data Protection Act 1984 on 1 April 1985. To say that this legislation has not been a success would be wrong, but it would be fair to say that the rights and obligations it creates are not widely known.

The Data Protection Act 1984 (the '1984 Act') was passed in order to ratify the UK's signature of the Council of Europe Convention for the Protection of Individuals with regard to Automatic Processing of Personal Data. The aim of the Act is to regulate the processing by automatic means of personal data – that is, data about living individuals. Organisations processing such personal data must register as data users with the Data Protection Registrar, stating what types of personal data will be held and for what purposes, from whom it will be collected, to whom it may be transferred and to which countries it may be transferred.

This lack of public awareness about the rights afforded to individuals under the 1984 Act is largely due to the fact that the then (Conservative) government had enacted the legislation somewhat reluctantly. The government had only conceded that data protection legislation was necessary to address concerns amongst industry chiefs that the UK was being perceived as a data haven,[11] a place which allowed free use of personal data. At that time it was assumed that being such a data haven was a barrier to international trade as there would be no protection of any personal data, such as customer names and addresses which are considered valuable, once the data were transferred to the UK. Enacting the 1984 Act allowed the UK to ratify the Convention (which it had signed in 1981); however, in one respect, it could be viewed as establishing a limited right to privacy[12] in the UK, a development which went far beyond the intentions of the government.

There are many offences created by the data protection legislation, the most notable of which is the offence of holding and processing data without the appropriate registrations being held. Where an organisation is found guilty of an offence it will be subject to a fine; however, the level of fines (currently £5000 maximum) has not proved sufficient to cause a real change in attitude amongst data users. An even more effective weapon available under the Act is deregistration, which would leave the data user unable to process personal data without committing an offence. In today's world, where data is all, it is not difficult to envisage that being unable to hold or process such data would have severe economic consequences for an organisation. However, the Registrar has to date never made use of this power and it is more than likely that use of this remedy would be too drastic. Although the Registrar does not shy from taking high profile cases,[13] it is quite possible that this would be a step too far for businesses to accept.

Data Protection Act 1998

Towards the beginning of the 1980s, the fact that there were different data protection regimes in the member states of the European Union and that in certain member states there was no legislation at all was identified as being a barrier to trade within the EU. As a result, a directive was proposed which sought to lay down a regime for data protection legislation within the EU.

This directive was developed over a long period of time,[14] but in 1995 the directive was finally agreed upon and it entered into force with effect from 24 October 1995. In terms of the directive, there was a three-year implementation period, meaning that member states had to amend their legislation or, where appropriate, enact completely new legislation to fulfil its requirements.[15]

Within the scope of this chapter we are seeking to review regulation of information and its impact and, whilst the intention is not to examine in detail the specific provisions of the new legislation, there are a number of elements which it is appropriate to highlight.

Aspects of the Data Protection Act 1998 Examined

One of the main issues surrounding the 1998 Act is the fact that its long genesis has meant that it is largely outdated in terms of today's technology even before it has been implemented. One notable feature is the regime that is being implemented in relation to transfers of personal data beyond the European Economic Area.

As a result of the directive, all member states (plus the three additional members of the European Economic Areas Norway, Liechtenstein and Iceland) are required to enact legislation in broadly similar terms – that is, on the basis of the directive. It is therefore assumed that within the European Economic Area there is an 'equivalent' level of protection for personal data. Article 1(2) of the directive provides that 'Member States shall neither restrict nor prohibit the free flow of personal data between Member States'. As a result, effectively free transfers of information may be made between member states; that is, they can be made without any consideration as to whether or not the personal data will be properly held after the transfer.

To give an example, if a multinational company operates within the European Economic Area with bases in Belgium and Austria and headquarters in the UK then, provided that the company has systems in place to comply with the legislation in each country – for example, appropriate registrations (or, to use the new terminology, notifications) have been made in the UK, Belgium and Austria – the company can transfer personal data regarding a customer from its office in Belgium to its headquarters in the UK and on to its other branch office in Austria without having to consider the protection being afforded to the personal data.

However, as already discussed, the most notable development in technology over the period in which the directive was being discussed was the development and acceptance of use of the Internet as a day-to-day business tool. An increasing percentage of business transactions are now carried out by communicating via e-mail and this is where the 'free' transfers regime breaks down. The Internet is an inherently unstable service but it was designed to survive nuclear attack and in order to do so it makes a feature of ensuring that any message sent via the Internet invariably uses an indirect route in order to communicate the message rather than choosing any direct route from A to B.

The net result of this is that, in sending a message from Edinburgh to Brussels via e-mail, there is no guarantee that the message will have gone directly; it is more than likely that en route the message may have gone via France, Brazil, the USA – in fact any country where there is a server connected to the Internet. Therefore, even before the data protection regime is fully implemented it could be said to be largely unworkable. As there is virtually no way of telling where information which was sent between Edinburgh and Brussels, and which theoretically is covered by the protections of the 1998 Act, will actually be sent en route then, technically speaking, sending any personal data via the Internet could be a breach of the 1998 Act.

On the other hand, while one of the fundamental data protection principles is that appropriate security arrangements are put in place,[16] there would be little merit in the Data Protection Registrar using the resources of her staff in simply trying to prevent messages being sent via the Internet. Data protection legislation needs to recognise the new technology: it is not going to prevent use of the Internet and therefore ways need to be sought (legally or technically) to address the specific concerns raised by the use of the Internet to send personal data.

From its inception the directive has caused considerable comment from beyond (and indeed inside) the EU, most notably from commentators in the USA. It is not, however, the fact that the directive is already outdated which has caused the greatest concerns but the fact that it prohibits transfers of personal data beyond the European Economic Area where the country where the personal data is to be received does not afford an 'adequate' level of protection.[17]

As an example, it is generally recognised that the regime for protection of personal data within the USA is not 'adequate' within the terms of the Data Protection Directive. The directive does give some indication of the features which can be examined in order to assess adequacy, however, even taking account of those features for which the US regime is lacking in appropriate protections. Most notably in the USA there is no federal legislation relating to data protection; instead the USA has taken a sectoral approach, only enacting legislation in relation to specific types of data protection – for example, credit reference agencies. Certain American states have enacted omnibus data protection legislation and transfers of data to those states could be said to be adequately protected. The USA has, however, seen the directive's restrictions on transfers of personal data as a barrier to trade and is concerned that the EU will not recognise that transfers of personal data to the USA will be adequately protected. The outcome of this debate has become involved in the latest US–EU trade disputes and as part of bigger issues it is difficult to know how this debate will be resolved.

Another feature of both the 1984 and the 1998 Acts is, as has already been mentioned, the fact that, generally speaking, most people are unaware of the rights which they have. Unless the position changes dramatically, it could be anticipated that the new legislation would not alter this situation. Without heightened awareness any new rights offered by the new legislation are unlikely to alter the position. In broad terms there is an increase in individual rights under the legislation, most notably the greater emphasis on the obtaining of specific consent from the individual to the holding of his or her personal data and the creation of a new category of 'sensitive personal data' where 'explicit consent' is required by the data user (data controller under the 1998 Act) before it can carry out any processing of such sensitive personal data.[18]

However, the types of enforcement action which can be taken by the Registrar (Data Protection Commissioner under the 1998 Act) against companies for failure to abide by the relevant provisions are to a large extent unaltered by the new legislation and therefore it is arguable that this is legislation without teeth. The greatest incentive for individual companies to adhere to the legislation will be a fear of bad publicity.

Given earlier discussion on the emphasis on use of digital media to record and store information, it is interesting to note that for the first time the 1998 Act will apply the data protection regime to the holding and processing of personal data which is held on manual – that is, paper – files. At the time the 1984 Act was enacted it was specifically decided to exclude paper files but the European Directive (and hence the 1998 Act) takes a different approach.The 1998 Act specifically includes information held on paper files, but only where they are held as part of a 'relevant filing system'[19] which means files in which information is held in such a way that individuals are used as references. An example would be a filing system where files are held in alphabetical order.

To a certain extent including information held on such paper files within a data protection regime might seem outmoded and largely obsolete but this would be to forget about the vast amounts of information already held on paper files which is likely to continue to be so held. To include paper files within the ambit of the legislation will impose a substantial burden on data controllers, not least in responding to a subject access request – that is, a request by a data subject to be given a copy of personal data held about them. Ensuring that the record of data held is complete will be a substantial task once it becomes necessary to ensure that all appropriate paper files have also been reviewed.

In summary, the 1998 Act will build upon regimes with which organisations are broadly familiar. There are, however, a number of further areas where it will seek to introduce a further burden on organisations in relation to how they hold their information. Unless individuals become more familiar with their rights, the additional administrative burden on organisations may in reality be minimal, but nonetheless compliance with the 1998 Act will require significant decisions to be made with regard to the organisation of personal data held.

Data Security

As has been seen, one of the big issues in relation to all aspects of digital storage and transfer of information is ensuring the security and integrity of that information at all stages of its life. The Data Protection Registrar a number of years ago identified that the two main challenges for data protection in the world of the Internet would be 'how to monitor and control, if necessary, transborder data flow; and how to ensure the security of transfers of personal data'.[20]

In a wider context, these concerns can be seen to be equally applicable to all forms of information transfer in a digital context. A dual approach can be taken to the issue of security, firstly by creating acceptable use policies for employees and others dealing with the information of the organisation or the public body to ensure that appropriate limits are placed upon the use and abuse of technology. However, relying on human intervention to ensure data security can only ever be part of the answer. The other element of the equation is to put in place appropriate technological solutions to provide additional protection. Indeed, it has been reported that more money is currently being spent on investigating questions of Internet security than most other information technology issues.[21]

However, the increasing sophistication of technology is also causing concern to law enforcement agencies, most notably the development of encryption technology. Encryption involves the coding of information in such a way that to an ordinary reader the information would make no sense. To give an example of simple encryption, the word 'Lqwhuqhw' is the word 'Internet' when encrypted by using the letter three letters further on in the alphabet; that is, a=d, b=e and so on. This encryption can be easily decoded but as technology has developed encryption is no longer so simple and increasingly more complex encryption products are being developed which require considerable time and energy to decode (if, indeed, this is possible at all).

It is the potential to withhold information or to make it inaccessible through use of encryption which causes concern for governments, most notably in its use by terrorist and criminal organisations. This debate began in the USA with the Clipper Chip[22] and government insistence on use of state-regulated encryption, but the debate was picked up on in Europe; however, the focus here has been on the role and regulation of independent bodies which would hold the encryption keys.

There have been various proposals from the EU in relation to electronic commerce, which have resulted in two draft directives, the draft directive on electronic signatures and the draft directive on e-commerce.[23] These attack different aspects of the perceived lacunae in current regimes and seek to create a mechanism for making electronic commerce more acceptable and secure.

At the same time as the EU has been seeking to address the issue of access and regulation of encryption, the UK (through successive governments) has been separately addressing this issue. The initial approach of the Conservative (Major) government looked at the issue of licensing of third parties and this aspect of the proposals has continued with the Labour government. With Labour, however, the regulation of encryption has become bound up with the development of e-commerce in the UK. The reason that governments are using e-commerce as a platform for raising concerns about encryption is that encryption technology can serve a double purpose of both security and identification. As already explained, encryption can provide security by making data unreadable without the relevant encryption keys but by ensuring that no two encryption keys are alike use of a particular encryption key can also be used as an identifier – that is, a digital signature – on the basis that use of that key means it came from a specific individual.

This is also a feature of the current draft Electronic Communications Bill (the 'E-Commerce Bill') that has recently been produced by the UK government.[24] This builds upon a number of consultation documents issued by both the previous and current governments, most notably the consultation paper produced in March 1999.[25] One feature that has aroused considerable discussion in Europe (and in the USA in relation to similar proposals) is the concept of allowing access by law enforcement agencies to encryption keys.

National governments and particularly law enforcement agencies are concerned that the use of encryption will allow international crime to boom on the basis that communication can be made safely and securely using encryption and it would take considerable efforts on the part of the law enforcement agencies to decode these communications. A number of proposals have been put forward to take account of this, most notably the concept of the 'trusted third party', an independent body which would hold a copy of the encryption key and would do so for a number of purposes, one of which would be the access by law enforcement agencies under a specific regime. One of the regimes which has been proposed as a model is the current regime under which warrants for telephone tapping are obtained and it has been suggested that a similar regime could be put in place to regulate access by relevant government authorities to encryption keys. Other potential roles for the trusted third party could include holding a copy of the key so that, if there was any situation where individuals had misplaced their encryption key, they could obtain a further copy from the trusted third party. Another element of the service could be the provision of certificates; that is, the trusted third party would produce a certificate saying that on a specific date the key in question was held by a particular individual and therefore the communication came from the individual named on the certificate.

One of the more controversial elements of the initial proposals was that such trusted third parties should be licensed; that is, only those individuals/organisations licensed by the government could provide this service. However, there was heavy criticism surrounding the proposal that the government licensing should be mandatory and the current proposals as enshrined in the E-Commerce Bill provide for voluntary, not mandatory, licensing of such trusted third parties.

While there is no doubt that the increasing use of encryption will resolve a number of issues relating to the security and integrity of information transfers in the digital era, there will still be important decisions to be made about what information is kept and the form in which it is retained or destroyed. For the government to achieve its aim of making the UK the best environment for electronic trading by 2002, a number of issues will need to be addressed in creating this environment, not least making sure the consumer/customer has no concerns about using e-commerce. Ensuring the integrity of a transfer of data goes part way to ensuring this, but there are other considerations which need to be addressed to ensure consumer confidence – for example, the issue of jurisdiction, or which law applies to a contract made on-line.

Other notable changes proposed by the Electronic Communications Bill which have been largely ignored in the controversy over the encryption proposals are the proposals which will give the government power to amend legislation where it perceives that there is a need to take account of electronic communication or document storage. Thus under Clause 8 of the draft Bill, 'the appropriate Minister may by order made by statutory instrument modify the provisions of any enactment or subordinate legislation in such manner as he may think fit for the purpose of authorising or facilitating the use of electronic communications or electronic storage (instead of other forms of communication or storage) for any purpose mentioned in subsection (2)'. Subsection (2) lists a number of purposes including where statutes require writing or delivery by specified means. This thus permits extensive changes to primary legislation by order, following the precedent of the Deregulation and Contracting Out Act 1984 which does, however, contain demanding special requirements of parliamentary scrutiny before such an order can be made.

Freedom of Information

Data protection legislation has to some extent helped create a more receptive environment for freedom of information (FOI) legislation. Though the coverage of such law is personal information, and so deals with us only as individuals, freedom of information has relevance to the individual and commercial activity alike. If the general issues of data security identified here and in the Introduction are addressed they will help secure the success of FOI in two principal ways: first, by developing a more informed and confident electorate that holds government in higher regard than at present because it is accountable by ensuring the authenticity of the data it provides; second, if the government's use of new methods of dissemination is supported through free access via public libraries and so on, this will empower new constituencies within the electorate.

Development of Current Legislation

It is access to information that gives power; either through propaganda or commercial advantage, or meeting a specific public interest so the balance of power between the provider and recipient needs to be scrutinised. How can trust between government and the public be fostered effectively if the public authorities are allowed to decide for themselves whether information should be disclosed in the public interest? Instigating trust in government information does not come from the existence of legislation but is earned through confidence in the enquiry process. Official secrecy forms a convenient focus for public fear about the activities of government:

> The idea of an informed and extensive public debate before decisions are reached seems to be deeply alien to the British political system.

> Secrecy is a fundamental part of the way British government works, the cement that holds the current system together. It is convenient for those in power because it enables them to take decisions well away from the glare of publicity, to ignore arguments which they find inconvenient and to suppress information that would be embarrassing ... Through a wall of secrecy government propaganda is pumped, masquerading as information.[26]

Understandably, the quality of public debate surrounding access to government information has suffered from the lack of informed discussion. There have been several recent high-profile cases[27] that confirm the need to redress the balance between government restrictions and public access.

After the publication of a White Paper on 'Open Government', a Draft Freedom of Information Bill, together with a Consultation Document, was published in 1999.[28] The consultation period ran until 20 July 1999 and the substantive Bill is in the 1999–2000 parliamentary programme. Section 72 of the draft Bill cites a commencement date of, at the latest, five years after the date of passing of the Act and it may be progressively introduced during that period. It aims to end secrecy and increase transparency through giving individuals the right to information held by the vast majority of public organisations, and those working on behalf of government. It would also give individuals the right to ask organisations covered by the Act to give other records or information on issues that are of interest.

There are several major discrepancies to note in this area: first, between what central government required of local government in the Local Government (Access to Information) Act 1985, and its subsequent revision in 1997, and what it was prepared to reveal about its own activities. Two key questions are, how well will people be able to discover what information exists and where can they find it? Guidance will be required, possibly through public libraries providing the network of equipment and expertise to retrieve the pertinent information. For example, Dundee City Council already has a network of 'PinPoint' terminals in libraries that offer touch-screen access to council information (events, council departments, contact information for elected members and also local organisations) and the assistance of trained librarians to help the enquirer.

The proposed Act will apply to information recorded in any form, but not in general to unrecorded information. In keeping with established practice, official (paper) record series are registered centrally (on a department level) but there are vast amounts of 'grey' record series that may not be part of a registered system. The growth in the use of PCs and other changes in the working practices have encouraged a move away from the construction of a single registered file in central registries holding vast amounts of paper. A 'complete' file of information may now include e-mail messages, graphics, video clips, spreadsheets, faxed documents and other digitally held data. In addition, the Act will not give a right of access to policy advice to government, including information forming the basis for such advice.

Some countries' FOI laws have been blunted by ministers possessing a final veto over decisions of the appeals body, a precedent the government rejected in the White Paper but included in the draft Bill in that, if information falls into an exemption from disclosure, the public authority will have discretion to disclose it if this is in the public interest. However, the Information Commissioner who will deal with complaints of non-disclosure will not be able to review this latter question. Therefore, the balance of power between the Information Commissioner, the ministry concerned and the secretary of state has changed and the commissioner will be less autonomous.[29] Recent government concessions may, however, lead to the commissioner having power to recommend discretionary disclosure, though not to compel disclosure.[30]

The first requirement to be met will be for the administrations covered to provide for the registration of record series, the 'publication scheme' referred to in cl.6(1) of the draft Bill. A record is registered when a set of data (metadata) relating to the record is entered in a database, as a data item would be entered for each of a range of predefined record characteristics.[31] Members of the public should be able to request records from departments from a standard set of data. The draft Bill proposed that members of the public have a right to have their enquiries answered within 40 days,[32] so a department's ability to meet this requirement is determined by the types of registration data it maintains. However, it now seems likely that a response time of 20 days, from the receipt of the enquiry, will be substituted, as proposed in the White Paper.[33] It remains to be seen whether there will be a standard way for the public to gain access to all government record series.

There exists a publicly accepted standard (Dublin Core) which outlines basic data for describing records, so it would seem logical that registration data common to departments should follow this or a similar agreed standard. There appear not to have been any additional funds forthcoming to improve the mechanics of record keeping (or file indexing), let alone improving the content! Departments may purchase packaged software to register all records in the same way that the central registries would have serviced paper file creation, registering and circulation in the past. However, any improvement in effectiveness requires a major re-think in the way official records are created and retrieved.

Public bodies will have numerous exemptions and the draft Bill provides us with only the general principles for the provision of information. This is, however, a milestone achievement in Britain,[34] bringing us nearer to the rights and privileges that residents of Australia, America, Ireland, Sweden and many other European countries have enjoyed for many years – in some cases decades.[35]

FOI interacts with and extends the Data Protection Act 1998, in relation to personal data held by public authorities. With some modifications and exemptions, it extends the individual rights and remedies available under the 1998 Act to all personal information held by public authorities, although, where information is personal information relating to a third party, it is exempt if disclosure would contravene the 1998 Act or if the data subject would have no right of access under it. It is unclear at present how third-party appeals against disclosure will be handled. The Local Government (Access to Information) Act currently provides protection against actions for defamation for disclosures relating to third parties. However, in the draft FOI Bill public bodies are not explicitly protected. It may not be possible for public bodies to gather enough detail about enquirers to know whether disclosure will cause litigation. It seems likely that the process for hearing third party appeals will be time-consuming and may be cumbersome to administer.

Currently, we have a double legislative mandate poised over organisational activities to regulate the accuracy and extent of data, whether it is personal information discoverable through data protection or freedom of information to provide access to other areas of decision-making activity in public life. There has not been much evidence of self-regulation in this area of market activity but government motives for introducing such a legislative move are rooted in its professed commitment to open government and to the information society. Its effectiveness in meeting these objectives has yet to be seen, especially when the tests and exclusions in the White Paper have multiplied in the draft Bill. The most obvious constituent group which will benefit from this Bill may be 'patients and pupils rather than litigants and political activists',[36] as their institutions will face the closest examination as fewer of the exemptions are likely to apply. However, policy advice, which is a potentially wide description, can remain reserved whether or not it might influence the workings of government.[37] This provides a wide safety net for both political and civil service acrobatics and has been very heavily criticised.[38]

One fundamental concern is how public bodies will meet the higher level of demand for information and the increased number of enquiries when many are already struggling to reduce the number of existing caseloads. Relevant public bodies will be able to charge[39] for part of the marginal cost of providing the information – a costly exercise for the sole enquirer – but this will not, in most cases, recoup the full cost of meeting the enquiry. Estimates of costs have been put at between £90 million and £125 million[40] to implement the system to log and manage the enquiries.

The most fundamental criticism of this Bill must be, however, that it is so riddled with tests and exclusions that the government will not have to reveal any more information than it is already bound to do under the existing Code of Practice.[41] Certainly, in the parliamentary discussion on 24 May,[42] the main exchange between Sir Norman Fowler and Jack Straw centred on the clauses that set out the exemptions, which go far beyond the need to maintain national security. The test for withholding information has been made easier and the robust right of access the White Paper promised – especially to policy formation or official investigations – has been restricted. The White Paper proposed that the test would be based on whether the disclosure of particular information would cause 'substantial harm', but it is proposed in the draft Bill that the test should be based on 'likely prejudice', clearly a weaker test.[43] It remains to be proven whether the delicate balance between extending the public's access to information, protecting privacy and confidentiality has been successfully achieved. The draft Bill contains a shorter list of public authorities than the White Paper, and access to information held by public corporations and privatised utilities seems to depend on the discretion of the secretary of state.[44]

The Scottish Perspective

The draft FOI Bill does not apply to the Scottish Parliament, to any part of the Scottish Executive, to the Scottish Parliamentary Corporate Body or to Scottish public authorities with mixed functions or no reserved functions.[45] The Bill will apply to UK public bodies operating in Scotland (such as the DSS or MOD) and to cross-border public authorities. However, the *Partnership for Scotland* document setting out the plans of the newly elected Executive contained a specific commitment to the early introduction of an effective freedom of information regime.[46]

The Scottish Executive has produced voluntary guidelines for the Scottish public sector organisations to adopt,[47] but it remains open to speculation whether the Scottish Parliament will liaise with the Information Commissioner to ensure coherent access to the model publication schemes required by cl.7 of the draft FOI Bill. Active dissemination of the publication schemes and supporting policies is a requirement in the draft Bill,[48] but the public authority may 'publish its publication scheme in such manner as it thinks fit'.[49] The precedent from the local government initiatives to open up access provides a fragmented picture.[50]

Freedom of Information: Conclusion

The concept that information produced by public bodies should generally be available to members of the public is not a new concept on the international scene, it has been a right for Swedish citizens since 1766,[51] and many countries follow a presumption of openness unless there is a specific reason for disclosure. As the experience of established FOI regimes shows,[52] there is usually a close operational relationship between the legislation that provides access to information and that which upholds privacy. FOI has a distinct relevance for business, not only to encourage confidence for those who deal directly with government but also to establish a more accountable relationship with government and commercial sectors as a whole. Will information about how government does business be readily available?

If enquiries lodged under the proposed FOI Act achieve much in the way of useful evidence once the Act is in force it will be in spite of the numerous exemptions, not because of the facility the Act provides for the citizen. It is interesting to speculate how accountable government can be made with such a fragmented and partial attempt to open up the process of its decision making. If information is not forthcoming can we be confident that it is because there is no legitimate way of discovering the answer or because it does not exist rather than that it is hidden through incompetence or malicious intent? The effectiveness of the enquiry process is thus at the heart of the legislation.

The draft Bill maintains the right of individuals to request access without having to prove a reason for their enquiry. Though there is a need for basic exemptions in defence, foreign affairs and personal privacy and there is more general provision for discretionary disclosure, there is no evidence at present to support confidence that this will be used generously to assist the enquirer. An independent arbiter exists in the person and office of the Information Commissioner, though in theory his/her power is now curtailed by the retention of the right of veto by ministers. The draft Bill, as it stands currently, is thus a weak measure, although the House of Commons Select Committee on Public Administration has made recommendations to ensure that it will be 'based more firmly on clear rights and less on discretionary duties'.[53] This requires a rebalancing of the draft Bill in the direction of the 'right to know'.[54] For example, it recommends the use of 'substantial prejudice', rather than just 'prejudice' as a test for the use of key exemptions.[55]

The legislation will be an initial novelty principally for journalists and those who have been frustrated by the current enquiry procedure, but the analysis of information provided will be key to assessing its trustworthiness. Anecdotal evidence from the Republic of Ireland suggests that one significant result of freedom of information legislation has been an increase in the care taken to record information through the more extensive use of office procedures and the closer registration of multi-media files which are physically dispersed.

Conclusion

As can be seen, the regulation of information as a result of the development of technology has become increasingly more important. However, there are conflicting interests – personal, legal, commercial and governmental – which need to be taken account of. As yet the balance has not been achieved. Technology is driving us forward but the legislation we are seeking to put in place fails, in many instances, to take account of the requirements of, and developments in, that technology. On the other hand, the increasing availability of information also requires increased awareness amongst users about the way in which the information can lawfully be used. While the freedom of information proposals are to be welcomed they do not change the attitude of the government which is to restrict access to information but at the same time ensure government (or law enforcement) access when required. Although the Data Protection Act 1998 will afford enhanced rights and remedies to individuals, unless there is a significant cultural change amongst data subjects it is unlikely that the new rights will be exercised and as a result the cultural change in organisations will be minimal. Data protection has come under scrutiny as a result of the implementation of the 1998 Act but, generally speaking, it is an area of information access which is largely ignored by data users and data subjects alike.

It may be that the government is correct to see e-commerce as the focus for change, particularly in the area of information storage and transfer. There is certainly no doubt that electronic methods of doing business will be increasingly used and it is important that this can be done in an environment which gives confidence to all. There is, however, a significant contrast between the approach being taken by the government in relation to making available its own information and its concerns about being unable to gain access to third party information, and it will be interesting to see if this dual approach can be sustained.

As technology makes access to information easier, issues of security become more important but, as discussed above, technological developments have also resulted in information overload. Without common reference standards for information storage there can be no meaningful information retrieval. Access to information could become irrelevant if appropriate information management systems are not properly established. From an organisational perspective it is in this area that more resources need to be focused to ensure that the legislation being put in place is not trivialised by an overwhelming amount of information.

Notes

1 Birkinshaw, Patrick (1996), *Freedom of Information: The Law, the Practice and the Ideal*, 2nd edn, London: Butterworths, p.5.
2 For example, Prescription and Limitation (Scotland) Act 1973, Companies Act 1985 and Taxes Management Act 1970.
3 The c:cure website is <http://www.c-cure.org./bsframes.htmin>.
4 *Ghost in the Machine – An Analysis of IT Fraud and Abuse*, Audit Commission Update Report, February 1998, p.1.
5 *Norwich Union* v. *Western Provident* (unreported) where Norwich Union paid £450 000 in settlement to Western Provident after its staff sent defamatory e-mails about Western Provident.
6 The School of Library, Archival and Information Studies at the University of British Columbia's *Protection of the Integrity of Electronic Records* identifies and defines the requirements for creating, handling and preserving reliable and authentic electronic records against different administrative, juridical, cultural and disciplinary points of view, see <http://www.slais.ubc.ca/users/duranti/>.
7 United States Federal Court of Appeals, *Public Citizen* v. *Carlin*, 6 August 1999, No. 97–5356, overturned a lower court's invalidation of the Federal Government's General Records Schedule (GRS) 20 which guided federal agencies on certain electronic records issues. For the decision and opinion of the Court of Appeals, see <http://www.cadc.uscourts.gov/common/opinions/199908/97–5356a.txt>.
8 Department of Trade and Industry (1999), *Promoting Electronic Commerce*, Cm 4477, London: HMSO.
9 Directive EC/95/46, OJ 1995 L281/31.
10 Reply to parliamentary question by Kim Howarth MP on 12 July 1999, 335 HC Debs, 73.
11 *Committee on Data Protection* (1978), Cmnd 7341, London: HMSO.
12 *Kaye* v. *Robertson* [1991] FSR 62 confirmed that there is no right to privacy as such under English law and the position is broadly similar in Scotland. However, insofar as the Data Protection Act prohibits holding of personal information without appropriate registration, it does give a right to privacy insofar as there is not a blanket permission to hold any personal data.
13 *Data Protection Registrar* v. *British Gas Trading*, decision of Data Protection Tribunal 5 May 1998, <http://www.open.gov.uk/dpr/dprhome.htm>.
14 The directive went through two versions: Commission Proposal – COM (90) 314 Final – SYN 287 (OJ 1990 C/277/03), Commission Proposal – COM (92) 422 Final – SYN 287 (OJ 1992 C/311/04).
15 Neither Greece nor Spain had an existing data protection regime.
16 Data Protection Act 1998, sch. 1, pt 1, para. 7: 'appropriate technical and organisational measures shall be taken against unauthorised or unlawful processing of personal data and against accidental loss or destruction of, or damage to, personal data'.
17 Ibid., sch. 1, pt 1, para. 8: 'Personal data shall not be transferred to a country or territory outside the European Economic Area unless that country or territory

ensures an adequate level of protection for the rights and freedoms of data subjects in relation to the processing of personal data.'

18 Ibid., sch. 3, para. 1.

19 Ibid., s. 1(1).

20 *Tenth Report of the Data Protection Registrar*, HC 453, 1993–4 p.3(n)(viii).

21 'Internet Security – Rival Products', *IT Law Today*, Nov./Dec. 1995, 8.

22 A proposal from the Clinton administration which involved a chip which would encrypt all messages sent electronically or over the phone. The government would only be able to decode the messages with a court order but, in order to unlock the code, two encryption keys would be needed. These two keys would be held separately by two different government agencies.

23 COM (1998) 297 final; COM (1998) 586 final.

24 *Promoting Electronic Commerce*, Cm 4477 (1999).

25 Department of Trade and Industry (1999), *Building Confidence in Electronic Commerce*, London: Department of Trade and Industry.

26 Ponting, Clive (1987), 'Secrecy and Freedom of Information', in Julia Neuberger (ed.), *Freedom of Information: Freedom of the Individual?* London: Papermac, p.1.

27 Notably the BSE Enquiry and the Matrix Churchill arms to Iraq affair, when the guidelines concerning the exports of arms overseas were altered without announcement to parliament. This led to the Scott Inquiry of 1996 (HC 115, published 16 February 1996). Clive Ponting , a former senior civil servant, came to prominence following his prosecution, under the Official Secrets Act, 1911, s.2, for disclosing information concerning government duplicity about facts relating to the sinking of the Argentinian warship, the *General Belgrano*. He was subsequently acquitted: *R* v. *Ponting* [1985] Crim LR 318. See also Birkinshaw, Patrick (1996), *Freedom of Information: The Law, the Practice and the Ideal*, 2nd edn, London: Butterworths, pp.79–81.

28 *Your Right to Know – The Government's Proposals for a Freedom of Information Act*, Cm 3818 (1997), London: HMSO; *Freedom of Information: Consultation on Draft Legislation*, Cm 4355 (1999), London: HMSO.

29 The commissioner's functions and responsibilities are identified in cls 40–43 of the draft Bill.

30 'Climbdown on Secrecy', *The Guardian*, 11 October 1999.

31 For example, a succinct textual description of the record, unique identification of the date of creation, author, organisation and so on.

32 This is 20 days longer than the period suggested in the White Paper and up to 11 days longer than in Canada, New Zealand and Australia.

33 'Climbdown on Secrecy' (n.30, above).

34 For a detailed assessment of the developments in this area, prior to the 1997 White Paper, see Birkinshaw, *Freedom of Information* (n.1, above).

35 For further information, see the Campaign for Freedom of Information website <http://www.cfoi.org.uk/>.

36 *The Times*, 25 May 1999, leader column, p.1.

37 For further comparison of the rights of access to policy advice, see *Access to Policy Advice under a Freedom of Information Act: A Discussion Paper*, CFOI April 1997, at <http://www.cfoi.org.uk/pdf/poladpaper97.pdf>.

38 See especially the Campaign for the Freedom of Information (CFOI) (n.35, above).

39 See cls 9, 12 and 13 of the draft Bill for detail on the fees payable.

40 Campaign for the Freedom of Information web-site (n.35, above).

41 *Code of Practice on Access to Government Information*, 2nd edn (1997).

42 332 HC Debs, 24 May 1999, cols 21–36.

43 See cls16–37 to identify the exemptions from the duty to disclose information.

44 See cl.38.

45 See the draft Bill, cl.2(4).
46 Scottish Executive News Release, 1076/99, 24 May 1999. For the Scottish Parliament discussion, see the Official Report, vol. 1, no. 11.
47 The *Code of Practice on Access to Scottish Executive Information* was published in July 1999 and is available at <http://193.32.28.91/library2/doc01/code.pdf>.
48 Draft bill, cl.6(1).
49 Draft bill, cl.6(5).
50 Scottish Consumer Council (1987), *Access to Information: How is the Act Working?*, prepared by Derek Manson-Smith, Glasgow; SCC measured the effectiveness and coverage of the Act in Scotland.
51 For a historical survey of FOI legislation around the world, see Oppenheim, Charles (1999), *The Legal and Regulatory Environment for Electronic Information*, 3rd edn, Tetbury; Infonortics, pp.170–72.
52 For further information from the USA, see, Birkinshaw, Patrick (1991), *Freedom of Information: The US Experience*, Hull: Hull University Law School.
53 Freedom of Information Draft Bill, HC 570, 1998–9.
54 *Ibid.*, para.53.
55 *Ibid.*, para.71.

15 Regulating Business and the Business of Regulation: The Encouragement of Business-friendly Assumptions in Regulatory Agencies

NOREEN BURROWS AND CHARLES WOOLFSON, *University of Glasgow*

Introduction

Over the past decade and a half the assumptions of regulatory agencies have been increasingly framed by the consideration of business interests. This chapter explores these assumptions as developed by the previous Conservative administration. It argues that such assumptions are being adopted with only minor modifications by the current New Labour administration. Certain common themes can be identified in the business-friendly exhortations of governments of both persuasions. Chief amongst these is the increasingly strong imperative to regulatory agencies that enforcement should not be 'over-zealous'.[1] Regulation, it is argued, should minimise costs and burdens on business, particularly small and medium-sized enterprises (SMEs).

The origins of the assumption that enforcement should be business-friendly are first examined. Legal mechanisms, both statutory and non-statutory, were used to introduce these assumptions. Three stages in this process can be identified. The first stage is the period from 1985 to 1993, when the Conservatives' general policy of deregulation was being developed. In the latter part of this period the Conservative administration was also developing its ideas on the Citizen's Charter, with its emphasis on openness and transparency of government agencies. The second stage is the period from 1994 to 1997. This period saw the introduction of the Deregulation and Contracting Out Act 1994 which was the high point of Conservative deregulatory policy. This Act introduced new forms of redress available to business which could potentially be exercised as a mechanism of inhibition in anticipation of proposed enforcement by regulators. The third and current stage began in 1997 and continues today. This period began with the rejection of the procedures introduced by the 1994 Act by regulatory enforcers themselves in a consultation on the extension of the procedures to a wide area of enforcement of activity, a rejection which was accepted by the New Labour government when it came to power in 1997. In this current phase, the inhibitory mechanisms of the Deregulation and Contracting Out Act are now being replaced by the introduction of an Enforcement Concordat seeking to create mutual understandings in a 'partnership' approach to regulation. These stages are examined in three policy areas: health and safety at work, the environment and food safety. An investigation of these areas demonstrates the translation of business-friendly assumptions into concrete policy outcomes.

The three policy areas which are discussed in this chapter are areas where UK governments have advocated the maintenance of high standards of public protection and effective enforcement. They are politically sensitive in that they are policy areas which command a high degree of attention from important interest and pressure groups as well as from the general public. They can generate high-profile issues where major incidents and breaches of the rules can lead to widespread public concern. Accidents at work, oil spillages and food scares all attract the scrutiny of press and public alike. Expectations of proper corporate or governmental behaviour increasingly underlie these concerns. Significantly too, these are areas where UK domestic legislation is increasingly influenced to a very great extent by European law and where the government is under an obligation, monitored by the European Commission and backed by the threat of action in the European Court of Justice, to implement and enforce European rules.

Stage 1: Working with Business (1985–93)

Freeing business from the perceived heavy burden of domestic and European regulation and the need to cut red tape was a central preoccupation of previous Conservative administrations. The first 'glimpse' of this policy was found in the Department of Trade and Industry (DTI) creation of the Enterprise and Deregulation Unit in 1985. However, by 1988, the DTI was able to announce only modest success for this initiative which, it was stated, had been working 'behind the scenes' in various government departments and agencies.[2] A relaunch of the deregulation initiative therefore took place in 1992 and a deregulation unit and 'task forces' were set up, this time under the overall control of businessmen rather than civil servants. The task forces identified many areas where regulations could be withdrawn or simplified, but they also looked to the potentially more significant area of enforcement culture. At the same time, the Citizen's Charter initiative, announced by the government in 1991, enunciated certain principles about the expectations 'citizens' could have in respect of levels and quality of public services. These two policy areas were brought together in *Working with Business: A Code for Enforcement Agencies*, published jointly by the Citizen's Charter and the Deregulation Unit in 1993.

Working with Business: A Code for Enforcement Agencies was personally endorsed by then Prime Minister John Major, who stated that it would apply to all government agencies and that it was to be forwarded to local authorities who would want to adopt these principles. In fact, the Local Government Management Board did adopt these principles in its own guide to good practice (1996), although there was some reluctance on the part of other agencies to adopt the Code as it stood.

The principles outlined in the Code were apparently straightforward. Standards were to be published, information was to be provided on the precise nature of the rule in question and how it would be applied, business was to be consulted to discuss compliance failure, enforcement staff were to be courteous and helpful, complaints procedures were to be established, and compliance costs would be minimised. Each enforcement agency was to publish its own code by 1 January 1994. The interests of business were to be served by cutting compliance costs and uncertainty. The interests of the citizen would be served by ensuring that regulations met their intended objectives and the tax burden would be reduced.

The significance of the Code in attempting to bring about a change in enforcement culture cannot be over-estimated. It is therefore worthwhile considering its legal status. Neither the Citizen's Charter initiative nor the deregulation initiative was based on any statutory authority. Citizen's Charter principles were set out in policy statements. For its part, the Deregulation Unit announced and directed policy by way of reports. The Deregulation Task Force was composed entirely of representatives of business appointed by central government. There was no statutory base for its existence. The Code was, therefore, one of that class of rules described as 'informal'. It contained instructions to officials from the prime minister, unlike other instructions to officials which come from ministers to the officials in their own departments or to agencies for which they are the sponsoring ministries. Such codes have been described as 'enabling rules'.[3] *Working with Business* may have been legally binding on agencies which are part of the Crown, but not on those agencies which act independently and which govern their own procedures. Refusal by an agency not part of the Crown to adopt the proffered regulatory principles, perhaps by adopting an alternative way of working, would not breach any legal rule unless that agency breached the terms of the statute which created it. Nonetheless, *Working with Business* as a code was intended to affect a large number of regulatory agencies: it was intended to have practical effects.

Government preference for resort to informal rules has been discussed extensively in the public law literature.[4] Craig offers a possible explanation as to why informal rules may be preferred to legislation.[5] He terms this 'a 'corporatist strategy' whereby government and major interest groups 'bargain independently of the legislature to attain a goal which both seek, but which may be opposed by other less powerful interest groups, and/or the legislature'. Certainly, given the business-dominated composition of the Deregulation Task Force, it is tempting to argue that such a strategy led directly to the explicitly business-friendly assumptions advocated in *Working with Business.*

Working with Business was a sufficient vehicle to set out the principles governing changing regulatory assumptions but it was not sufficiently prescriptive to enforce change on potentially unwilling or reluctant enforcement agencies. The Conservative administration therefore decided to turn to legislation to consolidate these changes.

Stage 2: Legislating for Business-Friendly Procedures (1994–97)

The legislative base giving powers to ministers to 'improve enforcement procedures' was provided in section 5 of the Deregulation and Contracting Out Act 1994. The hitherto informal rules were supplemented with formal powers. Section 5 empowers ministers (the Act is still in force) to issue orders addressed to enforcement officers or agencies requiring the use of business-friendly enforcement procedures. The minister could do this where he or she was of the opinion that a statutory provision, contained in primary or delegated legislation, had the effect of imposing restrictions or conditions on businesses and where enforcement procedures could be improved as far as 'fairness', 'transparency' and 'consistency' were concerned. Where legislation required consultation to be carried out before new regulations were to be introduced, the minister was required to carry out such consultation prior to issuing any order. Orders were to be made by way of statutory instrument. Nothing in section 5 was to preclude enforcement officers from taking immediate action where such action appeared necessary to the enforcement officer: for example, by way of the issue of a prohibition notice under section 21 of the Health and Safety at Work Act 'where there is a risk of serious personal injury'. Similarly, section 5 did not require an officer to disclose information which was contrary to the public interest.

The business-friendly procedures which a minister may require are set out in schedule 1 of the Deregulation and Contracting Out Act. Five different procedures are envisaged which relate to different phases in the enforcement cycle:

1 Where remedial action is required, the enforcement officer must provide a written notice which states the nature of the remedial action, the reason for it and the time limits within which the business must comply. The notice must also explain what constitutes a failure to comply and the nature of any enforcement action which could be taken, together with information on the rights of the business to make representations or to appeal against the decision of the enforcement officer. No enforcement action can be taken until the expiry of a period of notice to be determined by the minister in the order specifying the use of this procedure.
2 Where an enforcement officer takes immediate enforcement action or where he or she requires a business to take immediate remedial action incurring significant expenditure, the officer must issue a notice explaining why it was necessary to take such action.
3 Where an enforcement officer is minded to take any enforcement action against any person, he or she must provide a written notice stating that action is contemplated and the reason for the action and must allow, within a specified period, the business concerned to make written or oral representations in the presence of a person specified in the order. The enforcement officer must consider any such representations before action is taken.
4 Where enforcement action has been taken, and where a right of appeal is provided in the legislation, the enforcement officer must provide a written notice explaining how, where, within what time limits and on what grounds an appeal may be brought. The notice must also explain whether the enforcement action is to be stayed (in Scotland suspended) pending appeal.
5 Where enforcement action affects the position of third parties, in terms of outlay or costs or where goods or services are provided

by a third party, the order may specify that any of the procedures set out above should apply to such third parties.

Whilst it may be conceded that in their totality these procedures may be deemed to be good enforcement practice, and indeed the first two of these procedures have been routinely required in one form or another by enforcement officers, this would be to obscure the fundamentally innovatory thrust of the third procedure. It is the 'minded to' procedure which encapsulates the business-friendly orientation of the legislation. The controversial and problematic nature of this procedure can be seen from an examination of its introduction into the three policy areas under scrutiny. The procedures themselves, however, cannot be seen in isolation from the culture in which they were to operate. The Deregulation Task Force was anxious to bring about a change in the culture of enforcement. Its stated aim was to inculcate in every public servant the principle that 'deregulatory principles should be central to' his or her personal aims and objectives.[6] This change in culture means that the performance of enforcement officers should be measured in terms of 'impact, not activity'. In particular, the Deregulation Task Force recommended that the setting of targets for enforcement actions or prosecutions could not be used as the baseline for measuring the success of enforcement activity. The Task Force insisted that two principles should, in future, govern all enforcement agents. The first was that they 'treat minimisation of costs to business as a central aim'. The second was that the measurement of success or otherwise of an enforcement agency should be 'success in meeting the objectives of the regulation', rather than the measurement of outputs such as prosecutions.

Bearing these principles in mind, enforcement officers were faced with a difficult task when following business-friendly procedures. A new element of inhibitory restraint on regulators was being brought into the existing arena of 'negotiated compliance'.[7] The emphasis now was on finding a way for business to comply with a particular rule at minimal cost while offering new opportunities to challenge the day-to-day operational decisions of regulatory enforcement. The way in which these procedures were introduced is now examined in three policy areas: health and safety, the environment and food safety.

Health and Safety

The Health and Safety Commission (HSC) had responded to a report of the Deregulation Task Force Report of 1993[8] with a parallel review of existing health and safety provision. This review, conducted at ministerial request, concluded that 'there is little evidence that, despite the costs of compliance, the system is unduly burdensome for business'.[9]

This unanticipated outcome can in part be attributed to the fact that in the Health and Safety Commission an element of genuine tripartite (as opposed to Craig's bilateral) corporatism in the traditional sense remains. On the Commission itself, besides the employees there is TUC representation alongside a 'public interest' constituency via local authority representation. The review recommended that the core of the Health and Safety at Work Act, s.2(1), outlining the employer's duties should be preserved. New legislation should not result in the diminution of existing standards. Health and safety was clearly an area in which the straightforward introduction of business-led perspectives was problematic, not least for sections of business. It is clear from the minutes of evidence reproduced in the HSC review that business itself had reservations about the potential impacts of the removal of the existing floor of standards in this area.

Despite the lack of evidence that existing enforcement procedures were seen as unfriendly towards business, the HSC issued an *Enforcement Policy Statement* in October 1995 as part of the Citizen's Charter initiative.[10] The statement adopted the principles outlined in *Working with Business*. It sets out four guiding principles to inform Health and Safety Executive (HSE) enforcement strategy: proportionality, consistency, transparency and targeting. Proportionality is defined as relating enforcement action to risks and is said to be part of the concept of reasonable practicability which is enshrined in the Health and Safety at Work Act 1974. However, the HSC's *Enforcement Policy Statement* also explicitly incorporates compliance costs as part of the risk equation: 'some risks may be so trivial that it is not worth spending money on them'. Consistency is defined as taking a similar approach in similar circumstances to achieve similar ends. Given that enforcement of health and safety rules is divided between local authorities and HSE inspectors, consistency may prove difficult to achieve. To combat inconsistency, therefore, enforcing authorities are required to introduce 'arrangements' including liaison between enforcers. Transparency means helping duty holders to understand what is expected of them, but it is a particular duty on the part of enforcers to inform duty holders of essential legal requirements as distinguished from what is merely good practice. Finally, targeting means that enforcement officers will ensure that those whose activities give rise to the gravest potential risk, or where hazards are not well controlled, are given priority in inspections. Enforcers are required to develop 'systems' to enable such prioritisation to take place. As part of targeting, enforcement action is to be taken against the person(s) responsible for creating the risk.

Business-friendly as these procedures were intended to be, they did not conform completely to schedule 1 of the Deregulation and Contracting Out Act. It was at this point that ministers stepped in and 'asked' the Health and Safety Commission to bring its enforcement procedures in line with those in Schedule 1. The Act envisaged the use of an order made by a minister to apply the new procedures to existing regulatory areas. However, the HSC introduced the new procedures at the request of the government. In practice, discussion took place between officials from the Health and Safety Executive, the Cabinet Office Deregulation Unit and the former Employment Department. The HSC subsequently decided to adopt the business-friendly procedures and ministers, under these circumstances, decided not to use a statutory instrument to require their use.

Under the new procedures, where enforcement action was anticipated, local authority and HSE inspectors would first issue a 'notice of intention' (NOI) to issue an improvement notice rather than an improvement notice itself. Duty holders were to be given two weeks within which to challenge the decision to issue a notice and such a challenge could be made directly to the officer or to his or her manager. A new leaflet was produced setting out 'Your rights when health and safety inspectors take action' which was to be issued during an inspection or sent by post immediately thereafter. The Health and Safety Commission issued guidance to local authorities under section 18 of the Health and Safety at Work Act setting out these new procedures. The guidance was to be implemented by 5 February 1996. Simultaneously, instructions were issued to HSE inspectors to follow the new business-friendly procedures. The HSC also decided at this stage that, six months after their introduction, an evaluation of the new procedures would take place.

The evaluation of the new enforcement procedures, requested by the HSC, produced ambiguous results. The key focus of the inquiry was the new notice of intention (NOI) procedure giving businesses a right of representation before an improvement notice is issued.[11] Only 5 per cent of businesses surveyed had availed themselves of this opportunity, suggesting that the overwhelming majority of businesses did not regard existing procedures as unfriendly. A similar tiny proportion of businesses who received advisory letters approached the regulatory authority in an attempt to get the proposed action changed. Nearly a third of businesses did not read the new leaflet indicating their rights when health and safety inspectors proposed to take action. As many as one-fifth of businesses were not convinced of the advantages of the leaflet in clarifying the inspection and any subsequent action.

In terms of modifying the behaviour of enforcement officers in a business-friendly direction, the survey is somewhat less ambiguous. A substantial minority of inspectors (40 per cent) did not believe it helpful to have a leaflet telling business what rights they have and a slightly larger proportion did not believe that the new guidance/

instructions helped enforcement transparency and consistency. Only half thought it important to formalise enforcement practice in this way, whilst only one-fifth said the new guidance had affected the way they enforced the law. In the main, this was through an increase in the number of advisory letters, while one-third of inspectors reported a decrease in the number of improvement notices they issued and a similar proportion found the new procedures time-consuming. Overall, nearly half the inspectors commented on the additional administration and paperwork with which they were confronted, something of an irony given the government's explicit intention to reduce red tape.

The Deregulation Unit claimed that the results of this review demonstrated that 'the new procedures are effective both in giving business the right to make representations before an improvement notice is issued and in ensuring that they understood their rights when an inspector takes action'. Furthermore, it claimed that 'the Health and Safety Commission concluded that the new procedures were contributing to improved transparency and consistency in inspection and enforcement and that there was no evidence of any reduction in standards of health and safety'.[12]

These views were apparently contested at local authority level by the chief environmental health officers (CEHOs), whose departments are responsible for enforcing health and safety legislation in shops, offices and small business premises. The CEHOs commissioned their own evaluative study of the NOI procedures.[13] This latter study concluded that there was considerable opposition to the new procedures on the part of environmental health officers (EHOs), with only 10 per cent supporting the new procedures and only 1 per cent believing that they improved standards. In almost all cases, environmental health officers believed that they had been involved in increased paperwork and were required to carry out more than one visit to the same site. Furthermore, it appears that small businesses have become confused by the system, believing that the 14-day period specified in the NOI was the time limit in which they had to comply with the requirements laid out in it. This meant that they were spending more resources trying to meet a tight deadline rather than the normally much longer deadlines which would have been included in an improvement notice. Paradoxically, far from making enforcement more business-friendly, the procedures were creating a bureaucratic burden for enforcers while confusing business.

Environment

Business-friendly procedures were also adopted by the Environment Agency which was created by the Environment Act 1995. The 1995

Act is long and complex. Nowhere in its provisions is it possible to find any explicit mention of business-friendly enforcement procedures. However, the business-friendly assumptions of the administration can be seen in the general requirements of s. 39 of the Act which imposes a duty on the new Agency to have regard to costs and benefits in exercising its powers. The omission of a direct reference was surprising given that the Act was adopted only one year after the Deregulation Act, which set the benchmark for new regulatory agencies. Indeed, it is necessary to read between the lines of the Environment Act to discover the intention of government to require the Agency to follow the procedures set out in Schedule 1. Section 4 of the Environment Act states that it is to be the principal aim of the Agency to make a 'contribution' towards the objective of 'achieving sustainable development'. In order to achieve this aim, ministers are to give guidance with respect to the 'objectives' which they, the ministers, consider 'appropriate for the Agency to pursue in the discharge of its functions'. The Agency must 'have regard' to such guidance, and has the right to be consulted before any guidance is given. Drafts of guidance are to be laid before parliament. A negative resolution of either House would result in the minister not giving that guidance.

Howarth observes that specific guidance was issued in 1995 in two documents.[14] The significant guidance in relation to business-friendly procedures is contained in the Management Statement, two versions of which were published – the first in October 1994 and the second in December 1995. The 1995 version states:

> Ministers expect the Agency to implement environmental regulations in ways which deliver environmental objectives while not imposing unnecessary burdens on those it regulates. To do so, the Agency should seek constructive relationships with regulated bodies (or whose business activities are affected by its work) and their representatives. This should improve provision of advice on regulations, including its approach to enforcement and how to comply with these requirements.
>
> The Agency should develop a Code of Practice on the exercise of its regulatory responsibilities. This should promote fairness, proportionality, transparency and consistency of enforcement. It should reflect the principles of the Government's code for enforcement agencies ('Working with Business') and Schedule 1 of the Deregulation and Contracting Out Act 1994, while enabling the Agency to maintain effective environmental protection and to take immediate enforcement action where this is justified.[15]

Informed observers suggested that 'the instruction to the Agency to draw up a code of enforcement practice ... is believed to have been made at the insistence of the Government's Deregulation Unit'.[16] Ministerial guidance certainly seems to have reflected the assumptions being promoted by the Deregulation Unit. Furthermore, in January 1996, those same observers predicted that the code of practice would be ' likely to burden the Agency with red tape and discourage it taking prompt action against polluters'. If schedule 1 were to be translated fully into the Agency's code, it would be 'highly likely to inhibit regulators from resorting to enforcement action, or even suggesting remedial measures to companies. Inspectors will know that any such move will involve them in an extra tier of bureaucracy, and the Agency may have to create an "audit trail" of documentation to protect itself from claims in the courts or on appeal that it had not followed the enforcement procedures.'[17] Constitutional questions were raised about the controversial way in which the Department of the Environment managed to avoid parliamentary discussion on enforcement techniques by including an instruction to adopt the principles of schedule 1 in its Management Statement, rather than specifying the procedures themselves in the 1995 Act, thereby avoiding debate on the relevance of the procedures to the work of the Environment Agency. Furthermore, the text of the code itself avoided parliamentary scrutiny since it was adopted for internal Agency guidance.

The Environment Agency adopted its Enforcement Policy Statement in April 1996. In this statement it is said that the Agency's view of enforcement derives from its former constituent bodies: the National Rivers Authority, Her Majesty's Inspectorate of Pollution and local authorities with responsibility for control and discharge of sewerage. The policy is influenced by the need to harmonise procedures adopted formerly by those agencies and to integrate earlier regulatory regimes as well as complying with obligations imposed by its Management Statement. As one might expect, therefore, the principles of enforcement came to be derived from a variety of sources. However, the actual model for the Environment Agency's Policy Statement is, in fact, the *Enforcement Policy Statement* of the HSC. A straightforward textual comparison of the two statements in respect of the principles of enforcement shows that the HSC statement has merely been borrowed and slightly rewritten to accommodate the Environment Agency's remit. The principles of proportionality, consistency, targeting and transparency are set out almost word for word. Compare, for example, the HSC basic statement on proportionality to that of the Environment Agency:

> Proportionality means relating enforcement action to the risks. Those who the law protects and those on who it places duties (duty holders) expect that action taken by enforcing authorities to achieve compliance should be proportionate to any risks to health and safety and to the seriousness of any breach (HSC).

> 'Proportionality' means relating actions to the risks and costs. Those whom the law protects and those on whom it places duties expect that action taken by the Agency to achieve compliance should be proportionate to any risks posed to the environment and to the seriousness of any breach of the law or relevant licence or consent (Environment Agency).

This kind of comparison can be made with virtually the whole text of the Environment Agency enforcement policy statement. The conclusion to be drawn is not so much that there has been a harmonisation and integration of previous regulatory regimes in the area of environmental law but that there is harmonisation and integration of approaches across regulatory authorities. What needs to be examined is whether the Environment Agency will be as vigorous in its enforcement policy as, for example, the National Rivers Authority had been or whether cross-regulatory agency harmonisation will lead to a less tough enforcement policy.

The guidance issued to the Environment Agency also contained practice guidance for warranted officers. ('Warranted officer' is the term used to describe environmental inspectors by the Environment Agency; the term 'inspector' is used in the Act). This guidance follows closely the procedures set out in schedule 1 of the Deregulation Act. The Agency's policy creates specific rights for those on whom the law places environmental duties: in particular, the right to a letter, on request, explaining what needs to be done and why when warranted officers express an opinion that something needs to be done; the right to a 'minded to' notice and the right to be heard before any formal action is taken, a written statement where immediate action is required explaining why certain actions are necessary and the right to be informed of any appeals mechanisms. A leaflet setting out 'Your rights when Environment Agency warranted officers take action' is also to be presented by warranted officers whenever visits to premises are made. Any letters must set out the status of advice – that is, whether it is good practice or a legally binding obligation. Where remedial action is required there is a right to make representations within ten working days to the warranted officer's manager and no action should be taken within this ten-day period unless immediate action is justified by the risk. Enforcement notices should only be issued after an operator has been given the right to make representations to the warranted officer's manager who should discuss with operators what they must do to comply with the law. Any representations made must be examined in a fair and fresh manner. The Environment Agency will monitor warranted officers to ensure that a leaflet has been given to every operator where visits are made; that, where enforcement notices are to be issued, 'minded to' notices have been used; and that representations are properly considered.

Food Safety

Food safety has become one of the most politically sensitive areas in recent years, particularly with regard to enforcement. Food safety enforcement is carried out by local government inspectors in each local authority. In England, enforcement is divided between Trading Standards Officers and Environmental Health Officers. In Scotland and Northern Ireland, and in most Welsh local authorities, enforcement is the responsibility of Environmental Health Departments. There was, therefore, no single agency which could introduce business-friendly procedures across the board. In these circumstances, the business-friendly strategy of the Conservative government was slightly different.

The business-friendly procedures were applied, in July 1996, to the provisions of the Food Safety Act 1990, using the formal mechanism of delegated legislation.[18] This is the only occasion to date when ministers have utilised the formal mechanism provided for in Schedule 1 of the Deregulation and Contracting Out Act. The minister chose to apply the same 'minded to' procedures as were applied to health and safety and the environment to the enforcement of food safety. The order requires authorised officers of an enforcement authority, before they serve an enforcement notice on the proprietor of a food business, to give the proprietor written notice stating that the officer is 'minded to' serve an improvement notice and the reasons for such action. In addition, the officer must allow the proprietor to make written or oral representations to the officer, the latter in the presence of a senior officer of the enforcement authority. The officer must then consider representations which are duly made. The order was adopted on 28 June 1996 and came into force on 19 July 1996.

The timing of this order may appear surprising in view of the problems of food safety and food hygiene in the UK. The BSE crisis had led to the imposition of a ban by Germany on the import of British beef and beef products in August 1995 after a lengthy dispute over the standards of quality control of meat products in the UK. Subsequently, the European Community imposed a worldwide ban (March 1996) and the subject of food safety became a major domestic, European and international issue. Four months after the order requiring the use of 'minded to' procedures came into effect, the first in a series of E-coli outbreaks was reported in Lanarkshire. This ultimately claimed 21 lives. In response, the government appointed Professor Hugh Pennington to report on the circumstances leading to these events and their policy implications for food safety.[19]

Pennington's report identified a number of factors which have raised serious questions about the nature of the enforcement regime in food safety – in particular the lack of certainty of how, why and by whom enforcement is to take place. He listed, as factors leading to this uncertainty, the disruption of local authority functions as a result of local government reorganisation and a lack of earmarked resources in times of reduction of public spending. More significantly, in the context of this chapter, he pointed to changes in government policy since 1990 (the date of the adoption of the Food Safety Act) as a result of the need to enforce EU single market measures and of UK government deregulatory initiatives. Pennington concluded that 'this has created uncertainty amongst EHOs about the overall policy approach to enforcement ... the apparent desire on the part of the government for a light touch to enforcement has left EHOs uncertain about the policy imperatives and their expected roles'. Pennington concluded, in addition to asking for additional resources for EHOs, that 'It seems to us unacceptable, particularly in current circumstances, that EHOs should be in any doubt about the need for anything other than rigorous enforcement of food safety standards, which should be clear and unambiguous'. One of his final recommendations was that 'the Government should give a clear policy lead on the need for enforcement of food safety measures'. Pennington took up this theme again in an interview in the *Times Higher Education Supplement* in June 1997, when he stated that 'enforcers have to cope with a legal milieu that sometimes places too heavy a burden of proof on them. They also have to face hostility from those they regulate'.

In rejecting the 'light touch' approach in the matter of food safety, Pennington argues for a return to a strict enforcement regime. Said Pennington:

> In considering these issues, we recognised and understood the Government's general policy presumption against prescription and in favour of deregulation to reduce the regulatory burden on small businesses. In the case of food hygiene, the Government's aim has been for simple and proportionate legislation that does not dilute the overall level of public health protection. We felt, however, that the need to promote safety in food production and to safeguard public health has to be accepted as a special case where the balance requires a greater degree of prescription.[20]

The Conservative government's response to the inquiry accepted many of the recommendations of the report. Significantly, it said nothing on the issue of 'light touch' enforcement. However, before those recommendations could result in policy innovations, the Conservative government lost power.

Stage 3: The Concordat, Rethinking Enforcement (1997 to Date)

In the dying days of the Conservative government, the Deregulation Unit initiated a widespread consultation on whether to extend the business-friendly procedures to an extensive range of areas in trading standards, care services and environmental health.[21] The responses to that consultation showed unequivocal opposition to the introduction of business-friendly procedures by those entrusted with the enforcement of a wide variety of statutory provisions. There was also far from complete support from those who might be described as the objects of regulation, the vast majority of respondents in this category being businesses or trade associations. Indeed, among this group there was strong concern that lax enforcement would erode the protection offered by regulation to legitimate business. In particular, concerns were expressed about the potentiality for a rogue's charter for counterfeiters and other breaches of standards. Table 15.1 summarises the responses. For the purposes of this analysis, responses were categorised as being made by regulators and business. They were then analysed as being either broadly supportive or broadly unsupportive towards introducing business-friendly procedures. The percentages are rounded to the nearest whole number.

Table 15.1 Responses of regulators and business to proposals to extend business-friendly procedures

		Percentage of responses from group
Responses from regulators		
Broadly supportive	11	6
Broadly opposed	166	94
Total	177	
Responses from business		
Broadly supportive	65	70
Broadly opposed	28	30
Total	93	
Others	31	10
Total number of responses	301	

The consultation was not a true empirical study in any sense of the word and it is difficult to summarise the views. However, it is clear that the 'regulators' were opposed to the introduction of further levels of bureaucracy, particularly where these were likely to inhibit their regulatory functions. This was the view taken by most respondents, but it was those who had responsibility in matters of care for the elderly, in the control of infectious diseases and protection of the environment who were most concerned. Another level of concern related to the interface between the function of regulators as enforcers, and as providers of evidence in potential criminal prosecutions. In this respect, it was clear that enforcers felt that the issuing of informal notices would impinge on any subsequent attempt to gain objective evidence of an infringement of the law in view of the procedures under the Police and Criminal Evidence Act 1984 which applies in England and Wales.

Businesses, on the other hand, were interested in any procedure which might help clarify what they perceive as the often convoluted legislation which governs them. They also took the view that uniformity in enforcement across the country might be achieved if the business-friendly procedures were extended. However, the nearly one-third of businesses which were opposed to the extension of such procedures were in that sector which relied on trading standards officers to protect them against rogue traders. In these responses there was a generally supportive view taken of the way in which trading standards officers went about their business. This section did not want trading standards officers to condone, in any way, illegal behaviour. The Conservative government did not have the opportunity to act on these proposals which were, therefore, inherited by the incoming government.

On taking office, the New Labour government disbanded the Deregulation Unit and replaced it with a Better Regulation Unit. In an interview with *The Observer* in June 1997, the minister responsible stated that the new government 'while still pursuing the campaign against red tape ... would have to persuade people that some rules are there for their benefit. We want to persuade people that we should have sensible, coherent rules on issues from transport to food safety for their own protection.' Good regulation, it was claimed 'could benefit us all – it is only bad regulation that is a burden'. The new government's strategy was to be based on 'ensuring that regulations are necessary, properly costed, practical to enforce and straightforward to comply with'.[22]

As regards enforcement culture, the new government stated that the results of the consultation exercise discussed above 'clearly supported the principles 'underlying business-friendly assumptions. The government's concerns, however, were in relation to 'bureaucracy and inflexibility'.[23] An Access Business Group was early established to build on the 'consensus' between regulators and business about the *principles* of good enforcement. The Access Business Group was charged with developing a new 'Enforcement Concordat' setting out the principles of good enforcement as an alternative to the use of section 5 of the Deregulation and Contracting Out Act 1994. The Enforcement Concordat was published in March 1998 and set out the principles of 'good' enforcement policies. The Concordat attempts to balance the need to protect the public, the environment or specific groups as against the need to promote a thriving economy. Some of the principles outlined in the new Concordat are well rehearsed; proportionality and consistency are inherited from previous enforcement statements. The Concordat, however, stresses the need for regulators to meet performance targets in their work and to be open and friendly in their approach, with rights of appeal against them. As regards procedures, the 'minded to' procedures are replaced by 'an opportunity to discuss the circumstances of the case' unless immediate action is required. A 'regulatory conversation'[24] therefore replaces the 'minded to' notice introduced by section 5 of the Deregulation and Contracting Out Act.

The Concordat defines new terms of conversational engagement[25] between regulators and the regulated. These new terms have as their vocabulary the previous principles of proportionality and consistency but, in place of formal mechanisms of redress, they articulate business-friendly assumptions in terms of openness, plain language, consultation with stakeholders and helpfulness. This involves 'actively working with business, especially Small and Medium Sized Businesses, to advise on and assist with compliance'. Where enforcement does take place, rights of appeal against formal action remain. However, what is new is the whole tenor of the language that is used. It is no longer predicated on the assumption that the key objective is to prevent over-zealous enforcement. Rather, the Concordat seeks to provide a framework of conciliation before formal enforcement action is taken in which 'officers will provide an opportunity to discuss the circumstances of the case and, if possible, resolve points of difference'. It is clear that the new government has already embraced many of the business-friendly assumptions of its predecessor. However, New Labour has given a distinctively different inflection to the regulatory discourse with an emphasis on the creation of a 'partnership' approach with business.

These principles of the Concordat received a further restatement in the Better Regulation Guide.[26] In line with the Concordat, regulators are enjoined to 'allow opportunities to resolve differences before enforcement action is taken' (see Part 1, Enforcement Regime, para. 4.5). However the Better Regulation Guide goes further than the government's initial approach to 'better regulation' by proposing a reiteration of the previous administration's emphasis on 'risk-based' cost–benefit analysis approaches to regulation in the form of the need for a prior regulatory impact assessment. In a direct echo of the previous Conservative government, the Better Regulation Guide specifically proposes 'do nothing' as the first option for regulatory proposals, followed by a cascade of non-regulatory alternatives ranging from legal review to a deregulation order, improved information, non-mandatory codes of practice, self-regulation, the use of economic incentives, risk-based insurance or risk-pricing. In the event that direct regulation is the preferred option, consideration should be given to Europe-wide or international-level regulation 'to ensure the UK competes on a level playing field' (para. 1.14).

Signalling the government's 'genuine concern' to 'tackle over-regulation',[27] the Better Regulation Unit was duly transformed into the Regulatory Impact Unit. Under instruction from the trade and industry secretary there was henceforth to be a presumption against regulation, requiring future regulatory proposals to be justified at the highest levels. Nevertheless, despite these developments, business complaints continued to grow. These concerned New Labour's employment law reforms, the introduction of a national minimum wage and working time regulations, as well as self-assessment for tax purposes, and left the government open to damaging charges of 're-regulation by stealth'.[28] Such fears were acknowledged by the creation of yet another task force within the Department of Trade and Industry, this time led by Lord Haskins, chairperson of Northern Foods, with business people and others seconded to it. This in turn was followed by a series of 'summits' in the spring of 1999 between the trade and industry secretary and business leaders to impress upon them the seriousness of the government's endeavours. At the same time a White Paper on *Modernising Government* and the issuing of a consultation document, *Proposed Amendments to the Deregulation and Contracting Out Act 1994*, put forward proposals to increase powers under the Act to review primary legislation through the use of secondary legislation. Also included was the notion of 'sunsetting regulation', the idea that even were new regulation to be found necessary, after a prescribed period such regulation might be permitted simply to wither away. Like much else in the area of regulation, the Blair administration had borrowed this innovation from the US example.

While 'minded to' procedures were not reinstated, section 5 of the act was to remain essentially intact. In sum, what had changed, if anything, was the vocabulary of enforcement rather than its basic assumptions, a change of form rather than substance. This is now reflected in the approach of both the Health and Safety Commission and the Environment Agency.

Health and Safety

The *Quinquennial Prior Options Review of the Health and Safety Commission and Executive* was carried out in 1996/7. It spanned the demise of the previous government and the arrival of the new, and offers some interesting comments on the nature of enforcement. The *Review* reaffirms the bedrock assumption that 'the market alone cannot maintain adequate, fair and consistent standards of health and safety'.[29] The case for government intervention is uncontested. However, the *Review* accepts that there is a perceived inconsistency in enforcement and recommends that further scrutiny be carried out of the enforcement role of local authorities. In line with the change in emphasis of the new government, the HSC reviewed its own enforcement procedures in early 1998 and decided to withdraw its 'minded to' procedures. As from 1 April 1998, when inspectors propose to issue an enforcement notice they first discuss any breaches of the law with the duty holder, and an opportunity to discuss the matter with an inspector will be provided. It is only after such a 'regulatory conversation' has taken place that an improvement notice will be issued, providing an explanation of what needs to be done. These procedures mirror those outlined in the new Concordat and the Better Regulation Guide.

Environment

The Environment Agency consulted widely on its enforcement policy and a new Enforcement Prosecution Policy was adopted in November 1998. The 'minded to' procedures were repealed and are replaced by 'an opportunity to discuss what is required to comply with the law before formal enforcement action is taken'. This new policy also reflects the 'partnership' approach outlined in the Concordat and Better Regulation Guide.

Food Safety

The proposed Food Standards Agency also illustrates the approach of the new government to issues relating to enforcement. The White Paper recognises the 'need to introduce greater openness and more consumer involvement' into the work of government departments in food safety.[30] Local authorities will retain the obligation to enforce legislation on food safety but the new agency will work with them to try to ensure consistency in enforcement practices. The guiding principles in relation to enforcement are to be set out in legislation and in management practice, but to some extent they have been pre-determined in the White Paper. The new Food Standards Agency, while acting independently of sectoral interests, will be required to take only those actions which are proportionate to the risks involved and pay due regard to costs as well as benefits to those affected by regulation, and it must avoid over-regulation. When legislation was finally brought forward it enshrined yet a further 'modernising' principle which was to become an increasing feature of New Labour's approach to regulation, the notion of self-funding regulatory agencies (SEFRAs) which earn revenue from charging for regulatory services. It is at least arguable that the developing enforcement culture of the new Agency will be informed by the spirit of the Concordat and the Better Regulation Guide.

Conclusions

The introduction of the assumption that regulators ought, in principle, to be business-friendly in their approach to the enforcement process was an innovation introduced by the Conservative government as part of its deregulation strategy. At first informal, and then statutory, means were employed as a way of influencing, persuading and ultimately ensuring that these assumptions entered the language and culture of key regulatory authorities. Even though statutory powers were rarely used, the existence of section 5 of the Deregulation and Contracting Out Act was sufficient to ensure that the will of the government and its Deregulation Unit and Task Force prevailed. However, there was a clear resistance to an approach which tied the hands of regulators and led to little improvement for business. The perception that regulators were 'unfriendly' or unduly over- zealous was not universal and was difficult to prove.

The change of government has signalled some developments in the approach to regulation, particularly in the recognition that 'good' regulation is essential. The new government has also listened to the regulators themselves and has quietly shifted away from the use of section 5 procedures towards a less formal and less confrontational approach. Regulators will now attempt a conciliation in an attempt to resolve disputes before proceeding to use more coercive mechanisms of enforcement. However, the basic assumption that the work of enforcement agencies should be informed by business-friendly attitudes remains the same. The cultural shift from Conservative to New Labour is procedural rather than substantive. Under the Conservative administration, regulators were to reorient themselves in a business-friendly direction and to limit their zealous pursuit of possible infringements. In order to persuade them to stand back from the enforcement process, they were required to surmount a number of bureaucratic hurdles before taking action. The new government has admitted the need for good regulation but it is still persuaded of the need to limit regulation. Indeed, New Labour's Better Regulation Unit, now renamed as the Regulatory Impact Unit, has gained enhanced powers. As much, if not more so than its predecessor, the government has been particularly sensitive to the charge that it is over-burdening business with regulation. There is therefore an ambiguity in current government policy which, on the one hand, seeks a rational and systematic approach to enforcement of regulation but, on the other hand, does not wish to be seen to interfere unduly in the affairs of business. In this sense, whether New Labour will represent a departure from the preceding administration remains to be seen. It may be, paradoxically, that the genuine attempts by New Labour to improve regulation through greater consistency, transparency and so on may be undermined in the longer run by the inherited business-friendly assumptions regarding both the role of regulation and its enforcement philosophy fashioned by the previous administration.

Notes

1 Page, A. (1995), 'Deregulation and Contracting Out Act c.40', in *Current Law Statutes*, London: Sweet & Maxwell.
2 Department of Trade and Industry (1988), *Releasing Enterprise*, London: DTI.
3 Baldwin, R. (1995), *Rules and Government*, Oxford: Clarendon.
4 Hewart, G. (1929), *The New Despotism*, London: Benn; Ganz, G. (1987), *Quasi-legislation: Recent Developments in Secondary Legislation*, London: Sweet & Maxwell.
5 Craig, P. (1994), *Administrative Law*, London: Sweet & Maxwell.
6 Deregulation Task Force (1996), *Report 1995/96*, London.
7 Bartrip, F.W.J and P.T. Fenn (1983), 'The Evolution of Regulatory Style in the Nineteenth Century British Factory Inspectorate', *Journal of Law and Society*, 10, 201.
8 Deregulation Unit (1993), *Deregulation: Cutting Red Tape*, London: Deregulation Unit.
9 Health and Safety Commission (1994), Health and Safety Commission Review of Regulation Main Report, London: HSC.
10 Health and Safety Commission (1995), *Enforcement Policy Statement*, London: HSC.
11 Health and Safety Executive (1996), *Review of Health and Safety Enforcement Procedures: HSE Contract Research Report No. 119/1996*, London: HSE.
12 Deregulation Unit (1997), *Proposals for the Introduction of Business Friendly Enforcement Procedures for Trading Standards, Care Services and Environmental Health Legislation*, London: Deregulation Unit.
13 Environmental Health (1997), 'CIEH and HSC produce data clash on "minded to" notice', March; Environmental Health News (1997), 'Only 10 per cent of CEHOs back the "minded to" notice', 14 February.
14 Howarth, William (1997), 'Self-monitoring, Self-policing, Self-Incrimination and Pollution Law', *Modern Law Review*, 60, 200.
15 Environment Agency (1996), *The Environment Agency: Management Statement*, OP/OP/008 version 1 05/96.
16 Environmental Data Services Report (1996), 252 *ENDS* 3.

17 *Ibid.*
18 Deregulation (Improvement of Enforcement Procedures) (Food Safety Act 1990) Order 1996, S.I. 1996 No. 1683.
19 Pennington Group (1997), *Report on the Circumstances Leading to the 1996 Outbreak of Infection with E.Coli O157 in Central Scotland, the Implications for Food Safety and the Lessons to be Learned,* Edinburgh: The Stationery Office.
20 *Ibid.*, para. 4.11.
21 Deregulation Unit, *Proposals* (n.12, above).
22 Better Regulation Unit (1997), *Access Business,* <http://www.open.gov.uk/co/bru/access.htm>.
23 Eagle, Angela (1997), 'Interview with Angela Eagle', *Safety Management,* November.
24 Black, Julia (1998), 'Talking about regulation', *Public Law,* 77.
25 *Ibid.*
26 Cabinet Office (1998), *The Better Regulation Guide,* <http://www.cabinet - office.gov.uk/bru/brg_contents.htm>.
27 *Financial Times,* 20 May 1999.
28 *Financial Times,* 3 June 1999.
29 Department of the Environment, Transport, Regions (1998), *Quinquennial Prior Options Review of the Health and Safety Commission and Executive,* London: HMSO.
30 Ministry of Agriculture, Fisheries and Food and the Department of Health (1998), *The Food Standards Agency: A Force for Change,* Cmnd 3830. London: HMSO, (para.1.16).

16 Regulation and Markets Beyond 2000: Conclusion

LAURA MACGREGOR, TONY PROSSER AND CHARLOTTE VILLIERS, *University of Glasgow*

In the Introduction to this book we emphasised that we would be using a broad concept of regulation which would extend beyond the subjects which are traditionally seen as those of regulatory intervention, or at least of 'command and control' regulation. We emphasised that there are close links with competition law, and indeed that competition law can be seen itself as a form of regulation. This revealed a central theme; rather than regulation being an external constraint on markets, regulation can also constitute markets and, indeed, some forms of regulation are necessary for market creation and for the policing of markets to ensure that they remain competitive. We thus adopted a concept of regulation which is as broad as possible to include these activities. We also stressed that regulation is not an activity of an undifferentiated state; the activity of regulation can be undertaken at a large number of different levels, ranging from international organisations to private bodies. In particular, the concept of self-regulation is a complex one, usually involving a combination (often unstable) of public and private actors with law-setting boundaries for private regulation and providing guarantees for its operation.

The Nature of Regulation

The contributions in this book have amply demonstrated these themes. A number of further themes have now become apparent from them which can supplement the discussion of regulation in our Introduction. The first is that areas where there is apparently no formal regulation or little regulation of any kind are in fact subject to forms of regulation which are less apparent than in more conventionally regulated fields. This can be illustrated vividly from genetic testing. In that area we witnessed that, despite genetic testing being a newly developing activity, there nevertheless exists a network, albeit rather chaotic and disordered, of different regulatory controls. These include at one level general laws that can be applied to genetic testing even though they were created in a different context and for different reasons, such as for employment or consumer protection. Another level of controls includes specific regulatory measures that have been implemented within the industry itself by specially constituted committees such as the Gene Therapy Advisory Committee. The implications of this are twofold. The first is the theme which we have been stressing so much: that regulation is not limited to 'command and control' or the use of officially sanctioned legislative programmes. The second is that those introducing new regulatory schemes must be aware that they are not simply sowing virgin fields, for there are likely to be informal networks already operating and so the interaction of formal and informal techniques may give rise to difficulties. We saw something of this kind in another context when the history of environmental regulation was described; here essentially common-law concepts of nuisance proved a considerable disadvantage when transposed to more modern legislative schemes with somewhat different purposes.

Technological Development

The second theme which emerged strongly from this book is the relationship between regulation and rapid technological change. Important examples are genetic testing once more, information, telecommunications and transport. Of course, it would be banal merely to conclude that regulation and technological change are often found together; this would be obvious as areas of rapidly developing technology are precisely where public concerns resulting in official intervention are likely to be found. Rather, we can draw two conclusions which may be less familiar. The first is to echo the point made above: even if an area is in the course of rapid technological development, it is unlikely that it will be an empty space waiting for regulation to arrive. Even where no formal regulatory scheme has existed in the past, informal norms are likely to play a major role, for example through standards created by ethics committees in medical and genetic research. Indeed, what has been more common is that technological change has resulted in claims that it is being hampered by outdated and inappropriate regulatory forms.

We see examples of this in our discussion of the regulation of business and the better regulation initiatives, of electricity, of telecommunications and of transport once more.

This brings us to our second sub-theme, which is that it is incorrect to see regulation and rapid technological change as incompatible. Thus regulation is sometimes presented as being unable to cope with such change, the implication being that this is best left to the flexibility of the market with its particular ability to encourage innovation. Apart from the areas covered in this book, such a claim is characteristic of criticisms of media regulation as standing in the way of the rapid increase in consumer choice offered by digitalisation.[1] Yet some forms of regulation are necessary to permit innovation. Once more this is the case in genetic testing; it can also be seen in the case of transport, where the absence of effective regulatory arrangements for buses and the extreme lack of coordination in the privatised rail network created serious problems. This does not of course mean that the same regulation must be applied as in the past, and indeed we have seen examples of innovative regulatory responses such as taxation of energy consumption and new approaches to competition law. What it does mean is that we should not assume that a simple withdrawal in favour of the market will lead to satisfactory outcomes where technology is rapidly developing. The mechanisms for encouraging such development are far more complex than this, as we are seeing from the case of electronic communications and electronic commerce, where clarification of the allocation of intellectual property rights and such matters as electronic signatures and consumer liability have become urgent. The successful resolution of these questions is necessary for reasons of economic efficiency and the reduction of transaction costs.

Social questions are also raised by technological change, and once more a number of examples has been given here, including some in genetic testing, transport and energy. The debate is most advanced in relation to telecommunications liberalisation where, as the two chapters on the subject in this volume show, the recognition of social requirements may impose limits to liberalisation (as appears from the US experience) or may require the opening of markets to run in harness with the development of protections for universal service.[2]

The Importance of Competition

This leads to our third theme, again through the exemplification of a general point made in the Introduction to this book. An important and growing role of regulation is to create the conditions within which markets can operate. In this sense regulation cannot be separated from general competition law. This can be illustrated clearly from the current reform of UK competition law in the Competition Act 1998 as described in our Introduction. At first sight this might seem to be distinct from regulation. Yet the implementation of the prohibitions on anti-competitive agreements and practices and abuse of dominant position contained in the Act are very similar to actions previously taken by regulators under utility licence provisions; the changes to the powers of regulators are essentially remedial and procedural, though important nevertheless. There is no clear reason for assuming that the generalisation of these powers removes their regulatory nature. Indeed, this point is reinforced by the granting of concurrent powers to the utility regulators to enforce the prohibitions in their own sectors. Moreover, they also involve regular interventions by the competition authorities in private activity; the fact that they are designed to shape market behaviour in order to keep markets open does not mean that they are any less examples of regulatory interventions.

We have seen much evidence of the interaction of competition law and the work of other regulatory authorities in this book. This appears most clearly, perhaps, in the examination of the nascent essential facilities doctrine where action to the same ends has been taken by the European Court of Justice, by the European Commission and by both specialist sector regulators and general competition authorities. The message of Chapter 2 is that the complexity of the solutions required makes the courts an unsatisfactory source of regulatory solutions, something which has been amply demonstrated in other contexts also.[3] An even stronger illustration of the use of regulation to provide the opportunities for markets to operate successfully is through the attempts to create Trans-European Networks; as Sam Hamilton points out in Chapter 3, this is a prerequisite for the full establishment of a single European market, especially in the utilities sector. That objective is still a long way from realisation except in the field of telecommunications, but at least the problem is being addressed. National experience shows, however, that market creation is not simply a matter of ending the effect of national boundaries; as other chapters have shown, there has been a particular need to develop such markets within particular national systems, especially where provision of services has previously been the task of publicly owned monopolies. Thus in the UK the privatisation of electricity was carried out in a way which limited competition in generation and in supply as well as in the natural monopoly functions of transmission and distribution. The utility regulators themselves have played a major role in moving from this to a system of competitive markets, and even when a new market-based system for wholesale electricity trading comes into operation an essential part of this will be regulatory supervision.

A rather different type of market creation can be found in the discussion of public procurement. Here compulsory competitive tendering, 'best value' and other measures have moved many areas of procurement from administrative process to the incorporation of at least some elements of a competitive market. This process has been characteristic of other areas of government as well, such as the organisation of the National Health Service and market testing in central government, and has now been extended to the European level by the procurement directives.[4] As our contributors document, this has hardly been free from difficulties, but has had a substantial effect in opening up the tendering process and providing an information system on market opportunities.

Information and Disclosure

This issue of information and disclosure has emerged as of particular importance, figuring also, for example, in corporate governance and financial services. Chapter 11, on corporate governance, highlights the prominence of disclosure requirements as a key mechanism for accountability and control. For example, statutory provisions for disclosure of directors' remuneration exist alongside more detailed requirements in the Combined Code implemented by the London Stock Exchange. The contribution on financial services (Chapter 12) illustrates the point once more that ensuring a proper degree of openness is important both to achieve economic efficiency through ensuring that markets do respond properly to consumer signals and also to protect consumers from exploitation, as forcefully illustrated in the scandal of pension mis-selling. The use of tax as an economic incentive implies a degree of information availability which might not be achievable in practice; on the other hand, a success of the European procurement regime has been to increase information flows. The coverage of information governance (Chapter 14) shows the importance of rational systems for information governance in the private sector together with an effective scheme for access to governmental information. There must be some doubt as to the extent to which either is being achieved. Moreover, all these chapters illustrate the importance of trust both for the operation of markets and for effective regulation.

Policing Markets

As the procurement example makes very clear, the creation of markets is not the end of the process, for they need continued policing to keep them open. Once more we have seen substantial discussion of this task in the contributions above, notably in relation to essential facilities, electricity and financial services. The message here is that policing competition is not only a task for the general competition authorities, for in each of those areas specialist bodies have taken the lead. Indeed, as Chapter 2 suggests, specialist bodies may be well placed to undertake this sort of policing as they will have important informational advantages over a generalist body through contact with their specialist sectors over a range of matters; they may also have special expertise, as in the area of genetic testing. They may also be better placed to understand the limits to competition imposed by the requirements of public service.[5]

Different Regulatory Techniques

The opening up of markets has thus not led to a decline in regulation, though of course particular regulatory requirements may have been lifted and, indeed, this has been a well-publicised governmental objective. Instead, there has been the use of different forms of regulation designed to shape markets for economic and social objects rather than to replace them. This has also been reflected in developments in the institutional sources of regulatory action. The traditional approach has been to associate regulation with the state, normally conceived of as central government. In this book, however, we have not come across many examples of direct 'command and control' by government departments. The area in which central government has been most closely involved is that of ensuring that emissions are reduced sufficiently to meet the Kyoto targets. However, here the UK government has proceeded not by 'command-and-control' but by the use of tax incentives. The use of such techniques has an apparently sound economic rationale, but, as our contributors show, their practical application is extremely difficult, in particular because of informational difficulties. In a rather different sense, the use of concepts of nuisance derived from the common law has caused serious difficulties in relation to environmental law.

As a result, as well as the failure of regulation to wither away, in some regulatory areas 'command-and-control' regulation remains the most appropriate solution. This is most apparent in the case of transport, where assumptions made at the time of rail regulation that economic incentives would be sufficient to coordinate the rail network have not been proved justified. The greatest success in achieving such coordination seems to have come from the Passenger Transport Authorities retained from an earlier era, and steps are now being taken to introduce a more familiar form of regulation for the system as a whole with reform of the powers of the Rail Regulator (and his relationship to government) and the creation of the Strategic Rail Authority. Elements of 'command and control' can also be seen in environmental regulation and, arguably, in financial services.

In other cases moves towards self-regulation have taken place. To reiterate a point made above, self-regulation is not a simple concept, nor does it always mean freedom for private actors to regulate themselves. It can range from a system with minimal public intervention to one in which strong constraints are set by law and in which there is extensive power for government to intervene.[6] The first is in fact very rare; the example usually cited is that of the UK press, but in fact regulation by the industry takes place against the background of an extensive body of law dealing with issues such as defamation and confidentiality.[7] A particularly instructive example is that of financial services. Here the system which existed after the Financial Services Act was presented as one of self-regulation, partly to ensure industry acceptance.[8] However, even from the beginning it required an extraordinarily detailed and complex body of law, and was administered by what were public authorities in all but name. The presentation of the scheme as one of 'self-regulation' helped to destroy its legitimacy and it is now being replaced by a system which is more clearly part of a public regulatory system. A further example in which an attempt to delegate regulation to industry actors has resulted in a lack of transparency and, indeed, efficiency is that of the electricity pool, also now in the course of reform.

In other areas, self-regulation has been regarded as more successful. In the area of corporate governance, self-regulation is regarded, at least by those in industry, as more effective than burdensome legislative control. This might stem from the fact that corporate law principally aims to be 'facilitative' rather than limiting or preventive. Furthermore, some of the 'self-regulatory' bodies have in reality very weighty sanctions at their disposal, so that there is little incentive for corporate managers to break their standards. Nevertheless, these claims could be qualified by the example of directors' pay, in which self-regulation does not appear to have achieved the degree of control hoped. Consequently, the 'threat' of legislative intervention looms continually.

Better Regulation

One overarching theme in recent discussion of regulation has been the development of an ostensibly business-friendly regime, especially in relation to the enforcement process. The initial assumptions of this process were quite unrealistic in that they expected that 'deregulation' would be possible on a large scale. The more recent regime since the change of government has replaced this assumption with a belief that the aim is better regulation rather than no regulation. It has also led to a much more developed set of procedural guidance for the regulatory process through the development of the Better Regulation Guide. This would suggest that some of the themes suggested in this book have in fact also been reflected in government policy. However, our contributors suggest that this may be undermined by assumptions derived from the earlier approach stressing business friendliness at the expense of the participation of other groups, although the Guide does make it explicit that, for example, the needs of the voluntary sector are also to be considered in deciding whether to lift regulatory burdens, and there has been some widening of the membership of the Task Force to reflect this. Once more the key point to be made is that it is important not to confuse changes in the form of regulation or the lifting of regulatory burdens through reform of particular rules with the ending of regulation in all its forms. One advantage of the Better Regulation approach is that it should at least enable different forms of regulation in each context to be examined in the round.

In Search of a New Concept of Regulation

We commenced this book by discussing definitions of regulation and suggested that most which had been adopted have been unduly narrow. The contributions here have confirmed this view, and that regulation is not confined to 'command and control'; nor is it opposed to markets, but regulation is frequently necessary in order to constitute and police them. Nor is regulation necessarily carried out by public authorities: it can take the form of private ordering; no clear distinction can be drawn between public regulation and self-regulation. The key elements in what we have described as regulation are thus as follows. Firstly, there is a 'conscious ordering of activity'.[9] This is what distinguishes it from the typical market ordering, which like all ideal types is rarely to be found in real life. Secondly, there is some reference to economic activity, thus distinguishing regulation from, for example, ordering of artistic creation. This will normally relate to the allocation of resources, but is not incompatible with the existence of markets, for regulation may constitute, organise, police or supplant those markets. Thirdly, regulation will be institutionalised. This does not mean, of course, that the institutions involved must be public in nature, for we have seen important examples of private ordering in this book. Nor need formal law be used; informal norms may be just as important. Nevertheless, this institutionalisation differentiates regulation from individual transactions within the market-place.

This is perhaps the nearest we can usefully come to a concept of regulation. For all its faults, emphasising the breadth of the concept should provide a more fruitful approach for future studies than would one which restricts regulation to interventions in markets by state institutions.

Regulation beyond 2000?

We end by mentioning two further themes. First, the issue of regulation is clearly not only relevant to the UK. Most of the contributions to this book have revealed that regulation is of concern abroad and on a European or an international scale. Very few areas remain untouched by European initiatives. Other activities have also been the subject of international conventions. This fact highlights that we are dealing for the most part with cross-frontier markets. This is especially true in those areas that are touched by dramatic technological developments, not least in the fields of telecommunications and genetic testing. More cooperation is demanded between different states in order for knowledge and resources to be used efficiently. Ultimately, this may require formal intervention since policing of standards is more difficult across frontiers, even with the existence of better communications and transport opportunities. Distances may still limit trust, so that stronger frameworks for control become more necessary. Nevertheless, there still remain issues of enforcement and what kinds of sanctions will be appropriate when we are dealing with matters at an international level. This presents new challenges for international diplomacy at industry and at state level.

The last paragraph leaves us to speculate about what we might expect beyond 2000 from regulation. At the very least we can confidently predict that regulation will not wither away in any areas. What we might hope for is more rational regulatory structures rather than a chaotic and fragmented grouping of statutory and non-statutory rules. How these different forms of regulation interact must be carefully considered, including how different institutions may best operate together. This is dependent on context, of course, but also requires international examination, and the force of developing international markets calls for rationalisation on a very broad scale. Such an approach does not contradict an important role for delegated regulation and self-regulation, merely that we be clearer about regulatory rationales and the most appropriate division of regulatory labour. We hope, by showing the range of different types of regulation, to suggest that there is much scope for learning from experience of a large number of different regulatory techniques and institutions. This is not to say that there are no overarching concerns for achieving effective and legitimate regulation, and we have pointed to a number in this chapter – notably, availability of information. Rather than future debate following the dead-end road of a stark choice between markets and regulation, we hope it will be concerned with building democratic values and effectiveness into the vast range of institutions which span both.

Notes

1 For a discussion and critique of this view, see Goldberg, D., T. Prosser and S. Verhulst (eds) (1998), *Regulating the Changing Media: A Comparative Study*, Oxford: Clarendon, esp. chs 1 and 9.
2 See also Sauter, W. (1998), 'Universal Service Obligations and the Emergence of Citizens' Rights in European Telecommunications Liberalization', in M. Freedland and S. Sciarra (eds), *Public Services and Citizenship in European Law*, Oxford: Clarendon, pp.117–43.
3 For a striking example of a court being asked to take on economic analysis beyond its competence, see the opinion of the Privy Council in *Telecom Corporation of New Zealand* v. *Clear Communications Ltd* [1995] 1 NZLR 385.
4 See Harden, I. (1992), *The Contracting State*, Milton Keynes: Open University Press.
5 For a statement of these points in greater detail, see Prosser, T. (forthcoming), 'Competition, Regulators and Public Service', in B. Rodger and A. MacCulloch (eds), *The Competition Act in Perspective*, Oxford: Hart Publishing.
6 The classic account of the different degrees of self-regulation possible, with the use of coregulation and enforced self-regulation, is Ayres, I. and J. Braithwaite (1992), *Responsive Regulation: Transcending the Deregulation Debate*, Oxford: Oxford University Press.
7 See, for example, Gibbons, T. (1998), *Regulating the Media*, 2nd edn, London: Sweet & Maxwell, ch. 3.
8 Moran, M. (1988), 'Politics and Law in Financial Regulation', in C. Graham and T. Prosser (eds), *Waiving the Rules: The Constitution Under Thatcherism*, Milton Keynes: Open University Press, pp.56–72.
9 Daintith, T. (1997), 'Regulation' in R. Buxbaum and F. Mádl (eds), *International Encyclopedia of Comparative Law*, Tübingen: Mohr Siebeck, vol.XVII, 10–12.

Index

For Product Safety Concerns and Information please contact our EU representative GPSR@taylorandfrancis.com Taylor & Francis Verlag GmbH, Kaufingerstraße 24, 80331 München, Germany

Batch number: 10725973

Printed by Printforce, the Netherlands